Dedicated to our wives:
Terri Mae Saunders and
Virginia Lyons Friesen

Canadian Society in the Twenty-First Century

A HISTORICAL SOCIOLOGICAL APPROACH

Trevor W. Harrison
University of Lethbridge

John W. Friesen
University of Calgary

Toronto

National Library of Canada Cataloguing in Publication

Harrison, Trevor, 1952–

    Canadian society in the twenty-first century : a historical sociological approach / Trevor W. Harrison, John W. Friesen.

Includes bibliographical references and index.

ISBN 0-13-087224-5

    1. Canada—Civilization. 2. Canada—English-French relations.
3. Native peoples—Canada. 4. Canada—Civilization—21st century—Forecasting.

I. Friesen, John W. II. Title.

FC95.5.H37 2004   971   C2003-902589-6
F1021.2.H37 2004

Copyright © 2004 Pearson Education Canada Inc., Toronto, Ontario.

All rights reserved. This publication is protected by copyright, and permission should be obtained from the publisher prior to any prohibited reproduction, storage in a retrieval system, or transmission in any form or by any means, electronic, mechanical, photocopying, recording, or likewise. For information regarding permission, write to the Permissions Department.

ISBN 0-13-087224-5

Vice President, Editorial Director: Michael J. Young
Executive Acquisitions Editor: Jessica Mosher
Executive Marketing Manager: Judith Allen
Associate Editor: Patti Altridge
Production Editor: Martin Tooke
Copy Editor: Martin Townsend
Proofreader: Dana Kahan
Production Coordinator: Heather Bean
Page Layout: Heidi Palfrey
Cover Design: Anthony Leung
Cover Image: Corel Stock Photo Library, Corel Corporation

Statistics Canada information is used with the permission of the Minister of Industry, as Minister responsible for Statistics Canada. Information on the availability of the wide range of data from Statistics Canada can be obtained from Statistic Canada's Regional Offices, its World Wide Web site at http://www.statcan.ca, and its toll-free access number 1-800-263-1136.

1 2 3 4 5   08 07 06 05 04

Printed and bound in Canada.

Contents

Acknowledgements ix

Preface xi

Chapter 1   Introduction: What is Society?   1
The "Problem" of Society   3
Country, State, Nation   4
Back to Society   8
Globalization, the State, and Society   10
Theorizing Social Relationships   12
Thinking Theoretically: Canada's Game   15
Methodology: Sociology and Why History Matters   16
   Key Terms   18

PART 1   CANADA AND QUEBEC   19
Questions   20

Chapter 2   Living with the Consequences of 1760   21
Introduction   21
The Age of Mercantilism   22
The Rise and Fall of New France   23
The Proclamation Act and the Quebec Act   26
Being *Canadien*   27
The Loyalists and the Constitution Act of 1791   28
The Conquest's Economic and Political Impact   29
The Rebellions of 1837–38   31
Lord Durham and the Act of Union   33
Conclusion   34
   Key Terms   35

Chapter 3   One Hundred Years of Solitudes   36
Introduction   36
English Expansion and the Isolation of Quebec   37
Nationalism and Social Change in Quebec, 1867–1960   40
Clashing Nationalisms and Quiet Revolutions   44
Commissions and the "Three Wise Men"   45
The FLQ Crisis and Its Aftermath   47
Conclusion   48
   Key Terms   48

Chapter 4   The Constitutional Years   49
Introduction   49
Sociology and the Canadian Constitution   50

The Election of the Parti Québécois   52
The Language of Quebec Nationalism   53
A Study in Personal Agency: The 1980 Referendum   54
The 1982 Canadian Constitution   57
Quebec, Mulroney, and the Meech Lake Accord   59
Is Quebec a "Distinct Society"?   60
The Defeat of the Meech Lake and Charlottetown Accords   63
Conclusion   65
   Key Terms   66

Chapter 5   Beyond the Solitudes?   67
Introduction   67
A Near-Death Experience: The 1995 Quebec Referendum   68
After the Referendum   70
The Sovereignty Question Today   72
Society, Nation, Modernity, and "Self"   75
Solutions to the Impasse   77
Thinking the Unthinkable: Separation   78
Quebec and the "Other" Anglophone State   80
Conclusion   81
   Key Terms   81

Part 2   Canada and the United States   83
Questions   84

Chapter 6   The Making of English Canada   85
Introduction   85
The Birth of Two Nations   86
The War of 1812   89
The Making of English Canadian Identity   90
The Monroe Doctrine, Manifest Destiny, and American Exceptionalism   91
The Political Economy of British North America, 1800–1866   93
Canada and the American Civil War   97
Confederation   98
Conclusion   100
   Key Terms   100

Chapter 7   English Canada in Transition   101
Introduction   101
The "American System" and the National Policy   102
Immigration and the Peopling of the West   104
Between Two Empires   108
A World Interrupted: Canada and the First World War   109
Canada, 1919–1929   111
The Depression Years, 1929–1939   113
Canada and the Second World War   118
Conclusion   118
   Key Terms   119

Chapter 8   Postwar Canada and English-Canadian Nationalism   120

Introduction   120
Canada and the United States in the Cold War Era   121
From State to "Welfare" State   123
The Canadian Welfare State in Perspective   125
Women in the Changing Canadian Society   127
Labour Markets, Immigration, and Multiculturalism   128
The Rise of English-Canadian Nationalism   132
Economic Nationalism: Theory and Practice   134
Political Ideology in Canada   136
The New West   137
The Economic Crisis of the Canadian State   140
The Rise and Fall of Canadianization, 1972–1982   143
Conclusion   145
   Key Terms   146

Chapter 9   Canada in the Age of the American Empire   147

Introduction   147
Adopting Free Trade   148
Assessing the Long-Term Impact of Free Trade   150
Canadian Social Stratification and Inequality   156
Canada and the United States: A Comparison   160
The Global Context   162
The American War on Terrorism   164
Reflections on State and Empire: The Case of the United States   165
War, the Bush Doctrine, and Its Consequences for Canada   167
Conclusion   168
   Key Terms   169

Part 3   Canada and the Aboriginal Nations   171

Questions   172

Chapter 10   When Cultural Worlds Collide   173

Introduction   174
Pre-Contact Lifestyle   174
First Contact   176
The Fur Trade   178
The Indigenous People's Response   180
The Introduction of Agriculture   181
Colonization   183
The Reserve System   186
Aboriginal Education   188
Life in a Residential School   191
Conclusion   194
   Key Terms   194

Chapter 11 Keepers of the North 195

Introduction 195
A Portrait of the North 196
The People 197
The Coming of the Europeans 202
The Yukon Gold Rush 204
The Second World War and the Postwar North 206
Northern Visions 208
Conclusion 211
   Key Terms 211

Chapter 12 The Road to Oka 212

Introduction 212
The Royal Proclamation Act 213
Confederation 214
The Numbered Treaties 215
White Paper, Red Paper 217
Aboriginals and the 1982 Constitution 219
The Penner Report and the Notion of Self-Government 222
The Meech Lake and Charlottetown Accords 222
The Oka Crisis 224
Conclusion 225
   Key Terms 226

Chapter 13 The Search for New Learning Paths 227

Introduction 227
Portrait of the Aboriginal Peoples Today 228
The Royal Commission on Aboriginal Peoples 232
Healing the Past: Dealing with Residential Claims 234
The Indian Act 234
Aboriginal Self-Government and Self-Determination 236
Land Claims and Modern Treaties 238
Aboriginal Versus Non-Aboriginal Cultural Values 241
Education, Identity, and Cultural Survival 245
Conclusion: A Two-Way Learning Path? 246
   Key Terms 247

Chapter 14 Conclusion: Canada–A Twenty-First Century Society? 248

Introduction 248
Issues and Challenges in Canadian Society 249
   Key Terms 252

Appendix 1 Canadian Federal Election Results Since Confederation 253

Appendix 2 Canadian Prime Ministers, and Major Policies Since Confederation 255

Bibliography 257

Index 283

Acknowledgements

I want first to thank the many students to whom over the years I have taught courses about Canadian society, and whose perceptive questions have often taught me even more. Specifically, I want to acknowledge those students in my winter 2002 Sociology 101 class at the University of Alberta and my spring 2003 Sociology 2010 class at the University of Lethbridge, who were subjected to early drafts of this text while it was in process.

I would like also to thank those friends and academic acquaintances who stimulated over these many years my evolving thoughts about Canadian society, in particular Claude Denis and Gordon Laxer.

Special thanks must go to Andy Wellner, who first encouraged me some years ago to propose this book to Pearson Education. I subsequently want to thank Patti Altridge, Nicole Lucach, Jessica Mosher, and John Polanszky for their assistance in producing the final text. I would be remiss if I did not also thank my copy editor, Martin Townsend, whose efforts gave my words a ring of heightened clarity, and my proofreader, Dana Kahan, for her attention to detail.

I also want to mention the assistance of Marie-Josee Lalonde and Georgette Gaulin at Statistics Canada, Joanne Noel and Elise Chodat of the Department of Indian and Northern Affairs, and Cara Marshall of Industry Canada for assistance in gathering information for me.

I would also like to acknowledge Dr. P.B. Waite for the use of his words quoted in Chapter Six, Mrs. Thelma Lower for the permission to reproduce information from R.A. Lower's *Western Canada: An Outline History*, and John Robert Colombo for the use of various quotations from *Colombo & Company*.

Thanks also are due to Paul Lawton who, as my assistant this past year, worked on the valuable test bank. I apologize to any whose contributions I have unintentionally overlooked.

Finally, I must also acknowledge the support of my wife and children over the years. They are a constant source of inspiration and cause for my dedication to bettering Canada.

T.W.H.

I owe a debt of thanks to the late Russell Wright, curator of the Blackfoot Museum at Old Sun College at Siksika, Alberta, where I still teach from time to time. Russell was my mentor during many a lunch hour.

My formal introduction to First Nations communities actually began at the invitation of the Rev. Dr. John Snow, chief of the Wesley/Goodstoney First Nations band at Morley, Alberta. Several decades ago he invited me to bring students to Morley for regular visits while he shared information with them about his people. This practice culminated in an annual conference on Native education at Morley in the years 1970–1985.

I would be remiss if I did not acknowledge the assistance of my wife, Virginia Lyons Friesen. She has always accompanied me on my research trips while at the same time completing her doctorate in sociology of education. During the last decade we visited virtually every First Nations reserve from the Canadian prairies to Texas and were always graciously received. We owe much to the people of these communities, who welcomed us and shared information with us.

Finally, I want to thank my students at the University of Calgary for enrolling in my various classes in Aboriginal history and education and appearing interested. Their enthusiasm for the topic has served as a constant source of encouragement for me.

J.W.F.

Preface

Its [Canada's] strength—you might even say what makes it interesting—is its complexity; its refusal of the conforming, monolithic nineteenth-century nation-state model. That complexity has been constructed upon three deeply rooted pillars, three experiences—the aboriginal, the francophone and the anglophone.
—philosopher John Ralston Saul, 1997

As century's end approached, anxiety gripped Canadians over the country's future. Free trade with the United States remained controversial, despite an election dominated by the issue only a few years before. Quebec's place within Canadian confederation was still unsettled. Regional discontent continued to foment, especially in Canada's West. The uncertainties within Canada were matched on the international scene by free flows of capital, mass migrations of workers and displaced populations, the instability of governments, and ongoing regional wars.

1999? Actually, the year was 1899. Yet then, just as today, Canadians were also filled with hope and excitement. Canada was rapidly industrializing. Immigrants were pouring into Canada, especially the West, beginning the third phase of the National Policy. Canadian writers and artists were on the verge of discovering an "authentic" Canadian voice. Little wonder that Sir Wilfrid Laurier predicted that the twentieth century would belong to Canada.

Of course, there were also doubters, such as the English-born journalist Goldwin Smith. In 1891, Smith published *Canada and the Canadian Question*. Canada was impossible, he said; the conflict between English Canada and French Canada was intractable.

Smith's dire prediction was in good company. Scarce a decade has passed in the last 200 years that Canada's imminent demise has not been predicted. In the 1960s and 1970s, a serendipitous alliance of conservatives (George Grant), liberals (Walter Gordon), and social democrats (Melville Watkins) agreed that Canada was imperilled by American economic control. Others feared the rise of Quebec nationalism and of western regionalism. In the 1980s and 1990s, a plethora of books returned to familiar themes of French-English discord (see Brimelow, 1986; Gairdner, 1990) and creeping Americanization (see Martin, 1993a), while new perceived perils, such as multiculturalism (Bissoondath, 1994) and Aboriginal autonomy (Smith, 1995), were added to the mix. Yet, amidst the fears and doubts, a new confidence—even cockiness—also emerged, as witness Molson's popular "I Am Canadian" advertisement. The age-long quest to define, and therefore defend, Canada continues.

This book is about Canadian society: what it is today, how it became what it is, and some of the tough questions Canadians are likely to face in the twenty-first century.

The book is divided into three sections. These sections deal with what John Ralston Saul argues are the three main pillars of Canadian society: the aboriginal, francophone, and anglophone. Each of these pillars constitutes a kind of "master narrative" that has shaped Canadian society. Thus, Part One (Chapters Two through Five) examines francophone Quebec's relationship with the rest of Canada; Part Two (Chapters Six through Nine) examines English Canada's relationship with the United States; and Part Three (Chapters

Ten through Thirteen) examines Canada's Aboriginal peoples' relationship with non-Aboriginals. Clearly, other relationships, based on differences of gender, ethnicity, race, and class (for example) inform Canada's past and present, and cannot—should not—be ignored and are included here. The relationships highlighted by the three sections, however, provide a narrative structure for understanding the manner in which Canadian society has been shaped and—some would say—is now threatened.

The term *narrative* is used intentionally. A state, country, nation, or society—these terms are taken up in Chapter One—is a product of collective storytelling. As Edward Said (1993: xiii) has remarked, "... nations are narrations." The story of Canadian society enlists all the usual literary devices: myths (The Conquest); metaphors (are Quebec and Canada "two solitudes" or "Siamese twins"?); symbols (Canadian hockey, the maple leaf, the fleur-de-lis); heroes, villains, and tragic figures (Louis Riel is all three, depending upon whom you ask); and recurrent subtexts (regional alienation, Americanization). Of necessity, the story of Canadian society must also be historical if only because what we remember (or think we remember) provides the foundation for current understandings. For societies, no less than individuals, the child is parent to the adult. In the Canadian rendition, only one thing is missing from the usual story: an ending. Canadian society is a story in progress.

Of course, just as ten people seeing an accident will provide ten different accounts of what happened, there is no single view of the nature of relationships in any society. Dominant groups, buttressed by wealth and power, possess a particular understanding of existing relationships and act according to that understanding. Subordinate groups have their own views, upon which they also act. Sometimes, though not often, these subordinate views gain acceptance and become the new orthodoxy. Ultimately, the story of Canadian society is not singular at all; at best, it is a moving collage of conflicts and compromises between individuals and groups; of interests and ideas, memories and myths.

To guide understanding of the subject, this book's introductory chapter explores the meaning of society and several of its conceptual "siblings": country, state, and nation. Chapter One also introduces the concept of globalization and its potential impact upon societies such as Canada's. The chapter also provides students with a brief summary of central approaches in sociology: structural-functionalist theory, conflict theory, feminist theory, and symbolic interaction theory. Finally, Chapter One also provides a methodological justification for the use of history in sociological investigation.

For hundreds of years—longer in the case of Aboriginal peoples—people in this part of North America have been creating, together and alone, a story as broad as the prairie landscape, as deep as the Hudson Bay basin, and as rich as ore from the Canadian Shield. It is a story worthy of many books. This is one of them.

chapter one

Introduction: What is Society?

In every generation Canadians have had to rework the miracle of their political existence. Canada has been created because there has existed within the hearts of its people a determination to build for themselves an enduring home. Canada is a supreme act of faith.

—historian A.R.M. Lower, 1946

Ours is not the only nation which has out-travelled its own soul and now is forced to search frantically for a new identity. No wonder, for so many, the past Canadian experience has become not so much a forgotten thing as an unknown thing.

—novelist Hugh MacLennan, 1974

How could we have believed that there is such a thing as time, the self, or the nation?

—author John Gray, 1994

The final two decades of the twentieth century saw stability give way to uncertainty. The Cold War came to an abrupt close. The spectre of communism ended with neither a bang nor a whimper; it simply vanished. In 1989, the Berlin Wall fell. Shortly thereafter, communist regimes throughout Eastern Europe, including the Soviet Union itself, also collapsed. Capitalism won the Cold War almost by default.

The collapse of communism, however, was only part of broader, interrelated economic, political, and socio-cultural changes occurring throughout the world. Under the rubric of *globalization*, production moved to underdeveloped countries where wages were meagre and labour and environmental standards were low. Consumption, too, became internationalized. Finance capital ricocheted around the world at breakneck speed. Mergers and takeovers became ho-hum news. Everything—oil, wheat, cars, televisions, guns, drugs, sex, or human organs—seemed to be a tradeable commodity. Stock markets and unemployment rates fluctuated wildly. The threat of nuclear war receded but was replaced by localized ethnic wars (Rwanda, Indonesia), sanitized displays of high-tech "peacekeeping" (the Gulf War, Kosovo), and finally in September 2001 terrorist attacks on New York and Washington followed by the U.S.-led war in Afghanistan and, later, Iraq.

Through television and the Internet, people knew more than ever about what was going on around them and perhaps also, as a result, felt more powerless. Many complained of being chronically stressed and not having enough time. Suicide rates climbed in most countries, rich and poor alike. Although life expectancies rose nearly everywhere (except in Russia and Africa), birth rates dropped. Corporate CEOs, political leaders, and cultural icons rose, became heroes, then stumbled and fell. In the world Monopoly game of the late twentieth century, some went straight to jail. Everywhere, uncertainty reigned.

Canada was not immune to change. Economically, Canada embraced trade liberalization with the signing of the Free Trade Agreement with the United States in 1989 and, later, the North American Free Trade Agreement, which added Mexico. The following decade involved a period of wrenching economic restructuring. Jobs disappeared in the primary and secondary sectors, but new ones emerged in both the low- and high-end service sectors. Historic Canadian companies, such as Eaton's, disappeared, many taken over by foreign (mainly American) corporations. Throughout the 1990s, Canada was buffeted by a series of recessions, and unemployment rose to double digits for most of the decade before falling abruptly to an 18-year low. Absolute wealth increased, but the gap between rich and poor grew larger. Food banks proliferated and homelessness became a nightly news story.

Politically, Quebec's place in Confederation remained unsettled. Efforts to resolve the impasse failed in 1982, 1990, and 1992, resulting in the nearly successful Quebec referendum on sovereignty in 1995. But unrest was not centred solely on Quebec-Canada issues. Regional discontent, especially in western Canada, continued to foment, reflected in the emergence of the Reform and then Alliance parties. Aboriginal people, too, became more restive, demanding redress of historic wrongs. Old institutions—the Senate, the Supreme Court—were increasingly called into question. New forms of governance were debated, and a new territory, Nunavut, was created.

Socially, Canada's population was aging, placing increasing pressures upon social programs such as health care and income security. Family structure was also changing. Families became smaller, common-law and single-parent families more common, same-sex couples—grudgingly—more accepted. Gender roles continued a century-long redefinition, but gender inequalities in many areas of life continued. Rural Canada continued its retreat, epitomized in the plight of small, independent farmers, but a counter-movement also occurred in the form of urbanites fleeing to the imagined security of suburbs and acreages. Crime rates declined, but personal insecurities and fear of crime increased.

Culturally, Canadians cut a wide swath in the new global world. Canadian films garnered a larger audience, and Hollywood itself was flush with Canadian actors, writers, directors, and technicians alike. At home, Canadian musicians became distinctive, particularly in their regional voices, while abroad the likes of Alanis Morissette, Shania Twain, and Céline Dion became household names. Side by side with these successes, however, were notable losses. Rights to market the image of the RCMP were sold to the Disney corporation (Dawson, 1998). The same American corporation purchased a National Hockey League franchise in Anaheim, California, while Canadian cities in the league either disappeared or were relegated to second-rate status. The purpose of the CBC in a multimedia universe was increasingly questioned.

In this context of enormous changes and challenges, age-old questions—and assertions—resurfaced about Canadian identity and the country's future. These concerns frame this text. In particular, this text deals with the thorny problem of Canadian society. Given Canada's geographical vastness, its historical and cultural diversity, and its political and social complexity, how can anyone hope to grasp Canadian society? What sense does it make to even speak of "Canadian society" at a time when—we are repeatedly told—cultural, economic, and political borders are breaking down (Ohmae, 1990)? The vastness of the problem has led one sociologist to recently comment that "the task of 'constituting society,' of creating knowledge about, and articulating a wholist account of, the total society, is no longer central to current concerns of sociologists in Canada" (Whyte, 1992: 313). To paraphrase Frisby and Sayer (1986: 121), Canadian society would seem "too grand an abstraction by far for modern sociological tastes."

The reader is thus forewarned: in opening this text, you begin the daunting task of journeying into a territory that many scholars avoid, where existing maps may be unclear, where the terrain is constantly shifting, where fact and myth coexist, and where abstractions run wild. To assist in this journey through Canadian society, this introductory chapter provides a set of rudimentary tools: terms, concepts, theories, and an explanation of historical sociology as a method of study. Learn to use these tools well. The chapter begins with an attempt at defining the object of study.

THE "PROBLEM" OF SOCIETY

What is society? At first, the question may seem strange. After all, we use the term *society* frequently. But try to touch it or point a finger at it. It cannot be done, of course, because—unlike a rock, for example—society is not a concrete thing; it is an abstract concept.

This comparison touches on the first problem with the concept of society. Abstract concepts can be very powerful tools for assisting us to think about complex social phenomena. Abstract concepts become problematic, however, when we begin to think of them as actually existing materially, a process of delusion referred to as **reification**. Many of the terms we will deal with in this chapter, such as *state* and *nation*, share with *society* the frequent problem of being reified.

A second problem with the term *society* is its diverse meanings. Take, for example, the following definition of the term appearing in *Merriam-Webster's Collegiate Dictionary*[1] (2003: 1115):

> **1** : companionship or association with one's fellows : friendly or intimate intercourse : COMPANY
> **2** : a voluntary association of individuals for common ends; *esp* : an organized group working together or periodically meeting because of common interests, beliefs, or profession **3 a** : an

---

1. By permission. From M*erriam-Webster's Collegiate® Dictionary*, 10th Edition ©2003 by Merriam-Webster, Incorporated (**www.Merriam-Webster.com**).

enduring and cooperating social group whose members have developed organized patterns of relationships through interaction with one another **b** : a community, nation, or broad grouping of people having common traditions, institutions, and collective activities and interests **4 a** : a part of a community that is a unit distinguishable by particular aims or standards of living or conduct : a social circle or a group of social circles having a clearly marked identity <move in polite ~>; <literary ~>; **b** : a part of the community that sets itself apart as a leisure class and that regards itself as the arbiter of fashion and manners **5 a** : a natural group of plants usu. of a single species or habit within an association **b** : the progeny of a pair of insects when constituting a social unit (as a hive of bees); *broadly* : an interdependent system of organisms or biological units.

Such a definition is very broad. Clearly, Canada is not a society like that of a group of plants or the progeny of insects, or even that of individuals who believe in a "flat earth." Moreover, the problem of definition is only partially remedied by adding a descriptive modifier, such as *Canadian*.

When sociologists refer to society, they often mean something more narrowly defined, yet conceptually larger. A popular introductory text in sociology (Macionis and Gerber, 1999: 87), for example, states that "the concept of society refers to people who interact in a defined territory and share culture." Another popular introductory text (Kendall et al., 1997: 6) states: "A society is a large social grouping that shares the same geographical territory and is subject to the same political authority and dominant cultural expectations." This definition suggests that a society's social boundaries are co-existent with its political boundaries. But which political boundaries are to be used: federal, provincial, municipal?

This question points to a third problem with the concept of society: where does one society end and another begin? Denis (1993) notes, for example, that while Canadian society courses are common throughout Anglo-Canadian universities, Quebec's francophone universities focus on Quebec society courses. Even a recent anglophone text (Fournier et al., 1997) deals with Quebec society. Add to this the fact that the University of Calgary has since included an Alberta society course in its curriculum and we may acquire some understanding of the frustration voiced by Denis:

> Where does it stop? If "English Canada" and Quebec can both be distinct societies within Canada, which is itself a distinct society relative to (or within?) the U.S., does this also mean that American society is within... etc.? In this socio-geographic chain, shouldn't a number of statements be mutually exclusive?

A fourth problem with the concept of society is its conflation with several other concepts, notably those of country, state, and nation (see Denis, 1993). Note above, for example, the inclusion in *Merriam-Webster's* of *nation* in its definition of society, and Kendall's equation of the concepts of country and society. How can we distinguish between concepts such as country, state, and nation? And how are they related to the concept of Canadian society?

COUNTRY, STATE, NATION

Turning once again to our *Merriam-Webster's* dictionary, one of its definitions of *country* is as follows: "a political state or nation or its territory" (2003: 266). In other words, country *equals* nation *equals* state. There are problems with this formulation, as we will see. For now, however, we will define a **country** as *a territorial area, politically recognized as a country both by people within the territory and by governments outside it, on the basis of historical, material, and geographical factors* (see Lane and Ersson, 1994; Deutsch, 1980).

TABLE 1.1	Canadian Population, by Province and Region, 1851–2002 (in thousands)											
Year	CANADA	Nfld[1]	PEI	NS	NB	Que	Ont	Man[2]	Sask[3]	Alta[3]	BC	YT	NWT	Nun[4]
1851	2436	n.a.	63	277	194	890	952	n.a.	n.a.	n.a.	55	n.a.	6	n.a.
1861	3230	n.a.	81	331	252	1112	1396	n.a.	n.a.	n.a.	52	n.a.	7	n.a.
1871	3689	n.a.	94	388	286	1192	1621	25	n.a.	n.a.	36	n.a.	48	n.a.
1881	4325	n.a.	109	441	321	1360	1927	62	n.a.	n.a.	49	n.a.	56	n.a.
1891	4833	n.a.	109	450	321	1489	2114	153	n.a.	n.a.	98	n.a.	99	n.a.
1901	5371	n.a.	103	460	331	1649	2183	255	91	73	179	27	20	n.a.
1911	7207	n.a.	94	492	352	2006	2527	461	492	374	393	9	7	n.a.
1921	8788	n.a.	89	524	388	2361	2934	610	758	588	525	4	8	n.a.
1931	10 377	n.a.	88	513	408	2875	3432	700	922	732	694	4	9	n.a.
1941	11 507	n.a.	95	578	457	3332	3788	730	896	796	818	5	12	n.a.
1951	14 009	361	98	643	516	4056	4598	777	832	940	1165	9	16	n.a.
1961	18 238	458	105	737	598	5259	6236	922	925	1332	1629	15	23	n.a.
1971	21 962	531	113	797	643	6137	7849	999	932	1666	2241	19	36	n.a.
1981	24 820	575	124	855	706	6548	8811	1036	976	2294	2824	24	48	n.a.
1991	28 031	580	130	915	746	7065	10 428	1110	1003	2593	3373	29	61	n.a.
1996	29 672	561	136	931	753	7274	11 101	1134	1020	2781	3882	32	68	25
1998	30 248	545	137	936	753	7324	11 387	1138	1025	2907	3997	32	41	26
1999	30 509	541	138	941	756	7351	11 528	1143	1026	2960	4028	31	41	27
2000	30 791	538	138	942	756	7382	11 698	1146	1022	3010	4060	31	41	28
2001	31 111	534	139	943	756	7418	11 895	1149	1017	3059	4102	30	41	28
2002	31 414	532	140	945	757	7455	12 068	1151	1012	3114	4141	30	41	29
% (2002)	100	1.7	0.4	3.0	2.4	23.7	38.4	3.7	3.2	9.9	13.2	0.1	0.1	0.1

Sources: Adapted from the Statistics Canada publications *Historical Statistics of Canada*, Catalogue 11-516, 1983, Series A2-14, and *Canada Year Book*, Catalogue 11-402, 2001, Table 3.2, p. 3.2; from the Statistics Canada Web site at **www.statcan.ca/english/Pgdb/demo02.htm**; and from *Canadian Global Almanac 2000* (1999: 42), "Population of Provinces and Territories," reprinted with permission from Macmillan Canada an imprint of John Wiley & Sons Canada, Ltd.

1. Newfoundland figures before Confederation in 1949 are not included.
2. Population figures for Manitoba before 1871 are included in those of the Northwest Territories.
3. Population figures for Saskatchewan and Alberta before 1901 are included in figures for the Northwest Territories.
4. Population figures for Nunavut before 1996 are included in the Northwest Territories.

TABLE 1.2 Canadian Population, by Gender and Age, 2002 (in thousands and percent)

	Total	0-4	5-9	10-14	15-24	25-34	35-44	45-54	55-64	65-74	75+
Male	15 553	873	1023	1081	2170	2231	2655	2291	1517	1021	6905
%	49.5	2.8	3.3	3.4	6.9	7.1	8.5	7.3	4.8	3.2	2.2
Female	15 861	832	972	1027	2070	2182	2627	2306	1566	1144	1134
%	50.5	2.7	3.1	3.3	6.6	6.9	8.4	7.3	5.0	3.6	3.6
Total	31 413	1705	1995	2109	4240	4414	5282	4597	3083	2165	1825
%	100	5.4	6.3	6.7	13.5	14.0	16.8	14.6	9.8	6.9	5.8

Source: Adapted from Statistics Canada's CANSIM database, *Population by sex and gender.* Table 051-0001, on the Statistics Canada Web site at www.statcan.ca?english/Pgdb/demo10a.htm.

Note: Discrepancies between totals and percentages are caused by rounding.

In these terms, Canada is a country consisting of ten provinces and three territories, spanning 9 976 140 square kilometres. This makes Canada the second largest country in the world, next to Russia (formerly, the Russian Federation), which spans 17 075 200 square kilometres, and just ahead of the People's Republic of China (9 596 960 square kilometres). Compared with Russia and China, however, Canada is quite sparsely populated, with roughly 31.5 million people (see Table 1.1, page 5, and Table 1.2). By comparison, Russia's population is 145 million while China's population is 1.28 billion (*Time*, 2002: 743, 748, 844).

Defining Canada, Russia, or China as countries is unproblematic because each has diplomatic recognition of its sovereignty from the rest of the world. Contrast this reality with that of the Kurdish people, whose would-be homeland is divided among the countries of Iran, Turkey, and Iraq, or, for that matter, the small but militant Aryan Nations movement in the northwest United States, neither of which is likely to gain country status in the near future.

A term frequently employed offhandedly as synonymous with *country* is that of *state*. However, *state* is also often used when referring to issues of governance and the use of political power. In the former sense, an individual might argue that Canada *is* a state. In the latter sense, however, the same individual might ask what kind of state Canada *has* and what its characteristics are.

The latter meaning of *state* is rendered even more diverse in scholarly accounts. For example, pluralist theorists tend to ignore the state altogether, choosing instead to narrowly analyze the formal institutions of government (such as parties, legislatures, bureaucracies), which they view as open to the influence of competing political interests (see Orum, 1989: 180–85). By contrast, neo-Marxist scholars, such as Miliband (1969) and Poulantzas (1973), have tended to view the state more broadly, the former seeing the state as an instrument of capital accumulation, the latter as a relatively autonomous ensemble of social and political institutions. For others, like Skocpol (1979), the state is a wholly autonomous actor with its own powers, goals, and interests.

In each of these interpretations, the state is described more or less as a thing. Recent definitions of the state, however, have taken a more radical turn. Beginning with Abrams (1988), the state has increasingly been described as an abstract concept, the reification of which is itself a weapon for enacting, legitimating, and ultimately condoning "violence" (Sayer, 1987; Denis, 1989).

Despite important differences, the definitions reviewed here agree that the concept of state has something to do with the exercise of political power. In this text, therefore, a **state** is defined as *a set of institutions successfully claiming a monopoly over political rule-making and the legitimate use of violence and coercion within a given territory, i.e., a country* (see Weber, 1958: 78; Lane and Ersson, 1994: 30). The important question of the impact of globalization upon states is taken up below.

The third term requiring definition is *nation*. Note, at the onset, how the terms *nation* and *state* are often linked together, that is, as *nation-state*. (Note, also, how the *Merriam-Webster's* definition above equates the concepts of country and nation.) We have looked at the meanings of *country* and *state*. What exactly is a nation?

A **nation** is defined as *a mass of individuals who define themselves collectively as a people*. But on what bases might individuals define themselves as a nation?

Two types of nations are often defined: civic nations and ethnic nations (Webber, 1994). Civic nationalism is determined by citizenship. Membership in the civic nation, at least in theory, is open to anyone. By contrast, ethnic—sometimes also termed *tribal*—

nations are based on supposedly fixed biological (e.g., racial) and cultural (e.g., linguistic or religious) markers. Note, however, the malleability of even these markers. Biological descriptors are particularly uncertain measures of difference, and people can readily acquire a new language, convert to a different religion, or adopt new cultural practices.

Both civic and ethnic nations are tied to a specific territorial homeland. In the case of civic nations, however, the territorial referent is quite concrete: no territory, no citizenship. By contrast, ethnic nations may continue to exist, even thrive, after the territorial homeland has disappeared from political maps. Both civic and ethnic nations, however, constitute what Anderson (1983) terms *imagined communities*. A person can never know all the other members of his or her nation. Rather, the other members are idealized figments, our relationship with them the product of collective stories that we tell each other.

As stated above, the term *nation* is often conflated with *state* to produce *nation-state*. This conjoining of these terms is both unfortunate and imprecise. It is unfortunate because the notion of the nation-state suggests that every nation must be a state, and that every state must consist of only one nation. The consequences of this belief can be seen in the actions of the Nazi regime in Germany (1933–45) and in the Balkan and African wars of the 1990s. But the term *nation-state* is also imprecise in describing reality. As Hobsbawm (1992: 186) notes, no more than a dozen of today's 180-plus countries house only a single ethnic or linguistic group. Indeed, van den Berghe (1992) argues that only Japan, Swaziland, and Somalia are genuine nation-states.

As Laxer (2000: 56) points out, most countries are heterogeneous and "cannot, even mythically, pretend all citizens are kith and kin." A lot of countries, in fact, are "state-nations," that is, states organized (and perhaps one could say "created") by their own nations of people, while other nations are "stateless." In short, the assumption that country *equals* state *equals* nation is historically, politically, and socially constructed. Determining the exact fit between these terms in any particular case is a matter of empirical reflection. This point brings us to Canada.

A central thesis of this text is that, while Canada is indisputably a country, it is one founded on not one but three historic nations—English, French, and Aboriginal—and consequently requires a complex federal state structure. Efforts to make Canada conform to the European model—for example, repeated attempts by the English majority to coerce and otherwise assimilate either the French or Aboriginal peoples—have usually foundered, threatening Canada's continuance. The text's second thesis, however, is that these internal differences over nation and state, combined with external threats of absorption by the United States, have rendered Canada unique among twentieth-century countries. The result, in turn, is a country in which civil and state relations are also unique; in short, something that we may consider a society.

BACK TO SOCIETY

The concept of society emerged in the nineteenth century. **Sociology**, *the study of society*, arose at the same time. For early sociologists, the concept of society was meant to locate the site of the many changes wrought, both directly and indirectly, by the Industrial Revolution and the rise of capitalism. For Karl Marx (1818–1883) feudal relationships, based on tradition and fealty, were being replaced by capitalist relationships, based on private property and the cash nexus (Marx, 1977a). For Ferdinand Tonnies (1855–1936), rural and small-town life was being replaced by urban life, and kinship and tradition were being replaced by anonymity and self-interest (Tonnies, 1957). For Emile Durkheim (1858–1917), the changes were marked by a transformation in the basis of social solidarity from similarity-in-kind ("mechanical solidarity") to differentiation and, hence, greater interdependence ("organic solidarity") (Durkheim, 1964). For Max Weber (1864–1920), traditional authority was giving way to legal-rational forms of authority, reaching its apex in bureaucratic institutions (Weber, 1958).

Early on, however, the concept of society also came to define "one half of an antithetic tandem in which the other is the state" (Wallerstein, 1997: 315). Wallerstein adds:

> In this formulation, the state could be observed and analysed directly. It operated through formal institutions by way of known (constitutional) rules. The 'society' was taken to mean that tissue of manners and customs that held a group of people together without, despite or against formal rules. In some sense, 'society' represented something more enduring and 'deeper' than the state, less manipulable and certainly more elusive.

This perspective is very much alive today. Consider, for example, how often you have heard someone—perhaps on a radio talk show—denounce the state for doing something at variance with the interests of society. For many people, including academics, society is an abstract concept defined by its opposition to another abstract concept, the state.

It was not always the case, however, that society and state were viewed as separate (and perhaps opposed). Knuttila and Kubik (2000: 34–37) suggests, for example, that both Auguste Comte (1798–1857), who first coined the term *sociology*, and Durkheim, who held the first chair in sociology, viewed the state as an integral part—*but only a part*—of a functional modern society. From this perspective, society and state are not merely "coterminous" (Giddens, 1984); they are indivisible.

Recently, Denis (1989) has argued forcefully for a restoration of the links between the two concepts. For him, "'states' are a historically specific type of society, whose institutions take the legal-constitutional discursive form which has enabled capitalism to rise—*a state is not in (or above) society, a state is a society*" (1989: 347–48, italics added). Similarly, Teeple (1995: 15) has argued that the form of state that has emerged since the Second World War in most Western countries, the welfare state, "can also be seen as a capitalist *society*... " (italics in original).

This formulation may seem at first extreme, positing that "the (capitalist) state is everything, and everything is the (capitalist) state." Yet it is hard to think of any activity today that is not codified, regulated, approved, and occasionally prohibited in some way by the state, often for the purposes of enabling markets. This is true whether speaking of a state-capitalist country such as the "communist" People's Republic of China, the social democratic country of Sweden, or the laissez-faire capitalist country of the United States.

It is also true of Canada. The creation of Canada—of Canadian *society*—cannot be understood without reference to the role of the state. A prime example of this is the National Policy of 1878 (see Part Two), which dramatically altered Canadian economic development and immigration policy. The real challenge in conceptualizing state and society as one thing involves determining which social actors have gained either influence or outright control of the state's machinery at given times and what this has meant, in turn, for defining and shaping socio-cultural, economic, and political relations within Canada.

What, then, is society? A **society** is defined as *the product of relatively continuous and enduring interactions, within a political territory, between people more or less identifying* *themselves as members of the society, these interactions being maintained by an ensemble of political, economic, cultural, and other institutions, the sum of such interactions being in excess of interactions occurring with similarly defined societies external to the given territory.*

This definition raises several points requiring elaboration. First, note that societies, like states and nations, are processes, not things. Whether any of these labels has substantive meaning for a group of people is dependent upon the maintenance of "relatively continuous and enduring interactions." We may presume further that, on balance, positive interactions are more fruitful than negative interactions. Second, note also that individuals may have either greater or lesser attachment to a society, just as they may have greater or lesser attachment to other social groups (such as the family) or may have different reasons for feeling they are part of a group. Third, note the important role of various institutions in acting as intermediaries between individuals, small groups, and society as a whole. Fourth, note that no society today is hermetically sealed off from external influences. This last point is brought home in recurrent discussions of globalization.

GLOBALIZATION, THE STATE, AND SOCIETY

The term *globalization* became popular in the late part of the twentieth century as a shorthand means of describing global integration. But what does globalization actually mean? In brief, **globalization** is defined as *a series of interrelated economic, political, and cultural changes, sometimes contradictory and even opposed, occurring throughout the world* (see Harrison, 1999). Economically, globalization involves a complex series of worldwide exchanges in labour, trade, technology, and capital (Stubbs and Underhill, 1994; Laxer, 1995) and the reorganization over space of production itself (Mittelman, 1996; Lairson and Skidmore, 1997). Politically, globalization similarly manifests itself in increased interconnectedness and interdependence among countries, though not necessarily unification (Boyer and Drache, 1996). Culturally, globalization involves the spread of primarily Western liberal practices and notions of individualism and civil and political rights, as well as consumerism (Mittelman, 1996; Boyer and Drache, 1996; Robbins, 1999).

A central debate surrounding globalization has been its impact upon the state. One school of thought holds that globalization has severely curtailed the power and capacity of states, if not actually signalled their outright demise. Economic historian Eric Heilbroner (1992: 60), for example, exclaims:

> The global market system stretches beyond the political authority of any single government. Faced with a network of connections that escape their powers of surveillance and regulation, national governments become increasingly unable to cope with the problems that arise from the intrusion of the global economy into their territories....

Stated another way, it is argued that "the national state has become too small for the big problems of life, and too big for the small problems" (Bell, 1993: 362). In partial consequence, the state is being "decomposed" by globalization from above (by transnationals, the World Bank, the International Monetary Fund, and so on) and the reemergence of smaller communities from below (McDonald, 1994: 241). In effect, arguably, nation and state are decoupling (Paquet, 1997: 36), perhaps devolving into smaller, regional states (Ohmae, 1990).

Note that the state's supposed decline is not viewed equally by everyone. Some applaud the decomposition of the state as allowing for greater economic efficiency and consumer choice (Ohmae, 1990) and the end of state-orchestrated violence (Rummel, 1994; van den Berghe, 1992). Others, however, fear that the state's eclipse will result in the sweeping away of 200 years of hard-won civil, political, and social rights (Teeple, 1995). Likewise, some believe that the fragmentation of states signals the decline of civic nationalism and its replacement by renewed forms of tribalism (Barber, 1996), perhaps even anarchism and terrorism as witnessed in the attacks on New York and Washington in September 2001. Arthur Schlesinger, Jr. (1997: 10), historian and former special assistant to U.S. President Kennedy, remarks:

> The world today is torn in opposite directions. Globalization is in the saddle and rides mankind [sic], but at the same time drives people to seek refuge from its powerful forces beyond their comprehension.... The faster the world integrates, the more people will huddle in their religious or ethnic or tribal enclaves.

If traditional states are in decline, does this mean their powers of regulation and coercion are simply dissipating? A second school of thought argues, rather, that globalization has resulted in the powers previously held by territorial states being transferred to undemocratic quasi-states—transnational corporations—and other unaccountable international organizations (see Robbins, 1999: 132; Strange, 1996; Korten, 1995). From this perspective, the state itself is being globalized (Albrow, 1997: 172). In the words of David Korten (1995: 54), "Corporations have emerged as the dominant governance institutions on the planet...."

Clearly, the outright demise of the state or its resurrection at the global level would have important implications for societies such as Canada's. What might be the fate of Canadian society in such a world? Malcolm Waters (1994: 233) provides a succinct answer: "If the nation-state is dissolving, or at least attenuating, then so too must national societies...." One logical extension of this dissolution is that national societies will be replaced by a global society, also known as "the global village." Is such a thing possible, or is this merely Utopian theorizing?

A third school of thought suggests that both the death of the state and the inevitability and even originality of globalization have been greatly exaggerated (Laxer, 1995). From this perspective, the world economy has not been globalized but rather "internationalized," with states themselves the architects of reorganizing capitalist production. Moreover, while many of the world's largest economies are not countries, but corporations (Robbins, 1999: 137), the latter are not stateless, let alone "virtual." Most multinationals retain headquarters in the core states, especially the United States. Put another way, states peripheral to the world capitalist economy were weak before globalization and remain so now, while states that were central to that economy likewise remain powerful actors despite globalization (Burbach et al., 1997: 19).

Globalization has not left states unscathed. Technological and organizational changes and the freer flow of capital associated with the growth of multinationals have had an impact on state roles, functions, and policies (see Jessop, 1993; Teeple, 1995). Nonetheless, in this view, states still remain central actors, organizing economic life, providing political legitimacy, and exercising social control over populations (Boyer and Drache, 1996).

Likewise, Canada and Canadian society have not been untouched by globalization. As a wealthy but semi-peripheral country, Canada faces the additional challenge of residing next to the most powerful empire in world history, the chief engine of globalization. Yet Canada remains a sovereign country, with its own symbols and political state intact. And within these geographic and political boundaries, Canadian society also continues to exist as an object worthy of study.

As noted previously, sociology arose in the nineteenth century in an effort to explain the rise of industrial society. How might sociology be useful in examining the challenges facing Canadian society in an era of globalization?

THEORIZING SOCIAL RELATIONSHIPS

Students approaching sociology for the first time are frequently confounded by an array of theories. This reaction is both unfortunate and unnecessary. Theories are like tools. A wrench is a poor instrument for hammering nails. Likewise, a hammer is useless for sawing wood. But, used properly, a wrench or a hammer can be very helpful.

The same goes for theories. Theories are neither good nor bad. They are either useful or not in assisting us to sort out and understand particular phenomena.

The sociological "tool box" contains several theories for understanding how individuals and groups (large and small) interact. For students at a beginning level of instruction, four theoretical perspectives are particularly useful: structural-functional theory, conflict theory, feminist theory, and symbolic interaction theory.

Structural-functional theory can be traced back to the work of Emile Durkheim and Herbert Spencer (1820–1895), an English sociologist. For both Durkheim and Spencer, societies were analogous to the human body. Just as the skeleton and various organs fulfill specific functions necessary for survival, so do the various structures and institutions of human society—the church, family, schools, the state—fulfill functions necessary for the continuation and survival of that society (Parsons, 1951). An institution's function may be *manifest* or *latent* (Merton, 1968). For example, schools are manifestly intended to educate students, but they also act to control young people and socialize them for later participation in the labour market.

Structural-functionalism draws our attention to how various social elements are interconnected. A change in one part of society—for instance, a downturn in the economy—may thus have unforeseen consequences for other parts (Merton, 1968), such as family structure. Where change in one sphere occurs, and other spheres are not able to adapt, or do so slowly, disequilibrium or *dysfunctions* may occur. In general, however, the theory suggests that the interconnectedness of functions slows the rate of social change.

The second perspective, **conflict theory**, has its roots in the work of Karl Marx and Max Weber. Marx, whose writings underpinned the notion of social revolution during the twentieth century, argued that world history was the result of class struggle. By this, he meant that conflict between classes resulted in social change. Weber's contribution to conflict theory was to suggest that conflict is not necessarily based on class alone, but also upon differences in status and power. Today, conflict theory involves also recognizing the many non-class bases of inequality and conflict, such as ethnicity, language, region, age, and gender (Curtis et al., 1999). Frequently, conflict cuts across several lines. For example, labour conflict at a bank may involve workers and management (class conflict). At the same time, it is likely that the majority of low-level employees are female while upper-level managers are male (gender conflict).

As suggested in Box 1.1, structural-functional and conflict theories are the yin and yang of sociological perspectives.

BOX 1.1 | **The Essential Elements of Structural-Functional and Conflict Models**

The Structural-Functional Model:

1. Every society is a relatively persisting configuration of elements.
2. Every society is a well-integrated configuration of elements.
3. Every element in a society contributes to its functioning.
4. Every society rests on the consensus of its members.

The Conflict Model:

1. Every society is subjected at every moment to changes; social change is ubiquitous.
2. Every society experiences at every moment social conflicts; social conflict is ubiquitous.
3. Every element in a society contributes to its change.
4. Every society rests on constraints of some of its members by others.

Source: R. Dahrendorf (1958).

Both structural-functionalism and conflict theory are referred to as "macro" theories. In other words, these theories examine society as a whole from a high vantage point. Large groups, defined by class, occupation, or gender (for example), are the abstract objects of investigation.

By contrast, the two other theories to be examined here, feminist theory and symbolic interaction theory, often take a more mid-range or, particularly in the latter case, "micro" approach to social analysis. Though only recently introduced into sociology, the roots of **feminist theory** go back at least two centuries to the writings of such figures as Mary Woolstonecraft (1759–1797) and Harriet Martineau (1802–1876). Woolstonecraft's *A Vindication of the Rights of Women*, published in 1792, advanced the Enlightenment case for human equality and promoted the specific legal and social rights of women. Martineau translated Auguste Comte from French into English in 1853, later wrote on the evils of slavery and the need for better laws to protect factory workers, and also fought for greater gender equality and the right of suffrage (Macionis and Gerber, 1999: 316; Macionis et al., 2002: 12).

In practice today, there are several variations on the feminist approach. Morrow (1994: 18), for example, lists liberal, socialist, Marxist, radical, and post-modernist approaches, to which Harman (2001: 175) adds maternal (or conservative) feminism, pointing to such historical figures as Nellie McClung and Emily Murphy (see Chapter Seven) as representatives. Whatever the specific approach, however, feminist theory places gender at the centre of sociological analysis, and in doing so draws our attention to how patriarchal institutions and culture (including much previous research in sociology) have often rendered women and women's experiences—such as unpaid labour and the acceptance of male violence directed against women—invisible.

While ideas drawn from feminist theory can be employed at various levels of analysis, **symbolic interaction theory** more often deals with interactions within small groups or organizations. Symbolic interaction is a sociological offshoot of social psychology. While social psychological concepts are embedded in the work of Marx, Weber, and Durkheim, symbolic interaction theory is chiefly a product of American pragmatism, particularly the work of George Herbert Mead (1863–1931) (see Morrow, 1994: 13; also Collins, 1982). Whereas both conflict and structural-functional theories emphasize the structures within which action occurs or is constrained, symbolic interaction theory emphasizes the constructed nature of reality and the interpretation of meaning. In this sense, the methodological approach of Weber (1958), known as ***verstehen***—that is, *an understanding of the meaning that others attach to events, symbols, and experiences*—is entirely congruent with this theory. The major tenets of feminist theory and symbolic interaction theory are reviewed in Box 1.2.

BOX 1.2 — The Essential Elements of the Feminist and Symbolic Interaction Models

The Feminist Model:

1. **Patriarchy**—*the system of male domination in society*—and not biology determines in large degree a person's opportunities in life.
2. Ideas should be related to action.
3. The cultural division of human beings into two opposing and limiting spheres (male and female) must be replaced by a reintegration of people allowing for all individuals to develop all human traits.
4. Laws and cultural norms that promote sexual violence (e.g., abuse, harassment, pornography) and **sexism**—*the belief that one sex is inherently superior to another*—and that otherwise limit the opportunities of women or prevent possession of their own bodies must be opposed.

The Symbolic Interaction Model:

1. Human beings act toward things on the basis of meanings that things have for them.
2. The meaning of such things is derived from, or arises out of, the social interaction that one has with one's fellows.
3. These meanings are handled in, and modified through, an interpretive process used by the person in dealing with the things he or she encounters.

Sources: The feminist model is drawn from Macionis et al. (2002: 233–248); *Symbolic Interactionism*, second editon, by Charon, © Reprinted by permission of Pearson Education, Inc., Upper Saddle River, New Jersey.

The importance of meaning for action can be shown by a practical example. It is hard to imagine people sacrificing their lives for a piece of cloth. Defined as a flag, however, a piece of cloth is an object with symbolic properties for which many have died in wars.

How might a sociologist use structural-functional, conflict, feminist and symbolic interaction theories? A typically Canadian example makes the case.

THINKING THEORETICALLY: CANADA'S GAME

The theory you choose as your lens for examining a topic will provide you with particular questions and insights. Let's take hockey as an example. From a structural-functional point of view, a sociologist might examine the functions that hockey plays in our society. She or he might emphasize that hockey provides a source of national pride and cohesion, such as occurred in 1972 when Paul Henderson scored the goal that clinched Canada's defeat of the Soviet Union. Our sociologist might also remark on the role of hockey (and sports in general) in providing a safe outlet for male aggression, both at the interpersonal level and (as a substitute for war) between countries. She or he might finally note that hockey has traditionally provided a means of social mobility for working-class youth.

A conflict perspective forces us to examine professional hockey quite differently. The National Hockey League (NHL) player walkout in 1994 highlighted a conflict between capitalist owners and workers (albeit, very well paid ones). Analyzing the events that led to the Winnipeg Jets moving to Arizona in 1996 (see Silver, 1996) provides a similarly provocative view of corporate capitalism in an age of globalization. Alternatively, a conflict theorist might note that professional hockey seems to be stratified along ethnic lines. For example, most players in the NHL are Caucasian. The first black player in the National Hockey League was Willie O'Ree with Boston in 1958. Since then, black and Aboriginal players in the league have been few and have sometimes faced racist taunts from other players and fans.

By contrast, a sociologist employing a feminist perspective might note how women's hockey remains marginalized (despite the Canadian women's team's gold-winning victory at the 2002 Winter Olympics) and how female players appear to receive publicity only when they are sexually attractive. The feminist perspective might also draw our attention to how hockey, and sports in general, often enforce and reward a kind of male machismo whose aggressiveness is sometimes carried into the personal lives of players, with dire consequences for girlfriends, spouses, and children.

Finally, a sociologist working from a symbolic interaction perspective might concentrate on the meanings that fans bring to hockey. What, for example, is the process by which an individual becomes a fan? How is it that people come to see their own success as reflected in a team? How do people at a hockey game learn to act like fans (and not like uninformed wannabes)? From the players' point of view, what is the process by which one becomes accepted as a team member? What is team bonding, and how is it achieved?

None of these theories is exclusive. For example, a sociologist might argue that recent fan disenchantment (a symbolic interaction perspective) is linked to the increased corporatization of professional hockey (a conflict argument) and the subsequent breaking of the irrational—but very real—emotional bonds of solidarity (a structural-functionalist's concern) that fans have traditionally felt for their teams.

METHODOLOGY: SOCIOLOGY AND WHY HISTORY MATTERS

The methodological approach used in this text is termed **historical sociology**. Many students are familiar with sociology as the study of society, but often this understanding is focused upon society as it exists *at the moment*. This focus is comparable to that of a 35-mm camera taking a snapshot. By contrast, the focus of historical sociology is comparable to that of a movie camera. An underlying assumption of historical sociology is that *our material institutions, actions, and beliefs are shaped, though not determined, by past events and our understanding (or misunderstanding) of those events.*

The study of history is not fashionable today. At the end of the Cold War, the title of a best-selling book proclaimed "the end of history" (Fukuyama, 1992). About the same time, a line from a popular song spoke of "watching the world wake up from history." The fact is, we live in an anti-historical period. Modernism, with its endless emphasis upon newness, regards history as irrelevant. To ascribe any power, meaning, or obligation to history may even be viewed as a kind of personal affront to individualism and self-achievement. In the words often attributed to Henry Ford, Sr., "History is bunk."

Think for a moment, however, about the role of history—and memory—in your own life. Consider your own personal relations with others. Do you begin each meeting with your friends anew? Of course not. Your friendship is based on experiences, ideas, and feelings you have shared. In short, you have a history together. If you were to suddenly lose that history—if you contracted total amnesia, for example—the friendship would also be lost.

Looking around us, we can see where history continues to play a role in shaping current events: long-simmering disputes in Ireland, the Middle East, and Kashmir provide ample evidence. Likewise, the echoes of history can be heard in the breakup of Yugoslavia in the 1990s. Not even the United States—surely the world's most proudly modern country—can escape history, as witness the plethora of Hollywood movies that continue the socio-analytic function of coming to terms with *the* meaning of the Vietnam War.

But what of Canada? In an oft-quoted remark, Prime Minister W.L.M. King once stated regarding Canada, "If some countries have too much history, we have too much geography." As John Gray (1994: 124) notes, such arguments really mean that Canada "lacks *European* history," conveniently ignoring 50 000 years of Aboriginal existence in North America. But even by Eurocentric standards, the argument is false, as one glance at Quebec's licence plates will attest: "Je me souviens" (I remember). Remember what? History: the Conquest.

We need not refer, however, merely to centuries-old history. Ask Aboriginal Canadians about the continuing impact of residential schools, some of which remained open until the early 1980s. Or ask Albertans about the National Energy Program of 1980–84 and how it still colours a widespread understanding of political relations between that province and Ottawa.

Note, however, a difference between the facts of history and people's understanding, valuation, and interpretation of history. People may agree on the former, but not on the latter. Alternatively, they may disagree about *both* the facts *and* the meaning of events. In this sense, "History is contested terrain" (Francis, 1997: 12). It is not "dead" but, rather, a source of constant rediscovery, recreation, reinterpretation—and *power*. As George Orwell (1983: 886) wrote in his novel *1984*, "Who controls the past controls the future, who controls the present controls the past."

History may, of course, trap us. It *is* possible for some countries to have "too much history," to be (as it were) stuck in the past. But not remembering—living in a state of amnesia—is also a trap. The big questions are the following: Who determines "official" history? Are unofficial, alternative, and even multiple histories heard and respected within the society? And what are the lessons—myths, really—that a people construct around their collective histories?

Ultimately, history *determines* nothing (Carr, 1990). Our understanding—our *imagination*—of it, however, locates us, both individually and collectively, in time in the same way that geography locates us in space. Put another way, our understanding of history organizes material in a manner that helps us interpret current events. Without this temporal context, meaning and meaningful action become impossible (see Rickman, 1961; Dilthey, 1961).

Moreover, the consequences of historical events (as set down in institutions, treaties, laws, etc.), as well as our understanding and interpretation of these events, often set off chains of meaning and action long after the specific events themselves have ceased. Thus, for example, two lines can be drawn—one leading directly, the other indirectly—from the Royal Proclamation of 1763. The first of these lines leads to the Oka Crisis of 1990 and the recent passing of the Nisga'a treaty in British Columbia (Chapters Twelve and Thirteen). The second of these lines leads to the Meech Lake Accord and the Quebec referendum of 1995 (Chapters Four and Five).

Historical memory is all around us, even in Canada. Canadian humorist, economist—and historian—Stephen Leacock once remarked, "I never realized that there was history too, close at hand, beside my very own home. I did not realize that the old grave that stood among the brambles at the foot of our farm was *history*" (quoted in Colombo, 1994: 112). History is located in our texts and photographs, in the myths and jokes we tell each other, in the formal institutions present at our birth and surviving long after we have passed away. Historical memory acts upon and through us, often most powerfully when we are not conscious of its force.

One way of understanding the role of history in shaping Canadian society is to employ a methodological technique termed **counterfactual history**.

What is counterfactual history? While often condemned as a parlour game, counterfactual history properly employed is not just history "made up." Rather, it is based on factual information and interpretive and extrapolative logic, held together by a historical sociologist's imagination.

The use of counterfactual history is not new (Honan, 1998). Recalling, for example, the events that led to the dissolution of the Austro-Hungarian Empire in 1918, Oscar Jaszi (1961: 380) wrote:

> Opposed to the materialistic point of view, I accept the... reversibility of the historical process, and regard the chief utility of all historical and sociological investigations to be to admonish us of the alternative possibilities of history.

Counterfactual history provides a means of separating what is important in history from that which is merely incidental. It alerts us to the importance of history by asking the question, what if people involved in an event had made different decisions, or events had otherwise transpired in different ways? The reader is invited throughout this text to ask similar questions about Canada. What if New France had not been surrendered to the British in 1763 (Chapter Two)? What if the Meech Lake Accord had been passed in 1990

(Chapter Four)? What if the Liberals had won the 1988 election and overturned the Free Trade Agreement (Chapter Nine)?

Finally, counterfactual history also alerts us to the fact that individual people and the decisions they make matter; again, that history does not determine the present. For Canadians at the start of the new millennium, repeatedly advised that globalization is inevitable and that the invisible hand of the marketplace cannot be resisted, reminders of personal efficacy are to be valued.

KEY TERMS

conflict theory
counterfactual history
country
feminist theory
globalization
historical sociology
nation
patriarchy
reification
sexism
society
sociology
state
structural-functional theory
symbolic interaction theory
verstehen

part one

Canada and Quebec

The threat that Quebec would one day leave Canada has been around for more than a hundred years. Since the 1960s, the threat has produced a veritable cottage industry of reports and books on the topic. For a brief moment, however, on the evening of October 30, 1995, it seemed that the time of debate had reached a climax. Like deer caught in winter headlights, stunned Canadians watched the results of Quebec's referendum on sovereignty unfolding on their television screens.

In the end, the No side narrowly defeated the Yes side by less than a percentage point (50.6 percent to 49.4 percent), a mere few thousand votes. For supporters of sovereignty, the sadness of defeat was lessened by the true believers' faith that next time their side would win. For federalists, nervous relief dampened the ecstasy one would expect of victory. By the skin of its teeth, Canada had narrowly escaped a venture into unknown, uncertain, and—some argued—dangerous territory.

The 1995 Quebec referendum came at the end of more than a decade—some would say 200 years—of social and political wrangling. In 1982, Quebec refused to sign the new Canadian Constitution. Subsequent failures to meet Quebec's demands in 1990 (through the Meech Lake Accord) and in 1992 (through the Charlottetown Accord) set the stage for the later sovereignty referendum.

The chapters that follow examine the history of English-French relations in Canada, how that relationship has structured Canadian society as a whole, and why a country reputed by many outsiders to be "the best in the world" in recent years has come perilously close to dissolving.

QUESTIONS

Several important questions frame this examination:

- What are the issues behind Quebec nationalism? What are its historical, cultural, and political roots?

- How has Quebec influenced the structure of Canadian society? How has Canadian society changed Quebec?

- Why have constitutional issues in Canada been so divisive? More broadly, what is the sociological meaning of constitutions for societies?

- Why did Quebec nationalism reawaken in the 1960s? Why has it declined since the 1995 referendum? Is the decline permanent or will Quebec separatism resurface?

- Must Canada and Quebec (English and French) remain, in the metaphor of Hugh MacLennan, "two solitudes"? Or are other metaphors possible?

- Why is English Canada threatened by Quebec nationalism?

- What are the connections between Quebec separatism and globalization?

- What would happen if Canada and Quebec were to separate?

chapter two
Living with the Consequences of 1760

Valour gave them a common death / history a common fame / posterity a common monument.
—words on the Wolfe and Montcalm Monument, Quebec City

I die without remorse; all that I desired was the good of my country....My efforts have been for the independence of my compatriots....I die with the cry on my lips: Long live Liberty! Long live Independence!
—Chevalier de Lorimier, Patriote, before his execution, 1838

I expected to find a contest between a government and a people: I found two nations warring in the bosom of a single state.
—Lord Durham's Report, 1839

INTRODUCTION

The Meech Lake Accord's failure in 1990 and the subsequent Quebec referendum on sovereignty in 1995 brought into sharp relief two very different views of Canada. Is Canada a partnership of two founding peoples, the French and English, or even a third, the First Nations peoples (see Part Three)? Or is Canada a federation of ten equal provinces (Quebec and the others)? Most francophone Quebecers believe the former, sometimes referred to as the "two nations theory." They further believe that, as a minority nation within Canada, they have a historically distinctive patrimony that must be protected; that they constitute a "distinct society" within Canada.

Thanks to decades of political wrangling, many people in English-speaking Canada know something of the history of Quebec-Canada and French-English relations. But this knowledge is often partial or inexact. In any case, facts do not automatically produce meaning; even less do they constitute truths.

This chapter goes beyond the historic facts to explore the emotional and symbolic meaning of English and French relationships in Canada, and the early evolution of these unique relationships. Embedded in the discussion are important sociological questions regarding dominant-subordinate relationships and the responsibilities and consequences imposed upon conquerors and conquered alike by history.

THE AGE OF MERCANTILISM

Between 1689 and 1763, the French and the English fought a series of wars. The last of these wars (1756 to 1763) was known in Europe as the Seven Years War, but in British North America, as the French and Indian War (Hofstadter et al., 1957: 64). North America was merely one outpost, albeit an important one, in these wars. To understand these wars, it is necessary to reflect briefly on the political economy of European expansion beginning in the fifteenth century.

Before that time, the basic structures of European society had remained fundamentally unchanged since (roughly) the collapse of the Roman Empire (see Manchester, 1992). In Thomas Hobbes's memorable phrase, life was "poor, nasty, brutish, and short." People lived predictable lives in small rural communities. Families were large, class structures and age and gender roles were fixed, trade was local, and barter was the chief means of exchange.

Slowly, however, European feudal society began to change. Central to the changes were the growth of states in which power was centralized and monarchs became all-powerful, a corresponding decline in the temporal power of churches (though religion itself remained important), and the emergence of a new merchant class. In earlier times, churches had frowned upon trade, especially such practices as the granting of monopolies, usury, and profiteering (Hofstadter et al., 1957: 4). Between the sixteenth and eighteenth centuries, however, there arose a new economic arrangement. Now, the new merchant class and the state encouraged commercial trade. Merchants paid the state levies and taxes, and even lent money at favourable rates to support the state's armies. In return, merchants induced states to enact policies, including war, designed to protect their business interests (LaHaye, 1993: 534).

The new economic arrangement was called **mercantilism** (Hofstadter et al., 1957; La Haye, 1993; Norrie and Owram, 1996: 17–18). The chief aim of mercantilist policies was to preserve the mother country's supply of precious metals and to make it less vulnerable during times of war. Colonies were fundamental to mercantilist policy. In practice, because mercantilism and colonialism also meant the enrichment of one state and its merchant allies at the expense of other states and their business friends, conflict was a frequent result. In North America, the conflict primarily involved the English on the Eastern seaboard and around Hudson Bay and the French in Nova Scotia and along the St. Lawrence, the colony of New France. The indigenous people of the region soon found themselves caught up in the conflict.

THE RISE AND FALL OF NEW FRANCE

The history of New France begins in 1534. That year, Cartier first made landfall on the shores of the Gaspé Peninsula (see Miller, 2000). Like the Spanish far to the south, Cartier came in search of gold. He was discredited, however, when the "gold" he brought back from his third voyage (1541–42) turned out to be iron pyrites. Diverted by a series of European conflicts, France temporarily forgot about North America (Morton, 1997: 24).

Early in the next century, however, France returned in the person of Samuel de Champlain. A "navigator, soldier, visionary," "a Protestant turned Catholic by conviction," and "a man of Renaissance curiosity and eternal fortitude" (Morton, 1997: 25), Champlain in 1608 founded a trading post at what is now Quebec City. Thus New France began.

From the beginning, the post's survival was perilous. Life was harsh. Efforts by Champlain to forge alliances with the Huron Confederacy brought the colonists into conflict with the Huron's chief enemies, the tribes of the Iroquois Confederacy. Despite Champlain's efforts to build a colony, Quebec City in 1627 still had fewer than a hundred people. In that year, France's chief minister, Cardinal Richelieu, formed a private company made up of a hundred merchants and aristocrats. The *Compagnie des Cent-Associés* was given a monopoly over the fur trade in exchange for promises to colonize the territory (Moore, 2000).

Still the settlement did not thrive. Military threats continued. In 1629, an English trading company seized Quebec City; it was returned to France in 1632 only after diplomatic negotiations (Moore, 2000). The fact is, Quebec City and the surrounding area was far less politically and economically valuable to France than its posts in Cape Breton, Nova Scotia, and Newfoundland that protected the valuable cod fishery. Dickinson and Young (1993: 15) note that, until 1760, "France imported far more cod than fur and the fishery employed many more seamen and ships than all other French colonial trade combined" (see also Eccles, 1993a: 163). By contrast, New France's fur trade economy was unstable. European demand fluctuated according to fashion. Supply was equally unpredictable. Weather conditions, the needs and good fortune of Aboriginal suppliers, the actions of middlemen (Norrie and Owram, 1996: 43), conflict between Aboriginal tribes, exacerbated by competition between the French and Dutch trading companies in Port Albany: all these things affected supply. In the 1630s, disease decimated the Huron population, delivering another blow to the trade (Dickinson and Young, 1993: 19; Innis, 1962; Morton, 1997).

In 1650, about 1200 French colonists lived in New France (Dickinson and Young, 1993: 67). In theory, the Huron Confederacy's destruction opened up new opportunities to attract French immigrants into the fur trade and agriculture. However, war and the *Cent-Associés'* near bankruptcy prevented the colony from taking advantage of the changed circumstances (Moore, 2000: 121–122). In 1663, the colony's population was still only around 3000 people. That year, Louis XIV dissolved the company and made New France a royal colony. An active immigration policy was pursued. Encouragement and financial inducements were given to disbanded military officers and their men, civilian workers, and—in an effort to redress a long-standing gender imbalance in the colonies—women. By 1681, the population of New France was 10 000. Most of Canada's francophone population today traces its roots to these original 10 000 inhabitants (Moore, 2000: 127–129; also, Dickinson and Young, 1993). New France's population thereafter increased primarily from births rather than immigration.

Growth and development create their own problems and natural contradictions. After 1663, the internal contradictions and conflicts facing New France mounted: Catholic church versus state; rural versus urban; fur trading versus agriculture and industry. In the words of historian Desmond Morton (1997: 27), "Were the people of New France to be habitants, cultivating their small colony in the valley of the St. Lawrence, or were they to be voyageurs, carrying the fur trade, Catholicism, and French influence throughout the continent?" Yet the colony also began to develop. Visitors to New France in the mid-eighteenth century regularly commented on its growing prosperity and cultural sophistication (Eccles, 1993b).

In 1756, however, New France faced a growing threat from England and its southern colonies. The 13 British colonies that eventually became the United States had a more developed and diverse economy than New France. Agriculture and commerce were thriving. The English colonists—roughly 1.5 million compared with New France's 75 000 (Eccles, 1993a: 171)—were eager to expand into the Ohio Valley. There, however, they faced a belt of French forts constructed along the Ohio and Mississippi rivers, established both to support the fur trade and to hem off British expansion (Innis, 1962: 88–89; Morton, 1997: 30; Eccles, 1993a: 163). In 1754, a series of armed clashes occurred between British and French forces. These events partially set off the Seven Years War that began two years later (Dickinson and Young, 1993: 47; Eccles, 1993a: 163).

As the war began, the English in North America possessed several advantages over the French. Besides a larger population in the colonies, the English also had a larger and more powerful navy, with which they could blockade the French colonies, and a larger standing army. In 1756, there were roughly 22 000 English regulars and militia in the colonies, to which were later added another 20 000 regular troops. By contrast, New France had no more than 7 000 regular troops, and perhaps another 15 000 militiamen and Aboriginal allies (Dickinson and Young, 1993: 48; Moore, 2000: 185; but see also Eccles, 1993a: 171).

Despite these overwhelming odds, the French in the early stages successfully defended their colony, in part because the British had difficulty in marshalling their superior resources. Gradually, however, the British gained the upper hand. In 1758, the British seized the fort of Louisbourg in Nova Scotia. The following summer, a British fleet sailed up the St. Lawrence, while troops on the ground scorched the countryside (see Box 2.1).

BOX 2.1 | State Terrorism, 1759

Terrorism is *the deliberate use of acts of violence or the threat of violence by individuals, groups, or the state for the purpose of furthering political ends.* We tend to think of terrorism as a recent phenomenon (see Chapter Nine). In fact, terrorism—especially state terrorism—is quite old, as shown in the following excerpt from the written account of the Sergeant Major of the 40th Regiment's Grenadiers (part of the Louisbourg Grenadiers). The passage deals with Wolfe's campaign against New France in the summer of 1759, leading up to the Battle of the Plains of Abraham in September of that year.

> The 15th of Aug. Captain Gorham returned from an Incursion, in which Service were employ'd, under his Command, 150 Rangers, a Detachment from the different Regiments, Highlanders, Marines, &c. amounting in the whole to about 300, an arm'd Vessel,

BOX 2.1 — State Terrorism, 1759 (continued)

three Transports, with a Lieutenant and Seamen of the Navy to attend him, of which Expedition they gave the following Account:

"That on the 4th of August they proceeded down to St. Paul's Bay, (which is opposite to the North Side of this Island) where was a Parish containing about 200 men, who had been very active in distressing our Boats and Shipping — At 3 o 'Clock in the Morning Capt. Gorham landed and forced two of their Guards; of 20 Men each, who fired smartly for Some Time; but that in two Hours they drove them all from their Covering in the Wood, and clear'd the Village which they burnt, consisting of about 50 fine Houses and Barns; destroy'd most of their Cattle, &c. That in this one Man was kill'd and 6 wounded; but that the Enemy had two kill'd, and several wounded, who were carried off. — That from thence they proceeded to Mal Bay, 10 Leagues to the Eastward on the same Side, where they destroyed a very pretty Parish, drove off the Inhabitants and Stock without any Loss; after which, they made a Descent on the South Shore, opposite the Island of Coudre, destroyed Part of the Parish of St. Ann's and St. Roan, where were very handsome Houses with Farms, and loaded the Vessels with Cattle; after which they returned from their Expedition."

The same Day 1 of our Schooners went from the Fleet below the Fall, and the French fir'd 8 or 9 Shot at her; but miss'd her. This Day a Party of young Highlanders came to the Island of Orleans from Gen. Monckton's Encampment; on Purpose to destroy all the Canada-Side. — The same Day our People set one of the Enemy's Floating-Batteries on Fire; — and in the Night General Monckton set the Town on Fire, (being the 4th Time) and the Flames raged so violently, that 'twas imagin'd the whole City would have been reduc'd to Ashes.

August 18th a Sloop and Schooner went below the Falls; the French hove Shot and Shells at them, but did 'em no Damage. The same Day the Enemy hove a Bomb from the Town, which kill'd one Man and wounded 6 more, — one Man had his Arm cut off by a Piece of the same Shell.

On the 20th the Louisbourg Grenadiers began their March down the main Land of Quebeck, in order to burn and destroy all the Houses on that Side. — On the 24th they were attack'd by a Party of French, who had a Priest for their Commander; but our Party kill'd and scalp'd 31 of them, and likewise the Priest, their Commander; They did our People no Damage. The three Companies of Louisbourg Grenadiers halted about 4 Miles down the River, at a Church called the Guardian-Angel, where we were order'd to fortify ourselves till further Orders; we had several small Parties in Houses, and the Remainder continued in the Church. — The 25th, began to destroy the Country, burning Houses, cutting down Corn, and the like: At Night the Indians fired several scattering Shot at the Houses, which kill'd one of the Highlanders and wounded another; but they were soon repulsed by the Heat of our Firing. — It was said that the Number of the Enemy consisted of 800 Canadians and Indians. Sept 1st we set Fire to our Houses and Fortifications, and marched to join the Grand Army at Montmorancy; the 3 Companies of Grenadiers ordered to hold themselves in Readiness to march at a Minute's Warning.

Source: Robert Henderson (n.d.). Reproduced with the permission of *The Discriminating General*, www.militaryheritage.com.

Gradually, Quebec City was isolated from the surrounding territory, and the siege began. Throughout the following months, the British led by General Wolfe conducted a constant bombardment of the city in hopes of forcing the French under General Montcalm out of their defensive position. Much of lower Quebec City was laid to rubble. The British also torched the surrounding countryside (Dickinson and Young, 1993; Dufour, 1990; Moore, 2000). Yet the French did not surrender.

Frustrated, Wolfe tried a final tactic. On the night of September 12, the British forces seized a path up the cliffs to west Quebec City, setting the stage for the historic battle of the next day, as related by Moore (2000: 188):

> On the Plains of Abraham, Wolfe's red-coated army formed one line, facing east towards the city. After some fierce skirmishing, Montcalm's troops in their white coats moved west towards them, drums beating, regimental banners flying. The two armies were roughly equal in numbers. These were precisely the conditions Wolfe had sought all summer, and in a battle that lasted barely fifteen minutes, the close-range volleys of his skilled regulars tore the French army apart.

Wolfe died that day in battle; Montcalm succumbed the next day to his wounds; and part of a national mythology was born (see Francis, 1997: 55–56). In effect, the war was over, although fighting continued for another year. In August 1760, Montreal capitulated, the French humiliation completed by a public surrender of arms (Dufour, 1990). The Treaty of Paris in 1763 formally ended the war. France ceded its former colony along the St. Lawrence to Britain.

THE PROCLAMATION ACT AND THE QUEBEC ACT

In 1760, New France, now known as Quebec, was in a state of ruin. Roughly a tenth of the colony's population had been killed (Moore, 2000: 188). Quebec City and the area around it were in ruins, the colony's economic infrastructure destroyed. Famine and disease were rampant. All in all, the war and its immediate aftermath were terrifying for the residents of the colony.

Adding to their abject circumstances was French fear of their conquerors. The French had good reason to fear the British. The torching of homes and villages along the St. Lawrence gave ample proof of the enemy's barbarity. The forced expulsion of roughly 6000 Acadian people in 1754 from what is now Nova Scotia, without compensation for their land, was also fresh on French minds (Dickinson and Young, 1993: 48; Conway, 1997: 12).

The French were surprised, therefore, by the generally courteous and respectful behaviour of the British. In the years between 1760 and 1764, Quebec was under martial law. Yet the British did little to interfere with French traditions, and indeed they helped in the province's reconstruction. In the words of Dufour (1990: 27), the conqueror's behaviour was "correct. Even exemplary."

The Royal Proclamation of 1763, however, gave the French a taste of the iron fist. Designed to assimilate the French, the Proclamation declared that Quebec henceforth would be governed by British institutions, with an elected assembly and British laws. British immigration would be encouraged. Finally, in an effort to head off further wars with Aboriginal peoples, the interior hinterland of the Ohio Valley was made a vast Aboriginal reserve (Innis, 1962; Dickinson and Young, 1993).

In an act of surprising civility, however, the British governor, James Murray, refused to enact many of the Proclamation's provisions. In part, Murray's actions were based on his recognition that the provisions were not enforceable. Eighty-five percent of the colony's inhabitants lived in rural areas beyond administrative control (Dickinson and Young, 1993). There was little likelihood soon of a wave of English immigration that might change the colony's predominantly French and Catholic character. Under existing British law, no Catholic could hold office, making impossible the notion of a representative legislative assembly. Montreal fur traders were already demanding that the Ohio Valley be reopened for business. Moreover, given growing unrest in England's southern colonies on the continent, the last thing the British needed was agitation in the north. But it is also true that Murray himself *actually liked and admired the French* and—setting a tradition followed for a time by his successors—acted, albeit paternalistically, as a protector of French interests (see Dufour, 1990; Conway, 1997). Conqueror and conquered were mutually seduced (Dufour, 1990).

Thus, in 1774, the British passed the Quebec Act, which altogether reversed the Royal Proclamation. The law was changed to allow Catholics to hold elected office. Seigneurial land tenure was confirmed. The colony's territorial boundaries were increased to include some of the First Nations territories. Catholics were given the right to practise their religion. The Catholic church was once more allowed to collect tithes. And while English criminal law was retained, French law was allowed in civil cases (Dickinson and Young, 1993: 55).

In a curious sense, the Conquest seemed to have changed little. Nonetheless, its effects were real. In the most profound sense, the Conquest forged a people, a sociological—but not a political—nation.

BEING *CANADIEN*

A people somewhat distinct from the European French was arising in the colony even before the Conquest. In contrast to the town-dwelling French administrators, the peasant farmers—habitants, as they called themselves—were mostly rural. In their everyday lives, they experienced greater independence and social equality, including gender equality, than people living in France (Rioux, 1978: 17–18). This basic equality, combined with isolation, the harshness of their existence, and the constant fear of attack by Aboriginals, developed among the habitants over time a strong sense of solidarity (Dickinson and Young, 1993; Rioux, 1978). By the 1750s, visitors to New France "claimed that a new kind of French people was emerging along the banks of the St. Lawrence" (Morton, 1997: 28), a people distinguished by different beliefs, customs, behaviours, and even dialect (Rioux, 1978: 24–25; see also Eccles, 1993b; Thompson, 1995). They called themselves habitants and *Canadiens*, and their country Canada. There was no need to copyright *Canadien* identity. By definition, *Canadiens* were French-speaking Catholics settled permanently along the St. Lawrence. Moreover, in their own minds at least, the territorial boundaries of their nation extended well beyond their colony's borders into areas traversed and imagined by French voyageurs and missionaries.

But distinctiveness, though necessary, is not a sufficient basis of nationalism. The Conquest transformed—though not all at once—New France's distinctiveness into nationalism (Cook, 1995: 86).

Try to put yourself for the moment in the shoes of a habitant after 1763. You have been conquered, not merely defeated by the English (Dufour, 1990: 31). Equally, you have not been merely orphaned by the mother country, but—as the Treaty of Paris cruelly attests—abandoned. The past cannot be reversed. Finally, to add to your confusion, your enemy is actually magnanimous in victory. As a conquered subject, you welcome the difference; the fact that you are not tortured, raped, and killed is clearly important. Still, as Dufour (1990: 31) remarks, the conqueror's magnanimity changes nothing; indeed, it actually makes your being conquered more humiliating, because now you must also be grateful.

New France in 1760, like the British colonies to the south, was growing apart from France and no doubt one day would have sought independence. But the Conquest truncated this normal development. Quebec's sense of self-identity was not positive, in the sense of one chosen by the people; rather, it was an identity thrust upon them, forged in war, trauma, and the torturous severing of the colony's umbilical cord from France. Time and circumstances conspired to make the Quebec's French population a distinct people—*les Canadiens*—before their time. By contrast, the few hundred British who occupied Quebec after 1763 remained, even to themselves, "the British."

The political circumstances were unstable, however. As the British feared, the American colonists in 1775 revolted. In the wake of the conflict, 40 000 United Empire Loyalists fled to the northern British colonies, about 10 000 of them settling in Quebec (Dickinson and Young, 1993). The contest for political, territorial, and economic power and national identity began again.

THE LOYALISTS AND THE CONSTITUTION ACT OF 1791

Imagine now that you are a United Empire Loyalist recently arrived in Canada. Your property in the Thirteen Colonies has been stolen by the revolutionary leaders who have distributed it among themselves, their friends, and small farmers in order to garner their political support for the new republic (Zinn, 1995: 83). Your physical health, and that of your family, is poor. By contrast with the 30 000 Loyalists who arrived in Nova Scotia by ship, you came to Canada by horse cart overland and on foot, bearing little. You are bitter and angry; a historian will later remark that "quarrelsomeness" marked your character and that of your compatriots (Brown, 1993: 246). You were loyal to Britain (you say to yourself and anyone who will listen) and now have lost everything (Morton, 1997: 65; but also see Francis, 1997: 56). The free land, clothing, and farming utensils supplied by the British administration (Dickinson and Young, 1993) do not assuage your bitterness.

Such, in part, was the view of the Loyalists as they arrived in the northern British colonies. Like the French, the Loyalists were a conquered people. In Canada, however, the roughly 10 000 who arrived found their humiliation enlarged by the fact that they were a minority surrounded by more than 70 000 French Catholics. For their part, the French were no more thrilled with their new neighbours, viewing them as an advance guard of future anglophone settlement. In an age when ethnic and religious bigotry were rife, the arrival of the Loyalists was like gasoline thrown on a fire.

Elsewhere, the arrival of Loyalists created similar tensions. In Nova Scotia, the Loyalists who arrived quickly swamped the existing population of 4000 New Englanders and Acadians. The 1000 Loyalists who arrived on the Island of St. John (renamed Prince Edward Island in 1799) equalled those already living there, but the 400 Loyalists who arrived on Cape Breton doubled that island's existing population (Brown, 1993: 241–242).

Anxious to prevent conflict, the British thus segregated the respective populations. Nova Scotia was divided and a new province, New Brunswick, created, while Cape Breton (temporarily) became a separate colony. The colony of Quebec likewise was divided.

The instrument of this latter division was the Constitution Act of 1791. The Constitution Act amended the Quebec Act but left intact many of the latter's provisions protecting the French language, the Catholic Church, French civil law, and the seigneurial system. The Constitution Act, however, divided the colony into Upper Canada (where many of the Loyalists had settled) and Lower Canada (French Canada), the term Canada having been historically another name for New France. The act further maintained strong executive power in the office of the governor, an executive council (made up of the governor's advisers), and a non-elected legislative council (a colonial House of Lords). But it also allowed, for the first time, popularly elected assemblies in both Canadas and extended the franchise. Finally, the act envisaged the creation of a colonial aristocracy, a state church, and public education. The first idea was soon abandoned, but substantial land holdings were set aside for the Anglican Church and education (Careless, 1970: 119–121; Dickinson and Young, 1993: 58–59).

Even at the time, the Constitution Act pleased few people. The merchants of Montreal had not wanted Canada divided. The English in Lower Canada did not like being separated from the English in Upper Canada. The agrarians and rising bourgeoisie in both Canadas did not like the act's openly mercantilist bent. Democrats, believing that the elected assemblies did not go far enough, railed against oligarchic rule. But perhaps the major flaw in the Constitution Act was that it institutionalized ethnic conflict (Cook, 1995: 87). Thereafter, as Quebec premier Pierre Chauveau would later remark, the English and French would meet each other only "on the landing of politics"—frequently in conflict.

THE CONQUEST'S ECONOMIC AND POLITICAL IMPACT

Social stratification is *the system by which a society ranks categories of people (e.g., by occupation, race, ethnicity, or gender) in a hierarchy involving inequalities of various sorts*. At the top of New France's stratification system before the Conquest were royal officials: the governor, the intendant (the business manager), and the senior military officers. The clergy were somewhat parallel to the royal officials, but after 1663 clearly subordinate in the final instance to the state. The seigneurs, some of whom came from the French nobility, came next in the social order, followed by a sizable middle class (composed of merchants and small venders), the urban working class, then the habitants (Eccles, 1993a: 42). (Note that women did not rank in this stratification system, or ranked very low.) The Conquest changed Canada's economic and political order. The degree and type of changes, however, are somewhat disputed.

One dispute involves the actual number of people who left New France. The articles of capitulation in 1760 gave inhabitants the right to return to France. Perhaps only a few hundred took advantage of the opportunity (Dickinson and Young, 1993: 50), perhaps 4000 (Eccles, 1993a: 173). Most of those who left were French bureaucrats and soldiers (though some decommissioned soldiers remained), quickly replaced by British bureaucrats and soldiers.

A second, more important dispute arose during the 1950s and 1960s over the Conquest's impacts upon New France's economic classes and the colony's future. Early on, scholars of "the Montreal School" (Saul, 1997: 19)—Maurice Seguin, Guy Fregault, and Michel Brunet—developed the **decapitation thesis** (Cook, 1995: 92; Dickinson and Young, 1993). This thesis holds that the Conquest had destroyed New France's "embryonic bourgeoisie" (Brunet, 1993; also Rioux, 1978: 39; Conway, 1997: 15). The English and Scots merchants subsequently stepped into the void left by the French bourgeoisie, while the French who remained retreated to a rural existence. There, dominated by the Catholic Church, they espoused conservative values inimical to capitalist development (Norrie and Owram, 1996: 61; Dickinson and Young, 1993). Thus Lower Canada's economic development was truncated.

In direct refutation of the decapitation thesis, a second argument holds that New France in 1763 had no "viable business community" (Dickinson and Young, 1993: 52), no middle class (Hamelin, 1993) to be destroyed. More recently, a synthesis of both arguments has emerged. This third argument suggests that the Conquest resulted in the departure of agents and merchants directly connected to France's trading companies, but that local merchants, storekeepers, and traders stayed. That is, the transatlantic French bourgeoisie was eliminated, but the local French bourgeoisie, albeit small, remained (Norrie and Owram, 1996: 63; also Dickinson and Young, 1993).

More broadly, these debates point to how historical interpretations can have current sociological and political significance. Reflecting on the political context within Quebec during the period of these debates, one can see that the decapitation thesis lent itself to support for the Quiet Revolution (Chapter Three) and sovereignty (Cook, 1995; Saul, 1997). By contrast, the second and third explanations, much less so.

There is no dispute, however, that Canada's economy immediately after 1760 was in crisis. The war's devastation, the permanent disruption of its mercantile (metropolitan-hinterland) arrangements with France, and the outbreak of wars with Aboriginal tribes on the frontier were all contributing factors. Within a short time, however, Lower Canada's economy began to rebound. The colony was rebuilt; the Aboriginal wars ended in 1763 (see Chapter Ten), restoring the Ohio Valley fur trade; and trade links were re-established, this time with Britain. Capital also began to enter Lower Canada from Britain and merchants in England's southern colonies.

The direct economic impacts of the Conquest should not be minimized. In the long term, however, the Conquest's social and political consequences were more important. The English after 1763 held the balance of power—**power** being defined as *the ability of someone to impose their will upon others even against their resistance* (see Box 2.2). The imposition of English will was a fact of life in Lower Canada, despite the newcomers' frequent conciliations and sensitivity to the French majority. With the arrival of the Loyalists after 1775 (see Chapter Six), ethnicity came to play an even greater role in Canada's social structure. The effects of ethnicity, however, were mitigated somewhat by the granting of elected assemblies under the Constitution Act of 1791, which opened up opportunities for a nascent *Canadien* political class.

By the early nineteenth century, ethnicity had become a defining feature of Lower Canada's system of social stratification. The English controlled the executive and judicial branches in the political realm, but the French dominated the legislative branch. The English controlled the upper reaches of the economy: international trade, banking, and finance. The French business class was restricted to local trade. At the lower levels, British labourers, contractors, and producers—often favoured by British administrators—competed with their French counterparts (Dickinson and Young, 1993: 114; Innis, 1962; Norrie and Owram, 1996). Finally, the habitant majority occupied the bottom level of Lower Canada's social structure (Rioux, 1978: 35).

> **BOX 2.2 — Means of Exercising Power**
>
> Power can be exercised by three means. Each means may succeed in achieving a given end in a particular situation. Each also has limits. Finally, the use of any one means of power does not exclude the simultaneous use of other means. The three means of power are:
>
> ***Force or the threat of force***, *also referred to as punishment or coercion.* The expulsion of the Acadians, mentioned earlier, the use of police at Regina in 1935 (Chapter Seven), and the governmental response to the Oka crisis (Chapter Twelve) provide examples of the use of force.
>
> ***Reward.*** Rewards may be pecuniary but not always. Status is a form of reward, for example. Because systems of social stratification (as discussed in this chapter and elsewhere) differentially reward individuals and groups on the basis of class, race, ethnicity, gender, etc., such systems are themselves means of power. Note: withholding instrumental rewards results in economic coercion—the use once more of force.
>
> ***Authority.*** Authority gains its power through being recognized as legitimate. Authority frequently coincides with the means of force and reward but often includes elements of tradition, law, status, or prestige. The **dominant ideology** (see Chapters Three and Eight) of any period tends to legitimize current power relations.

The ethnic division of Lower Canada was not merely social, but also demographic. Gradually, the English "captured" the urban portion of the colony, while the French retreated to the colony's villages and rural farms (Rioux, 1978). Early in the nineteenth century, 40 percent of Quebec City and 33 percent of Montreal were anglophone (Norrie and Owram, 1996: 98). In this context the Catholic church, especially its parish priests, grew in importance.

By the 1830s, these social, political, and economic divisions, built on a foundation of Conquest, had nurtured among Lower Canada's French population a growing sense of grievance and a rising spirit of nationalism. Finally, the grievances boiled over.

THE REBELLIONS OF 1837-38

In 1837, after years of political discord, and in the midst of a prolonged recession, rebellions broke out in both Upper and Lower Canada. The causes of the rebellions in the two Canadas were similar. Popular anger focused on the corrupt oligarchies who governed the provinces —the Chateau Clique in Lower Canada, the Family Compact in Upper Canada— and their political masters in London.

In Upper Canada, the rebels demanded "responsible government." They wanted real power to rest with an elected legislative assembly. The Upper Canadian rebels also wanted economic reform, believing—correctly—that current policies were designed to protect mercantilist interests. The rebels wanted instead increased immigration, greater access to capital, and more land opened up for agriculture (Careless, 1970; Norrie and Owram, 1996).

Though the movements in both Upper and Lower Canada were informed by liberal democratic ideals, inspired by the French and American revolutions (Rioux, 1978: 49; Cook, 1995; Conway, 1997; Romney, 1999), a fundamental difference existed between the two rebellions. In contrast with Upper Canada, the rebellion in Lower Canada was not only inspired by demands for representative democracy, but also nationalism (Conway, 1997: 22). In consequence, the conflict in Lower Canada could only be more serious—and bloody.

In Lower Canada, the rebellion's leader was Louis-Joseph Papineau, a member of the new middle class and Speaker of the Assembly. The rebellion occurred in several stages. In October 1837, Patriote leaders issued a Declaration of the Rights of Man, based on the American declaration of 1776 (Ouellet, 1993: 360). At St. Denis on November 23, 800 Patriotes defeated 200 British regulars. This was followed by a British victory two days later at St. Charles, then a massive British attack on the rebels at St. Eustache, north of Montreal, on December 14. Many of the rebels hid in the village church. The British, however, set the church alight and shot the rebels as they fled through the windows. Estimates of the number of Patriotes killed range from 58 to 100. The village of St. Eustache was razed. The fight continued into the countryside, where British irregulars left behind them a trail of scorched habitant homes, farms, and villages (Morton, 1997: 37; Dickinson and Young, 1993: 165; Conway, 1997: 29).

In the wake of the Lower Canada rebellion, martial law was declared, the Canadian constitution suspended, and a new Governor of British North America (Lord Durham) named (Dickinson and Young, 1993: 165). By now, Papineau had fled to the United States. The rebellion, however, soon flared anew.

In late November 1838, an invading rebel force entered Canada near Alburg, Vermont. Its leader, a follower of Papineau, declared Lower Canada a republic and issued a Proclamation of Independence. The border incursion was soon put down, but in November new insurrections broke out within Lower Canada. While a degree of leniency followed the first wave of rebellions in Lower Canada, no leniency was shown after the second rebellion. Twelve Patriotes were hanged and 58 deported to Australia's penal colonies, while two more were banished (Dickinson and Young, 1993: 167; Conway, 1997: 29; Wynn, 2000: 211–212).

By contrast, the rebellion in Upper Canada was, in the words of historian Jack Granatstein (1996: 29), a "small-bore affair." There, the rebellion was led by William Lyon Mackenzie, publisher, editorialist, and social critic. Since the 1820s, he had fought against the Family Compact and for democratic reform, to no avail. Finally, emboldened by events in Lower Canada—Mackenzie was in frequent contact with Papineau—the rebels took up arms in December 1837. On December 7, after a night of heated discussion at Montgomery's Tavern, 800 of Mackenzie's followers (mostly farmers, small-town tradesmen, and some professionals) marched up Yonge Street in Toronto. There, untrained militia recruited by Upper Canada's elite met them. Shots rang out. The rebellion soon ended. Mackenzie fled disguised as a woman to the United States—he would return 12 years later and be elected to the legislature—but two of his lieutenants died on the gallows. Ninety-two more of Mackenzie's followers were sent to the penal colonies, while hundreds more, disenchanted with the rebellion's outcome, eventually left for the United States. As in Lower Canada, a few cross-border skirmishes occurred in 1838, led by groups trying to liberate Canada from "the British yoke." In 1840, Mackenzie supporters also burned a British steamship at the Thousand Islands and blew up Brock's monument at Queenston

Heights. These events were mere sideshows, however. Upper Canada's rebellion was over (Morton, 1997: 49; Dickinson and Young, 1993; Conway, 1997: 23–25; Wynn, 2000: 217).

Neither rebellion had widespread popular support. The movements were primarily middle class in origin (Morton, 1997; Ouellet, 1993; Trofimenkoff, 1993), no match for the power of the state and its allies. In Upper Canada, the rebels were easily tainted with the labels "American" and "republican" (Granatstein, 1996). In Lower Canada, the movement's avowed anticlericalism evinced even stronger condemnations from the Catholic church (Trofimenkoff, 1993).

The rebels' final defeat in 1838 was decisive. French nationalism would not rise again with force until the 1960s (Cook, 1995). For Canada as a whole, defeat meant the stillbirth of liberal democracy (see Laxer, 1989; Trofimenkoff, 1993; Conway, 1997). Thereafter, conservatism—exercised both in the political-economic and religious realms—gained an increased hold on Canadian society.

LORD DURHAM AND THE ACT OF UNION

Appointed governor of all British North America in the midst of the uprisings, Lord Durham spent five months in Canada before resigning in anger. On his return to England, he produced his analysis of the rebellions, based on his time in Canada, including a ten-day steamboat trip and conversations with a few close acquaintances (Martin, 1993b: 444). Durham's Report on the Affairs of British North America condemned the ruling oligarchy, the abuses of land granting, and Anglican privileges in the colonies. The report dealt with a host of issues, from immigration to canal building (see Careless, 1970: 195). It further made some of the most derogatory statements ever directed at the *Canadiens*, for example this one (Lord Durham, 1839):

> There can hardly be conceived a nationality more destitute... than that which is exhibited by the descendants of the French in Lower Canada, owing to their peculiar language and manners. They are a people with no history and no literature.

Finally, Durham's report included a particularly memorable paragraph:

> I expected to find a contest between a government and a people: I found two nations warring in the bosom of a single state: I found a struggle, not of principles, but of races; and I perceived that it would be idle to attempt any amelioration of laws or institutions until we could first succeed in terminating the deadly animosity that now separates the inhabitants of Lower Canada into the hostile divisions of French and English.

Durham's analysis reflected European views of the time about the "necessary" relationship between state and nation (see Chapter One); as such, it is a textbook example of material reality being shaped to fit theory. Theories have consequences, and in this case two significant consequences flowed from Durham's report.

Durham's report contained two major recommendations: first, that the British North American colonies be granted responsible government; and second, that Upper and Lower Canada be united (Careless, 1970: 195). In effect, the sundering of the two colonies by the Constitution Act of 1791 would be reversed. There was now, however, an important difference. In 1791, the French had been in the majority; it was to protect the English minority that the colonies had been split. By 1840, however, the demographics had changed. Lower Canada still had the larger population, between 600 000 and 650 000, compared with

Upper Canada's population of 450 000 (Dickinson and Young, 1993: 181; also Conway, 1997). But virtually all of Upper Canada's population was anglophone, while approximately 150 000 people in Lower Canada were also of British heritage. Thus, the English could dominate in a united Canada. Moreover, Durham argued that English immigration should be strengthened to ensure over time the complete assimilation of the French, thereby blunting the nationalism that had fuelled the recent rebellions.

In 1840, the British government implemented much of Durham's report through the Act of Union, but what they did not implement was crucial. First, they denied outright responsible government, with the result that reformers in Upper Canada remained angry. Second, the union was not total. The Quebec Act's major provisions protecting French civil law, the rights of the Catholic church, and local control of education remained extant. Even more importantly, the Act of Union provided that Canada would be governed by an elected legislative assembly in which Canada East (Lower Canada) and Canada West (Upper Canada) would equally hold 42 seats (see Conway, 1997).

The seeds for further crisis, leading ultimately to Confederation in 1867, were thus sown. The French population would not—could not—be assimilated; indeed, the legislative structure actually gave the French minority power disproportionate to its numbers, power which they sensibly used, voting *en bloc*, to protect their interests. The English in Upper Canada, meanwhile, complained bitterly that they had cast off the oligarchic power of the Family Compact only to find themselves now dominated by Lower Canada and a French-speaking minority that was Catholic to boot (see Romney, 1999).

The rebellions of 1837–38 had seen French Canada conquered a second time. Both Papineau's dream of an independent French republic and Durham's hope of French assimilation were equally chimerical. Nonetheless, the conflicts remained. It would take the forces of modernity, a major depression, two world wars, and the rise of a new intellectual class before Quebec nationalism would again rise; but rise it would, in unexpected ways, with consequences for conquered and conqueror alike.

CONCLUSION

New France gave Canada its name, its history, and one of its languages; in the wording of Dufour (1990), its "heart." After 1840, however, the English increasingly put their stamp on the rest of Canada. A series of events symbolized the ongoing rejection of the French language and its near isolation to the province of Quebec: the hanging of Riel in 1885; the school acts adopted in several provinces, beginning with Manitoba in 1890; and of course the conscription crises of the two world wars.

Why does this matter? As many as five later aspects of Canadian society derive, directly or indirectly, from these events. First, history (beginning with the Conquest) helps explain Canada's system of stratification until recent times, with those of English ethnic origin disproportionately occupying elite positions and people of French (and other) ethnic origins disproportionately occupying lower rungs (see Porter, 1965; Clement, 1975; Nakhaie, 1997). Second, a historical perspective suggests why francophone Quebecers might feel a sense of grievance toward the rest of Canada (see Conway, 1997). Third, attention to historical context also sheds light on Quebec's continuing claims to linguistic, cultural, and religious distinctiveness.

A fourth, less obvious consequence of this early history is that no "strong national myth" could cement Canadian federalism, as in the United States (Balthazar, 1997: 45; see Part Two of this text). In the words of political scientist Reg Whitaker (1987: 23), "Nationalism as legitimation is a weak, derisory ploy in Canada." Any attempt by political demagogues to "fly the flag" has quickly run aground on ethnic divisions and the Canadian tendency, perhaps inborn, toward skepticism.

Finally, a fifth related consequence (which we shall explore further) involves the complex nature of Canadian federalism. Some of the Fathers of Confederation no doubt wanted to create a strong, centralized government, leaving the provinces with only meagre powers. Quebec's presence, however, as well as that of the smaller Maritime provinces, made this impossible. Canada's flexible and significantly decentralized system of powers and responsibilities—sometimes a benefit, sometimes not—is a product of efforts to solve real problems and conflicts between Canada's constituent communities.

To a degree, political institutions and cultural traditions before the 1950s restrained conflict between Canada's English and French communities. Where these might have proved insufficient to reduce conflict, social isolation—in Hugh MacLennan's felicitous phrase, the fact of "two solitudes"—provided additional restraint. But the world would not let the two communities go on this way. War and the relentless forces of modernity—capitalism, industrialism, secularism—were about to throw the separate worlds together.

KEY TERMS

authority
decapitation thesis
dominant ideology
force
mercantilism
power
reward
social stratification
terrorism

chapter three

One Hundred Years of Solitudes

English and French, we climb by a double flight of stairs toward the destinies reserved for us on this continent, without knowing each other, without meeting each other, and without even seeing each other, except on the landing of politics.
—Pierre Joseph-Oliver Chauveau, first Quebec premier after Confederation, 1876

He shall hang though every dog in Quebec howl in his favour.
—Prime Minister Sir John A. Macdonald, refusing to pardon Riel, 1885

Society must take every means to prevent the emergence of a parallel power which defies the elected power.
—Prime Minister Pierre Trudeau, at the peak of the FLQ Crisis, 1970

INTRODUCTION

In the spring of 1955, Canadians were transfixed by television pictures of hundreds of hockey fans rioting in the streets of Montreal to protest the suspension, for the rest of the regular season and playoffs, of Maurice "Rocket" Richard. Store windows were smashed, cars overturned, and property looted, leading to the arrest of 37 adults and four juveniles. The Richard Riot ended only when Richard went on radio and television the next day to ask the rioters to stop.

We noted in Chapter One the importance of symbols to societies. In 1955, Quebec was on the verge of "La Revolution Tranquil," the Quiet Revolution. In this context, the Richard Riot had little to do with hockey. Richard was hero to a French-speaking population dominated by an anglophone minority. For francophones, Richard's suspension was symbolic of this unequal and discriminatory relationship. In turn, the riot was a symbolic protest against 200 years of subjugation and humiliation (Dupereau, 1981). As we will see in this and subsequent chapters, however, symbols not only unite, they also divide. Indeed, much of French-English conflict in Canada can be viewed as a clash of symbols.

This chapter provides a necessarily short account of Quebec during the period between Confederation and the Second World War. It then provides a more detailed account of the events, individuals, and ideas that transformed Quebec, leading to the historic Quebec election of 1960 and the turbulent years of the Quiet Revolution, which ended with the FLQ Crisis of 1970—a moment when, once more, English-speaking Canada watched transfixed by events on their television screens. Competing concepts of nationalism are discussed.

ENGLISH EXPANSION AND THE ISOLATION OF QUEBEC

Confederation in 1867 recognized Quebec as distinct, with its own majority French-Canadian population, Catholic religion, and civil law tradition, combined with autonomous political powers. For many French-Canadians, the historic province on the shores of the St. Lawrence was their homeland. At the same time, significant French-Canadian communities existed outside Quebec, especially in New Brunswick, but also in Nova Scotia, Prince Edward Island, Ontario, and the western territories (Silver, 1997). Confederation partially disentangled issues of Quebec's governance from those of the other, majority-English provinces. Confederation did not, however, separate French and Catholic sensibilities from the issue of how their compatriots were treated in the other provinces, indeed, from the issue of respect.

Some French Quebecers in 1867 no doubt viewed diaspora French as "dead ducks"—to use Parti Québécois leader René Lévesque's expression of the 1970s. In their minds, only Quebec could provide security for French language and culture. Nonetheless, French-Canadians in general also viewed Canada as a bargain between French and English. Yes, Quebec for all practical purposes would always be the citadel of French culture in Canada. But the rights of French Catholics outside Quebec were also to be respected. By 1900, a broader understanding that "the two races" were not to be compartmentalized but rather forge a new nation had emerged within French Canada (Silver, 1997). Henri Bourassa, grandson of Louis-Joseph Papineau, was a chief spokesperson for this "pan-Canadian" view (Rioux, 1993).

Not all French-Canadians held this view; even less did English Canada. Alexander Muir's poem "The Maple Leaf Forever," written in the year of Confederation, says volumes about English Canada's view of the country just created:

> In days of yore, from Britain's shore, Wolfe the dauntless hero came, And planted firm Britannia's flag, On Canada's fair domain.

A hundred years of history had taught the English that the French could be neither defeated nor assimilated. However, the French could—it was believed—be contained. The

French could have their separate language, religion, and civil laws, but only in Quebec. The rest of Canada would carry a distinctly British stamp.

These conflicting views of Confederation, and of the rights of minorities, inevitably met on the political landing. The rendezvous did not take long to occur. At Red River in the western territories in 1869, Canadian and American expansionism ran headlong into an established community of Metis (see Chapters Seven and Ten). Led by a young intellectual and visionary, Louis Riel, the Metis firmly rejected American efforts at annexation, but also demanded from the Canadian government full provincial status and protections for their French language and Catholic religion. Prime Minister Macdonald's government acceded to the demands. Thus, the Manitoba Act was passed in 1870, guaranteeing French-language rights in the legislature and schools and the right to a Catholic education in the new province of Manitoba.

The battle for French and Catholic rights outside Quebec was not over, however. The social conflicts and political intrigues of 1869 were repeated again in 1885, this time against the wider canvas of the entire western territories. This time, the demands of Riel and the Metis, not to mention the concerns of Aboriginals and non-Aboriginals, were rejected. The "rebels" were hunted down and tried. Louis Riel was hanged amidst outcries from French-Canadian politicians and the Quebec press, who were convinced that he would not have been executed had he not been French and Catholic.

Riel's hanging was a blow to both French-Canadian and Metis hopes on the prairies. For French Quebecers, Riel's hanging symbolized their exclusion from the rest of Canada. Incensed by Prime Minister Macdonald's refusal to pardon Riel (see quotation, above), French Quebec thereafter staunchly refused to vote Conservative, save for the Diefenbaker landslide of 1958 and Brian Mulroney's equally massive electoral victories in 1984 and 1988 (Appendices One and Two). More than ever, French Quebecers retreated behind their provincial walls, where the Catholic church and conservative political leaders urged they remain (see Dufour, 1990; Rioux, 1993; Conway, 1997).

In the aftermath of 1885, immigrants quickly filled the west (see Chapter Seven, Table 7.1). In the early stages, many of these were from Ontario: English, Protestant, and often decidedly anti-Catholic. Soon, they were a majority. In 1890, the English-speaking and Protestant legislature of Manitoba abolished Catholic separate schools and declared French no longer an official language (Careless, 1970; Conway, 1997). Declared unconstitutional by the Supreme Court in 1979, this legislative act nonetheless served its purpose: in the interim, French was reduced to a minority language in Manitoba. The legislature of the North-West Territories in 1892 passed similar language legislation. In 1912, Ontario eliminated French from its public education system. In 1916, Manitoba broke an agreement made with Sir Wilfrid Laurier when he was prime minister and abolished French and any other language except English from its schools (Conway, 1997: 400; Silver, 1997: 244).

Throughout the twentieth century, the minority status of French-Canadians and the political impotence of Quebec within Confederation were thus reinforced again and again. Symbolically, French-Canadians were "put in their place," that is, the place of a vanquished people. Canada was British.

The maintenance of British constitutional symbols, such as the monarchy and the Union Jack, was particularly grating to French-Canadians. For nationalists, such symbols were constant reminders of defeat. For pan-Canadianists, such symbols revealed English-Canadians as slavish colonials unable or unwilling to get on with the task of creating a new nation. Tensions heightened in 1903 with the Boer War, leading to Bourassa's break with the Laurier government. French-English conflict escalated into a full-blown political crisis during the First World War (see Chapter Seven).

Many French-Canadians viewed the First World War as not Canada's fight, and were offended that English-Canadians had allowed themselves and the country to be dragged into the conflict. By contrast, many English-Canadians were still emotionally tied to the British Empire and could not understand the lack of a similar French-Canadian need to defend France. That the umbilical cord between French-Canadians and France had been severed in 1763 entirely escaped most people in English Canada, who viewed French-Canadians *en masse* as disloyal, if not cowardly.

As the war dragged on, the need for fresh troops (and British demands that Canada "pull its weight") caused Prime Minister Robert Borden's Unionist government to intensify its efforts at recruitment. These efforts were botched and led in 1916 to anti-recruitment riots in several Quebec towns. Amidst continued Quebec opposition, Borden the next year introduced the Military Conscription Bill, and called an election on the issue. Though many Canadians opposed conscription, farmers and labourers among them, the election results revealed a particularly massive fissure between Quebec and the rest of Canada (see Appendices 1 and 2). Borden's government won, but there were no French-Canadians from Quebec or Acadia among his MPs (Silver, 1997: 248). The will of the English majority ruled over the French minority: the Conscription Bill was passed. The riots resumed throughout Quebec (Careless, 1970; Conway, 1997).

In the end, only 60 000 men actually were drafted. A large number of French recruits—as many as 40 percent—did not report (Dickinson and Young, 1993: 245). Few of the conscripts reached the front before the war ended. Bitterness lingered, however, between the French and English communities.

The Conscription Crisis was reprised during the Second World War. In 1940, Prime Minister Mackenzie King won re-election, partly on a promise made to Quebec that he would not bring in conscription. Two years later, however, as casualties again mounted, he sought political absolution from his promise through a national referendum. Since the promise had been made to them alone, French Quebecers viewed the matter as one that should have been resolved only with them, not all of Canada (Silver, 1997). Nonetheless, the referendum was held. The outcome was quite predictable. Once again, Quebec was isolated. Quebec voted 73 percent against releasing King from his promise, while the rest of Canada voted 80 percent in favour of the release and, thereby, conscription (Conway, 1997: 47).

In the end, King's adroitness—some would say dithering—forestalled the sort of flare-up that had occurred in 1917. Though anti-conscription riots did occur in parts of Quebec, their intensity was less than in the previous war (see Fraser, 1967: 14). Most Quebecers understood King had gone the extra mile in attempting to meet their objections to conscription.

For many French Quebecers, the hanging of Riel, Canada's ongoing British connection, the conscription crises, and the school controversies symbolized their minority status within Confederation. Too often, when conflicts arose, Quebec's views and interests were ignored. By the late 1940s, the idea of a pan-Canadian, French and English Canada had all but retreated from Canada's political map. More than ever, Canada consisted of "two solitudes."

By then, however, the consequences of two world historical events were rapidly pushing the French and English communities together. The first event was the world wars of 1914–18 and 1939–45. The second event was the intervening economic depression (see

Chapter Seven). Both of these events had the consequence of enlarging and centralizing state power, the first in making Canada a giant war factory, the second in creating the liberal welfare state (Rice and Prince, 2000). A further consequence was the emergence from the Second World War (in particular) of a new spirit of nationalism in English-speaking Canada. The stage was thus set for a clash over the nature of Canada and Quebec's place within it. These changes in English-speaking Canada cannot be understood, however, without reference to changes also occurring inside Quebec.

NATIONALISM AND SOCIAL CHANGE IN QUEBEC, 1867-1960

Throughout the late twentieth century, federalists and sovereigntists in Quebec argued strongly about Quebec nationalism and its future (see below). They agreed, however, on one thing: Quebec's past (Couture, 1998: 48). Quebec after the Rebellions of 1837–38 (they argued) had been in a hundred-year "time warp" dominated by the Catholic church, a bourgeois and anglophone business establishment, and an anti-democratic and authoritarian state. The results were a reactionary and backward society (Trudeau, 1996). In the words of Rioux (1993), Quebec had been governed by an "ideology of conservation"— alternatively "conservative nationalism" or (reflecting the pronounced influence of the Catholic church during this period) "**clerico-nationalism**" (Cook, 1995: 91).

Conservative nationalism stressed French Quebec's unique cultural heritage. The past and rural life were glorified. Engaging in business or seeking material rewards, by contrast, was denounced. So also were Quebecers warned against leaving their homeland, either to the United States (though many did so) or Canada's opening West: there, the dragons of certain assimilation waited. Furthermore, French Quebecers were charged with a historic and sacred mission to defend and preserve their culture against the English, the last bastion (moreover) of "true" Catholic France. (It was viewed as "providential" that Quebec had been saved from the radicalism and anticlericalism that had befallen the mother country after the French Revolution of 1789.) Large families were applauded. Catholic, French-speaking, agricultural, and traditional: these were the idealized traits (federalists and sovereigntists both agreed in the 1950s) that marked Quebec society in the second half of the nineteenth century and continued largely unchallenged until the end of the Second World War (Rioux, 1993).

There frequently is a kernel of truth in generalizations. The Catholic church *did* grow more powerful after the failed rebellions, as was reflected in the Ultramontane movement, and continued to exercise considerable influence over Quebec society until the 1950s (Dickinson and Young, 1993). Anglophones *did* dominate Quebec's increasingly capitalist economy after 1880, especially its financial and manufacturing sectors. Quebec's political culture *was* strongly conservative, featuring at the extreme individuals like Abbé Groulx, whose anti-Semitism is legendary. Its political system likewise *did* have anti-democratic and authoritarian aspects. Women, for example, did not get the vote until 1940, civil rights were sometimes abridged, and the state's coercive powers were frequently used, particularly under the reign of Maurice Duplessis in 1936–39 and 1944–59 (see Black, 1977), against labour and in defence of private property (Dickinson and Young, 1993: 280-83).

Recently, however, Couture (1998) has challenged these depictions of pre-1960s Quebec. He argues that Quebec was never entirely homogeneous, nor much different from other Canadian provinces of the period. The Ultramontane movement had its counterpart in the Orange movement that swept Ontario and much of the West (see also Saul, 1997: 32). Into the 1960s, Canada as a whole was socially conservative and highly religious. With the exception of Saskatchewan after 1944 (see Chapter Seven), Canadian governments at all levels were business-oriented and, on occasion, authoritarian. Likewise, the economic and social changes (such as urbanization and industrialization) occurring in Quebec during the twentieth century were similar in broad terms to those in the other provinces.

Quebec's population grew from 1.36 million in 1881 to 2.36 million in 1921, then 5.25 million in 1961. Its percentage of the Canadian population declined from 31.4 percent in 1881 to 26.8 percent in 1921, but rebounded to 28.8 percent by 1961 (see Table 1.1). In part, this decline during the middle period resulted from decreased birth rates. Quebec's birth rates fell from a pre-industrial high of 50 per 1000 to 41.1 in 1884–85 to 29.2 in 1931–32, the period when Quebec was rapidly industrializing (Dickinson and Young, 1993: 199). Birth rates in rural areas remained higher than in urban areas, but high death rates, especially infant deaths, reduced overall population growth. During and after the Second World War, however, birth rates once more rebounded—part of the broader Canadian phenomenon known as the baby boom (Chapter Eight)—while life expectancy gradually increased.

The larger reason, however, for Quebec's relative decline in population during this period, compared with the rest of Canada, lay in immigration and emigration. The early twentieth century witnessed massive European immigration into Canada, especially the West (see Chapter Seven). At the same time, despite the exhortations of church leaders and politicians, many francophone people left the boundaries of Old Quebec. Fearful of their treatment elsewhere in Canada, but finding themselves unable to survive farm life economically, some were convinced to move into the Shield country north of the St. Lawrence. Thus began Quebec's period of northern expansion. Work in New England's lumber mills, however, proved a far greater attraction. Between 1840 and 1930, perhaps 900 000 Quebecers, along with many francophone people from Nova Scotia, moved (in particular) to the New England states (Cook, 1995: 91; see also Dufour, 1990).

Of course, immigrants also came to Quebec. This was not a new occurrence. The potato famine of the 1840s, for example, saw the arrival in Quebec of large numbers of Irish, many of whom as orphaned children were welcomed into francophone families (Dufour, 1990). Immigration intensified during the period 1911–15, resulting in large and thriving Italian and Jewish communities arising in Montreal (Dickinson and Young, 1993: 201–03). As in the rest of Canada, immigration declined during the two world wars and the intervening Depression years. After 1945, however, as immigrants streamed into Canada, many again located in Quebec. Indeed, the percentage of immigrants to Canada settling in Quebec increased steadily, from 13.6 percent in 1946 to 23.7 percent in 1951 and 23.6 percent again in 1961 (GRES, 1997: 97). Nonetheless, Quebec remained about 80 percent francophone, while the actual number of anglophones declined and became more confined to the Montreal region.

These demographic changes were accompanied by other social and economic changes. For example, agriculture was still an important element of Quebec's economy in 1891, employing 45.5 percent of Quebec's labour force. Even then, however, Quebec was rapidly industrializing. Quebec's transition from a rural and pre-industrial society to an urban, industrial society intensified in the early twentieth century, fuelled by the flow of foreign (mainly American) capital into Canada (see Chapter Seven). By 1941, agriculture in

Quebec employed only 19.3 percent of the workforce (Dickinson and Young, 1993: 209). As noted, some of the "surplus" workers left Quebec. Many more, however, found employment in manufacturing (based on Quebec's abundant hydro power) and resource extraction (especially timber and mining).

The decline in rural Quebec was matched in both relative and absolute terms by growth in urban Quebec. In 1901, 36.1 percent of Quebec's population lived in urban areas; by 1931, the figure was 63.1 percent (Dickinson and Young, 1993: 200). Montreal was the hub of much of this urban growth, spurred by the presence of the head offices for the Bank of Montreal, Sun Life, the Canadian National Railway, and the Canadian Pacific Railway. But other urban centres, many of them resource towns, sprang up across the province.

Again, however, the interrelated social and economic changes that Quebec experienced after Confederation and up until the end of the Second World War were not particularly unusual. Industrialization, urbanization, and assorted social changes occurred throughout Canada (see Chapter Seven). What made Quebec's situation different was that the changes it experienced brought into sharp relief the social, political, and ideological structures that had arisen around the Conquest.

As we have seen (in Chapter Two), Quebec after 1760 was stratified (among other things) along ethnic lines. Whether an individual was French or English influenced their occupational status, their class position, their chances at social mobility, even the town and neighbourhood in which they lived. Curiously, the arrangement "worked"—if that term can be used—after 1837–38 precisely because French and English did live in separate worlds.

Industrialization and urbanization disrupted this arrangement, forcing French and English into renewed contact and conflict. For example, industrialization created a (largely) **francophone proletariat**. At work sites, francophone workers found themselves in regular conflict with their anglophone bosses. Class conflict merged with ethnic conflict, creating a dangerous mix that finally exploded at the company town of Asbestos in 1949 (Finkel, 1997: 74). The Asbestos Strike became a symbolic rallying point for opponents of both the Duplessis government and an economic structure that favoured anglophone-dominated corporations.

Likewise, industrialization, mass communication, and rising levels of literacy also gave rise to new occupations and professional groups. Quebec's new francophone middle class felt thwarted in its aspirations for social and economic advancement (Taylor, 1993: 8-9; Rioux, 1993: 82).

Inevitably, these changes resulted in challenges to the old political order. These challenges came from trade unionists, progressive intellectuals (including some within the Catholic church), and members of the new middle class and were directed first at replacing the Union Nationale government of Maurice Duplessis. But the challengers also had broader goals of changing Quebec's role within Confederation.

The challengers were not homogeneous, however. In particular, each possessed a different ideological notion of Quebec's identity and its relation to the rest of Canada.

What is ideology? **Ideology** is *the set of assumptions, beliefs, explanations, values, and unexamined knowledge through which we come to understand reality* (Marchak, 1988: 1). At any given time, one ideology may dominate a society or a host of societies. Marx (1977a: 236) stated it eloquently: "The ruling ideas of each age have ever been the ideas of its ruling class." Beginning in the early 1950s, two ideologies began seriously competing for the hearts and minds of Quebecers.

The first of these ideologies was liberal, federalist, and anti-nationalist. Its leaders were Pierre Trudeau (1919–2000), a lawyer and political economist who rose to political prominence during the Asbestos Strike; and Gérard Pelletier (1919–1997), a long-time friend, journalist, and social activist. They founded a radical magazine, *Cité libre*, in 1950 to articulate their vision of Quebec's future in Canada. The magazine denounced the insularity and conservatism of Quebec. Though Catholic, the editors also denounced the power of the Catholic church. Finally, taking a stance that marked his entire career, Trudeau also denounced Quebec nationalism—indeed, all forms of nationalism, new and old—as retrograde, a reversion to tribalism. Trudeau's vision of Quebec and Canada was essentially liberal, ostensibly valuing the individual over the collective (but see Couture, 1998). He and Pelletier argued that Quebec had all the powers it needed under the British North America Act. What was needed to address Quebec's rising demands was for increased democracy within the province and greater power in Ottawa (McCall-Newman, 1982; Clarkson and McCall, 1990: Balthazar, 1993).

The second ideological strain challenging conservative Quebec was sovereigntist and nationalist. Quebec's intellectual class, especially historians, provided early impetus for the nationalist cause by reinterpreting the history of Quebec in light of neo-Marxist notions of class and colonial oppression. But other members of the new middle class, such as journalists, broadcasters, and teachers, also were prominent (Rioux, 1993; Cook, 1995). The old Quebec nationalism was cultural rather than political; largely unconcerned with economic development; based on a set of mainly Catholic values; inward looking and defensive; and rejecting of newcomers. By contrast, while the new nationalism shared with the old a belief in the French language and was perhaps even more dedicated to preserving the French fact in North America, it was otherwise opposed, even scornful, of Quebec's traditional culture.

Like the liberal anti-nationalists, the new nationalists favoured modernization and political reform. Unlike the liberals, however, the new nationalists were often stridently anti-clerical and highly secular, and their reforms extended into the economy. Most importantly, the new nationalists argued that French culture could only survive if Quebec had the powers of an autonomous state (Balthazar, 1993; Taylor, 1993; Conway, 1997: 52-53). These powers could be exercised within a loose federal arrangement; if not, however, so be it.

Embedded in this idea was an important transformation in identity. Prior to the Second World War, Canada's two identities, French-Canadian and English-Canadian, had existed (distantly) side by side. The war, however, fuelled a new sense of nationalism in English-speaking Canada and (by the close of the 1950s) increasing demands for an end to "hyphenated" Canadianism (see Chapter Seven). In Quebec, however, these demands and the increasing encroachment of the federal government into areas of provincial jurisdiction were viewed as threats. Quebec's long isolation and rejection by the rest of Canada produced finally an identity coincident with the new nationalism. The old nationalism identified with the French language and the Catholic faith; its people were *French-Canadian*. By contrast, the people of the new nationalism were *Québécois* (Webber, 1994: 49).

Revolutions require not only symbols but ideological justifications and blueprints. Quebec's Tremblay Report of 1956 provided both of these. The report became a bible for the Quiet Revolution. In four volumes, it "gave ideological and statistical support to provincial autonomy and to the idea that the Quebec government was the primary defender of a threatened culture" (Dickinson and Young, 1993: 283). In some ways profoundly traditional and nostalgic, the report nonetheless contained two ideas important to debates about Canada and Quebec ever since. First, the report gave voice to a belief already existing in Quebec that Confederation involved a pact between two equal peoples, French and English. Quebec was not thus "just one" of several provinces. Second, the Tremblay Report argued that Quebec was distinct from the other provinces and required jurisdictional autonomy in some areas into which the federal government was moving (Cook, 1995: 162).

Maurice Duplessis died in 1959. Jean Lesage's Liberals defeated Duplessis's Union Nationale government in June 1960. Quebec's Quiet Revolution had begun.

CLASHING NATIONALISMS AND QUIET REVOLUTIONS

Lesage's Liberal Party contained elements of both the new liberal and new nationalist factions. In time the marriage would break down. At first, however, the goals of replacing the Union Nationale and modernizing Quebec provided sufficient cement to hold the coalition together.

The Liberals in their first mandate moved to bring Quebec's public services (health, education, labour laws, social welfare) up to the level of the other provinces (Conway, 1997). Political changes were also made. The voting age was lowered from 21 to 18, new laws governing election expenses were passed, and patronage and gerrymandering were attacked. Much of English Canada applauded these steps. Two year later, however, Lesage won re-election using the slogan "Maîtres chez nous" (Masters in our own house). English Canada grew more wary.

The Liberals in 1962 called an election seeking a mandate to nationalize Quebec's private electric companies. The idea was that of René Lévesque (1922–87), a former journalist and prominent television commentator, now Lesage's minister of natural resources. Lévesque believed Quebec's distinctiveness could only be protected if francophone Quebecers had control over the economy.

Following their election win, the Liberals created Quebec Hydro. It quickly became a symbol of Quebec nationalism. Other measures followed, such as the creation in 1965 of the Caisse de Dépôt et Placement du Québec, made responsible for Quebec's own pension plan. These actions were popular among Quebec francophones who saw in economic nationalism a means of addressing entrenched inequalities between themselves and the English minority. Quebec's English-dominated business community viewed these actions with alarm, however.

English fears within Quebec were matched outside the province by English-speaking Canadians concerned that Quebec nationalism was becoming at odds with their ideal of "One Canada." Few Canadians were yet travelling across their country; the Trans-Canada Highway was not formally opened until the summer of 1962. Television and radio provided a kind of link, but also reinforced regional and cultural divisions. Indeed, French television in Quebec after 1950 became a chief breeding ground for cultural nationalism (Balthazar, 1993). In consequence, Canadian nationalism exhibited what Rotstein (1978) described as "mapism." That is, English-speaking Canadians had learned in school the country's shape on the map, but often knew nothing about the history or culture of their fellow citizens, especially those in Quebec. They knew only that Quebec was geographically at Canada's heart, and that Quebec nationalism now seemed to be threatening to tear out that heart.

For most Quebecers, Canada outside Quebec also remained a mystery; more than a century of parochial education had ensured that. The new nationalists did not harbour any hatred toward English Canada. (This could not be said regarding the dominant anglophone minority within Quebec, especially the business class.) In the main, French Quebecers were simply indifferent to the rest of Canada.

For a few Quebec nationalists, however, the pace of social and political change was too slow. In the early 1960s, the Front de Libération du Québec (FLQ) was formed for the sole purpose of taking Quebec out of Canada, by force if necessary. The FLQ and many of its sympathizers drew their revolutionary ideals from broader social currents of the time, in Canada and abroad. While in English Canada, anti-establishment politics focused upon opposition to the U.S., in Quebec the spirit of revolution focused on anglophone symbols and institutions and their supporters. In the revolutionaries' view, Quebec was still a colony. In the words of Pierre Vallieres (1971), francophone Quebecers were "White Niggers." They needed to be liberated.

In 1963, the FLQ began a terrorist campaign directed at symbols of English privilege and power. Banks were robbed, weapons were stolen, bombs exploded. The campaign began with the bombing of the Wolfe monument in Quebec City—what more symbolic target could there be? Over the next seven years the FLQ proceeded to other targets: McGill and Loyola universities; the Westmount district of Montreal; the Eaton's department store and the Montreal Stock Exchange; the RCMP and the Black Watch Regiment; a monument to Queen Victoria and the Queen's Printer. Six lives were lost. Some of the terrorists were caught, tried, convicted, and sentenced (Conway, 1997: 57).

The FLQ's tactics never had strong support in Quebec; indeed, they were denounced. The bombings served a purpose, however, in garnering English-speaking Canada's attention. Thus began English-speaking Canada's education on Quebec and the history of French-English relations.

COMMISSIONS AND THE "THREE WISE MEN"

In the context of growing civil strife in Quebec and rising angst elsewhere, Prime Minister Pearson's newly elected Liberal government in 1963 created the Royal Commission on Bilingualism and Biculturalism, also known as the Laurendeau-Dunton Commission after its co-chairs. In its preliminary report of 1965 and a final report, encompassing six books, the commission detailed the second-class status of francophones within Quebec and Canada's federal structures. In 1961, for example, unilingual anglophones had the highest average income in Quebec ($6049), followed by bilingual anglophones ($5929), bilingual francophones ($4523), and finally unilingual francophones ($3107) (Webber, 1994: 45; see also Conway, 1997). Most of Quebec's private sector economy was owned by anglophone Canadians or non-Canadians. Francophones were similarly disadvantaged in the federal civil service, significantly underrepresented and concentrated in the lower tiers of administration. Both inside and outside Quebec, English was the language of work in the federal service. Francophone hospitals, schools, and universities were inferior to those of anglophones (see also Porter, 1965). In short, the pattern of social stratification in Quebec, set in motion at the time of the Conquest (Chapter Two), seemed largely unbroken 200 years later.

Even before the commission's final report, acting on its preliminary recommendations and spirit, the Pearson Liberals took several steps. There was never any intent that all of Canada could or should become a completely bilingual country. At the level of federal institutions, however, an intensive French and English language training program was instituted for civil servants. In keeping with its demands for greater control over internal economic affairs, Quebec was allowed to opt out of the Canada Pension Plan (Webber, 1994). And a new Canadian flag also was created (see Chapter Eight), one that broke with Canada's long-standing fealty to Britain (Conway, 1997: 60).

These measures had their critics, both among Quebec nationalists who viewed the commission as obscuring their demands, and some in English-speaking Canada who were unsympathetic to francophone demands for equality. Yet, many English-speaking Canadians also accepted, even embraced, the administrative and linguistic changes.

More problematic was the commission's vision of Canada, specifically, the idea that Confederation involved a partnership of the French and English "nations." Very quickly, some academics, notably the eminent historian Donald Creighton (1970), denounced this **two nations theory** (a.k.a., **compact theory**) as revisionist. For them, Canada was not a partnership between the French and the English, but rather a partnership of equal provinces (see Romney, 1999). In Weberian terms, French- and English-speaking Canadians had a very different understanding of the basis of their relationship with the country. The resultant disagreement continues to frame Canada-Quebec relations and constitutional debates today (see Chapter Five).

Jean Marchand (1918-1988) was a prominent member of the Royal Commission on Bilingualism and Biculturalism. Already a well-known labour leader who had fought against the Duplessis regime and worked with Lesage's Liberal government, Marchand was approached by Prime Minister Pearson to run for the Liberals in the 1965 federal election. He agreed, but only on condition that his long-time friends Pierre Trudeau and Gérard Pelletier join him. They did, and the three were soon referred to as Quebec's "three wise men." Marchand, Pelletier, and Trudeau believed Quebec's demands for cultural protection could best be met by securing representation within Ottawa. For the Liberal party, Marchand and his associates also represented the resurrection of an old idea, dating back to Laurier and Bourassa, that Canada was both English and French. In English Canada, however, another message was frequently understood: that Quebec's new ministers would stop the nationalist agitation and put Quebec back in its place.

The year 1967 was Canada's centennial. English-speaking Canada was optimistic, its cheery enthusiasm captured by Bobby Gimby's song "Canada." All Canada and much of the world seemed to congregate that summer in Montreal, home of the "Man and His World" exhibition, to celebrate. But France's president, Charles de Gaulle, came to Canada in July on a state visit. Steaming up the St. Lawrence on a French cruiser, he disembarked at Quebec City and proceeded by cavalcade to Montreal. There, overcome by the occasion, speaking from the balcony of city hall, de Gaulle shouted "Vive le Québec libre!" The Canadian government was not amused with this break in diplomatic protocol—Quebec and Quebecers did not, in its view, require liberation—and quickly insisted on de Gaulle's exit (see Clarkson and McCall, 1990: 103–04). Nonetheless, for English-speaking Canadians the Quebec "problem" had reared its head once more.

In 1968, Pierre Trudeau succeeded Lester Pearson as leader of the Liberal Party and prime minister. As justice minister in the previous cabinet, Trudeau had reformed Canada's divorce laws and made liberal amendments to Criminal Code laws on abortion and homosexuality (Clarkson and McCall, 1990: 107). Now, in 1968, Canadians experienced what was termed "Trudeaumania" and became familiar for the first time with the word **charisma**, a term coined by Max Weber (1958: 295) meaning *an extraordinary quality of a person, regardless of whether this quality is actual, alleged, or presumed.*

As prime minister, one of Trudeau's first acts was to bring in the policy of official bilingualism. Following in the footsteps of Henri Bourassa, Trudeau held a pan-Canadian vision of the country, one in which French and English were equal from sea to sea. Quebec nationalism, he believed, would whither as francophones came to feel at home in the rest of Canada. Two years later, however, the Canadian state and society faced a serious challenge from those in Quebec who believed Trudeau did not understand their demands and was selling the rest of Canada a false vision.

THE FLQ CRISIS AND ITS AFTERMATH

On October 5, 1970, members of the FLQ kidnapped James Cross, a British trade commissioner. The terrorist cell quickly made seven demands in exchange for Cross's release. The Quebec and Canadian governments rejected all demands at first. They soon relented, however, granting one request: the broadcast and publication of the FLQ's manifesto.

Few Quebecers supported the FLQ's actions. Nonetheless, the manifesto—a broadly Marxist polemic laced with invective and humour—drew much applause. In its way, the FLQ touched on real frustrations and angers felt by francophones in the province.

Faced with unexpected public support within Quebec for the FLQ's position, the Quebec government declared on October 10 that no further concessions would be made to the kidnappers. A few hours later, the crisis escalated. Pierre Laporte, Quebec's labour minister, who had only months before nearly been elected provincial Liberal leader, was kidnapped by another FLQ cell acting independently.

Lévesque, union leaders, and some others began demanding negotiations with the FLQ for Cross's and Laporte's lives. Rejecting, however, the notion of a "parallel government," Pierre Trudeau ordered Canadian troops to be positioned in Ottawa and the province of Quebec. On October 16, the federal government declared the War Measures Act (WMA). Under this act, all civil rights and liberties in Canada were legally suspended. Those suspected of criminal offences were arrested without charge and held without bail and without trial. The focus was upon Quebec and those suspected of being FLQ supporters, but the act's application was wider. Under the WMA, 465 Quebec "supporters" were arrested, 403 of whom were released without charge. Of the remainder, 32 were charged but not prosecuted, while 18 were convicted of minor offences (Conway, 1997: 77).

The day after the WMA was declared, Laporte was murdered by his kidnappers. The killing intensified feelings of fear and panic, both inside and outside Quebec. Support for the Trudeau government rose, especially in English-speaking Canada. Feelings were more mixed in Quebec, but many also accepted the presence of tanks and the suspension of civil liberties without question.

Laporte's killers were eventually caught, tried, and convicted using regular police methods. Shortly thereafter, in early December, Cross was located and freed in return for his kidnappers' safe passage to Cuba. Over time, all of Cross's kidnappers voluntarily returned to Canada where they too were tried, convicted, and sentenced (*Maclean's*, 2000).

Thus, the FLQ Crisis—and the Quiet Revolution with it—came to an end. Today, the crisis and the imposition of the War Measures Act remain controversial (see Gagnon, 2000). Was invoking the WMA necessary? Or was it an overreaction? How is civil society best protected from threat? When is state coercion justified, and what are its limits?

In the short term, Trudeau's government received praise for its handling of the situation, while the use of violence to achieve sovereignty, never widely supported in Quebec, was thoroughly repudiated. Yet, if invoking the WMA was meant to render Quebecers fearful of pursuing nationalism, it utterly failed. Within a few years, support for Quebec nationalism among francophones was stronger than ever.

CONCLUSION

Quebec, as all of Canada, experienced unprecedented changes during the twentieth century, especially after 1945. Still largely Catholic and conservative at war's end, Quebec was essentially secular and liberal by 1970. Birth rates fell remarkably, divorce rates rose. Sexual mores and social views changed, becoming more liberal than those held elsewhere in North America.

Industrialization, long a fact in Quebec, also continued apace and expanded into the province's north, bringing Quebec society into increasing contact, and conflict, with its Aboriginal population. But economic development also remained uneven. After 1960, social stratification along French-English lines began lessening, and a new francophone bourgeoisie emerged. Rural-urban and gender differences remained, however.

These changes were not dissimilar to changes elsewhere in Canadian society during this period. The changes in Quebec were given cogency, however, by the fact they occurred against the historic backdrop of French-English relations starting with the Conquest. Moreover, Quebec's demands also coincided with, and reinforced, changes occurring in English-speaking Canada's structure, beliefs, and identity. Sometimes, English-speaking Canada even changed in response to demands it *imagined* French Quebec had made (for example, bilingualism). Throughout the 1960s, Canada and Quebec danced together, each reacting to the other, tailoring their steps, measuring the other's performance. Yet as the fall of 1970 ended they were seemingly more separate than ever. Ironically, conflict increased between the French and English groups as the two communities became less separate and more similar, as—to continue the metaphor—their steps became more synchronized. In 1970, no one could be certain how or when the dance would end.

KEY TERMS

charisma	francophone proletariat	two nations theory
clerico-nationalism	ideology	(a.k.a., compact theory)

chapter four

The Constitutional Years

The Magnificent Obsession.
—subtitle to Clarkson and McCall's 1990 examination of the Trudeau years and efforts at constitutional reform

Quebec constitutes, within Canada, a distinct society.
—Meech Lake Accord, 1987

The process of constitutional reform in Canada has been discredited.
—Quebec Premier Robert Bourassa, after the failure of the Meech Lake Accord, 1990

INTRODUCTION

Goa is a former Portuguese colony on India's western coast. In a country predominantly Hindu, Goa's population is largely Catholic, and much of its small population bears decidedly non-Indian names, like de Jesus. In other words, despite being surrounded by a dominant majority population, Goa, like Quebec, retains its distinct cultural identity.

One of this book's authors was travelling in Goa in the fall of 1976 when he heard the separatist Parti Québécois, led by René Lévesque, had been elected to govern

Quebec. Because he was a young, unilingual, and politically unaware westerner, the significance of the event escaped him then. He remembers, however, two francophone Québécois in their late 20s, also visiting Goa, who were elated by news of the PQ's victory and celebrated long into the night.

This chapter examines events in Quebec and the relationship between Canada and Quebec during the 20 years that followed the FLQ Crisis of 1970. As noted in the previous chapter, the FLQ crisis ended the Quiet Revolution in Quebec. Thereafter, nationalist and separatist impulses within the province took a less violent but, in the long term, potentially more lethal turn alternating between efforts to reform Canada's Constitution and threats of referenda on Quebec's independence. The period ended with the failure of the Meech Lake Accord in 1990 and the referendum defeat of the Charlottetown Accord two years later. The chapter begins with a discussion of sociology and its relationship to political constitutions.

SOCIOLOGY AND THE CANADIAN CONSTITUTION

The events of the 1960s, culminating in the FLQ Crisis in 1970, set off a profound rethinking of Canada's Constitution. Sociology and sociologists played a major role in this rethinking. This should not surprise us. After all, one of sociology's main interests involves **social norms**, *the more or less agreed-upon societal rules and expectations specifying ways of behaving in society*.

Constitutions fall under a specific type of norm: **laws**. The term **constitution** *refers both to the institutions, practices, and principles that define and structure a system of government and to the written document that establishes or articulates such a system* (taken from Hemberger, 1993: 189). A constitution defines a state's sphere of authority, the means of its governance, and claims that may be made in the political realm, broadly defined and contested. More broadly, constitutions represent symbolically a statement of spirit or intent, for example, that "all people are created equal." Beginning with the American and French revolutions, constitutions arose as a means of formally specifying the relationship between individuals and groups and their relationship to the modern state—a chief interest of early sociologists such as Tönnies, Weber, and Durkheim (see Chapter One). Finally, while some constitutions are more easily changed than others, none are written in such a way that they can be changed at whim. Constitutions are meant to represent a more-or-less firm statement of a country's legal foundation. By comparison, the American Constitution is relatively "fixed" while the Canadian Constitution is sometimes referred to as a "rolling compromise." Beginning in the 1960s, the roll picked up speed, with sociologists often giving it a push.

Until 1982, Canada's key constitutional document, of course, was the British North America (BNA) Act (later renamed the Constitution Act, 1867) creating the Dominion of Canada (Dunn, 1995) (see Chapter Six). Long before 1867, however, Canada's existence was structured by a series of constitutional acts: for example, the charter of the Hudson's Bay Company in 1670, the Royal Proclamation of 1763, the Quebec Act of 1774, the Constitution Act of 1791, and the Act of Union of 1841 (see Chapter Two). The BNA Act repealed some elements contained in these previous legal documents. Other commitments, however, remain in effect; for example, current Aboriginal land claims date from the Royal Proclamation Act (see Chapter Thirteen).

The BNA Act was repeatedly altered after 1867 to meet changing conditions and demands. A partial list of these changes includes the various acts that incorporated the lands of the Hudson's Bay Company and the North-West Territories into Canada, made Manitoba, British Columbia, Alberta, and Saskatchewan provinces, established the Yukon Territory, and brought Newfoundland into Confederation.

Constitutional reform stalled, however, after the 1920s, even as the need for it became greater. The Statute of Westminster in 1931 declared Canada (along with Australia, New Zealand, and South Africa) sovereign and equal to Britain. Canada, however, declined at that time to take control over the Constitution because the federal and provincial governments could not agree on how the Constitution would be amended in future.

Why was the issue of an amending formula problematic? The amending formula was problematic because it dealt with issues of power between levels of government and between government and individual citizens. For example, would the federal government be able constitutionally to make changes unilaterally? Or would provincial consent for constitutional changes be required? If so, how many provinces and would all provinces, large and small, be equal? If not provinces, would Canadian citizens have the ultimate say over constitutional changes through (for example) a Canada-wide referendum? How would the rights of smaller provinces and (in the case of Quebec) minorities be protected against the majority provinces or population? Would some elements of the Constitution be more easily changed than other elements? These were only some of the constitutional questions facing Canadian politicians after 1931. With no clear answers in sight, the Constitution remained "housed" in Britain, even as Canada symbolically distanced itself from Britain in other ways. (In 1950, for example, the British Privy Council ceased to be Canada's Supreme Court.)

Constitutional questions would not go away, however. Two issues with constitutional implications dominated federal-provincial relations in Canada during the 1950s. The first was the ongoing search for an amending formula. The second was fiscal relations between the two levels of government (Webber, 1994: 93), the latter a by-product of the federal government's control of revenues and the expansion of welfare state programs after 1945 (see Chapter Eight). With the Quiet Revolution of the 1960s, a third issue was added to the mix: Quebec's historical relation to the rest of Canada. Was Canada a Confederation of ten equal provinces, or was it a bargain between two nations, French and English (Chapter Three)?

The events of the Quiet Revolution, culminating in the FLQ Crisis, made obvious the necessity of resolving these issues. Quebec, however, was not the sole impetus for demands for constitutional change. In particular, the western provinces in the 1970s also demanded constitutional changes in two areas: first, "control over the taxing and marketing of natural resources"; and, second, "reform of federal institutions, especially the Senate" (Webber, 1994: 103) (see Chapters Eight and Nine). Quebec and many of Canada's "hinterland" provinces demanded *both* a greater devolution of federal powers and, concomitantly, more inclusion at the centre of federal decision-making.

The Trudeau government's interpretation of Canada's "problem" was quite different. Among developed countries, Canada was significantly decentralized already. The problem was not an excess of power at the centre, but too much power in the regions. Giving in to Quebec's nationalist demands would only feed more demands. Already, other provinces were piggybacking on Quebec's demands, threatening further weakening of the Canadian state. The solution to Canada's problems, in Trudeau's eyes, lay in constitutional reforms that would bring Quebecers and Quebec into the "Canadian nation" (see Balthazar, 1997).

By 1971, both the federal and provincial governments were seeking constitutional reform. At a federal-provincial meeting held in Victoria, the two levels of government appeared at last to have reached an accord on some principles for renewing Confederation. Premier Robert Bourassa faced strong opposition from nationalists, unionists, business groups, and the media, however, upon his return to Quebec. These opponents feared the agreement would enhance federal authority while reducing Quebec to the status of just another province. Constitutional reform thus was put on hold. In the absence of a constitutional solution to Quebec's demands, new coalitions of social and political forces soon arose in Quebec proffering different solutions to the Quebec-Canada "problem."

THE ELECTION OF THE PARTI QUÉBÉCOIS

On November 15, 1976, René Lévesque's Parti Québécois became Quebec's governing party, taking 71 of 110 seats and 42 percent of the popular vote (Conway, 1997: 86). The election was a startling turnaround for the PQ, who in 1973 had won only six seats (though they won 30 percent of the vote) in losing to Bourassa's Liberals. Much of English Canada panicked. The business community was particularly stunned, fearing equally the PQ's avowed separatism—Lévesque promised to hold a referendum on sovereignty sometime during his party's electoral mandate—and social democratic platform. What had happened?

In part, the PQ's election was the Liberal government's rejection. Bourassa's personal image had never fully recuperated from his handling of the FLQ crisis of 1970, when he was widely seen by francophone Quebecers as weak and ineffectual in defending their interests. More broadly, however, the PQ's election reflected a further evolution in Quebec society itself and in Quebec nationalism. By the 1970s, the economic changes undertaken during the Quiet Revolution were bearing fruit. New middle and entrepreneurial classes were emerging, dominated by francophone Quebecers. Labour unions, long suppressed in Quebec, were also growing in power, and labour militancy was on the rise, exemplified in an extreme manner by the intentional destruction by workers of the James Bay hydroelectric site in 1974. Quebec culture and arts, no longer insular or defensive, were also thriving. The PQ's positive message of creating a more autonomous, social democratic, and modern society appealed to a wide cross-section of francophones within the blue- and white-collar, intellectual, and cultural communities.

Like all Quebec political parties, going back to the previous century, the PQ was nationalist. But the PQ's nationalism was fundamentally different from that of previous Quebec governments. First, reflecting changes among Quebecers themselves, the PQ's nationalism was more positive and future-oriented than in the past (Dufour, 1990; Thompson, 1995). Second, where Quebec governments in the past had defended the French "nation"—albeit with its obvious homeland in Quebec, still within Canada—the PQ rejected both the notion of allegiance to Canada and to a broader pan-Canadian French nation (Webber, 1994: 101). For the PQ and many of its followers, there was only a Québécois nation, its interests represented by Quebec's quasi-state, on the verge of becoming a sovereign country. All that was needed to make Quebec sovereign was a decision by its people to assert their rights of self-determination.

Third, where the Union Nationale had been authoritarian and conservative, and the Liberals classically liberal, the PQ was unabashedly democratic socialist, as reflected in several progressive policies enacted during its first term in office. Labour laws were amended, outlawing strikebreaking and adopting the Rand formula (see Chapter Eight) for deducting union dues. Reflecting the strength of emergent feminism within the party, the rights of women also were extended (see Dickinson and Young, 1993: 319–26). Finally, Quebec's minimum wage became the highest in Canada, and the sales tax was removed on shoes, clothing, and furniture (Conway, 1997: 92). The PQ's most important moves, however, were in defence of the French language.

THE LANGUAGE OF QUEBEC NATIONALISM

Language is perhaps the chief element of national identity (see Chapter Five). Language symbolically represents continuity with the past and future. From a symbolic-interaction perspective, language is the chief vehicle for expressing a group's history, beliefs, and values, but from a conflict perspective, it is often also a contested terrain between the dominant culture and minority groups. The efforts of the Canadian government historically to eliminate Aboriginal languages and the recent efforts of Aboriginal peoples to relearn their languages provide instructive examples (see Chapters Ten and Thirteen).

Until the Constitution Act of 1982, only the BNA Act of 1867 (later renamed the Constitution Act of 1867) dealt constitutionally with language, and then only in Section 133 and in a limited context. Section 133 states that either French or English can be used in the legislatures of Canada and Quebec and courts under their authority, and that records and journals of both Parliament and the Quebec legislature must be bilingual. Section 23 of the Manitoba Act of 1870 replicated the Quebec provisions of the BNA Act (Dunn, 1995: 340–42), as did arrangements in the North-West Territories in 1874 (Cook, 1995: 153).

The cultural wars of the 1890s and early twentieth century saw English majorities abuse French language protections, however. Meanwhile, the majority French in Quebec found their social and cultural status gradually declining against the minority, and unilingual, anglophone population. In effect, where constitutional bilingualism existed it provided greater protection for English speakers, minority or otherwise, than it did French speakers.

By the 1960s, survival of the French language and culture in Quebec was further threatened by a combination of declining birth rates and rapidly increasing immigration into the province (Dickinson and Young, 1993; Fournier et al., 1997). Many of the new arrivals spoke neither French nor English. Surrounded by a North American sea of English, however, and experiencing the economic and social benefits of English within the province, most immigrants were choosing to speak English. Moreover, schools were pressed into the debate, as immigrants demanded their children receive education in English. For many francophones, their ancestral homeland and culture were once more under siege. Official bilingualism (enacted in 1969) did not address these fears. Indeed, official bilingualism was the answer to a question most francophone Quebecers had not asked, satisfying only Canadian nationalists outside the province. In 1968, violence broke out in Montreal between francophone nationalists and immigrant Italians over language instruction in schools (Dickinson and Young, 1993: 309; Thompson, 1995; Fournier et al., 1997).

The Bourassa government in 1974 attempted to deal with the issue through the Official Languages Act (Bill 22). Bill 22 made French Quebec's official language in certain key areas, such as business, labour, education, some professions, and public administration (Conway, 1997: 88). It did not demand the exclusive use of French, however. Education matters, for example, were left largely untouched, with immigrant parents still able to enroll their children in English-language schools.

After its election, the Parti Québécois moved quickly to remove any ambiguity concerning the status of French in Quebec. The Charter of the French Language of 1977 (Bill 101) made French the official state language and the "normal language of work, education, communications, and business." Bill 101 also restricted English instruction to those whose parents were educated in English in Quebec. (An exception was granted Aboriginal peoples, especially in the case of Aboriginal languages.) Bill 101 further placed limits on bilingual signs and restricted the use of English in business and government (see Fournier et al., 1997: 242–259; Dickinson and Young, 1993: 310; Webber, 1994: 100–101).

Anglophones within Quebec, of whom many had deep ancestral roots, felt themselves under attack. Their anger found support outside Quebec among English-speaking Canadians who could not understand the Quebec government's moves to make the province predominantly French at a time when they were (grudgingly) accepting bilingualism. Anger outside Quebec was aided and abetted by some English-Canadian politicians pandering to anti-French, anti-Quebec sentiment in search of cheap votes.

Supporters of Bill 101 pointed out, however, that its provisions dealt solely with Quebec's public and symbolic realms, not with cultural institutions (e.g., McGill University) or private interactions (Webber, 1994: 101). They further pointed out the failure of governments elsewhere to protect and promote the French language (see Conway, 1997: 96–97). However, few in English-speaking Canada listened to such arguments. Following the passage of Bill 101, Sun Life announced it was moving its headquarters from Montreal to Toronto. Other businesses soon followed. Many young anglophone Quebecers also left the province during this period (Morton, 1997).

By 1979, the Parti Québécois was entering the bottom half of its electoral mandate. It had been elected on a promise to hold a referendum on sovereignty that would make the Quebec state the political embodiment of that expression. Now, time was running out to fulfill the promise. The stage was set for the 1980 referendum and one of the most compelling political rivalries of the late twentieth century.

A STUDY IN PERSONAL AGENCY: THE 1980 REFERENDUM

One of sociology's ongoing central debates involves the relationship between individual behaviour and the constraints and imperatives of social structure. Do individuals really make a difference, or are we merely creations of our time and place? In a famous passage Marx (1977b: 300) once wrote that people "make their own history, but they do not make it just as they please, they do not make it under circumstances chosen by themselves, but under circumstances directly encountered, given, and transmitted from the past." C. Wright Mills (1961: 6) viewed agency and structure as a meeting place for what he termed the **sociological imagination**, *the ability "to grasp history and biography and the relations of the two within society."* From this perspective, Pierre Trudeau and René Lévesque can be seen as products of pre-war 1939 Quebec society and the political and ideological struggles of their time. Yet each also influenced the shape and manner of those struggles (Cook, 1995: 138).

Trudeau and Lévesque are often viewed as opposites: Trudeau the reasoned intellectual and committed federalist, Levesque the passionate "man of action" and Quebec nationalist. Certainly, their public styles were at odds (Clarkson and McCall, 1990: 198–200). Yet they were both children of the post-First World War French-Canadian bourgeoisie, had fought to end the Duplessis regime, and were social liberals dedicated to modernizing Quebec. Both believed in a "large role for the state in public affairs" (Chodos and Hamovitch, 1991: 195). Moreover, each in his own way represented a form of Quebec nationalism (see Dufour, 1990: 81), Trudeau as passionately as Lévesque, Lévesque in as calculated a manner as Trudeau. In their time, each elicited mixed public responses. Loved by francophone Quebecers, loathed by their anglophone counterparts, Lévesque was at the same time both respected and feared in English-speaking Canada. For his part, Trudeau likewise was loathed and hated, admired and respected, often by the same people. (The poet Irving Layton once wrote: "In Pierre Trudeau, Canada has at last produced a political leader worthy of assassination.") Yet Lévesque's death in 1987 resulted in a profound outpouring of grief in Quebec (Conway, 1997: 126), while Trudeau's death in September 2000 was mourned by much of Canada, his funeral perhaps the largest attended and watched in Canadian history (*Maclean's*, 2000).

In 1979, Trudeau and Levesque's visions of Quebec's relationship to Canada were on a collision course. Trudeau believed in a strong Quebec, but as a province among other provinces, within a bilingual Canada. As already noted, Trudeau held a pan-Canadian vision of a bilingual Canada, a vision with deep roots in Quebec (Chapter Three). But Trudeau's idea of a strong central state and constitutionally equal provinces also was very European, as well as American (see Dufour, 1990; Balthazar, 1997).

For many Quebecers, this vision of Canada was at odds with the historic reality of Quebec's relationship to the rest of Canada, going back at least to the Quebec Act of 1774. Perhaps worse, Trudeau's vision created a kind of straightjacket for constitutional change (Dufour, 1990). Many francophones supported Lévesque's vision of a strong Quebec with unique powers within a decentralized Canadian federation. By 1979, a sizeable number of Quebecers believed the only option, if their nation could not be protected within Canada, was Quebec independence.

Lévesque's vision of the Canadian federation was neither radical nor recent. Debates about how centralized or decentralized Canada should be, or about jurisdictional responsibilities, had gone on since before Confederation and were a key aspect of discussion at Charlottetown and Quebec leading up to 1867 (Moore, 1995; Romney, 1999) (Chapter Six). Beginning with the Depression and Second World War, however, Ottawa's role had increased in Quebec and Canada at large (Balthazar, 1997; Thompson, 1995). In the wake of Quebec's separatist threat, and faced with a stagnating economy in 1970s, the Trudeau Liberal government attempted to reassert federal authority both politically and economically. These actions elicited hostility from Quebec, as well as other provinces, especially in the West (see Chapter Eight).

In this context of renewed constitutional conflict, the federal government created the Task Force on Canadian Unity (Government of Canada, 1979), otherwise known as the Pépin-Robarts Report after its two chairs, former Liberal cabinet minister Marcel Pépin and former Ontario premier John Robarts. The Pépin-Robarts Report was tabled in early 1979 and called for a more decentralized and flexible federation, including the replacement of the Canadian senate by a House of the Provinces that would bring the provinces and regions into the national decision-making process. The Trudeau government immediately dismissed the report, however. Faced with increasing economic problems of rising unemployment and a skyrocketing debt, the Trudeau Liberals feared that meeting Quebec's demands would result in similar demands from the other provinces (see Clarkson and McCall, 1990; Webber, 1994). Decentralization would spur on centrifugal forces that would further delegitimize and weaken the Canadian State. The Trudeau government's rejection of the Task Force's recommendations set the stage for further constitutional confrontations.

The Ottawa-Quebec, Trudeau-Lévesque showdown was briefly postponed by the Liberal party's defeat in the 1979 federal election by Joe Clark's Progressive Conservatives. A few months later, however, Clark's minority government was defeated and the Liberals, led by a rejuvenated Trudeau, returned to office in the subsequent election (see Appendices 1 and 2). In the meantime, Lévesque's government had called for a sovereignty referendum to be held on May 20, 1980. The referendum question (cited in Chodos and Hamovitch, 1991: 192) read:

> The Government of Quebec has made public its proposal to negotiate a new agreement with the rest of Canada, based on the equality of nations; this agreement would enable Quebec to acquire the exclusive power to make its laws, levy its taxes and establish relations abroad—in other words, sovereignty—and at the same time to maintain with Canada an economic association including a common currency; no change in political status resulting from these negotiations will be effected without approval by the people through another referendum; on these terms, do you give the Government of Quebec the mandate to negotiate the proposed agreement between Quebec and Canada?

The PQ worded the question strategically to embrace the twin notions of increased sovereignty with which to defend and assert Quebec's nationhood and, at the same time, a continuing "association" with Canada, thus mitigating the economic, political, and social uncertainties of independence. The question also seemed to put off the hard step of actual independence. After all, the government was asking only for a "mandate to negotiate," while still giving separation a push (see Conway, 1997: 93).

The debates and speeches leading up to the referendum vote were impassioned, occasionally nasty. Families were divided, friendships dissipated (Chodos and Hamovitch, 1991: 193). In the end, 60 percent of Quebecers voted No to the referendum. Why did the first Quebec referendum result turn out as it did?

In part, for older francophone Quebecers, the question represented a kind of "Sophie's choice" between two heritages, Canada and Quebec, and—for that matter—between two respected "sons," Trudeau and Lévesque. Many Quebecers in general also feared the economic consequences of sovereignty, a fear magnified by the No side throughout the campaign. But the reasons for the referendum's outcome also were reflected in the demographics of the voters. Quebec's anglophones and allophones, who made up roughly 20 percent of the population, voted nearly *en masse* for the No side, meaning that francophone voters were split 50-50. In short, half of Quebec's large francophone population had publicly voiced their displeasure with their place in Canada's constitutional arrangements. Moreover, Yes supporters could take hope from the fact that the young and the educated among francophones had voted overwhelmingly in favour of the sovereigntist option (Conway, 1997: 105). The future seemed theirs to grasp.

For the moment, however, the referendum outcome left Yes supporters with a sense of bitterness and gloom, feelings of "collective trauma," and a mood of "political exhaustion" (Chodos and Hamovitch, 1991: 107). For No supporters, the predominant feeling was one of relief (Conway, 1997). They understood too well that, in the words of Balthazar (1993), Quebecers had said no to sovereignty but had not said yes to Canada.

In the closing days of the referendum campaign, Trudeau repeated promises that if the No side won he would work to revitalize Confederation (Clarkson and McCall, 1990: 236–39; Conway, 1997). The vote was not likely swayed by these promises, vague in any case. The referendum was fought "on the ground" by individuals and groups on both sides of the debate. Nonetheless, Trudeau's pledge, repeated the day after the referendum, set the stage for the most substantial revision of Canada's Constitution since 1867.

THE 1982 CANADIAN CONSTITUTION

Trudeau's statements before and immediately after the referendum were not clear, occasionally suggesting changes to federal institutions and a redistribution of powers. His only certain statement was that the patriated Constitution must contain a Charter of Rights and Freedoms. Such a charter had long been one of Trudeau's dreams. In February 1968, before announcing his run at the Liberal leadership, he had tabled a white paper in the House of Commons entitled "A Canadian Charter of Human Rights." Now, more than ever, he viewed the proposed charter as a means of ensuring the individual equality of all Canadians, especially against the "collective assaults of Quebec nationalism" (Conway, 1997: 108).

By long-standing tradition, however, Quebec held a veto over constitutional changes. Quebec did not oppose *per se* the constitutional entrenchment of individual rights; after all, Quebec had passed its own Charter of Human Rights and Freedoms in 1975 (see Fournier et al., 1997: 260–67). Quebec nationalists, however, feared Trudeau's Charter could be used against Quebec's national interests, for example in attacking Quebec's language laws.

Quebec's possible veto was not the Trudeau government's only problem. Many Conservative premiers also feared the Charter's application, believing that judicial activism would replace legislative supremacy. Several provinces also wanted changes in other areas. The western provinces wanted institutional reforms, notably dealing with the Senate. They also wanted clarification of provincial control over resources.

Finally, new actors also were appearing on the scene. Aboriginal Canadians, women's groups, and other social organizations also wanted input into constitutional changes.

In September 1980, the premiers and the federal government announced they had failed to agree on an amending formula. Not deterred, however, Trudeau announced his government's intention to proceed with unilaterally patriating the Constitution. A joint Commons-Senate committee held hearings throughout November and December on the proposed Charter of Rights and Freedoms.

In September 1981, however, Canada's Supreme Court ruled that, while the federal government could unilaterally patriate the Constitution, doing so "offended the federal spirit" (*Maclean's*, 2000; Clarkson and McCall, 1990). It was a strong judicial rebuke to Trudeau's plans. Thus, the federal government and provinces returned to talks in the fall of 1981.

As talks began that November, only the provinces of Ontario and New Brunswick supported the federal plans. The other premiers, known as the "gang of eight," posed a seemingly solid front. But the Trudeau government held a winning card. The public at large liked the idea of the Charter and wanted Canada's Constitution "brought home." In the negotiations that followed, the alliance of provincial premiers slowly began to crack. Equally important, Lévesque had agreed in the course of negotiations to give up Quebec's traditional constitutional veto. When the final agreement was reached on the Constitution, Levesque stood alone, Quebec—in the eyes of nationalists—defenceless (Clarkson and McCall, 1990; Conway, 1997).

The new Canadian Constitution, proclaimed on April 17, 1982, has six parts (Government of Canada, 1982; Webber, 1994; Dunn, 1995). Part One deals with the Canadian Charter of Rights and Freedoms. These rights and freedoms include the fundamental freedoms of conscience, religion, thought, belief, opinion, expression, peaceful assembly, and association; as well as democratic, mobility, legal, equality, and language rights. Part One makes French and English the official languages of Canada. It further designates New Brunswick Canada's only officially bilingual province. The Charter of Rights and Freedoms, however, also includes a "notwithstanding" clause allowing provinces to opt out of a provision if they choose.

Part Two of the Constitution Act, 1982, recognizes Aboriginal rights, including those existing by way of land claims, and formalizes the holding of conferences between first ministers and Aboriginal peoples (Chapter Twelve). Part Three commits governments to promoting equal opportunities for all Canadians, reducing regional disparities, and providing essential public services. Part Four commits the government to holding two future constitutional conferences on Aboriginal peoples and the representatives of Yukon and the Northwest Territories, since held. Part Five sets out a procedure for future amendments to the Constitution. Amendments may henceforth be done with the agreement of Parliament and seven provinces totalling 50 percent of the population. Part Six amends the British North America Act of 1867, renaming it the Constitution Act of 1867.

By and large, English-speaking Canadians seemed happy with the new Constitution. A Gallup poll in May 1982 found that 57 percent of Canadians viewed it positively, ranging from a high of 65 percent in Ontario to a low of 49 percent in Quebec, the latter figure skewed by overwhelming anglophone support in that province for the new act. The political elite outside Quebec were also generally pleased. The new Constitution clarified provincial powers over natural resources, a key sticking point for provinces such as Alberta. The Charter's application had been limited by the insertion, demanded by premiers Sterling Lyon of Manitoba and Allan Blakeney of Saskatchewan, of the "notwithstanding clause."

The PQ government and francophone nationalists in Quebec were embittered, however. The promises of constitutional renewal had been hollow. Ottawa and the rest of the provinces had gotten what they wanted. What had Quebec gotten? Quebec had been "humiliated," "betrayed," "stabbed in the back." Quebec had lost its traditional veto, and now was constitutionally defenceless against Canada's anglophone majority. The Charter of Rights and Freedoms, it was feared, could and would be used to advance anglophone rights and attack French language laws. Thus, the Constitution Act of 1982, meant to heal the rifts of past years, became yet another source of Quebec grievances. Lévesque's government refused to put Quebec's signature on the Constitution and did not participate in the ceremonies marking the occasion.

Whether the PQ would ever have signed a constitutional agreement is a moot point. Trudeau, the provincial leaders, and most Canadians outside Quebec doubted that a government dedicated to separatism would ever have signed. Yet, the referendum defeat had left the PQ with few options and Lévesque himself was viewed as a "soft" separatist.

As for the PQ, though re-elected in 1981, the period after 1982 saw the party's fortunes decline. Beset by a faltering economy, the PQ floundered, at odds with its union supporters, slowly withdrawing from its social-democratic ideals. Lévesque himself, his health diminished, seemed increasingly erratic. Age, disappointment, humiliation, and the shock of discovering just prior to the first ministers meeting in 1981 that his chief adviser and colleague, Claude Morin, had long been an RCMP adviser finally took their toll (Conway, 1997: 116).

By 1984, Lévesque seemed to have abandoned his commitment to either social democracy or sovereignty. Lévesque's old nemesis, Trudeau, had retired, replaced as Liberal leader by a former finance minister, John Turner. The Tories, meanwhile, also had a new leader, Brian Mulroney, a bilingual Quebecer with strong ties to international business. When Mulroney promised Quebecers a deal that would allow them to sign the Constitution "with dignity," Lévesque and Quebec nationalists as a whole threw their support behind the Tories.

QUEBEC, MULRONEY, AND THE MEECH LAKE ACCORD

The Mulroney Tories in 1984 routed the widely discredited Liberals, taking 211 (of 282) seats, 58 (of a possible 75) seats in Quebec (see Appendices 1 and 2). It was the largest number of seats ever won by a federal party, reflecting the broad sweep of Mulroney's electoral coalition, which featured at its core traditional conservatives, pro-business advocates of free trade, and Quebec nationalists.

No sooner was the election over than Mulroney moved to make good his promise to Quebecers on constitutional reform. By the spring of 1987, informal discussions had proved sufficiently positive that a federal-provincial meeting was held at Meech Lake, a resort a few miles outside Ottawa. Much to everyone's surprise, that meeting ended in a formal agreement being signed by the federal government and all the premiers. Five elements made up the Meech Lake Accord's proposed amendments to the Canadian Constitution (Balthazar, 1997: 54). These elements were

- restoring and enshrining in the Constitution Quebec's historical veto;
- enshrining the convention that Quebec holds three of nine appointments to the Supreme Court;
- limits on federal spending in provincial jurisdictions;
- increased powers over immigration; and
- recognition of Quebec as a "distinct society."

Signing the Meech Lake Accord did not immediately change the Constitution, however. Both Mulroney and the premiers were required to take the Accord back to the people, in the form of passage through their respective legislatures. The time frame for doing so was three years from the date when any one legislature passed the Accord, failure by any legislature (federal or provincial) to do so resulting in the Accord's rejection. Quebec passed the Accord quickly. The clock hence began ticking on its acceptance by the various levels of government.

Opposition to the Meech Lake Accord was slow in mobilizing, in part because the impact of constitutional changes is not always apparent and such documents are far from easy or enjoyable reading. Slowly over the next few years, however, opposition mounted. Three years after its signing, the Accord collapsed, dividing Canada more than any time since the FLQ crisis. At the extremes, anti-French bigots in English-speaking Canada attacked the Accord as a "sell-out" by Ottawa to Quebec, while nationalists in Quebec condemned the agreement as a "sell-out" by Bourassa's government of the French historical "fact." Lit by well-televised burnings of the Quebec flag in Ontario and the Canadian flag in Quebec, passions flamed brightly throughout the fall of 1989 and spring of 1990.

Opposition to the Accord was quite diverse and even, at times, contradictory, making defense of the Accord doubly difficult. In general, however, opposition centred on five main points (see Cohen, 1990; Smith et al., 1991; Webber, 1994). First, the Accord came under attack for "how" it was created, a process viewed by an increasingly aware, sophisticated, and less deferential public (Nevitte, 1996; Adams, 1998) as elitist. Second, federalists, led by Pierre Trudeau, denounced the Accord as dangerously decentralizing, threatening Canada's further balkanization. Third, opponents argued the Accord's granting of a veto to Quebec would prevent further constitutional reform, for example of the Senate, or to grant eventual provincial status to the northern territories. A fourth complaint was lodged against what the Accord did not contain. For example, minority groups, particularly Aboriginals and women, complained the Accord neglected their concerns and further entrenched inequalities.

The fifth and most politically important argument against the Meech Lake Accord, however, revolved around its "distinct society" clause. Why was the notion of Quebec as a **distinct society** so controversial in 1990? Why does it remain so today?

IS QUEBEC A "DISTINCT SOCIETY"?

At least on the surface, few could seriously argue that, culturally, Quebec is a province *comme les autres*. Two measures of culture, language and religion, make such a position difficult to maintain.

Linguistically, Quebec is the only domain in Canada and in North America in which the French language dominates, although New Brunswick is Canada's only officially bilingual province (see Table 4.1 below). In 1991 and 2001, French was the primary language of nearly 82 percent of Quebecers, but of only 4.7 percent of people outside Quebec in 1991, dropping to 4.2 percent in 2001. Today, for Canada as a whole, nearly 60 percent of people continue to claim English as their primary language, but the figure is almost 76 percent if Quebec is excluded. In this sense, terming Canada a "bilingual country" is misleading. Canada is marked at the federal level by **institutional bilingualism**. At the level of everyday usage, however, **territorial bilingualism** predominates, much as it does in Belgium or Switzerland (Dunn, 1995: 368–69).

Moreover, while the proportion of French speaking ability among non-Quebecers whose mother tongue is not French rose marginally between 1981 and 1991, from 10 percent to nearly 11 percent, the everyday usage of French in the home declined from 24.6 percent to 23.3 percent. Quebec was the only province to avoid a decline in everyday French usage (Harrison and Marmen, 1994: 17, 19). For francophones inside and outside Quebec, this decline reinforces fears of assimilation and suggests their worsening position within Confederation.

If language remains a significant marker of cultural difference, religion historically has also played such a role. Today, as indicated in Table 4.2, 45 percent of Canadians identify themselves as Catholic. This figure is also misleading, however. The largest majority of Catholics are located within Quebec. More than 85 percent of Quebecers identify themselves, at least nominally, as Catholic. By contrast, Canada outside Quebec still defines itself as largely Protestant, though other religions also are making gains.

TABLE 4.1	Population with English, French, or English and French Mother Tongue, Canada, Provinces, and Territories, and Canada less Quebec, 1991 and 2001 (in thousands and percent)												
	1991						2001						
	English	%	French	%	Both	%		English	%	French	%	Both	%
Canada	16 169.9	59.9	6 502.9	24.1	91.9	0.3		17 572.2	59.3	6742.0	22.7	122.7	0.4
Newfoundland	555.6	99.0	2.7	0.5	0.2	0.1		500.1	98.4	2.2	0.4	0.3	0.1
Prince Edward Island	120.6	94.1	5.6	4.4	0.3	0.2		125.2	93.9	5.8	4.3	0.4	0.3
Nova Scotia	830.1	93.2	36.6	4.1	1.7	0.2		834.3	93.0	34.1	3.8	2.6	0.3
New Brunswick	460.5	64.3	241.6	33.7	4.2	0.6		465.8	64.7	236.8	32.9	5.3	0.7
Quebec	599.1	8.8	5556.1	81.6	39.5	0.6		572.1	8.0	5788.7	81.2	55.4	0.8
Ontario	7380.4	74.0	485.4	4.9	31.4	0.3		8079.5	71.6	493.6	4.4	40.3	0.4
Manitoba	784.2	72.7	49.1	4.6	3.0	0.3		837.0	75.8	44.8	4.1	2.8	0.3
Saskatchewan	807.1	82.7	20.9	2.1	1.5	0.2		825.9	85.7	18.0	1.8	1.5	0.2
Alberta	2031.1	80.6	53.7	2.1	5.4	0.2		2405.9	81.8	59.8	2.0	6.3	0.2
British Columbia	2545.5	78.4	48.8	1.5	4.6	0.1		2865.3	74.1	56.1	1.5	7.5	0.2
Yukon	24.4	88.3	0.9	3.1	0.1	0.2		24.8	87.1	0.9	3.1	0.1	0.3
Northwest Territories	31.1	54.2	1.4	2.4	0.1	0.2		29.0	78.1	1.0	2.6	0.1	0.2
Nunavut*	—	—	—	—	—	—		7.4	27.6	0.4	1.5	0.1	0.1
Canada less Quebec	15 570.7	77.1	946.8	4.7	52.4	—		17 000.1	75.5	953.3	4.2	67.2	—

Sources: Adapted from the Statistics Canada publication, *Mother Tongue–20% sample data*, The Nation, Catalogue, 93-333, 1992, Table 1, pp. 10-11 and from the Statistics Canada Web site at www12.statcan.ca/english/census01/products/highlight/LanguageComposition/Index.cfm?Lang=E, Canada, Provinces and Territories.

Note: *Figures for Nunavut for 1991 included in Northwest Territories.

TABLE 4.2 — Population by Religion, Canada, Provinces, and Territories, and Canada less Quebec, 1991 (in percent)

	Catholic[1]	Protestant	Eastern Non-Christian[2]	Eastern Orthodox	Jewish	Other Religions	No Religion	United Church	Anglican	Other Protestant[3]
Canada	**45.7**	**36.2**	**11.5**	**8.1**	**16.7**	**2.8**	**1.4**	**1.2**	—	**12.5**
Newfoundland	37.4	61.0	17.3	26.2	17.6	—	—	—	—	1.6
Prince Edward Island	47.3	48.4	20.3	5.2	22.9	—	—	—	—	3.8
Nova Scotia	37.2	54.1	17.2	14.4	22.5	—	—	—	—	7.6
New Brunswick	54.0	40.1	10.6	8.5	21.0	—	—	—	—	5.4
Quebec	86.1	5.9	0.9	1.4	3.5	1.4	1.3	1.4	—	3.6
Ontario	35.6	44.4	14.1	10.6	19.6	3.8	1.9	1.8	—	12.5
Manitoba	30.4	51.0	18.6	8.7	23.4	1.5	1.9	1.3	—	13.7
Saskatchewan	32.5	53.4	22.8	7.2	23.5	—	2.0	—	—	11.0
Alberta	26.5	48.4	16.7	6.9	24.9	3.1	1.7	—	—	19.7
British Columbia	18.6	44.5	13.0	10.1	21.5	4.9	—	—	—	30.4
Yukon	20.2	43.0	8.7	14.8	19.5	—	—	—	—	34.3
Northwest Territories	38.1	50.0	5.7	32.1	12.2	—	—	—	—	10.4
Canada less Quebec	**32.1**	**46.5**	**15.0**	**10.4**	**1.2**	**3.2**	**1.5**	**1.1**	—	**15.5**

Source: Adapted from the Statistics Canada publication *Religions in Canada*, Catalogue 93-319, 1993, Table 1, pp. 8–17.

1. Includes Roman, Ukrainian and other Catholics. By far the largest group, however, are those belonging to the Roman Catholic faith.
2. Includes Islamic, Buddhist, Hindu, Sikh, and other Eastern non-Christian faiths. Some percentages may not add to 100 due to rounding.
3. Includes Baptist, Lutheran, and Pentecostal, as well as a host of smaller religious groups based in the Protestant faith.

Clearly, then, Quebec is distinct in terms of both language and religion from the rest of Canada. Moreover, this distinctiveness is historically and constitutionally grounded. (Remember, for example, that the Quebec Act of 1774 granted Quebec control over language and religion, and a distinctive legal system.)

Most English-speaking Canadians, inside and outside Quebec, acknowledge that the province of Quebec is distinct. Some even embrace Quebec's difference as a cornerstone of their identity. So why did the notion of "distinct society" lead to the failure of the Meech Lake Accord in 1990 and threaten Canada's survival?

Much of the furor revolves around the vagueness of society as a concept (Cook, 1995), as previously discussed (Chapter One). For example, does the phrase mean that Quebec is distinct? Or does it refer to the francophone community within Quebec?

Opponents, led by Preston Manning's newly created Reform party and Pierre Trudeau, successfully argued that the Meech Lake Accord's "distinct society" clause went against the notion of equality of the provinces, granting Quebec powers or claims to a status not held by others (Denis, 1993; Harrison, 1995). They further argued that "distinct society" status implied something greater than mere difference, that it could be used later on by Quebec governments to leverage further demands for nationhood and, perhaps, separate statehood.

Interestingly, hardline separatist factions in Quebec argued just the opposite. For them, Quebec was not merely a distinct society, but a sociological nation. The vapidity of "distinct society" was underlined by then BC Premier Bill Vander Zalm's comment that Canada was made up of "ten distinct societies" (see Bourgault, 1991: 35). In this context, Denis (1993) argues that "distinct society" seems merely a clever way of avoiding the "two nations" concept fundamental to the understanding of Canada held by many Quebecers.

At the more general level, the passions unleashed in English-speaking Canada by the notion of a "distinct society" can be traced to the fragility of Canadian identity itself. The author Joseph Conrad once wrote that underlying every great emotion is a great fear. What is English-speaking Canada's great fear? Just as Quebec's overarching fear has been assimilation into English Canada, Canada's fear has been a fatal embrace by the United States. For many Canadians, Quebec's assertions of difference and its refusal to "buy into" notions of Canadian nationalism threaten Canada's integrity. In the spring of 1990, English Canada's demands for uniformity, swelling in the aftermath of the recently signed Free Trade Agreement with the United States, ran up against Quebec's long-standing demands for respect and recognition of its differences.

THE DEFEAT OF THE MEECH LAKE AND CHARLOTTETOWN ACCORDS

The Meech Lake Accord unravelled under increasing pressure in the spring of 1990. The unravelling occurred simultaneously from both the top and the bottom, attacked at the one end by Trudeau, Manning, and the premiers of New Brunswick, Newfoundland, and Manitoba, and at the other end by popular, grassroots elements (Conway, 1997: 127).

The Accord's chief political problem lay in the long period for ratification: three years. Since 1987, new governments had been elected in New Brunswick and Newfoundland, while Gary Filmon's government in Manitoba had been reduced to a minority. New Brunswick's leader, Frank McKenna, and Gary Filmon demanded changes be made to the

Accord. Their demands were joined in April of that year by Newfoundland Premier Clyde Wells, who rescinded that province's previous ratification of the Accord.

As the Accord's ratification deadline (June 23) approached and tensions mounted, the Mulroney government created a special Commons committee to make recommendations for add-ons to the Accord. The committee's recommendations angered Quebec, however. The Meech Lake Accord was the minimum Quebec could accept to sign the Constitution. Now the Accord was being changed. The rest of Canada once more was "ganging up" on Quebec (Cohen, 1990; Conway, 1997). Anger in Quebec culminated in the resignation of one of Mulroney's key ministers, Lucien Bouchard, from the federal cabinet and the formation shortly thereafter of the separatist Bloc Québécois (Cornellier, 1995).

In a last-ditch effort to save the Accord, Mulroney in June called together a meeting in Ottawa of Canada's first ministers. The meeting was to last a couple of days. Instead, it dragged on for over a week. Between June 3 and 10, 1990, Mulroney and the premiers met in secret, appearing only infrequently—increasingly bedraggled, overwrought, and often unshaven—before television cameras to report on their progress in dealing with the emerging crisis. It was an amazing spectacle, one that heightened Canadians' fears that Canada was in crisis.

In the end, but only briefly, the crisis seemed averted. Under intense pressure, the recalcitrant premiers agreed to return to their provinces and ensure the Accord's passage. But such was not the case. Inflamed by Mulroney's glib comments a few days after the meetings that he had "rolled the dice" and counted on pressure to make the premiers to sign the agreement, Clyde Wells refused to put the Accord to a vote of the Newfoundland legislature. By then, however, the Accord was already dead. The death of the Meech Lake Accord really occurred in Manitoba at the hands of an Aboriginal MLA, Elijah Harper (see Chapter Twelve). Harper's refusal to give approval for fast-tracking the Accord through legislative debate meant there was no time to legally approve the Accord. Three years in process, the Meech Lake Accord died on the order paper (see Cohen, 1990; Conway, 1997) (Chapter Twelve).

The short- and long-term consequences of Meech Lake's failure were immense. Support for Quebec separatism (see Bourgault, 1991) and specifically the Bloc Québécois received an immediate boost (Cornellier, 1995). Elsewhere, in the context of fear and anger, the fortunes of the populist Reform Party also rose (Harrison, 1995). Three years later, the federal Tory party—its political coalition having evaporated—was dismembered, suffering the greatest electoral defeat by any government in Canadian history. In Quebec, the Tory limbs were torn off by the separatist Bloc, which, in a moment of supreme political irony, rose to the position of loyal Opposition to the victorious Liberals. The Reform Party led the slaughter in the West (see Appendix 1).

In the medium and longer terms, the failure to ratify the Meech Lake Accord left three principle concerns unresolved—Quebec's role in Canada, western Canada's growing sense of alienation, and Aboriginal self-government (Meekison, 1993)—and with no clear means of resolution. Thus Canada entered a time of constitutional fumbling, culminating in a historical footnote known as the Charlottetown Accord.

The Charlottetown Accord arose out of a meeting of English Canada's nine premiers in July 1992. It was meant to appease the various interests who had opposed the Meech Lake Accord. The Charlottetown Accord gave widespread new powers to the provinces, while limiting those of the federal government. It further proposed entrenchment of Aboriginal rights and creation of a Triple-E (equal, elected, and effective) Senate. Finally, the Charlottetown Accord relegated the notion of "distinct society" to a new proposed Canada clause, whereby its constitutional meaning would be constrained by commitments to "equality of the provinces" and "linguistic duality" (Conway, 1997: 140). The new Accord did not offer Quebec much. Nonetheless, Quebec Premier Robert Bourassa reluctantly accepted the agreement, with a few minor changes.

Like its predecessor, however, the Charlottetown Accord also failed. Stung by previous criticisms that the public had largely been excluded from ratifying the constitutional changes, politicians submitted the Charlottetown Accord to a rare Canada-wide referendum, held on October 24, 1992. The referendum's wording was standard throughout Canada, except in Quebec where that province enacted its own (though similar) referendum question. Seventy-five percent of Canadians turned out to vote, 55 percent voting No to the Accord, 45 percent voting Yes. The No side won in nearly every province, including Quebec, British Columbia, Manitoba, Saskatchewan, Alberta, and Nova Scotia, as well as Yukon. The Yes side only barely prevailed in Ontario.

Why did the Charlottetown Accord fail? In part, because after Meech Lake the chalice of constitutional reform already was poisoned. In part, also, Charlottetown failed because it was too unwieldy. It attempted to do too much, to address all issues, and be all things to all people at the same time. In the end, the best thing that could be said about the referendum result was that the Accord had been rejected throughout Canada, though the reasons for its rejection varied from person to person, and between Quebec and the other provinces.

The Charlottetown Accord's rejection thus ended for a time formal constitutional change in Canada. Many Canadians heaved a sigh of relief. Quebec's relationship to Canada still remained unresolved, however.

CONCLUSION

What would have happened had the Meech Lake Accord passed in 1990? No one can know for sure. While opponents argued passing the Accord would have put Quebec on the fast track to independence, more certain are three events directly resulting from its failure. Specifically, had the Meech Lake Accord been ratified, the Bloc Québécois would not exist as a political party, the Charlottetown Accord and referendum would have been unnecessary, and the Quebec referendum on sovereignty in 1995 (Chapter Five) would not have been held. It is additionally likely that, had the Meech Lake Accord passed, the Oka Crisis of 1990 (see Chapter Twelve) would have played out differently or at least had a different tone. We can further speculate that the Progressive Conservative Party may also have remained a stronger political entity than it is today, the Reform Party likely would have remained a smaller, regional party, and the Canadian Alliance Party would never have gotten off the ground (see Wills, 2000).

However, the history of societies (like that of individuals) is one of roads both taken and not. The failure of the Meech Lake Accord and its Charlottetown successor put an end to the era of formal constitutional change in Canada begun with the Quiet Revolution, but it did not end change. Canada was much different at the end of the constitutional years than it had been at the beginning, in part because of the Charter of Rights and Freedoms and promises made to Aboriginal peoples. But Canadians and Quebecers in 1992 also saw themselves differently from how they had done in 1970. Meanwhile, new and different pressures for change were coming from forces beyond the political sphere and even beyond Canada's borders. The old issues were dying or being recast. In time, the old warriors themselves would disappear. Before then, however, one more battle was to be fought, one more reprise of the referendum wars.

KEY TERMS

constitution
distinct society
institutional bilingualism
laws
social norms
sociological imagination
territorial bilingualism

chapter five

Beyond the Solitudes?

The time has come to reap the fields of history.
—preamble to Quebec's Sovereignty Bill, 1995

History goes in one direction—it doesn't stop, it flows like a river, immense, powerful. History is made by the will of the people. The history of Quebec is flowing. It flows toward sovereignty, my friends, because it is the solution.
—Quebec Premier Lucien Bouchard, 2000

In many respects, Canada suffers from the same ailments as Quebec. Like Quebec nationalism, Canadian nationalism is congealing under the weight of the myths and dogmas that are becoming obstacles to the nation's evolution.
—journalist Alain Dubuc

INTRODUCTION

Since 1970, Quebec and Canada had held constitutional negotiations designed to address Quebec's grievances and resolve their different visions of the country. The defeat of the Meech Lake and Charlottetown accords removed constitutional change—at least for a time—as a means of doing so. What options now remained? Effectively, there seemed only two options. Either Quebec could accept the status quo and perhaps sign the current Constitution, or it could reject the status quo and push for independence.

This chapter begins with an examination of the 1995 Quebec referendum, through which the Parti Québécois government sought a mandate to pursue this second option, and events since that time. Practical solutions to the Quebec-Canada conflict are detailed. More broadly, however, the chapter examines connections between individual and collective identity, and the power exerted by symbols and metaphors in shaping group solidarity and conflict. Finally, in anticipation of the book's next section, the issues of nation and state are reconsidered in the context of globalization and the threat posed by the United States to both Canadian nations.

A NEAR-DEATH EXPERIENCE: THE 1995 QUEBEC REFERENDUM

On October 30, 1995, Quebecers once more voted in a referendum on sovereignty. Canadians watching on their televisions saw their country come within a few thousand votes of being fundamentally changed, perhaps disintegrating altogether.

The referendum was presaged by three major events. First, the separatist Bloc Québécois elected 54 members to Parliament in the 1993 federal election, suggesting widespread support for independence (Appendix 1). Second, the BQ's provincial counterpart, the Parti Québécois, led by Jacques Parizeau, won the Quebec provincial election in September 1994 with a commitment to pursue sovereignty. Third, the PQ after much discussion tabled a draft bill on sovereignty, following which public consultations were held throughout Quebec during the early part of 1995 (Balthazar, 1997; Conway, 1997).

Debate within the sovereignty movement now centred on the question to be asked. Quebec Premier Jacques Parizeau, a sovereigntist hardliner, called for a clear and unambiguous question. His Bloc Québécois counterpart, Lucien Bouchard, called for a "softer" question, one that embraced a notion of continued association with Canada, arguing that Quebecers would be more likely to vote Yes in a referendum if assured of such ongoing relations. Discussions between Parizeau, Bouchard, and Mario Dumont, the leader of a small but influential party, L'Action Démocratique du Québec, led to an agreement on June 12 regarding the referendum question. The question asked: "Do you agree that Quebec should become sovereign, after having made a formal offer to Canada for a new Economic and Political Partnership, within the scope of the Bill respecting the future of Quebec and the agreement signed on 12 June 1995?" The referendum vote was set for October 30.

The referendum campaign formally began on September 11. As Quebec premier, Jacques Parizeau led the Yes campaign in the early stages, while Quebec Liberal leader Daniel Johnson led the No forces. It was clear from the start that the campaign would be close. Polls conducted since the 1994 Quebec election showed support for sovereignty stable at 45 percent (Conway, 1997: 214), a significant base upon which to build. Moreover, the sovereigntist camp believed the referendum question sufficiently benign as to attract "soft" voters.

For their part, federalists saw the question as vague, even duplicitous. No formal offers, acceptable to either side, would follow a Yes vote. A Yes vote would *de facto* result—as Jacques Parizeau stated—in Quebec being set "on the fast track to sovereignty."

Midway through the campaign, both campaigns' leaderships changed. Hoping to put wind in the sails of a becalmed campaign, Parizeau on October 9 ceded leadership of the

Yes campaign to Bouchard. Later, on October 25, in the face of polls showing a possible victory for the Yes side, Jean Chrétien entered the fray, promising to make the kind of constitutional changes Quebec had demanded since 1982 (Morton, 1997: 340). Chrétien's promises rung hollow, however, for many Quebecers. Trudeau had made similar promises just prior to the 1980 referendum (Chapter Four). Instead, the result had been the Constitution of 1982, unsigned by Quebec, which Chrétien had played a part in devising (Clarkson and McCall, 1990).

In short, in 1995, both Chrétien and Canada's political class more generally had nothing concrete to offer Quebecers. The defeat of the Meech Lake Accord (Chapter Four), in which Chrétien again had been instrumental, had foreclosed the possibility of constitutional renewal, at least for a time. All Chrétien and Canada's other leaders could offer was the status quo, liberally sprinkled with threats should the Yes side prevail (Conway, 1997: 219).

Moreover, even these threats were bound to be less successful than in 1980. First, Quebec's economy in 1995 was far more developed, and Quebecers felt more secure. Second, francophones made up a larger proportion of Quebec's business class in 1995 than in 1980. Though not stridently nationalist, many remained at least neutral in the 1995 sovereignty debate. Third, English-speaking Canada's constant reminders that Quebec is a net beneficiary of federal transfer payments (see below) fell on deaf ears. This is partly because such reminders are insulting, partly because many Quebecers do not believe this to be the case (Valaskakis and Fournier, 1995), and partly because many Quebecers outside the Montreal area do not directly see the benefits of these transfers, which often go to large corporations. The alleged dangers of separation are lost on people in the rural areas of Quebec, who often face double-digit unemployment.

As referendum day approached, many ordinary Canadians outside Quebec felt fearful, angry, bewildered, and powerless. On October 27, a unity rally was held at Canada Place in Montreal. The No-sponsored rally attracted between 30 000 and 150 000 people, many of them from outside the province, loudly declaring their love for Quebec. No doubt, these expressions of affection were sincere. But, as Balthazar (1997: 58) notes, "Since those Canadians had nothing to offer but their words of love, they gave Quebecers the image of an all-inclusive Canada that did not allow for the recognition of Quebec's uniqueness."

The impact of these events upon the referendum's outcome is uncertain. A study of polls conducted during the period suggests voting intentions remained fairly stable throughout and that the impact of Bouchard's increased prominence during the latter part of the campaign was negligible (see Fox et al., 1999). Likewise, the pro-federalist Montreal rallies may have made those in attendance feel better, or may have driven undecided voters into the Yes camp, or may have had no impact at all.

Few televisions in Canada were silent on referendum night, 1995. The Yes side took a seemingly commanding lead in the early stages, and jubilation reigned among its supporters. Gradually, however, the outcome turned as results came in from the Montreal Island. Nearly all of Quebec's eligible voters—90 percent (4.7 million people)—cast ballots. Of these, 50.6 percent voted No, while 49.4 percent voted Yes (Morton, 1997: 340). A swing of less than 30 000 votes would have changed the referendum's outcome (Young, 1998).

As in 1980, the 1995 referendum split not only Canada but also Quebec. The Yes side won strong support from francophones, about 60 percent of eligible francophone voters (compared with 50 percent in 1980). The Yes side also won strong support in Quebec City and rural Quebec, among the middle class and better-educated voters, and among union supporters. In contrast to 1980, the Yes side also received some support from business, though business in general remained on the sidelines of the sovereignty debate (Conway, 1997: 217). Polls conducted prior to the referendum also suggested that sovereignty appealed especially to those 35 to 44 years of age and males slightly more than females, though the gap had lessened (Trent, 1995). By contrast, the No side fashioned its close victory from about 40 percent of francophones and almost all anglophones and allophones, mostly located in Montreal (Fox et al., 1999), not to mention northern Quebec's small but politically powerful Cree and Inuit peoples (Conway, 1997: 219), thus opening up new and important ground for discussing the future of Aboriginal peoples within Canadian society (see Part Three).

As in 1980, English-speaking Canada sighed with relief, while Quebec's sovereigntists wept. There was bitterness on both sides. An obviously distraught Jacques Parizeau remarked on referendum night: "It's true we have been defeated, but basically by what? By money and the ethnic vote. All it means is that next time round, instead of us being 60 or 61 percent in favour, we'll be 63 or 64 percent" (quoted in Conway, 1997: 220; see also Balthazar, 1997; Morton, 1997). Reproached by colleagues and opponents alike for his divisive remarks, a remorseful Parizeau resigned the next day and was succeeded shortly thereafter as Quebec premier by Lucien Bouchard.

In broad statistical terms, Parizeau's observations leading to his resignation were correct. Francophones in Quebec *do* disproportionately favour sovereignty; non-francophones *do not*. His remarks, however, were divisive in singling out all members of Quebec's allophone community as being opposed to Quebec nationalism—indeed, being unpatriotic (Balthazar, 1997: 59). More broadly, Parizeau's comments once more unearthed debates within Quebec and the Parti Québécois itself about who is a true Québécois and the nature of Quebec nationalism.

As noted above (in Chapter Three), traditional Quebec nationalism was cultural and inward-looking. It traced its ancestry through bloodlines to the original 10 000 *Canadiens* of the St. Lawrence. The old Quebec nationalism was anti-modern and tribal. Old nationalism today is expressed linguistically through descriptions of people as either "Québécois pur laine" (literally, "pure wool") or "Québécois de souche" (later arrivals) (Ignatieff, 1993: 172).

By contrast, the new nationalism that arose in the 1950s was modern, democratic, territorial, and pluralistic. In theory, the new nationalism welcomes anyone living within Quebec's borders who is willing to accept the values of Quebec society. Most Quebecers today view their nationalism as civic, not ethnic (Ignatieff, 1993: 169; also Smith, 1998).

The debate over who is a Québécois continues in Quebec. In the fall of 1999, the Bloc Québécois released a policy document suggesting that language, culture, and history define Quebec identity, but that anyone living in an independent Quebec would enjoy equal rights (*Edmonton Journal*, 1999a). In early 2001, however, Lucien Bouchard's resignation was spurred by comments of a prominent PQ supporter singling out Quebec's Jewish community as opponents of sovereignty (Frank, 2001).

AFTER THE REFERENDUM

Despite defeat on referendum night, sovereigntists more than ever could believe the flow of history was with them. By contrast, Canadians in general at best could feel only relief.

Having won by the skin of their teeth, the federalist forces, led by Jean Chrétien's Liberal government, adopted after 1995 two approaches to counter Quebec sovereignty's appeal. These two approaches are often referred to as "Plan A" and "Plan B," or as Conway (1997: 227) describes them, the carrot and the stick.

Plan A involves attempts to show Quebecers that Confederation works and perhaps, in time, to win Quebecers' hearts and minds. The transfer since 1995 of administrative powers over immigration to Quebec (one of the Meech Lake Accord's five demands—see Chapter Four) is one example of Plan A at work. (These powers are also available for transfer to the other provinces upon demand.) The federal government also launched a series of programs, especially in higher education (for example, the millennium scholarships), designed to restore Ottawa's political and fiscal importance within the province. Other, more symbolic, examples of Plan A include the adoption by the House of Commons one month after the referendum of a motion recognizing Quebec as a distinct society (Balthazar, 1997: 59), and the Calgary Unity Declaration of the premiers in 1997 acknowledging the "unique character of Quebec society." Plan A has also involved—as in the 1960s (see Chapter Three)—the enticing of federalist Quebecers such as Stéphane Dion and Pierre Pettigrew to Ottawa. Other elements of Plan A include renewed efforts at pan-Canadianism through promotion, for example, of a private French television network in May 1999 (*Edmonton Journal*, 1999b) and federal efforts to expand French usage on-line (*Edmonton Journal*, 1999c).

By contrast, Plan B is a "tough love" approach to Quebec (Conway, 1997; Balthazar, 1997). Politically, the centrepiece of Plan B is Bill C-20 (The Clarity Act). Passed by the House of Commons in March 2000, The Clarity Act allows federal MPs to vote on both the clarity of the wording of any referendum question on sovereignty introduced by the Quebec National Assembly, and the clarity of any victory in a referendum, before beginning negotiations on Quebec sovereignty. In short, The Clarity Act renders a sovereigntist victory in any future referendum null until debated and passed by the House of Commons. Quebec nationalists, and sovereigntists in particular, view The Clarity Act as an infringement on Quebecers' rights to self-determination and the jurisdiction of Quebec's National Assembly. The Clarity Act further suggests Quebec's boundaries would be up for negotiation should a sovereignty vote be successful (*Edmonton Journal*, 2000a). For many Quebecers, in general, Plan B repeats an all-too-familiar pattern of trying to coerce French Canada into accepting the rules of Confederation.

For its part, the sovereigntist movement has been largely becalmed since 1995. The Bloc Québécois continues as Quebec's separatist voice in the House of Commons. It lost its status as Loyal Opposition (to the Reform Party) in the Canadian election of 1997, but it still captured 44 seats and roughly 38 percent of the popular vote in Quebec. In the 2000 federal election, the Bloc Québécois again took 37 seats and about 40 percent of the popular vote (see Appendix 1). At the provincial level, the Parti Québécois under Lucien Bouchard won re-election in 1998. Much of its focus, however, was on practical issues of governance, especially dealing with Quebec's deficits and cumulating debt. The party's *raison d'être*, independence, has largely been on the back burner, except in response to The Clarity Act and other perceived federal intrusions into Quebec's affairs. Even then, however, the separatist movement has been unable to mobilize an emotional response among Quebecers (*Edmonton Journal*, 2000b). The Parti Québécois suffered a serious internal blow with Bouchard's resignation as leader in early 2001, caused in part by continued debates over the nature of Quebec nationalism (see above) and frustration that he could not rekindle enthusiasm for sovereignty (Frank, 2001).

Since that time, Quebec politics have embarked on new territory. The spring of 2003 saw Jean Charest's Liberals elected to govern Quebec on a platform of economic stimulation and better relations with Ottawa. The Liberals are flanked on the left by the PQ and on the right by Mario Dumont's L'Action Démocratique du Quebec, a party whose ideology is similar to that of the former Mike Harris government in Ontario and the Ralph Klein government in Alberta (Pinard, 2003).

THE SOVEREIGNTY QUESTION TODAY

Beyond the immediate fate of political parties, how strong is the appeal of Quebec sovereignty today? The question begs comparison.

Compared with the 1960s and 1970s, sovereignty today invokes little passion in Quebec. The reason in part is that Quebec nationalism has gone beyond a need to redress past wrongs (Ignatieff, 1993). Most of the political, economic, and cultural grievances expressed during the Quiet Revolution have been addressed. Economically, French-Canadians in general, and francophone Quebecers in particular, no longer experience the second-place status relative to English-Canadians once identified by Porter (1965) and the Royal Commission on Bilingualism and Biculturalism (Government of Canada, 1969). Quebec's long-term unemployment rate remains generally two percentage points above the Canadian average (Riddell and Sharpe, 1998: S36, Table 1A). In partial consequence, average incomes in Quebec remain below the Canadian average, though ahead of several other provinces. In 2000, the average wage earner in Quebec made $29 385, about 94 percent of the Canadian average, while full-year, full-time earners in Quebec averaged $39 150, or about 90.6 percent of the Canadian average (see Table 5.1).

Likewise, as technically a "have-not" province, Quebec also receives transfer payments from the federal government, though per capita far less than the Atlantic region or Manitoba. For the fiscal year 2003–2004, for example, the federal government will transfer through various programs $1.4 billion ($2662 per capita) to Newfoundland, $385 million ($2747 per capita) to Prince Edward Island, $2.2 billion ($2371 per capita) to Nova Scotia, $2.0 billion ($2619 per capita) to New Brunswick, and $2.5 billion ($2175 per capita) to Manitoba. By contrast, Quebec will receive $13.1 billion ($1758 per capita), while Saskatchewan will receive $1.5 billion ($1434 per capita), British Columbia $5.7 billion ($1367 per capita)), Ontario $14.9 billion ($1225 per capita), and Alberta $3.8 billion ($1225 per capita). Per capita funding in Canada's north is far higher again, ranging from around $15 000 per person in Yukon and the Northwest Territories to slightly over $24 000 per person in Nunavut (Department of Finance Canada, 2003).

Today, however, economic circumstances are less tied than in the past to ethnicity. Within Quebec—in contrast to the 1960s—much of the bourgeoisie is francophone, and like the Canadian bourgeoisie at large, the Quebec bourgeoisie is wedded to breaking down rather than defending national borders. Likewise, among workers, those of French ethnicity (in Canada as a whole) actually earned significantly more than workers of British ethnicity in 1991 (Lian and Matthews, 1998).

Clearly, there remains racial and ethnic discrimination in Canada (Fleras and Elliott, 2002). Today, however, the demographic factors with the most direct impact on income

TABLE 5.1 Average Earnings, All Earners and Full-Year, Full-Time Earners, Canada, Provinces and Territories, 1980, 1990, and 2000

	All Earners					Full-Year, Full-Time Earners				
	1980	1990	2000	% Change 1990–2000	% Canadian Average 2000	1980	1990	2000	% Change 1990–2000	% Canadian Average 2000
Canada	**22 229**	**29 596**	**31 757**	**7.3**	**100.0**	**40 943**	**41 013**	**43 231**	**5.4**	**100.0**
Nfld. & Lab.	23 530	22 017	24 165	9.8	76.1	37 082	37 703	37 806	0.3	87.5
PEI	20 210	21 546	22 303	3.5	70.2	32 575	34 812	33 381	–4.1	77.2
NS	24 422	25 587	26 632	4.1	83.8	35 892	37 518	37 800	0.8	87.4
NB	23 501	24 173	24 971	3.3	78.6	35 705	36 828	35 982	–2.3	83.2
Que.	29 285	28 516	29 385	3.0	94.0	39 726	38 569	39 150	1.5	90.6
Ont.	29 360	32 181	35 185	9.3	110.8	41 103	43 831	47 247	7.8	109.3
Man.	25 988	25 859	27 178	5.1	85.6	36 888	36 017	36 549	1.5	84.5
Sask.	27 460	24 159	25 691	6.3	80.1	38 901	33 901	35 252	4.0	81.5
Alta.	31 857	29 241	32 603	11.5	102.7	44 659	40 540	44 080	8.7	102.0
BC	31 950	30 170	31 544	4.6	99.3	45 389	42 439	44 231	4.2	102.3
Yuk.	33 554	31 402	31 526	0.4	99.3	48 672	45 359	44 605	–1.7	103.2
NWT	—	—	36 645	—	115.4	—	—	51 823	—	119.9
Nun.	—	—	28 215	—	88.8	—	—	48 017	—	111.1

Source: Data adapted from the Statistics Canada Web site at www.statscan.ca/english/IPS/Data/96F0030XIE2001013.htm.

Note: Earnings not adjusted for inflation.

inequality (besides education) are Aboriginal ancestry (Chapter Thirteen), gender, marital status and, increasingly, age. Income and poverty rates are particularly high for single-parent female-headed families and single, widowed, or divorced female seniors (Morissette and Zhang, 2001). Recent immigrants also have lower earnings, even when education is controlled, than long-term immigrants or Canadian-born individuals (Statistics Canada, 2003a).

Politically, francophones since the 1960s have used their strength in Quebec (particularly) to make gains within the elite positions in Canada's political and labour sectors (Nakhaie, 1997). By contrast, while those of British background continue disproportionately to dominate elite positions within Canada, it might be argued that British Canada as a sociological construct no longer exists (Gwyn, 1996).

Quebec's success in stemming the cultural threat is harder to measure. Though the percentage of French-speaking people in Quebec has stabilized at roughly 80 percent (see Chapter Four), many francophone Quebecers remain "linguistically insecure" (Thompson, 1995: 78). They fear particularly the impact of allophone immigrants to Quebec who might choose English rather than French as their adopted language. But this level of insecurity is lower among younger Quebecers, used to the protections provided by Quebec's language laws (Chapter Four). Moreover, recent census figures suggest that in fact allophone immigrants are today actually strengthening the French language in Quebec by opting to adopt that language (*Globe and Mail*, 2002). Finally, Quebec today has more powers over immigration than in the past, with which the provincial government is actively attempting to recruit immigrants from francophone countries (*Edmonton Journal*, 1999d).

Beyond Quebec, the world has also changed dramatically since the time of the Quiet Revolution. Liberation politics, drawn from Third World experiences and the writings of Franz Fanon and Che Guevara, today have less appeal. Few Quebecers today, most especially young people, argue that their province is a colony. In this time of globalization, as the world seems drawn closer and closer together by economics, technology, and trade deals, the very notion of sovereignty seems unclear. (What does independence mean? What would Quebec gain through sovereignty that it does not already possess?) Meanwhile, recent examples of ethnic nationalism run amok (in Yugoslavia, for example) provide stinging counterpoints to the ideal of independence. (What would an independent Quebec lose?) Finally, many young Quebecers increasingly see themselves—not unlike young people elsewhere—as individual consumers and mobile workers. A CROP/Environics poll conducted in the fall of 2002 found that 63 percent of Quebecers aged 18 to 44 identify with neither the federalist *nor* the sovereigntist sides (*Edmonton Journal*, 2002).

Research conducted since 1995 is consistent on four points (Trent, 1995; *Edmonton Journal*, 1999e, 2000b; Johnson, 1999; Macpherson, 2000; Dubuc, 2001). First, the vast majority of Quebecers—as many as 80 percent in one poll—oppose holding another referendum. Second, few Quebecers believe a referendum on sovereignty would pass if held today. Third, support for sovereignty during "normal" periods fluctuates between about 40 and 46 percent. Support for sovereignty rises only when Quebec feels attacked or rejected by English Canada (as during the Meech Lake crisis), when the idea is presented in the abstract, or when the definition of sovereignty is unclear. Fourth, a large number of Quebecers harbour the apparently contradictory beliefs that Quebec and Canada have reached an impasse *and* that federalism can be renewed.

Looked at another way, about a third of Quebecers are consistent federalists. Another third are hard-core *indépendantistes* who identify with the Quebec state. The remaining third of Quebecers are torn between choosing the Quebec nation or the country of Canada, a predicament captured in the oft-quoted joke of Quebec comedian Yvon Deschamps that, "All we want is an independent Quebec within a strong and united Canada" (Colombo, 1994: 224). It is on this third of Quebecers that the outcome of any sovereignty referendum hinges.

English-speaking Canada for two centuries has believed Quebec nationalism would disappear. Federalist politicians have fuelled these beliefs for the past 30 years, often after yet another crisis has shaken the Canadian federation. Yet, Quebec nationalism and the idea of an independent homeland continue to stir within Quebec. Why is this the case? The answer lies in the fact that the issue of French-English, Quebec-Canada relations within the country cannot be addressed solely by material or even constitutional changes alone. The basis of the issue lies in such non-tangible, but immanently sociological, issues as self-identity, mutual respect, and the need for recognition.

SOCIETY, NATION, MODERNITY, AND "SELF"

Who are you? That is, what are the elements that make up who you are, speaking to you and others of your "self"? This is a distinctly sociological question, one that emerged in the nineteenth century with modernity. Riesman et al. (1950) note, for example, that notions of individual identity make little sense in pre-modern, feudal societies, where ideas, norms, behaviours, expectations, and outcomes are fairly rigidly controlled by tradition. In the Middle Ages, to use the popular phrase of the 1960s, no one would have declared an intention to "find myself." People of that earlier era were told (directly and indirectly) who they were from the time they were born. By contrast, in modern societies, individuals not only *seem* more free of social restraints, they are also expected to find and express their particular uniqueness.

What are the building blocks used in this construction? In modern societies, the cache of materials is seemingly endless, drawn from television, the Internet, magazines, and so on. For Marx, writing in the mid-nineteenth century, class was the primary factor in a person's identity "kit"; for Durkheim, occupation was central. For feminist scholars today, gender is a chief source of one's identity as well as one's world view. But other factors—religion, ethnicity, education—may also provide salient materials informing an individual's self-identity.

From a sociological point of view, several points about individual identity must be noted. First, individual and collective identities are mutually constructed. In a real sense, no one simply chooses an individual identity. Rather, an identity arises out of membership in a group (Tajfel and Turner, 1986). Second, both individual and collective identities are highly malleable (Cook, 1995: 235). The importance of an identity may lessen over time for a person or group, or events may lead an individual or group to rediscover and reassert their roots. Third, individual identities are neither singular nor exclusive. A person may simultaneously see him- or herself as Italian, a doctor, a soccer player, a conservative, and gay or lesbian.

What does the issue of individual and collective identity have to do with Quebec and Canada? Simply this: Quebec's national culture, broadly conceived, provides many Quebecers with essential materials for their personal identities. André Laurendeau (1985) argued that "the homogenizing influence of the United States put in question the very existence of both Canadian [French and English] cultures."

This notion is at odds (at least on the surface) with dominant Anglo-Saxon culture, where private and public spheres are viewed as separate, the individual is sacrosanct, and "the state and civil society are typically understood as facing off against each other" (White, 1997: 22). Pierre Trudeau's denunciations of Quebec nationalism as tribal (Chapter Four) were rooted in a supposed separation of individual self and society (Couture, 1998). Hence his desire to entrench the Charter of Rights and Freedoms in the 1982 Constitution as a means of protecting individuals from collective oppression.

Separating the spheres is difficult, if not impossible, however. Note, for example, that the Charter of Rights and Freedoms deals with both individual and collective rights (Cook, 1995: 234). Likewise, the policies of official bilingualism and multiculturalism enacted by Trudeau similarly protect collective rights over language and culture (Webber, 1994; Couture, 1998).

It is therefore inaccurate to argue a necessary opposition exists between the rights of collectives and those of individuals, represented by Quebec and English-speaking Canada, respectively. Repeated surveys show Quebecers have at least as much deep regard for individual rights as other Canadians. Indeed, Quebecers are generally quite liberal in their acceptance of individual differences (Denis, 1993). At the same time, English-speaking Canadians also possess an, albeit understated, sense of collective identity, as evidenced quickly if someone tells them they are "just like" Americans.

If the sociological (and political) problem between Quebec and Canada doesn't lie in an opposition between individual and collective rights, it lies even less in an absolute separation of the French and English cultures. French and English identities (and others) in Canada include elements of each other (Dufour, 1990; Webber, 1994; Saul, 1997). Notes Dufour (1990: 81), "Almost by definition, the Quebec identity comprises a more or less significant, more or less conscious, Canadian component." And again: "English is a deeply ambivalent and perturbing element of the Quebec identity" (1990: 97). A majority of Quebecers (though less among francophones) still see themselves simultaneously as Quebecers *and* as Canadians (see Smith, 1998), though the former generally takes precedence in their identity structures.

What, then, underlies the conflict? Simply that the right of Quebecers *to possess* a distinct identity be recognized and respected by the rest of Canada (Taylor, 1993; Coulombe, 1998).

There is an apparent paradox in this demand, for—as Taylor (1993) and Ignatieff (1993) note—Canada and Quebec have never been closer. Quebec was "more distinct" before the Quiet Revolution than it is today. Throughout Canada, regional differences on social factors and values have been lessening for decades (see Goyder, 1993: Baer et al., 1993), a product of modernization. The paradox of diminishing differences and escalating demands for recognition is partly explainable, however, if we consider globalization's impact upon states and nations (see Chapter One).

On the one hand, globalization has accelerated the process of homogenizing cultures. On the other hand, it has left many national groups feeling uneasy and compelled to overemphasize and protect remaining distinctions. The weakened capacity of states—especially multinational states, such as Canada—to protect them, has further pressed national cultures to seek shelter in smaller units. Moreover, in line with the contention of Bell (1993: 362) that national states today are both too big and too small to deal with important issues, sovereigntists argue an independent Quebec would be better able to adapt to the demands of the global marketplace (see Bourgault, 1991; PQ, 1994).

Such claims are debatable but ultimately beside the point. The question is, is it possible for English-speaking Canada to acknowledge Quebec's distinctiveness in a meaningful way; to grant recognition and respect for Québécois identity; and to give Quebec sufficient powers for its survival within Canada's existing state structures (see Taylor 1993; Denis, 1993; Coulombe, 1998)? Or does the flow of history lead inexorably to Quebec sovereignty?

SOLUTIONS TO THE IMPASSE

Ignatieff (1993: 147) remarks, "If federalism can't work in my Canada, it probably can't work anywhere." How might Canada and Quebec get beyond the consequences of their mutual histories? Three solutions short of Quebec leaving Confederation are frequently discussed.

The first solution is that of more or less maintaining the **status quo**. Status quo supporters argue, however, that Canadian federalism is adaptable, as attested by the country's survival over 130 years. They further point to the gradual decline of separatist sentiment. Indeed, they argue, the periods of greatest English-French discord have occurred usually in the context of efforts to enact grand constitutional changes.

By contrast, critics of the status quo argue that Confederation today is less flexible than it once was. In consequence, Canada is unable to deal with such problems as Quebec separatism and regional alienation, especially in western Canada (Dufour, 1990: 20), or the problems of adapting to the global economy (PQ, 1994). Critics further note that Quebec nationalism is a resilient force. The recent apparent calm in Quebec-Canada relations is certain, at some point, to be replaced by a new crisis threatening Canada's future.

The second proposed solution to the Canada-Quebec impasse is **asymmetrical federalism**. Taylor (1993) argues philosophically that asymmetrical federalism recognizes the reality of Quebec's distinct historical, legal, and cultural place within Canada, that is, that it never was a province "just like the others." How would asymmetrical federalism work? Laxer (1992; 2001) and Webber (1994: 230) suggest that Quebec be given constitutional powers over areas it views as necessary for preserving its national identity, while these same powers for Canadians elsewhere remain "housed" in Ottawa. In effect, Quebec would have more powers than the other provinces, but it would not have powers over the citizens of other provinces, nor would Quebecers have more powers than other Canadians. The change would require two sittings of the House of Commons: an all-Canada sitting, in which Quebec MPs would participate, and a separate sitting in which Quebec MPs would not participate. Resnick (1991) similarly proposes a government and parliament of the Canada-Quebec Union to deal with issues in common, including international affairs, but also separate "national" governments and parliaments for Canada and Quebec. Both Resnick and Conway (1997) further suggest asymmetrical federalism be combined with other political reforms. Such changes might include reform (Resnick) or abolition (Conway) of the Senate, as well as fixed electoral dates and the replacement of Canada's first-past-the-post electoral system with proportional representation (Conway, 1997: 245).

Critics, however, launch three arguments against asymmetrical federalism (see Cook, 1995: 242–245; also Valaskakis and Fournier, 1995). First, in a practical sense, such a change is unacceptable to the other provinces and most Canadians, as attested by English-speaking Canada's response to the Meech Lake Accord. Second, Canadian federalism already is asymmetrical in certain respects. Further asymmetry would weaken Canada's federal principle as other provinces quickly sought the same powers. Third, by making Quebec City more important to Quebecers, an action not wholly endorsed by many Quebecers themselves (*Edmonton Journal*, 2000b), the path would be set for further separatist agitation.

The third solution is **decentralization**. Decentralization could be minimal, returning to the situation of Canada prior to the Great Depression and two world wars, during which the powers of the federal government grew (Rice and Prince, 2000; see Chapter Seven). Or decentralization could be more extreme. Anticipating a Quebec separatist victory in a sovereignty vote, Gibson (1994), for example, suggested a radical decentralization of powers *before Quebec left*. In Gibson's "Plan C," Ottawa would be reduced to a "service centre," a relatively powerless clearing house for functions residual to those of the provinces.

The appeal of decentralization as a solution is that it meets Quebec's demands while also maintaining a strict equality of the provinces. Decentralization also appeals to provincial rights advocates in general, political leaderships in the "have" provinces, and those concerned with regional alienation (Manning, 1992; Gibbins and Arrison, 1995). Finally, decentralization seems for many an inevitable and positive adaptation to globalization. Courchene (1996), for example, argues in favour of the principle of **subsidiarity** (namely, *that unless there is a valid reason to the contrary, state functions should be exercized by the lowest level of government*) and suggests (1998), as do others (Resnick, 2000; Ibbitson, 2001), that decentralization would strengthen Canadian federalism. Resnick (2000) takes the decentralization argument even further, suggesting Canada be reconfigured as a country with three tiers rather than a community of equal provinces. These three tiers would include six provinces (the four Atlantic provinces and Manitoba and Saskatchewan); three region-provinces (Ontario, Alberta, and British Columbia) with large populations and significant resources; and one nation-province (Quebec).

Decentralization also has critics, however. First, it is argued, Canada already is the world's most decentralized federation (Valaskakis and Fournier, 1995). Second, most Canadians still believe in a strong role for the federal government, particularly in areas of social policy, a belief underscoring much of the opposition to the Meech Lake and Charlottetown accords. They further believe the federal government provides one of the few "checks and balances" to provincial power, and vice versa (see Taylor, 1993).

More broadly, decentralization raises the spectre for many critics of Canada's further fragmentation. With Ottawa rendered powerless, the "have" provinces would go one way, the "have-nots" another, and Canada would dissolve into multiple and conflicting fiefdoms. Laxer and Harrison (1995) argue that decentralization would allow the United States and large corporate interests to play regions and provinces off against each other. In consequence, national programs, such as medicare, would all but cease to exist; people's identification with Canada would lessen; and Canada's profile in the world would diminish. Courchene (1996) counters that fragmentation could be resolved by giving the provinces *not only more powers* but also *more responsibilities* for the implications of their policies. Such a solution would seem likely to lead to conflicting mandates and constituencies, however.

THINKING THE UNTHINKABLE: SEPARATION

Countries, states, nations, and societies change. Nothing is ordained to last forever. Goldwin Smith (1891) predicted over a hundred years ago that Canada one day would splinter into its French and English halves, with the English part joining the United States.

Such predictions have become a staple of Canadian political analysis ever since (see Simeon, 1977; Brimelow, 1986; Young, 1995).

The vast majority of people outside Quebec and a plurality of people within that province oppose outright Quebec independence. There are some, however, both inside and outside Quebec, who support separation. The arguments put forward by Quebec sovereigntists are familiar, ranging from alleged economic benefits to the belief that Quebec is a nation and must become a state in order to chart its own historic course (Parti Québécois, 1994). At the same time, a number of anglophone scholars and assorted pamphleteers argue that Quebec's separation is something to be embraced rather than feared. Their arguments are diverse. Brimelow (1986) reiterates Smith's (1891) argument of historical destiny. Bercuson and Cooper (1991), and many others, argue that Quebec wields too much political influence in Canada and that the country would be economically better off if the province left. Anti-French, anti-Quebec sentiments often lurk close to the surface of such desires, but not always. A tinge of sadness, for example, underlies the contention of Scowen (1999) that it is time to "say goodbye." For him, Quebec's view of itself as a nation is simply incompatible with Canada as a "civil association."

What would Canada and Quebec look like if they separated? In descriptive terms, Canada would cover 8.4 million square kilometres, nearly 85 percent of its previous size, though the Atlantic provinces would be separated from Ontario (Young, 1995: 9; Scowen, 1999), and have a population of more than 23 million, 50 percent of which would be located in Ontario (see Table 1.1). Quebec would cover 1.5 million square kilometres and have a population of about 7.5 million people. The economies of both Canada and Quebec would still be large. For Canada, *sans* Quebec, in 1997, the **gross domestic product** (GDP)—*the total value of all goods and services produced by a country in a year*—was $473 billion, while that of Quebec was $185 billion (*CGA*, 1999: 27 and 356). Indeed, Quebec today ranks among the world's 30 leading economies (Ramonet, 2001). These figures, however, assume no massive transfers of land either way, no large movements of population, and no disruptions to either economy resulting from political unrest. These are big assumptions.

Setting aside the possibility of violence (see Gibson, 1994; Monahan, 1995; Martin, 1999a), several key issues would need immediate address. These issues would include territorial boundaries (Reid, 1992: 37–66); division of public assets and debts, the latter roughly $580 billion in 1998 (*CGA*, 1999: 206; see Valaskakis and Fournier, 1995: 84; Scowen, 1999: 128); and determination of citizenship (Bourgault, 1991; Scowen, 1999). A further key issue would be jurisdiction over and responsibility for Aboriginal peoples (Bourgault, 1991; PQ, 1994; Gibson, 1994; Conway, 1997; Scowen, 1999). These issues would only scratch the surface, however. Deeper questions would remain for the citizens of both countries.

Canada and Quebec would both require new constitutions. Quebec could achieve this task more easily than Canada (*PQ*, 1994). By contrast, constitutional renewal in Canada would require far more actors and a fundamental rethinking of the country's purpose and structure. The process also would be psychologically wrenching for Canadians, who suddenly would find their identity and "home" taken away.

Both countries also would have to refashion their international relations. Quebec's task in this case would likely be more difficult than Canada's, though Quebec sovereigntists assume international recognition, a seat at the United Nations, and partnership in all agreements previously signed by Canada would be automatically forthcoming (Bourgault, 1991;

Turp, 1993; *PQ*, 1994). Finally, both Canada and Quebec would need to consider their changed relationship to the United States.

QUEBEC AND THE "OTHER" ANGLOPHONE STATE

Bourgault (1991: 24) notes, "In Quebec, pro-American feeling is probably stronger than in the rest of Canada." At first, this may seem curious given the virulent antipathy between New France and the New England states in the years prior to the American Revolution (Chapter Two). After this time, however, Quebec's contacts with the United States gradually became more positive. The American Revolution's ideals appealed to Quebec's intellectual class and fuelled the rebellions of 1837–38 (Conway, 1997). From Papineau to Louis Riel, French-Canadian "rebels" repeatedly sought safe haven across the border. Nor were they alone. Throughout the nineteenth and twentieth centuries, francophone emigrants, too, chose the eastern United States over the Canadian West.

Meanwhile, American capital also streamed into the province, stimulating Quebec's industrialization (Chodos and Hamovitch, 1991). The fact that Prime Minister Brian Mulroney grew up in a Quebec town built by American investment and was president of an American branch plant before entering politics (Sawatsky, 1991) is symbolically significant.

The rise of English nationalism in the 1960s (Chapter Eight) in counterpoint to Quebec nationalism further pushed (unwittingly) many Quebecers into the American embrace. Anglo-Canadian desires for a strong central government found little support among Quebecers, who viewed the concept of One Canada and the federal state with suspicion. Closer economic links with the United States were furthered by economic development after the Quiet Revolution, especially the expansion of hydroelectric power during the 1970s, and by the sovereigntist argument that less dependence upon Canada enhanced the separatist project. Thus was premised in part Quebec's support of the Free Trade Agreement in the 1988 federal election, or so thought some of English-speaking Canada's nationalists (see Resnick and Latouche, 1990).

Like people everywhere, Quebecers are large consumers of American culture. Likewise, many Quebecers, including many of its elite, also spend considerable time in the U.S., especially Florida (Cook, 1995: 229). For them, visits to the rest of Canada hold little attraction, though this sometimes changes when Quebecers do venture into the other provinces.

Quebec's unconscious relationship with the United States raises interesting questions. André Laurendeau (1985) argued that "the homogenizing influence of the United States put in question the very existence of both Canadian [French and English] cultures." Unlike English-speaking Canadians, few Quebecers seem concerned about this influence. Some have argued, however, that Quebec's distinct culture has survived against American influence precisely because of its protected place within Canadian Confederation (Dufour, 1990; Resnick, 1991; Valaskakis and Fournier, 1995). More recently, Brunelle (1999) and Ramonet (2001) have further suggested that the sovereignty question has distracted Quebecers from examining the impact of neo-liberal globalization and Americanization upon Quebec society, and the problems it might face after separation. (One interesting sidelight to the American war in Iraq in March 2003 was the sudden rise of anti-American sentiment in Quebec, which—of all Canadian provinces—most opposed the war.)

Interestingly, many of the same arguments can also be made regarding English-speaking Canada: that it has insufficiently valued the role of the French language and culture in differentiating Canada from the United States. Could either Quebec or Canada alone long withstand the assimilating influences of the American giant? This question and others are addressed in Part Two.

CONCLUSION

Canada and Quebec have travelled a long way since 1960, let alone since 1763. Sometimes in conflict, more often than admitted in co-operation, each has shaped the other. Canada's institutions, its decentralized system of governance, its tolerance of cultural differences (not to be overstated), and much of its identity are built upon French foundations. For its part, Quebec—the territory in which the French "fact" was suppressed and contained, and therefore incubated—also contains a hidden English element. Together, Canada's French and English "nations" have withstood absorption into the United States and built, by nearly any standard, one of the best societies on earth.

Canada, it is often said, is an experiment (Bernard, 1996; Conway, 1997; Saul, 1997). Is it possible to break the European model of nation *equals* state *equals* country *equals* society? Is it possible to conceive and create a state structure in which two nations—three, counting the Aboriginal peoples—exist harmoniously and prosper, housed within a single country? A state structure in which majority, minority, and individual differences are embraced and respected, and yet political and social coherence are maintained? We leave the last words to Conway (1997: 252):

> If we can continue our unique experiment in seeking unity through diversity, if we can retain the two great cultures [French and English] together in one federal or confederal structure, Canada could yet become a model for all the world.... [I]f we fail, it will not be a disaster. Life will go on....But the Canada we could have become... will be lost, perhaps forever.

The world watches.

KEY TERMS

asymmetrical federalism
decentralization
gross domestic product (GDP)
status quo
subsidiarity

part two

Canada and the United States

In 1996, at a time when English Canada's psyche was still bruised from the 1995 Quebec referendum, the *Globe and Mail* ran a story headlined "Might Canada as a distinct society disappear?"

Fears of American absorption are not new. Beginning with the American Revolution and for several decades thereafter, Canada faced twin threats of military takeover by the United States and annexation movements within its own borders. The creation of Canada in 1867 was presaged by American political and economic threats. The onset of a recession later in the century led to Goldwin Smith's thesis, stated in *Canada and the Canadian Question* (1891) that Quebec and Canada were bound to part ways, Canada inevitably joining the United States. An American scholar, Samuel Moffett (1972), in 1908 published *The Americanization of Canada* stating a similar thesis.

Part Two of this book examines Canada's complex and often ambivalent relationship with the United States. On the one hand, Canada's relationship has been marked by fears of takeover. On the other hand, the United States is also a land of fascination and allure for Canadians. How close can Canada come to the United States without triggering a fatal embrace?

The chapters that follow trace the political, economic, and cultural moments defining this relationship. Sometimes, such as during the development of the Canadian economy in the nineteenth century or at the time of Roosevelt's New Deal in the 1930s, the United States has been considered a positive model for Canadian society. At other times, however, such as during the turbulent period of the 1960s, the United States has been seen as a negative model. The result has been a relationship that, if traced, would show two ships occasionally running parallel, occasionally tacking quite differently into the future.

The next chapters, however, do not focus solely on this external relationship. They also examine Canada's internal development and deal with such issues as regionalism, the evolution of corporate capitalism, and the development of the Canadian welfare state. Along the way, other changes in Canadian society are also detailed, such as Canada's class structure, the role of women in Canadian society, and immigration policy.

Finally, Part Two examines the issue of Canada's survival in a rapidly globalizing world dominated by the American empire and the problems of building a "better country" in North America in the wake of the terrorist attacks in New York and Washington in September 2001 and the subsequent wars in Afghanistan and Iraq.

QUESTIONS

- How are Canada and the United States similar? In what ways are the countries different?

- What is ideology? Do Canadians and Americans share similar values and beliefs?

- What is the nature of the Canadian-American relationship? How has it changed over the years?

- How has the United States influenced Canada's internal politics, economy, and culture?

- How has Canada attempted to develop separately from the U.S.? What has been the role of the state in this process?

- How has Canadian society—as a whole—participated in its own development? What changes have occurred in the course of this development?

- Why did free trade come about and what does globalization mean for Canada?

- What particular problems does the so-called "war on terrorism" pose for Canada?

chapter six

The Making of English Canada

[T]he American continents, by the free and independent condition which they have assumed and maintain, are henceforth not to be considered as subjects for future colonization by any European power....[W]e should consider any attempt on their part to extend their system to any portion of this hemisphere as dangerous to our peace and safety.
—U.S. President James Monroe, Annual Message to Congress, 1823

It is our Manifest Destiny to overspread the continent allotted by Providence for the free development of our multiplying millions.
—newspaper editor John O'Sullivan, *United States Magazine and Democratic Review*, 1845

When the experiment of the 'dominion' shall have failed—as fail it must—a process of peaceful absorption will give Canada her proper place in the great North American Republic.
—publisher Horace Greeley, *New York Tribune*, 1867

INTRODUCTION

The phrase "the world's longest undefended border" is an overused metaphor for describing Canada's relationship to the United States. No Canadian prime minister,

American president, or accompanying journalist leaves home without some variation on it. While the phrase is not entirely incorrect—though who can say, given events since the terrorist attacks of September 2001—it is historically misleading.

Canadians and Americans forget that their mutual relationship began less cordially, with a war. The American Revolution spawned not only the United States but also Canada (Lipset, 1990). From then on, until 1871, the threat of American invasion was real and Canadians had frequent cause to anticipate war (Winks, 1998: 3). Even after, until at least 1936, the American Department of Defense regularly updated invasion plans for Canada (Rudmin, 1993).

This chapter traces the development of English-speaking Canada from 1775, when the American Revolution began, until Confederation in 1867. The chapter concentrates on the early troubled history of relations between Canada and the United States and on how events in the United States helped spawn the creation of Canada in 1867. Specifically, this chapter shows that Canadian society has developed socially, economically, and politically both for internal reasons and as a defensive response (see Aitken, 1959) to the American threat. Finally, the chapter begins the process of defining English Canada's identity.

THE BIRTH OF TWO NATIONS

The American War of Independence, popularly known as the American Revolution, began at Lexington, Massachusetts, on April 18, 1775, and ended with the Treaty of Paris in 1783. Why did the American colonists revolt in 1775?

The American Declaration of Independence of 1776 (*Time*, 1999: 64) provides a useful starting point for answering the question. Like all revolutionary tracts, the Declaration does not shy away from rhetoric: "The history of the present King of Great Britain is a history of repeated injuries and usurpations, all having in direct object the establishment of an absolute Tyranny over these States." The Declaration lists a series of specific complaints: the general suspension of natural and constitutional rights, unjust trials, press ganging, the denial of political representation, unlawful taxation, the prevention of trade, the growth of colonial bureaucracy, general harassment of the people, and the "quartering of large bodies of armed troops."

Many of these complaints were justified. The American colonists believed strongly that a paternalistic and authoritarian British monarch and his administration had breached constitutional rights guaranteed by the English Bill of Rights (1689).

Taxation was a particularly vexing issue. From the late seventeenth century on, the English Crown and Parliament had imposed a series of taxes on the colonies. At first purely regulatory in nature, after 1763 taxation became a means of generating revenues (Hofstadter, 1958: 3–4). The colonists were unaccustomed to paying revenue-raising taxes and, in any case, viewed them as potentially ruinous. The colonists also believed that the taxes had been imposed without their consent given either directly or indirectly, through the will of Parliament (Hofstadter et al., 1957: 42).

The British viewed taxation differently. "The empire was expensive; costly wars had been fought to acquire and defend it; still more money would have to be laid out in the future to garrison it" (Hofstadter, 1958: 3). In short, it was time for the colonists to shoulder their fair share of state expenses.

Though frequently the tax measures were withdrawn under protest, or otherwise circumvented by the industrious colonists (see James, 1997), taxes were certainly a major sore point leading up to the Revolution. Anti-tax protests were common. In several instances, such as Boston in 1770, there was violence between British troops and civilians. These confrontations invited further repressive measures. Troops were posted, and dissenters were dealt with harshly.

Nonetheless, as James (1997: 107–09) notes, "Americans in 1774 enjoyed considerable freedom," including a free press, rights of assembly, and the right to travel. Indeed, these freedoms provided much of the basis for the Revolution's success. While the issues listed in the Declaration were important, they were not intractable before 1775. There was little support for independence, even less for war (Zinn, 1995: 76).

The reasons for this lack of support are easy to discern. The American Revolution was less a nationalist fight against foreign oppression than a family squabble. Nine-tenths (James, 1997: 101) of the colonies' 2.5 million people (*Time*, 1999: 798) were of British descent, many of them "excessively proud of their Britishness" (James, 1997: 100). At least a third of the American colonists were staunch Loyalists to the Crown, while another third were probably neutral throughout the conflict (Zinn, 1995: 76). Many of the colonists were not sure why they were fighting (Hofstadter, 1958).

Why, then, did the American colonies revolt? The general answer is, ironically, that the conclusion of the war with France in 1763 removed a major threat to the colonies. In simple terms, the British Empire had outlived its usefulness. But this explanation only provides a context, not a substantive cause for the Revolution.

More to the point, the consequences of managing the peace created enormous and unexpected conflicts between the British and certain colonists, especially in New England (see Orchard, 1998). The colonies that would become Canada were integrally involved in these disputes. Two sections of the Declaration of Independence make clear this connection (see *Time*, 1999: 65). One of the two sections reads:

> For abolishing the free System of English Laws in a neighboring Province, establishing therein an Arbitrary government, and enlarging its Boundaries so as to render it at once an example and fit instrument for introducing the same absolute rule into these Colonies.

The second important section of the Declaration reads:

> He [the King] has excited domestic insurrections amongst us, and has endeavoured to bring on the inhabitants of our frontiers, the merciless Indian Savages, whose known rule of warfare, is an undistinguished destruction of all ages, sexes and conditions.

The reference in both quoted sections is to the Quebec Act of 1774. As we've seen (in Chapter Two), the Quebec Act restored to the French Canadians and the Catholic Church certain privileges removed in 1763 by the Royal Proclamation Act. The resurrection of French Catholicism in North America provoked hysterical alarm among the overwhelmingly Protestant colonists whose memories of sectarian conflict were fresh. James (1997: 105) notes that, in early 1775, "the New England backwoods buzzed with rumours that Popery was about to be imposed...." Among the colonists, Papal fears alone might have seemed sufficiently provocative. But the Quebec Act also extended the boundaries of Quebec into the Ohio-Mississippi Indian Territory, thereby limiting the expansionist ambitions of American agrarians, investors, and land speculators, including George Washington, Thomas Jefferson, and Benjamin Franklin (see Orchard, 1998: 14).

Why did the British extend Quebec's boundaries? In part, they did so under pressure from merchants in the Montreal-based fur trade (Innis, 1962: 176). But the British also extended the boundaries in hopes of reasserting control over lands designated in the Royal Proclamation Act of 1763 as specifically "reserved" for Aboriginals: the lands west of the Appalachian Mountains (see Chapter Twelve). The expansion-minded colonists had consistently ignored the Royal Proclamation Act, resulting in renewed conflict with the Aboriginals of the Ohio Valley. The British meant through the Quebec Act to curtail settlement in the volatile region. In the minds of the colonists, however, the Quebec Act had merely incited further conflict with the Aboriginals, whom the colonists hated and wanted removed from the territory; hence, the Declaration's rather florid statements quoted above.

The Quebec Act was passed in the summer of 1774. Shortly thereafter, in September 1774, a Continental Congress was convened to devise a slate of measures in retaliation to the Quebec Act (James, 1997: 105). Events thereafter continued apace. The Revolution's first volleys were fired only days before the Quebec Act was to have come into effect (May 1, 1775).

The war dragged on for six years. It was fought by unconventional means by untrained colonists and conventional means by the trained British troops. Long periods of idleness and boredom were punctuated by brief battles of horrific savagery on both sides.

In June 1775, the Americans launched a two-pronged attack on Canada. One American army, led by General Richard Montgomery, went along Lake Champlain and captured Montreal, forcing Governor Carleton to flee to Quebec City. A second army, led by General Benedict Arnold, landed in Maine and proceeded to the shores of the St. Lawrence where both armies then joined in an assault upon Quebec City. The siege failed the following May, however, when a flotilla of British troops arrived. The American forces withdrew (Conway, 1997; James, 1997; Orchard, 1998).

Thereafter, the war never seriously threatened Canadian territory. Nonetheless, the American colonists believed throughout that Canada would soon join them in open revolt. The invasion of Canada in 1775, for example, was "advertised as a war of liberation" (James, 1997: 113). When the American Articles of Confederation were written in 1777, a special Canada provision (Article 11) was even included, which read:

> Canada, according to this confederation, and joining in the measures of the United States, shall be admitted into, and entitled to all the advantages of this Union: but no other colony shall be admitted into the same unless such admission be agreed to by nine states.

The idea that Canada might join the rebellion was not far-fetched. The people in Nova Scotia, linked by trade and family connections to the New England states, briefly considered joining the cause (Winks, 1998: 3). Likewise, many within Montreal's English-speaking business class supported the revolutionary cause (Morton, 1997). The larger French-Canadian community—clergy, seigneurs, and merchants alike—remained neutral, however. As the British had hoped, the Quebec Act ensured its neutrality.

Which side would emerge victorious was not quite certain until 1778, when France, ever desirous of revenge upon Britain for losses suffered in 1763, joined the conflict. With French assistance in the form of both troops and a naval blockade, the Americans won the last great battle of the war at Yorktown, Virginia, in October 1781 (Hofstadter et al., 1957: 108–09; Zinn, 1995: 79).

The Treaty of Paris saw England recognize American independence. The treaty further set America's borders at the Mississippi River on the west, the 31st parallel (just above Florida) in the south, and the Great Lakes in the north. The treaty also acknowledged American rights to Newfoundland's fisheries. England, however, retained joint privileges with America in navigating the Mississippi. The Americans further agreed to compensate British creditors for private debts owed them and to recommend that individual states restore Loyalist property (Hofstadter et al., 1957: 109–10).

Many Americans in 1783 viewed Canada as a natural extension of their colonies, and wanted to remove British influence entirely from the continent. The United States, however, was not strong enough, politically or militarily, to press such demands (Horsman, 1993). Moreover, at least some Americans may have viewed a continuing British presence in North America, for all its drawbacks, as a kind of bulwark against possible French and Spanish expansion (James, 1997: 119). For these reasons, Canada remained standing. But it was a Canada quickly changing, and soon facing renewed threats from its American neighbour.

THE WAR OF 1812

The Treaty of Paris did not end disputes between Britain and its former American colonies. A major source of conflict was ended with the signing in 1794 of Jay's Treaty, which saw Britain evacuate the forts it had maintained in the Ohio Valley in defence of the Montreal fur interests (Horsman, 1993: 297). Setting a pattern that would repeat itself again in 1814 (the Treaty of Ghent) and in 1846 (the Oregon Treaty), trade—and good relations—with the United States was far more important to Britain than trade with Canada. The interests of Montreal's fur traders, and Canada generally, were expendable (Couture, 1993: 232).

Still, irritants remained and were heightened after 1793 by the outbreak of yet another war between Britain and France. In their zeal to defeat the French (this time in the person of Napoleon), the British were soon seizing American ships that traded with France, arresting escaped British seamen, and pressing American seamen into Royal service (Berton, 1980; Horsman, 1993). Understandably, Americans viewed Britain as not only harming American trade but also breaching American neutrality and sovereignty (Bowler, 1993). America's still fragile honour was at stake (Horsman, 1993: 279).

Once more, the Aboriginal people also featured prominently among American complaints. The British, it was alleged, were encouraging their Aboriginal allies, led by the Shawnee chief Tecumseh (see Chapter Ten), to attack American settlers (Bowler, 1993: 298; Hofstadter, 1958: 227; Berton, 1980; Morton, 1997; Granatstein, 1996).

As such "provocations" mounted, war fever gripped the United States. During the American congressional debates of 1811 and 1812, legitimate complaints gave way to overblown rhetoric that Canada must be liberated. Finally, President Madison declared in June 1812 the beginning of a second War of Independence (Morton, 1997: 42).

Once again, the Americans believed Canada would be an easy conquest. Former President Thomas Jefferson stated confidently that "The acquisition of Canada this year... will be a mere matter of marching" (Colombo, 1994: 29).

As in 1775, such confidence was not ill-placed. In 1812, there were only half a million people in British North America compared with 7.5 million in the American states (Morton, 1997: 33). Moreover, two-thirds of Upper Canada's population were newly arrived Americans (Bowler, 1993: 302), largely indifferent to the war. The British themselves were occupied in fighting Napoleon. In short, the War of 1812 seemed like one that the United States could not lose. Yet they did.

The War of 1812 was fought almost entirely in Upper Canada, though it strayed occasionally into Lower Canada, spawned a few memorable sea battles, and touched off a miniboom in maritime smuggling (Bowler, 1993). Along Upper Canada's main front, the war began in a gentlemanly fashion, continuing indifferently at times—along the invisible border, truck, trade, and personal contacts continued largely unabated—but became more savage as time progressed (Berton, 1980). In April 1813, the Americans sacked and burned York (now Toronto). In revenge, British forces in August 1814 captured and burned the U.S. Capitol building and the presidential mansion at Washington.

In the end, a combination of three things saved Canada from American takeover: American military ineptness, French-Canadian and Aboriginal support at key moments, and the end of the Napoleonic wars in Europe that freed regular British troops to come to Canada (Berton, 1980: 27; Morton, 1997: 42; Horsman, 1993).

The Treaty of Ghent in 1814 formally ended the war. The pre-existing borders were restored; the problems that began the war were forgotten or soon disappeared. In the words of historian Desmond Morton (1997: 43), "The war changed no boundaries, brought no reparations, avenged no wrongs." The Battle of Waterloo and Napoleon's subsequent banishment to St. Helena ended Britain's need to seize ships and impress seamen. The severely weakened Aboriginal tribes were no longer a threat to the Americans or an impediment to settlement.

The War of 1812 gave English Canada its first heroes: Major-General Isaac Brock and Chief Tecumseh (who both died in battle), as well as Laura Secord (Morton, 1997; Bowler, 1993; Orchard, 1998). The war also strengthened British resolve to protect its North American colonies. It further solidified the alliance of the French, English, and Aboriginal peoples, who had fought side by side against the Americans, though the last of these received the least reward for their sacrifices (see Chapter Ten). Finally, and most importantly, the war of 1812 forged a sense of English Canada as a community and the beginnings of its distinct identity.

THE MAKING OF ENGLISH CANADIAN IDENTITY

We have briefly to reacquaint ourselves with the Loyalists (Chapter Two), especially those 10 000 or so who settled in Canada and caused its division in 1791. Our first impressions were not favourable. Contemporaries used the words "quarrelsome" and "bitter" to describe them. It is time, however, to revisit the Loyalists, to ask, "Who were they?" and, more importantly, "What became of them?"

To the first question: the Americans portrayed the Loyalists as an "elite of Anglican clergy, bureaucrats, and merchants living off government favours" (Dickinson and Young, 1993: 70), an image the Loyalists themselves later encouraged. The image was incorrect, however. The Loyalists were not fundamentally different from the Americans who stayed behind. Most were subsistence farmers, disproportionately young, often poor and illiterate. While most were recent immigrants from Britain, the Loyalists also included Germans, Dutch, and French-Canadians (Dickinson and Young, 1993: 70; Brown, 1993: 244, 247; Granatstein, 1996: 15). The Loyalists also included approximately 3000 escaped black slaves who settled in Nova Scotia and almost 2000 Iroquois who settled north of the Great Lakes, where the city of Brantford today commemorates the name of their leader, Joseph Brant (Wynn, 2000: 220).

The American Revolution did not merely create two nations; it also created two myths. Not *all* Americans were democrats; not *all* Loyalists were monarchists. Most people on both sides were indifferent, confused, and scared, caught up in events beyond their control (see Granatstein, 1996: 13).

Yet the Loyalists quickly began to believe their own myths—which brings us to the second question: "What became of them?" A couple of quotations will point us toward an answer.

The first is taken second-hand from Christian Dufour (1990: 54), who cites a Canadian history text used in English high schools in the 1930s as it concludes the episode of the American invasion of 1812: "Once again, the American invaders were repelled, as in 1776, as in 1690." But, asks Dufour, "How can the British Canada that drove back the Americans in 1812 be linked to the New France that stood up to the English in 1690?" Put another way, who were the "Americans" in 1690? They were, of course, the English. (The specific date 1690 refers to a famous incident in which Governor-General Louis Frontenac defeated the invading army of the Bostonian Sir William Phips.)

The second quotation is from historian P.B. Waite, recalling his days as a schoolboy in Belleville, Ontario, in the early 1930s. In the quotation, Waite (1997: 13) remembers situating his identity within Canada's history:

> We mapped the voyages of Champlain, of La Salle....We rejoiced in the story of Phips' demand... and Frontenac's reply....Thus did we English-*Canadiens* fight the Americans and their British allies. And we continued to be *Canadiens*....
>
> Then suddenly, oddly, sharply we became English. It was something of a wrench. Wolfe had laid siege to Quebec in the summer of 1759 and all that summer we stayed with Montcalm fighting off the British. Then, early on the morning of 13 September 1759, we changed sides. We crossed the St. Lawrence with Wolfe and the British in the dark, silent boats, we fought with the British regulars on the Plains of Abraham; and though we mourned both Montcalm and Wolfe, by the time of Montcalm's death the next morning we were already on our way at last to being English-Canadians.

What became of the Loyalists? They were upon their arrival defeated, humiliated; indeed, not unlike the French they found in the new land. But they found in the French something of particular value: the French had an identity, one ready-made for appropriation; an identity, moreover, shaped by being the first anti-Americans. Thus, the Loyalists became *Canadiens*, and Canadians became (by Loyalist definition and thereafter) anti-Americans.

Of course, we cannot lay the whole weight of appropriation upon the Loyalists. In most provinces, the Loyalists soon found themselves a minority (they never were a majority in Quebec). The sole exception was New Brunswick. Even there, however, the Loyalists after 1812 found themselves engulfed by other immigrants. In 1812, only one-fifth of Upper Canada's population of 100 000 was Loyalist in origin (Brown, 1993: 247; see also Wynn, 2000: 221). Nonetheless, the Loyalists' myth of rejecting American takeover and their incorporation of French Canada into their identity structure began the process of forging in English Canada a distinctive identity (Brown, 1993; Granatstein, 1996). After 1812, the people of British North America, at last, had something in common: British and French alike, Aboriginal and black, they were *not* Americans.

THE MONROE DOCTRINE, MANIFEST DESTINY, AND AMERICAN EXCEPTIONALISM

The Treaty of Ghent did not end tensions between the United States and Britain's North American colonies. Conflict was blunted, it is true, by the signing in 1817 of the Rush-Bagot Convention, which prohibited large warships on the Great Lakes, and by the 1818

Convention, which clarified somewhat the boundary lines. The existing line was extended westward from the Lake of the Woods to the Rocky Mountains along the 49th parallel (Careless, 1970: 134–135).

American expansion continued unabated, however, fuelled by the demands of a growing population (9.6 million people in 1820) (*Time*, 1999: 796) and a changing economy. But American expansion also invoked as its justification the notion of "liberating" land and people from the foreign and colonial yoke—even when the people involved did not want to be liberated and viewed the Americans as aggressors. Thus, President James Monroe in his message to Congress in December 1823 coined what become known as the **Monroe Doctrine** (see opening quotation above), *the doctrine that declares that the Americas are to be free of foreign influence and that the United States will act to prevent such influence.* American expansion also was justified by *a religious belief that the new country was divinely ordained with a special mission to cover North America.* The term for this belief, **manifest destiny**, was first coined in 1845 by editor John O'Sullivan (see quotation above), but the idea itself had long been believed by many Americans. In turn, such beliefs paved the way for what is often termed **American exceptionalism**, *the belief held by many Americans that the United States cannot be judged by the same standards as other countries* (see Chapter Nine).

America expanded steadily across the continent throughout the first half of the nineteenth century. The process was always similar. American trade with and exploration of new territories was soon followed by immigration. Soon, the American land speculators, merchants, and settlers would complain about the actions of local government officials (usually Spanish in origin); then they would lobby Washington to intervene. Covert aid would follow. In time, the existing government would be dethroned (sometimes with the help of American troops), the populace would "ask" to be annexed, and the United States would oblige. Thus, Florida was seized from Spain in 1819; Texas, after years of internal intrigue inspired by the American government, also from Spain in 1845; and New Mexico and California, following an American-provoked war, from Mexico in 1848 (Hofstadter et al., 1957: 181–182 and 279–281; Orchard, 1998: 32–33). The war with Mexico doubled the size of the United States, not incidentally on the eve of the California gold rush.

Canada was not immune from American intrigues and claims. War nearly erupted in the 1820s after Maine's governor declared New Brunswick's timberlands part of the state and ordered U.S. troops to seize the territory (Orchard, 1998: 30). In a prelude to the Mexican wars, the United States in 1844 also claimed, by dint of biblical injunctions, the Oregon territory. The dispute was settled in 1846, again under threat of war, on grounds favourable to the Americans. This dispute was followed in 1859 by the so-called Pig War over the San Juan Islands in Puget Sound, which ended in 1873 with the United States gaining sole ownership of the islands (Lower, 1983: 66–88; 75). By the 1850s, also, American settlement in the Red River Valley was bringing pressures in that region for annexation to the United States.

In these ventures, the biggest losers were the Aboriginal people (see Chapter Ten), who were vilified, pacified, assimilated, and often hunted down, sometimes to extinction. (Before becoming American president in 1832, Andrew Jackson earned a well-deserved reputation for savagery directed at Aboriginal people, whom he terrorized and killed by the thousands, before taking more than two million acres in northern Alabama [Wright, 1993: 211–212]. Another future president, Abe Lincoln, while sympathetic to the situation of blacks, thought the Aboriginal people unredeemable and fought briefly as a young man in the vicious Illinois Black Hawk wars of the 1830s.)

By 1853, the United States had nearly achieved its present territorial size. Alaska was added in 1867 and Hawaii in 1898. The only territory in North America unincorporated into the United States was what the French author Voltaire once called "a few acres of snow": Canada (quoted in Colombo, 1994: 18).

THE POLITICAL ECONOMY OF BRITISH NORTH AMERICA, 1800-1866

To the unreflecting eye, the British colonies in 1800 must still have seemed not much more than a frozen wasteland. The combined population of the five British North American provinces in 1805 was about 360 000. Of this total, about 230 000 resided in Lower Canada, 46 000 in Upper Canada, 54 000 in Nova Scotia, 25 000 in New Brunswick, and 5000 or so in Prince Edward Island (Careless, 1970: 122; Norrie and Owram, 1996: 84, 119; Dickinson and Young, 1993). Newfoundland's total population in 1805 was just short of 20 000, but this number included a large number of semi-permanent residents engaged in the seasonal fisheries (see Norrie and Owram, 1996: 75).

The end of the Napoleonic wars, however, saw Britain hit by a depression and rising unemployment. Thus, the colonies—except Newfoundland, which itself entered a period of stagnation until the 1850s (see Norrie and Owram, 1996)—after 1815 experienced a massive wave of immigration that lasted four decades. Between 1815 and 1850, nearly 800 000 mainly British immigrants arrived in Canada: "discharged soldiers and half-pay officers from Wellington's armies, Irish weavers and paupers, Scottish artisans and dispossessed crofters, English country labourers and factory workers" (Careless, 1970: 147).

Few British immigrants settled permanently in Lower Canada. Those that did settled mainly in the Eastern Townships and the growing cities of Montreal and Quebec. Elsewhere, however, British immigration left a permanent mark. Scottish immigration especially filled Nova Scotia, competing with the settled Loyalists and pre-Loyalist New Englanders, and Prince Edward Island; while the Irish, especially after the 1840s, filled New Brunswick (Careless, 1970: 148).

Immigration effects were felt most, however, in Upper Canada. There, British immigration rose steadily after 1820, dropped in the mid-1830s due to cholera and the province's political troubles, then rose again sharply during the 1840s. Though all elements of British society—"English, Welsh, Lowland and Highland Scots and Catholic and Ulster Irish" (Careless, 1970: 149)—arrived, it was perhaps the Irish who left the greatest impression. Driven from their homeland by poverty, overcrowding and, finally, the potato famine, the Irish soon found employment building canals and, later, the railroads (Morton, 1997: 54; also Pentland, 1991; Norrie and Owram, 1996).

American immigration to the British colonies generally declined during this period due to American westward expansion. A sole exception to this pattern was the relatively large influx into the Maritimes and Upper Canada of American blacks escaping slavery during the 20 years leading up to that country's Civil War (see below). By 1861, there were about 60 000 blacks in British North America (Winks, 1998: 8; see also Kelly, 1997).

As a consequence of immigration and births, British North America's population by 1851 had grown to over 2.4 million; by 1861, 3.2 million. Upper Canada now had the largest population—nearly 1.4 million—followed by Lower Canada (1.1 million), Nova Scotia (331 000), New Brunswick (252 000), and Prince Edward Island (61 000) (see Table 1.1).

Immigration to the colonies, however, began declining in the early 1850s, and by the 1860s was actually outpaced by people leaving Canada. Indeed, from 1851 to 1901, for example, while 1.9 million people entered Canada, 2.2 million left, primarily for the United States (McKie, 1994: 26).

The British colonies' problem in attracting and retaining people was simple: their economies were insufficiently able to compete with the expanding and rapidly industrializing neighbour to the south. Though economic development occurred, the British colonies generally lacked investment capital; their transportation systems were substandard and internally not integrated; and their separate economies exhibited many of the instabilities characteristic of staple-based, export-driven economies.

Newfoundland, for example, remained an imperial outpost, not even a colony, until 1824. And, though the granting of responsible government in 1855 coincided with a period of growth lasting until the mid-1880s, its economy remained dangerously one-dimensional. In 1858, for example, 89 percent of Newfoundland's labour force worked in the fishery, a statistic that remained relatively constant over the next decade, indicating a single-industry dependence that would sink the Newfoundland economy two decades later (Norrie and Owram, 1996: 78–79; 350–351).

The situation elsewhere in the colonies was less bleak but still no cause for optimism. The American Revolution spurred a short-lived economic boom. Nova Scotia's timber industry developed around pine masts for the British navy; shipbuilding, formerly concentrated around local markets, also grew to service trade with the West Indies; and internal markets, especially for agricultural products, arose around the province's increased population, inspired in part by Loyalist immigration. Subsequently, the Napoleonic Wars produced a second Maritime boom, as Britain increased its colonial imports. The fisheries remained important, but forestry also now developed in New Brunswick and spurred forward economic linkages: sawmills and (especially) shipbuilding. By 1860, the Maritimes were one of the world's premier shipbuilding centres. Other important industries developed at the time included Nova Scotia's trade in coal and agricultural produce (Norrie and Owram, 1996: 79–80; 86).

The years, especially after 1815, were not kind to Lower Canada. The fur industry entered a period of decline following the signing of Jay's Treaty in 1794 and left the St. Lawrence valley altogether following the merger in 1821 of the North West Company with the Hudson's Bay Company. Wheat became a major export item to Britain and the West Indies during the late eighteenth century, but early the next century it too entered a period of permanent decline occasioned by recurrent crop failures (see Trofimenkoff, 1993: 384) and increasing competition from Upper Canada (see below).

These losses were partially offset by other sources of economic growth, notably timber (Norrie and Owram, 1996) and power generation. Also, the two major urban centres of Quebec City and Montreal increased in size and importance, the former economy based on shipping, the military, and services; the latter on industry and finance. But much of the province remained rural—indeed, became even more disproportionately so during the century (see Chapter Three)—and underdeveloped, while the benefits of industrialization went almost entirely to the anglophone bourgeoisie.

By contrast, Upper Canada's situation grew decidedly more hopeful as the nineteenth century progressed. The province was at first economically dependent on British administrative expenditures in the form of direct handouts: subsidies and claims to Loyalists and military and civil construction. In the words of Norrie and Owrams (1996: 123), "the British government subsidized the initial stages of settlement in Upper Canada." The arrival of the "late Loyalists" (Americans newly arrived in the early 1800s) and of British immigrants after 1820 provided both labourers and consumers. Local domestic markets developed and the timber industry grew. But wheat was Ontario's real story.

Small amounts of wheat were already being shipped down the St. Lawrence as early as 1794 (Norrie and Owram, 1996: 124). During the War of 1812, however, wheat became a major export to Britain. Though wheat sales declined after the war, a new market was soon found in Lower Canada, then later again in Britain and the United States. Wheat exports from Upper Canada rose by 500 percent during the 1840s and then doubled again, peaking in 1861 (McCallum, 1991: 11).

The importance of wheat to Upper Canada's economy cannot be overestimated. In 1820, over 95 percent of the province's population was still rural (Norrie and Owram, 1996: 126). Locally produced wheat thus fed Upper Canada's population without resort to imports. Capital acquired through exports of surplus wheat, especially after 1840, later fuelled industrial development (McCallum, 1991).

Instances of economic development and diversification aside, the British colonies in the mid-1850s were marked by uneven development and export dependency. Nova Scotia's export trade was spread between the other British North American colonies, the United States, and the West Indies. New Brunswick's export trade was heavily tied to Britain. Prince Edward Island's export trade was moderately tied to the other colonies. The Province of Canada's economy was based on agricultural and forestry exports, primarily to Lower Canada and the United States. All of the colonies imported a larger percentage of their manufactured goods (Norrie and Owram, 1996: 91).

The colonies' resultant economic instability fuelled ongoing political demands, particularly from the Province of Canada's business class, for either annexation by the United States or (at the very least) a reciprocity agreement with the U.S. that would ensure stable markets. In 1854, they got their wish.

Understanding how the Reciprocity Treaty of 1854 came about requires a brief discussion of changes in economic thinking that had occurred since the eighteenth century. As you will remember (Chapter Two), New France was founded primarily as a mercantilist adventure. Two centuries later, however, mercantilism was under increasing attack. Adam Smith (1986) launched the first attack in his classic text *The Wealth of Nations,* which, fittingly, came out in 1776, the same year as the American Declaration of Independence. The latter stated a liberal interpretation of political freedom. Smith's text similarly argued for a liberal interpretation of economic freedom.

Smith directed three specific arguments against mercantilism. First, he argued that free trade between countries was mutually beneficial. Second, he argued that trade enhanced specialization in production, leading to increased efficiency. And third, Smith denounced mercantilism on the basis of the "collusive relationship" it encouraged between governments and the merchant classes (La Haye, 1993: 535).

Smith's arguments found fertile ground in Britain during the American Revolution. Many British already viewed the colonies as expensive to maintain, administratively and militarily. Now they were a political headache, as well.

The outbreak of the Napoleonic Wars in 1793 brought mercantilism a temporary reprieve, as Britain became dependent upon its colonies for food and materials; for example, Maritime fish and timber. After 1814, however, Smith's ideas—now augmented by a young economist, David Ricardo—gained momentum. Slowly at first, then with greater alacrity, mercantilism's regulatory walls collapsed. In 1833, Britain abolished colonial slavery, thus creating "free labour." "Free trade" followed in the 1840s with the repeal of timber duties, the Navigation Acts, and the Corn Laws (Norrie and Owram, 1996: 173). Britain's policy of preferential trade with the North American colonies ceased after 1846.

Free trade made perfect sense from the British point of view. Britain, after all, was the first modern industrialized capitalist country. Moreover, it was still a great empire possessing the world's most powerful fleet.

Elsewhere, including the United States, Adam Smith's ideas had far less appeal (Laxer, 1989; Watkins, 1991) (see Chapter Seven). The ending of protected markets by free trade was viewed with especial fear in Britain's North American colonies. How did this affect the security of the colonies' exports? The panic found its climax in April 1849.

The Canadian government had been moved the previous year from Kingston to Montreal, the site of Canada's business establishment. In 1849, the Reform government of Baldwin-Lafontaine passed a bill compensating Patriotes and innocent victims of the Rebellions of 1837–38 (see Chapter Two) for losses suffered during the conflict. Montreal's English business class, already feeling abandoned by the British government's adoption of free trade and fearing a recession, stormed and burned the new parliament buildings, and threatened the governor general, Lord Elgin (Careless, 1970: 203; Morton, 1997: 56–57). A manifesto circulated in favour of annexation to the United States. In Chatham, New Brunswick, meanwhile, inhabitants "marched through the streets on July 4, 1849, firing pistols in the air and singing 'Yankee Doodle'" (Wynn, 2000: 207).

Annexation was nowhere very popular. Within weeks, talk of joining the United States subsided. By then, gold had been discovered in California, and the North American economy entered a period of growth that continued until the early 1870s. Nonetheless, many in the colonies remained concerned about securing access to the large American market.

The Reciprocity Treaty of 1854 was the result. The treaty came into effect in 1855 and lasted until 1866, when the United States terminated it. Specifically, the treaty eliminated the tariff on natural products, including fish.

The signing of the Reciprocity Treaty blunted demands by Montreal merchants for annexation (Winks, 1998: 4). The decade following witnessed rapid economic growth throughout the British colonies (Aitken, 1959). This period featured the increased economic integration of the St. Lawrence lowlands, the extension of the agricultural area of southern Ontario, the beginning of manufacturing in Ontario and Quebec, and the development of a railroad system from the Detroit River to the Atlantic seaboard.

How responsible was the Reciprocity Agreement for this period of prosperity? The question is not easily answered. On balance, however, reciprocity seems to have increased the overall volume of trade between the two countries and specifically to have benefited British North American trade in wheat, oats, and flour (Norrie and Owram, 1996: 184–185; see also Careless, 1970; Laxer, 1989).

By the 1860s, however, Americans increasingly viewed reciprocity with alarm. Business interests pressured the American government to abrogate the agreement. American politicians noted, with some accuracy, that Canada was doing very well by the agreement. Ultimately, however, the Reciprocity Agreement collapsed for reasons political—and military—rather than economic.

CANADA AND THE AMERICAN CIVIL WAR

As the debate over the Meech Lake Accord and "distinct society" heated up in 1989, Reform Party leader Preston Manning repeatedly borrowed American President Abraham Lincoln's phrase warning of the perils of a "house divided" (see Harrison, 1995: 173). In the overheated aftermath of the 1995 Quebec referendum, parallels between Canada's situation and events leading up to the American Civil War in 1861 were again advanced (McPherson, 1998). The discerning of Canadian parallels, or parables, in the American Civil War was not new. The war was very much on the minds of Canadian politicians in 1864 as they began deliberations on Confederation.

The American Civil War (1861–65) previewed wars soon to come, introducing trench warfare, advanced weaponry (for example, the Gatling gun), and calculated terrorism against civilians. To this day, American deaths during the Civil War (623 000) outnumber the total of American deaths in all the wars since (Zinn, 1995: 232; *Time*, 1999: 398). As in later wars, a modern invention, the camera, "brought home" the Civil War to those far removed, including the people of British North America.

British North America was affected by events in the United States even before the war began. In the months leading up to the conflict, some American officials suggested that a war with Britain over Canada might prove a useful diversion and unite the squabbling states. Other Union officials argued that, in the event of losing the South, the conquest of Canada would make for an adequate replacement (Morton, 1997: 61; Winks, 1998; see also Marquis, 2000).

In the beginning, most people in the British colonies supported the North, believing that the war was intended to abolish slavery (Winks, 1998). As the war went on, however, sympathies in the colonies became more conflicted. It became apparent that ending slavery was incidental to the Union's crusade. The war's first purpose was to save the Union (Hofstadter, 1958). The South's argument that individual states had voluntarily entered into a Confederacy in 1776 and therefore retained the right of self-determination, including the right of exit, struck a more responsive chord in the British colonies than did the North's federalist alternative.

Inevitably, the British colonies also found themselves caught up in the war's actual dynamics. To the North's displeasure, the British continued to trade with the South. The South also used the colonies as a staging ground for raids against the Union, both by land and sea (Winks, 1998; Marquis, 2000). In retaliation, and much to British annoyance, Northern forces also breached the Canadian border in pursuit of the rebels. Throughout the American Civil War, many in Canada feared, and some in the Confederacy actively hoped, that Britain would be dragged into war with the Union (Winks, 1998).

Nor did fears lessen with the conflict's end. British and colonial officials noted the United States had a battle-tested army of 2.3 million men—nearly equal to the entire population of the province of Canada (Martin, 1993c: 560)—which now could be turned north. Facing the American army was a regular military force of a little more than 19 000 (Winks, 1998: 282) and perhaps another 10 000 militia. Elaborate plans were made and discussed throughout 1864–65 concerning Canada's defence (see (Winks, 1998: 351–52). These plans became more urgent when Irish raiders, the Fenians, began invading Canada (with at least tacit American support) in 1866 (McCue, 1999).

Most British officials, including Prime Minister Gladstone, accepted the obvious: Canada ultimately was not defensible against American attack. So, to avoid provocation, Britain in 1871 removed all its troops from Canadian soil. But the American Civil War, and the threats of invasion that followed, provided the psychological context (Martin, 1993c: 559) for getting on with a task long debated: Confederation (see also Winks, 1998: 379; and Moore, 1997).

CONFEDERATION

Confederation in 1867 was intended to address three problems. First, Confederation was meant to provide an "effective defence" against the threat of American invasion. (The fact that such a defence was no more possible after Confederation than before is incidental.) Second, Confederation was meant to create an economic union. Economic union was made necessary by the American government's suspension of the Reciprocity Treaty in 1866 in response to British support for the South during the Civil War. Third, Confederation was meant to deal with French-English political instability in the Province of Canada, where 12 governments had fallen in 15 years (see Moore, 1997; Romney, 1999).

Confederation began as a discussion of Maritime union at Charlottetown, Prince Edward Island, in June 1864. Almost immediately, however, these discussions expanded to include plans for a broader union of all British North America. A follow-up meeting at Quebec City in October that same year drafted the union's essential features. The Quebec Resolutions were then taken back to the individual colonial legislatures for debate and ratification (see Careless, 1970: 243–249: Norrie and Owram, 1996: 207–209; Moore, 1997; Silver, 1997; Romney, 1999).

Confederation's blueprints, and the British North America (BNA) Act of 1867, which legally constituted the federation, drew heavily from "British precedent and practice" (Norrie and Owram, 1996: 210), including an elected federal parliament and a system of jurisprudence based on the British model. Also, the British monarch remained the formal head of state, and the highest court for judicial appeals remained in London. But Confederation also drew upon practices already employed in the Province of Canada and the American model.

From the Province of Canada was adopted the idea of tariffs, an important element of the National Policy soon devised (see Chapter Seven). Likewise, many of the Dominion's banking regulations copied legislation developed in the Province of Canada (Norrie and Owram, 1996: 211).

From the American model came the idea of the Senate. Like the American Senate, which represents individual states (Hofstadter, 1958: 76–77), the Canadian Senate was meant to represent the provinces (Moore, 1997: 108–09). Unlike American senators, however, Canadian senators were not to be elected. Why not? In part, the reason is that the Canadian Senate was modelled also on the British House of Lords; in part it was also that an appointed Senate left obvious opportunities for patronage—a current criticism. But the Fathers of Confederation, such as George Brown, also feared that elected senators would possess legitimacy equal to the elected members of Parliament, threatening the principle of "one person, one vote" (see Moore, 1997: 108; Romney, 1999).

The Fathers of Confederation also discerned in the American experience, specifically the recent Civil War, an object lesson (Winks, 1998) on the perils of decentralized government. Here, however, the perceived lesson could only partially be applied (Moore, 1997; Silver, 1997; Romney, 1999). Certainly, Sir John A. Macdonald desired to construct a strong central government, but this was not possible. Neither the Maritime provinces, nor especially Quebec, would accept a strongly centralized federation.

The result was a Confederation in which jurisdictional powers were divided between the federal government and the provinces. The federal government was given powers over national defence, postal services, the census and statistics, currency and banking, navigation and shipping, fisheries, criminal law, the regulation of trade and commerce, weights and measures, bankruptcy and insolvency, and taxation. Provincial governments were given powers over two areas that would become particularly important later on, health and education, as well as generally local matters, such as property and civil rights, civil law, municipal governments, licences, and the chartering of companies, as well as direct taxation for government costs. All residual powers lay with the federal government. Finally, the federal government was further charged with responsibility to ensure equitable fiscal assistance to all the provinces to meet their constitutional functions (Careless, 1970: 254–255; Norrie and Owram, 1996: 209–210).

There was no great outcry of public support in 1867 for Confederation; in some quarters there was significant opposition. Newfoundland and Prince Edward Island rejected Confederation (Careless, 1970: 246; Norrie and Owram, 1996: 208), while New Brunswick and Nova Scotia were only slowly brought on side (Careless, 1970; Moore, 1997). In Canada East, opposition only shrivelled in the face of implicit and explicit promises by the Conservatives and their leader, George Cartier, that Confederation offered the French a sovereign homeland within a federated state (see Silver, 1997; Romney, 1999). Only Canada West—festering under the Act of Union, demanding separation from entanglements with Canada East and a system of "Rep by Pop," its gaze fixed on westward expansion—greeted Confederation with something like passion.

Thus, on July 1, 1867, the Dominion of Canada was proclaimed. Housing roughly four million people—mainly French and English, Catholic and assorted flavours of Protestant—the new country covered 370 045 square miles (958 416.5 square kilometres)—a tenth of British North America. Small clusters of minority populations were growing, however, presaging Canada's multi-ethnic mix of the next century.

Montreal, the site of trade and finance, was the country's largest city, with more than 100 000 people. It was followed by Quebec City (59 699), Toronto (56 092), Halifax (29 582), and Saint John (28 805) (Morton, 1997: 12–19). But the majority of people still lived and worked on rural farms and in small villages.

A significant manufacturing base was developing (Laxer 1989), but most manufactured goods were still imported and staple exports (fish, wheat, and trees) still ruled Canada's economy (Norrie and Owram, 1996: 208). Indeed, the new Dominion remained largely pre-industrial, even pre-capitalist. Probably few people realized immediately they had become subjects of a new country. Even less did the indigenous people of the West and the North know they too would soon be absorbed into something called Canada (see Chapters Ten and Eleven).

CONCLUSION

English Canada was born as a fragment cast off by the American Revolution. The United States became English Canada's Other, a place of mystery, awe, and fear. Where few differences marked the Loyalists from other Americans in 1775, war, politics, and economics erected borders that, in time, also took on a cultural and psychological reality. Separate histories make separate peoples: attempts to unite East and West Germans after the Cold War provide a contemporary example.

Confederation made concrete the idea of Canada. Shortly thereafter, American efforts at conquering Canada militarily ceased almost entirely. As Governor General Vincent Massey later noted, "the disparity of population has made armaments for one country futile and for the other superfluous." Yet Canada's future remained uncertain beside the American behemoth that, on the shores of the twentieth century, was flexing its muscles. Much remained to be done if the new country was to thrive.

KEY TERMS

American exceptionalism manifest destiny Monroe Doctrine

chapter seven

English Canada in Transition

We often say that we fear no invasion from the south, but the armies of the south have already crossed the border. American enterprise, American capital, is taking rapid possession of our mines and our water-power, our oil areas and our timber limits.
—Sara Jeanette Duncan, *The Imperialist*, 1904

I am for [reciprocity] because I hope to see the day when the American flag will float over every square foot of the British North American possessions clear to the North Pole.
—Champ Clark, speaker of the U.S. House of Representatives, 1911

Air force operations from a base in the Great Lakes area would be capable of dominating the industrial heart of Canada, the Ontario peninsula.
—American commander of the Army-Air Force, in secret testimony to the U.S. Congress supporting the building of a border air base, 1935

INTRODUCTION

Despite Confederation, Canada immediately after 1867 faced two great challenges: constructing a viable national economy and securing the western region from American advances. Between 1867 and 1905, two internal wars were fought, the economy was transformed, immigrants entered the country in droves, and five new provinces joined the Dominion: Manitoba (1870), British Columbia (1871), Prince Edward Island (1873), and Saskatchewan and Alberta (both 1905).

Over the following 40 years, Canada fought in two world wars and suffered through a major economic depression. Canada also changed structurally. Corporate capitalism took hold, mass consumerism flourished, and class conflict intensified. Canada became more urbanized. Women entered the workforce as never before. Slowly, a fledgling sense of Canadian nationalism began emerging from the broad shadows cast by Britain and the United States. This chapter examines these and other events, ending with the Second World War.

THE "AMERICAN SYSTEM" AND THE NATIONAL POLICY

Confederation in 1867 was meant in part to deal with Canada's recurrent economic problems and the threat of American expansion (Chapter Six). But the new country still faced the question of what specific policy should be adopted to meet these goals?

Looking around the world today, models of economic and social development are dominated by "globalization," based on economic liberalism and free trade. In the nineteenth century, however, several models competed. The **British system**, with ideas similar to current neo-liberalism, provided one model, but outside England it was widely rejected. A **European system** of economic development existed, based on activist government policies, investment banks, and technical education (Watkins, 1991), but it was largely unknown and culturally distant from the Canadian experience. A third model, however, known as the **American system**, existed next door and was therefore more familiar to Canadian business and political leaders.

The American system employed three elements: high tariffs to protect domestic manufacturers; expanded transportation systems (especially railroads), built through federal contracts and guaranteed loans to private operators, and designed to bring products to market; and immigration to supply domestic markets (Hofstadter, 1958: 250; also Laxer, 1989; Watkins, 1991). In 1878, the Conservative government of John A. Macdonald ran on a platform of economic development based on the American system and renamed the National Policy.

The National Policy's specific elements were not new to Canada. Tariffs, for example, were already an established tradition in Upper and Lower Canada by the time of Confederation. Thus, in 1879, tariffs were raised from 17.5 percent to 29 percent on a host of manufactured and agricultural goods, and in 1887 they were raised again (especially) on iron, steel, farm machinery, and textiles (Norrie and Owram, 1996: 249). Likewise, railway construction was by then another Canadian tradition going back to the boom years of 1850–1859 (Norrie and Owram, 1996: 191). What was fundamentally different about the National Policy, compared with previous economic policies, was its broader aim of nation-building, specifically incorporating the western territories into Canada.

Canadian politicians and the people of Ontario specifically had long viewed the lands west to the Pacific as theirs to occupy. By the 1860s, however, competing notions of manifest destiny were evident along the 49th parallel. In British Columbia, 30 000 people were attracted to the Fraser Valley and Cariboo by the discovery of gold in 1857 (Norrie and Owram, 1996: 213; see also Easterbrook and Aitken, 1988). Many of these immigrants were Americans, veterans of the recent California boom, who began pressing for annexation to the United States (see Morton, 1997).

Similar pressures were exerted at Red River (later Winnipeg). Between 1850 and 1860, the population of Minnesota, just south of Manitoba, increased by 2730 percent (Winks, 1998: 4). As arable land filled up, Americans pushed further northward into the Red River area, where in 1869 they too pressed for statehood. Caught between the Canadian and American visions for the West were the Aboriginals and Metis (see Chapter Ten). In both cases, Sir John A. Macdonald's vision won out, aided by the use of force in Manitoba and the promise of a railway in British Columbia.

Between the two newest provinces lay the vast North-West Territories. The Territories had long been the Hudson's Bay Company's preserve. Especially after its merger with the rival North West Company in 1821, the entire region (including British Columbia) had fallen under the company's control. By the 1860s, however, the fur trade was dying, and the West was coveted by Canadian politicians—for whom the National Policy was already a gleam in the eye—not to mention Americans with their own plans for the Territories.

In 1870, the Hudson's Bay Company formally transferred the Territories to Canada, and settlement of the western region slowly began. Immigrants began settling in the "postage stamp" province of Manitoba (so-called because of its shape). When the best land was taken, later settlers pushed further westward into the Territories. In 1883, however, land prices soared, the CPR faced bankruptcy, and immigration stopped (see Morton, 1997). The word secession was heard in British Columbia (Conway, 1994: 25).

The hard times were even harder for the West's Aboriginal and Metis people. The buffalo were disappearing, the fur trade no longer provided a secure living, and unscrupulous traders were wreaking havoc on the people. In 1885, rebellion in the Territories provided the Canadian government with justification to send in troops (see Chapter Ten). The long-promised rail link to British Columbia was completed in time to facilitate their arrival.

Thus, by 1885, Canada had expanded to fill the top shelf of North America from sea to sea. The National Policy's alleged economic benefits, however, had yet to be realized: public debt was rising, markets were failing, immigration stalled. Why was the National Policy slow in delivering expected results?

Several factors limited Canada's economic takeoff. First, beginning roughly in 1873 and lasting for six years, the increasingly integrated world economy entered a prolonged slump that reduced demand for Canadian commodities and hindered the necessary flow of investment capital into Canada (Hobsbawm, 1995: 86–87; Lairson and Skidmore, 1997; Saul, 1969). Second, the National Policy depended upon the development of western agricultural land, specifically for wheat exports. But development of the Canadian West could not proceed until the more productive lands of the American West were "used up" (Morton, 1997) and new strains of wheat were developed to meet the Canadian prairies' harsh climate and short growing season (Norrie and Owram, 1996: 227; also Laxer, 1989). Third, public debt acquired throughout the early nineteenth century meant that the Canadian government after 1867 employed private interests to build railroads by granting them monopoly rights and free land (Laxer, 1989). The companies, however, restricted railroad construction to areas of profitability and limited land development to keep prices high, with the result that the massive immigration necessary to make the National Policy viable never occurred.

By 1890, the mood in Canada was sour. Many felt the National Policy had failed. Demands were renewed for a reciprocity treaty with the United States; some called for outright annexation.

The federal election of 1891 was held in this context of uncertainty. The Liberal Party under Wilfrid Laurier ran on a platform of unrestricted reciprocity with the United States (Morton, 1997; also Norrie and Owram, 1996). By contrast, the Conservatives under Sir John A. Macdonald appealed to anti-American and pro-British sentiments (see Granatstein, 1996) in successfully arguing that free trade would inevitably lead to Canada's political annexation, and won.

Canada's first free trade election occurred just as the world economy was rebounding. After 1896, investment capital was freed up and circulated throughout the world at an unprecedented rate (Laxer, 1995). Internationally, consumer demand increased, while production also expanded in the wake of the second industrial revolution (Norrie and Owram, 1996: 223).

Canada shared in the prosperity, though unevenly: Aboriginal peoples in particular were left out (see Part Three). Fuelled by the Yukon Gold Rush (see Chapter Eleven), increased mining in the Canadian Shield, the development of the newsprint industry, and large scale hydroelectric developments on the Great Lakes and the St. Lawrence, Canada (especially southern Ontario) between 1900 and 1913 experienced its second economic boom (Aitken, 1959). While Canada's real GNP grew at a compound rate of only 2.38 percent during the period 1870–1896, between 1896 and 1913 it grew at a rate of 6.48 percent (Norrie and Owram, 1996: 218). Both a cause and a consequence of this boom was the fact that the National Policy's third element, immigration, at last took off.

IMMIGRATION AND THE PEOPLING OF THE WEST

Pre-Confederation, in 1861, 3.2 million people lived in British North America. Canada's population stood at only 4.8 million (Table 1.1) 30 years later. By contrast, the population of the United States during roughly this same period rose from 31.4 million to 62.9 million (*Time*, 1999: 796). Nature and geography, mercantilist policies, and American competition held Canada's population growth at bay. Indeed, so unattractive was Canada relative to its southern neighbour during the 50-year period 1851–1901 that only 1.9 million people entered Canada while 2.2 million left, most of them to the United States (McKie, 1994: 26).

By 1896, however, the American West was virtually filled and a recent depression over. In Ottawa, the new Minister of the Interior, Clifford Sifton, fervently pursued immigration. The West's indigenous people by 1900 had largely been pushed aside (see Chapter Ten). Now, the prohibitive land regulations (Laxer, 1989) were changed, the railways were forced to open up land for settlement, and irrigation construction was proceeded with, especially in the arid region known as the Palliser Triangle (see Norrie and Owram, 1996: 227). Above all, Canadian immigration was promoted as never before. The result was the largest influx of immigrants in Canadian history. More than 1.5 million immigrants entered Canada between 1901 and 1911 (McKie, 1994: 28; Hall, 1977); another 375 756 arrived in 1912, and 400 870 more in 1913 (see Table 7.1).

The immigrants came primarily from three main areas: the United States, Great Britain, and Europe. Of these groups, the first two were viewed as particularly desirable. American immigrants had capital, goods, and prairie farm experience, and they could "fit in" ethnically into Canada. Thus, the number of American immigrants to Canada increased from 2400 in 1897 to 12 000 in 1899. Between 40 000 and 50 000 Americans annually entered Canada during the years 1902–05 (Hall, 1977: 70). For their part, British immi-

TABLE 7.1 — Immigration to Canada, 1852–2001

Year	Immigrants	Year	Immigrants	Year	Immigrants	Year	Immigrants	Year	Immigrants
1852	29 307	1877	27 028	1903	138 660	1928	166 783	1953	168 868	1978	86 313
1853	29 464	1878	29 807	1904	131 252	1929	164 993	1954	154 227	1979	112 093
1854	37 263	1879	40 492	1905	141 465	1930	104 806	1955	109 946	1980	143 135
1855	25 296	1880	38 505	1906	211 653	1931	27 530	1956	164 857	1981	128 639
1856	22 544	1881	47 991	1907	272 409	1932	20 591	1957	282 164	1982	121 176
1857	33 854	1882	112 458	1908	143 326	1933	14 382	1958	124 851	1983	89 188
1858	123 339	1883	133 624	1909	173 694	1934	12 476	1959	106 928	1984	88 271
1859	6300	1884	103 824	1910	286 839	1935	11 277	1960	104 111	1985	84 334
1860	6276	1885	79 169	1911	331 288	1936	11 643	1961	71 689	1986	99 325
1861	13 589	1886	69 152	1912	375 756	1937	15 101	1962	74 586	1987	151 999
1862	18 294	1887	84 526	1913	400 870	1938	17 244	1963	93 151	1988	161 494
1863	21 000	1888	88 766	1914	150 484	1939	16 994	1964	112 606	1989	191 493
1864	24 779	1889	75 067	1915	36 665	1940	11 324	1965	146 758	1990	216 396
1865	18 958	1890	82 165	1916	55 914	1941	9329	1966	194 743	1991	232 744
1866	11 427	1891	30 996	1917	72 910	1942	7576	1967	222 876	1992	254 817
1867	10 666	1892	29 633	1918	41 845	1943	8504	1968	183 974	1993	256 741
1868	12 765	1893	20 829	1919	107 698	1944	12 801	1969	161 531	1994	224 364
1869	18 630	1894	18 790	1920	138 824	1945	22 722	1970	147 713	1995	212 859
1870	24 706	1895	16 835	1921	91 728	1946	71 719	1971	121 900	1996	226 039
1871	27 773	1896	21 716	1922	64 224	1947	64 127	1972	122 006	1997	216 014
1872	36 758	1897	31 900	1923	133 729	1948	125 414	1973	184 200	1998	174 159
1873	50 050	1898	44 543	1924	124 164	1949	95 217	1974	218 465	1999	189 922
1874	39 373	1899	41 681	1925	84 907	1950	73 912	1975	187 881	2000	227 313
1875	27 382	1900	41 681	1926	135 982	1951	194 391	1976	149 429	2001	250 346
1876	25 633	1901	55 747	1927	158 886	1952	164 498	1977	114 914		
		1902	89 102								

Sources: Citizenship and Immigration Canada publications *Citizenship and Immigration Statistics 1996*, Cat. No. MP22-1/1996, Ottawa: Citizenship and Immigration; and *Citizenship and Immigration Statistics 2003*, Cat. No. C&I 291-07-02E, p. 3, www.cic.gc.ca/english/pub/index-2.htm#statistics. Adapted with the permission of the Minister of Public Works and Government Services Canada 2003.

grants, with the exception of the Irish, were viewed as loyal to the Crown. The immigration boom attracted large numbers of people from the rural areas of England and Scotland. By 1901, however, the great wave of British immigration, fuelled in the early nineteenth century by a population boom in the Old Country, was already declining. Thus, hesitantly, Canadian immigration officials expanded their search for immigrants beyond the traditional anglophone countries, into northern and eastern Europe.

Certain ethnic groups, however, remained restricted from entering Canada. These groups included "Negroes," "Orientals" (including East Indians), "Galicians" (meaning eastern Europeans), Italians, and Jews whom, it was argued, were urban people who could not adjust to the demands of prairie life and who, in any case, would not fit into Canadian culture. In the case of the Chinese, government policies were explicitly racist. Good enough to be employed as cheap labour in building the railroads, then later in British Columbia's mines and forestry industry (Morton, 1997: 122), Chinese immigrants were not considered good enough, however, to become citizens. The first of several "head taxes" was enacted on the Chinese in 1885 to prevent workers from being able to afford bringing over family members (Hall, 1977: 78).

Immigration moved in waves across the prairies, leaving distinctive cultural traces that remain today in every province. Between 1871 and 1891, Manitoba's population increased from 25 000 to 153 000, rising to 461 000 by 1911 (see Table 1.1). The early days saw Anglo farmers and expatriate elements of Ontario's upper class settle in southern Manitoba (Lower, 1983: 195), though a sizable Icelandic contingent also moved to Manitoba in 1873, settling north of Winnipeg. Later, European immigrants who arrived, finding the best land already taken, settled in the north and west of the province, while Anglo-Americans moved into the southwest (Widdis, 1997). But these waves of immigrants to Manitoba were not only ethnically distinct. Over time, they also transformed Manitoba's class structure and political culture. By the start of the First World War, Winnipeg had developed a strong working class culture, the product of British and eastern European immigrants, paving the way for the strike of 1919 (see below) (Wiseman, 1993).

The combined population of the entire Territories in 1871 was about 48 000 (not including Aboriginal people). By 1901, Saskatchewan's population alone had risen to 91 000, while that of Alberta stood at 73 000. Ten years later, these provinces' populations had risen to 492 000 and 374 000, respectively (Table 1.1). Before the turn of the century, there existed significant francophone populations in Saskatchewan's north and southwest. Like western Manitoba, however, the early twentieth century saw Saskatchewan settled by the second wave of Anglo and European immigrants, not to mention (in the province's southwest) American immigrants (see Wiseman, 1993; Widdis, 1997).

Alberta, too, at the turn of the century had a large francophone population, located mainly in the northeast. In the late nineteenth century, however, Anglo-American immigrants moved into southern Alberta, bringing with them populist notions of direct democracy, as well as strong beliefs in possessive individualism (Harrison, 2000) that remain part of the province's political culture today (see Chapter Eight). American influence in the south was further strengthened after the discovery in 1914 of oil at Turner Valley, a harbinger of events to come. But other ethnic groups also arrived. The mining communities of the southern Crowsnest Pass, for example, filled with southern (especially Italian) and eastern Europeans, while the province's north similarly experienced an influx of central and eastern Europeans.

British Columbia's population growth was slower, but steadier. Approximately 36 000 people (not including Aboriginals) lived in BC at Confederation in 1871, rising to 179 000 by 1901 and 393 000 by 1911. Much of this non-Aboriginal population was English and Scottish in origin, via Canada's Atlantic region; others were American. In the early stages, settlement was tied to the coastline and Vancouver Island. Later, settlers spread inland, along paths set by the railways. These late arrivals, employed in construction and resource extraction, brought a distinctive working class consciousness (see Robin, 1993). At the same time, sizable numbers of Chinese and Japanese immigrants also came.

There were other distinctive populations throughout the West who were unable or unwilling to be "fitted" easily into the dominant British mould. Black communities developed early on, for example, in Breton, Alberta, and around Maidstone, Saskatchewan. Catholic, Anglican, and other Protestant religious orders dominated Canadian religious and cultural life. Nonetheless, some persecuted religious minorities also found a home in the West. With the moral and financial support of Count Leo Tolstoy, some 7400 Doukhobors arrived in Canada between December 1898 and April 1899, settling near Yorkton and Prince Albert, Saskatchewan (Mayes, 1999). Other religious minorities— Mennonites in southern Manitoba, Hutterites throughout western Manitoba and southern Alberta, and Mormons in southern Alberta—also arrived.

National concern focused on how best to assimilate what sociologist Howard Angus Kennedy in 1907 termed the "new Canadians," whom James S. Woodsworth in 1909 called the "strangers within our gates" (Woodsworth, 1972). Outside Quebec, Canada's immigration and other policies (for example, education) at the time enforced **Anglo-conformity**— the requirement that subordinate group members express outward compliance with the values and practices of the dominant British group—and reflected broad public sentiment and fears of social discord.

In the early 1900s, "Canadians were more provincial than cosmopolitan, more openly biased than politically correct, and each social grouping more protective of its niche in society" (Lyon, 1998: 26). Small differences, even the neighbourhood one lived in, were magnified in importance. Thus, there existed a recognized pecking order even within the British "tribes." (Those of Irish Catholic descent were decidedly last.)

In extreme cases during the period 1901–1911, **racism**, the belief that one racial category is innately superior or inferior to another, and **xenophobia**, the fear of what is strange, resulted in anti-immigrant riots in several cities (see Palmer, 1982). Anti-Asian riots broke out in Vancouver during the recession year of 1907 (Whitaker, 1991), for example. In most cases, however, public reaction took the form of occupational or social exclusion, or snickering at the new immigrants' "exotic" and "peculiar" lifestyles. Groups kept to their own turf. Finally, we should keep in mind the well-meaning, if often paternalistic, efforts of many individuals, voluntary agencies, and church groups who assisted the new immigrants' adjustment to Canadian life.

The immigration boom ended in 1913. That year, more than 400 000 immigrants landed on Canada's shores. The world economy was slowing down, however, and the war that followed ended immigration almost entirely. In 1914, only 150 484 immigrants entered Canada, and the number declined further during the war years (see Table 7.1, above).

The wartime decline in immigration was presaged in May 1914 by the arrival in Vancouver harbour of a former collier ship, the Komagata Maru. Immigration officials met the ship, which carried 376 East Indians, mainly Sikhs, and refused the migrants entry. The ship was held in port for two months, its passengers detained while a Canadian warship kept watch. Finally, 21 of the migrants were allowed to disembark. The rest, however, returned to India on the ship. Arriving there in September, they were greeted by British gunfire. Eighteen died (Jensen, 2000).

BETWEEN TWO EMPIRES

Why were new immigrants viewed as such threats during this period by many in English Canada? First, English Canada in 1900 certainly was parochial and ethnocentric. Second, however, English Canadians remained anxious over the country's future. As we have seen, Canada's hesitant economic development after 1867 had raised questions not only about the National Policy but Confederation generally. Fears that Canada was destined to be annexed by the United States were fuelled by those, such as the liberal historian and journalist Goldwin Smith, who positively embraced the idea (see Smith, 1891).

A group of eminent intellectuals argued for strengthened ties to the British Empire. These "**Canadian imperialists**" (alternatively, **imperial nationalists**)—among them novelist Sara Jeannette Duncan, Presbyterian minister and educator George Monro Grant, humorist and political economist Stephen Leacock, and educator Sir George Robert Parkin—idealized the Loyalist legacy, especially elitism and anti-Americanism. Nostalgic for a simpler life and opposed to the raw materialism, industrialism, and urbanism represented by the United States (Cook, 1995), the imperialists saw Canada as having a kind of religious "mission" on earth (Berger, 1976; Romney, 1999).

Canadian imperialism and its organizations had some successes in pressuring the Canadian government to increase ties with the Crown. In 1897, for example, Prime Minister Wilfrid Laurier (elected the previous year) re-established British preferential trade (Norrie and Owram, 1996: 249). In 1899, to the chagrin of his French-Canadian supporters, Laurier also sent Canadian soldiers overseas to fight alongside Britain in the Boer War (Miller, 1999).

After 1900, however, American influence upon Canada increasingly replaced that of Britain. Trade and investment figures from these early decades highlight America's increased influence.

Throughout the late nineteenth century, Canada's trade with the United States and Britain steadfastly shifted toward the former. While British import and export trade with Canada continued to grow during this period, its overall importance to the Canadian economy declined relative to that of the United States. By 1891, Canadian imports from the United States surpassed those from Britain and thereafter never looked back. Export trade took longer to shift, picking up additional steam during the First World War as Canadian industry met British wartime demand. By 1921, however, Canadian exports to the United States, like imports, also surpassed those to Britain (Marchildon, 1995; see also Alford, 1996: 38–39).

This shift in trade was in part reflected in the amount and form of British and American investment in Canada. Canadian economic development historically has relied upon massive amounts of foreign capital. The boom after 1896 involved especially huge investments, with foreign capital flows into Canada increasing from 2.1 percent of GNP in 1897 to a high of 17.7 percent in 1912 (Norrie and Owram, 1996: 241). Until 1922, Britain was Canada's chief source of investment capital. That year, however, American investment totalled $2.6 billion (50 percent of total foreign investment), compared with $2.5 billion (47 percent) from the U.K. (Norrie and Owram, 1996: 324; also Marchildon, 1995; Li, 1996). Thereafter, American investment in Canada, both in actual dollars and as a percentage of foreign capital, was never overtaken.

From early on, an important difference existed between American and British foreign investment. Foreign investment takes two forms: **portfolio investment** (for example, long-term investments, such as bonds and loans) and **direct investment**: the actual ownership of productive property. British investment took predominantly the portfolio form. By contrast, American investments abroad were predominantly direct in nature. In Canada, direct investment involved the buying up of Canadian resources and firms or establishing branch plants. This meant, in practice, that American capital had greater control than British capital over the Canadian economy as a whole, but especially in certain areas of the economy—automobiles, newsprint, metals, and petroleum—that would become important in the twentieth century. The increasing number of American firms in Canada also helps explain the rising level of exports to, and imports from, the United States: American firms were trading with themselves.

As always, Canada's need for capital and the prospect of jobs were balanced against the fears of American control leading to annexation (see the Sara J. Duncan quotation above). These fears reached a symbolic climax in 1911.

In 1910, Laurier became the first Canadian prime minister to visit western Canada. There, he heard repeated complaints from farmers regarding the National Policy's tariff. Remembering his defeat in 1891, but still dedicated to the liberal notion of open markets, Laurier's government worked out a limited reciprocity agreement with the United States (Norrie and Owram, 1996: 250). Laurier believed the Conservatives under Robert Borden would not seriously oppose the agreement, as they had for years held out hopes of gaining a similar agreement.

The American House of Representatives and Senate gave the agreement swift passage. But the outspoken remarks of several Congressmen that the agreement would hasten Canada's annexation (see Champ Clark quotation above) soon became front-page news in Canada. The election that followed saw Laurier's Liberals defeated by a potent mixture of fear, anti-Americanism, and protectionism (see Granatstein, 1996; Orchard, 1998; Norrie and Owram, 1996). The issue of free trade hence disappeared from public debate, revived only in the late 1980s by the Conservative government of Brian Mulroney (Chapter Nine).

Outside Quebec, Canada in 1914 remained decidedly British, but American economic, cultural, and geopolitical influence over Canada was gradually increasing. The war that followed reinforced this emerging pattern.

A WORLD INTERRUPTED: CANADA AND THE FIRST WORLD WAR

In 1914, years of political posturing, unbridled jingoism, and imperial competition resulted in war. Estimates for the number of people killed in the First World War (1914–18) range between 8.5 and 16 million; the number of wounded is estimated at more than 21 million (Stearns, 1975: 277–78; *Time*, 1999: 399). Russia's casualties were the greatest, made even greater by the revolution and the famines that followed. But Germany, France, and Britain also suffered enormous costs, including in effect the wasting of an entire generation. Many who returned bore wounds that were not always physical. In strictly monetary terms, the total direct costs of the war were $180 billion, the indirect costs, $151 billion—substantial amounts for the time (Langer, 1948: 951).

Canadian losses amounted to 60 661 Canadian troops dead, among them a host of "war poets," such as John McCrae. Nearly as many Canadians died throughout 1918–19 as a result of a worldwide influenza epidemic, an indirect result of the war. Another 1600 people were killed (6000 more wounded) at Halifax harbour on December 6, 1917, when an ammunition ship collided with a freighter, exploding with the force of an atomic bomb and destroying much of Halifax.

European places like Ypres, Passchendaele, and Vimy Ridge entered Canada's history, while a small number of individuals—mainly "air aces" like Billy Bishop, William Barker, and A. Roy Brown (who shot down the "Red Baron," von Richthofen)—became household names for a time. Small towns and villages throughout Canada erected monuments to the dead that still stand, augmented later by more names from other wars. Some towns were named after the battles (such as Vimy, Alberta); however, Berlin, Ontario (founded by people of German ancestry, but now afraid to admit their heritage), was renamed in 1916 after a British war hero, Field Marshall Lord Kitchener, who had died at sea.

Beyond the obvious losses of men, money, and material, the war had several major impacts on Canada, some more immediate that others.

First, the war altered Canada's position relative to other powers within the international state system. The Russian, German, Austro-Hungarian, and Turkish empires were destroyed; the British Empire was hobbled. By contrast, the United States, already the world's leading economy in 1914 (Norrie and Owram, 1996: 223), ended the war as the world's leading creditor country (Palmer, 1957: 691), second only to Britain as the world's chief direct investor (Dunning, 1983), and in military matters an increasingly formidable power. A series of invasions and military coups after 1898, underpinned by the Monroe Doctrine, had ensured that, in the Americas especially, the United States reigned largely unopposed (Zinn, 1995: 399).

Second, the war discredited old institutions and traditional authorities, especially in Europe but also in Canada, paving the way for the rise during the 1920s and 1930s of new political ideologies and parties. Third, at the same time, the role of the state in Canadian society (as elsewhere) expanded. Canadian government spending on goods and services, for example, rose from 10 percent of GDP in 1913 to 14.5 percent of GDP in 1914, remaining at that level throughout the war (Norrie and Owram, 1996: 300). The bureaucratic infrastructure of government also expanded. On the revenue side, the Canadian government introduced business and personal income taxes, a temporary wartime measure that soon became a permanent part of Canada's fiscal landscape.

Fourth, the First World War accelerated in all countries a series of social changes. Women, for example, entered the labour force, especially the growing public bureaucracies (Lowe, 1987). As in most combatant countries, women in Canada also gained the vote (1918). The year previous, Louise McKinney was elected to the Alberta legislature, becoming the first woman to hold such an office in the British Empire. But there were other social changes, notably the continued decline in rural life and the growth of cities (see below), a gradual shift from primary production to secondary manufacturing and services, and the expansion of wage labour.

Fifth, the Conscription Crisis (see Chapter Three) became part of the panoply of grievances dividing French and English in Canada. Sixth, the war slowed immigration to Canada—indeed, killing off many who might have come—thus cutting off an important leg of Canada's National Policy.

Finally, the war also sparked in English Canada a fragile sense of independent nationalism. In 1914, Canada was still very much a British colony. Britain's declaration of war meant that Canada was itself immediately at war, its troops under British command. By 1918, however, there existed a distinct Canadian Corps led by Canadian officers. Canada's separate signing of the Treaty of Versailles in 1919 and garnering of a seat in the newly founded League of Nations further symbolized the country's growing independence from Britain.

CANADA, 1919-1929

The troops returning in 1919 were greeted by high unemployment, rising inflation, declining wages, and mounting anxiety. In the spring of 1919, a dispute in Winnipeg between labourers in the metal and building trades and management over collective bargaining rights, better wages, and working conditions escalated into a General Strike of 30 000 workers, lasting 40 days. The strike encouraged sympathy strikes (particularly in the West) involving another 88 000 workers. It ended on June 25, amidst lingering images of the RCMP on horseback charging into a crowd of strikers at the corner of Portage and Main—causing 30 injuries and at least one death—and federal troops occupying the streets of Winnipeg (Conway, 1994: 90–93).

There also was anxiety in rural Canada, especially in the West. Mass immigration between 1901 and 1911 (see above) had transformed the prairie landscape and, in less than two decades, had led to Ontario's being supplanted as Canada's wheat-growing region (see Morton, 2000: 28; Norrie and Owram, 1996: 233). This transformation came at a cost, however.

The West, reliant upon a single commodity, was particularly at the mercy of world markets. When wheat prices collapsed at the end of the war, Canada's agrarians revolted at the ballot box. The United Farmers of Ontario won the election in 1919. Subsequently, the United Farmers of Alberta gained office in 1921 and the United Farmers of Manitoba in 1922. Meanwhile, at the federal level, the newly founded National Progressive Party in 1921 elected 65 MPs, the most successful showing by a federal "third party" until the Reform Party in the 1990s (see Appendix 1). Among Progressives elected was Canada's first woman parliamentarian, Agnes Macphail.

Why the widespread discontent following the war? The explanation lies in a series of social and economic trends that, beginning in the early twentieth century, were rapidly transforming Canadian society.

Think for a moment about life in mid-nineteenth-century Canada. Family and community were the focal point around which people's lives revolved. Except for arriving immigrants, people travelled little in their lifetime. Much of Canada was still rural (80 percent in 1871). The family was still the site of production and consumption, gender roles were largely fixed, markets were mainly local, and few people were full-time wage labourers. Well into the late nineteenth century, small, paternalistic, family-operated businesses—what Marx termed the "petite bourgeoisie"—dominated the Canadian economy, while family farms were the norm.

After 1900, however, a new form of capitalism emerged: corporate capitalism. Moving beyond the limitations of either petite bourgeois or mercantile or industrial capitalism, **corporate capitalism** (sometimes also termed **monopoly capitalism**) is large-scale, highly capitalized, centralized, and non-competitive (Heron and Storey, 1986; Li, 1996). Between 1900 and 1920, for example, the number of manufacturing units in Canada fell from 76 000 to 22 000 (Li, 1996: 16; also Morton, 2000: 29). Similarly, the number of Canadian banks went from 36 in 1900 to 22 in 1914 to 10 in 1928 (Li, 1996: 20). Canada was quickly transformed from a society of petite bourgeois agrarians and nascent small-time industrialists into one in which large-scale manufacturing (especially in the automobile industry) and services began playing an increasingly large role. At the same time, industrialization and economic development were unevenly distributed and thus increased regional divisions in Canada.

The rise of corporate capitalism had particular impacts in shaping Canada's labour market. Demand for labour grew. Thus, the number and percentage of wage labourers in the overall labour force grew rapidly (see Li, 1996: 34). As in the past, labour demand was met in part by new immigrants. But immigration during the 1920s did not recover to pre-war levels. Instead, labour demand was met largely through natural population growth, rural migration—hence, in part, the farmers' revolts of 1919–22—and a largely untapped source: women.

The period leading up to the 1920s saw women increasingly enter the workforce. Between 1911 and 1921, the participation rate for females of 14 to 65 years of age rose from 16.6 to 19.9 percent, compared with a rise from 82 to 89.7 percent for males in that age group during the same period. By 1931, the participation rate of females in the labour force was 23 percent, compared with 87.2 percent for males (calculated from Denton, 1983). Women's jobs, however, were mostly located in the low-paying clerical jobs that arose in the burgeoning bureaucracies of the state and corporations (Lowe, 1987; Krahn and Lowe, 2002).

The situation of women was changing at the political level, too. In 1929, five women—Irene Parlby, Louise McKinney, Henrietta Muir Edwards, Emily Murphy, and Nellie McClung—won an especially important legal battle when the Judicial Committee of the Privy Council in Britain (then Canada's highest court) overturned an earlier ruling by the Supreme Court of Canada and declared that women were "persons" under the law and therefore could hold any public office (Bellamy and Irving, 1981).

Meanwhile, corporate capitalism was also changing Canada's workplaces and workplace relations in important ways. This period saw the introduction to the workplace of new forms of organization. Bureaucratic principles and management techniques based on Frederick Taylor's principles of **scientific management** (see Box 7.1) were introduced into factories and soon also into white-collar work. These organizational forms increased managerial control over workers and deskilled workers in the name of efficiency and higher profits (see Krahn and Lowe, 2002).

In the long run, concentrated capitalism meant also concentrated labour, resulting in the rise of trade and industrial unions. In the short run, however, these changes led to growing alienation and intensified class conflict, as occurred at Winnipeg.

Technology, the war, the increasing role of the state, and the rise of corporate capitalism changed Canada in other ways during this period. Canada gradually became more urbanized. In 1901, 62 percent of Canadians still lived in rural areas. By 1921, however, an

> **BOX 7.1** **The Six Elements of Scientific Management**
>
> 1. Shift the decision-making responsibility for doing a job from workers to managers.
> 2. Use scientific methods to determine the most efficient way of executing a job and redesign it accordingly.
> 3. Provide a detailed description of how to perform each step in a job.
> 4. Select the best worker to perform the job.
> 5. Train workers to execute the job efficiently.
> 6. Closely monitor workers' performance.
>
> Source: *Work, Industry and Canadian Society*, fourth edition, by Krahn and Lowe (2002: 230) ©2003. Reprinted with permission of Nelson, a division of Thomson Learning: **www.thomsonrights.com**. Fax: (800) 730-2215.

equal number of Canadians lived in urban and rural areas (see Table 7.2). Canada's urbanization had begun.

In 1901, Montreal (population 328 172) and Toronto (population 209 892) were still Canada's largest cities. The next largest city was Quebec City, with 68 840 people. Over the next ten years, however, Winnipeg sprang up from 42 340 to 136 035 people, while Vancouver grew from 29 432 to 120 847. By 1921, Hamilton and Ottawa also exceeded 100 000 people, joined in 1931 by Quebec City (see Norrie and Owram, 1996: 334).

Mass consumption became a reality in the 1920s (Bell, 1996: 66; Robbins, 1999). The automobile was the chief symbol of the new consumer society. Cars had been around for decades. By the 1920s, however, mass production technology, low cost, and easy credit made it possible for more people to own a car. The number of cars registered in Canada increased from 275 000 in 1918 to 1.9 million in 1929 (Norrie and Owram, 1996: 327), a growth rate far outstripping even the United States (see Hofstadter et al., 1957: 642).

By the 1920s, British influence, though still strong, was waning; the pull of American culture was increasing. Many of Canada's corporations were American-owned. Faintly, however, a more independent Canadian culture was stirring within English-speaking Canada, spearheaded by artists such as Emily Carr and the Group of Seven. Prints of these artists' paintings soon appeared in banks and magazines across the country, promoting images of their land that few Canadians could actually know.

The first half of the 1920s in Canada, as elsewhere, began with a recession. By contrast, the years between 1925 and 1929 were a time of prosperity, marked by illegal gin, Charleston-dancing flappers, the new "Model A" Ford, and jazz. Then, suddenly, the prosperity ended.

THE DEPRESSION YEARS, 1929–1939

In October 1929, the New York stock market crashed. Stock values on the New York Stock Exchange alone fell by 40 percent (Palmer, 1957: 780), and 10 percent of private wealth vanished, virtually overnight (Norrie and Owram, 1996: 296). Despite repeated statements by government officials in Canada, the United States, and elsewhere that the economy was sound, the crisis soon spread. As industrial and finance capital collapsed, production fell,

TABLE 7.2 | Canadian Rural and Urban Population, 1871-2001 (in thousands)

Year	Canada	Urban		Rural					
		Total	%	Non-Farm	%	Farm	%	Total	%
1871	3689	722	19.6	n.a.	n.a.	n.a.	n.a.	2967	80.4
1881	4325	1110	25.7	n.a.	n.a.	n.a.	n.a.	3215	74.3
1891	4833	1537	31.8	n.a.	n.a.	n.a.	n.a.	3296	68.2
1901	5371	2014	37.5	n.a.	n.a.	n.a.	n.a.	3357	62.5
1911	7207	3273	45.4	n.a.	n.a.	n.a.	n.a.	3934	54.6
1921	8788	4352	49.5	n.a.	n.a.	n.a.	n.a.	4436	50.5
1931	10 377	5469	52.7	1670	16.1	3238	31.2	4908	47.3
1941	11 507	6271	54.5	2123	18.4	3113	27.1	5236	45.5
1951	14 009	8817	62.9	2423	17.3	2769	19.8	5192	37.1
1961	18 238	12 700	69.6	3465	19.0	2073	11.4	5538	30.4
1971	21 962	16 410	76.1	3738	17.3	1420	6.6	5158	23.9
1981	24 820	18 436	75.6	4867	20.0	1040	4.3	5907	24.3
1991	28 031	20 907	76.6	5583	20.5	807	3.0	6390	23.4
2001	30 007	23 908	79.7	n.a.	n.a.	n.a.	n.a.	6098	20.3

Sources: Adapted from the Statistics Canada publication *Historical Statistics of Canada*, Catalogue 11-516, 1983, Series A67-69 and A75-77; and *Population and Dwelling Counts (On-Line)*; and from the Statistics Canada Web site at www12.statcan.ca/english/census01/products/standard/popdwell/Table-UR-PS.cfm; and the *Canadian Global Almanac 2000* (1999: 49), "Canadian Urban and Rural Population" (as taken from Statistics Canada), reprinted with the permission from Macmillan Canada, an imprint of John Wiley & Sons Canada, Ltd.

Notes: *Urban* is defined as persons living in a built-up area having a population of 1000 or more and a population density of 400 or more per square kilometre *Rural* is defined as persons living outside "urban areas." *Rural farm* is defined as persons living in rural areas who are members of households of farm operators. *Rural non-farm* is defined as persons living in rural areas who are not members of households of farm operators.

and unemployment rose, resulting in more uncertainty, a further decline in consumption and yet more layoffs throughout the industrialized, capitalist world.

During the Depression's worst period (1932–33), the **unemployment rate** (generally calculated as *the number of people unemployed and actively looking for work divided by the total number of labour force participants*) reached 22 to 23 percent in Britain and Belgium; 24 percent in Sweden; 27 percent in the United States; 29 percent in Austria, 31 percent in Norway; 32 percent in Denmark; and no less than 44 percent in Germany (all rates from Hobsbawm, 1995: 90–93). Canadian unemployment officially peaked in 1933 between 25 and 30 percent (Rice and Prince, 2000: 48). How much official statistics underestimate the problem is open to question, however.

Canada suffered uniquely in the Depression because, first, its economy was export dependent, second, its range of exports was small and lacked diversification, and third, its chief export market was the United States, a country that during the Depression became highly protectionist (Norrie and Owram, 1996: 354). Canada's economy was insufficiently developed, self-contained, and integrated to withstand the shocks. In consequence, during the period 1929–33, Canadian industrial production fell by half, exports by two-thirds, and construction by 90 percent (Rice and Prince, 2000: 48).

Within Canada, the Depression hit the West hardest. The region's economy was particularly dependent on wheat for export. Additionally, much of the West experienced a long, harsh drought. The worst-hit area was southwestern Saskatchewan, where the combined effect resulted in the abandonment of farms by an estimated quarter of a million people during the 1930s (Berton, 1991: 291). For the Maritimes, in semi-permanent recession since the 1880s, the Depression hardly seemed a change.

The Depression halted, even reversed for a time, years of social change in Canada. Barter, for example, partially replaced the money economy. Cars morphed into horse-drawn carriages, nicknamed (after Prime Minister R.B. Bennett) "Bennett buggies." The process of urbanization slowed. Immigration to Canada all but ended; indeed, for the first time since the nineteenth century, more people left Canada than entered (McKie, 1994). Most Canadians did not mind, however. Anti-immigrant sentiment in the 1930s was high. The Canadian government took special steps to halt the entry of people viewed as communist agitators and "trouble makers," or people who were deemed as not fitting in. In a replay of the Komagata Maru incident, the Canadian government in 1939 refused the embarkation of 907 Jews aboard the liner St. Louis, resulting in their return ultimately to Nazi Germany's death camps (Abella and Troper, 1982; Whitaker, 1991).

The Depression damaged Canada's social fabric. Crime rates rose. The year 1931 witnessed an "unprecedented wave of bank holdups" (Berton, 1991: 88). Fuelled by Prohibition south of the border, booze became a growth industry throughout Canada, from the Maritime ports to the cities of southern Ontario to the Crowsnest Pass region of Alberta. Mothers and fathers, desperate and afraid, sometimes killed their children and then committed suicide. Birth rates, already dropping in the 1920s, declined further, to 3.0 per thousand in 1936 and 2.8 in 1941 (see Li, 1996: 155), figures not seen again until the 1960s. In the 1930s, few people wanted to have children, not knowing if they could care for them.

Yet Canadians' sense of being part of a larger society also expanded during the Depression. Some young Canadians experienced the country first-hand, hopping freight cars and travelling from community to community in search of work (Berton, 1991). Others learned about Canada and the world at large through the cinema, though in the main the silver screen provided, not access to, but an escape from reality. By contrast, radio played a major role in incorporating Canadians into society. Bennett's government recognized in the early 1930s the importance of radio in nation-building and so created the Canadian Radio and Television Commission. Radio manufactured an "imaginary collective," creating and sharing common experiences for Canadians from coast to coast, related to a host of events, from Foster Hewett's hockey broadcasts to disasters both real and fake (the "War of the Worlds"), to human interest stories (the Dionne Quintuplets).

Bennett's government expanded the role of the state in other ways, notably the creation of the Bank of Canada and the Wheat Board. In areas of economic and social concern, however, Bennett during the early years of the Depression followed the policies of his American counterpart, President Herbert Hoover, in steadfastly arguing that governments could not—should not—do anything to interfere in the economy. In both countries, problems of the poor, the hungry, and the unemployed were thrown back on local authorities and charities. The role of governments was to balance budgets, protect private property, and maintain social order.

As in the United States (Zinn, 1995), there were in Canada strikes and protests by workers throughout the decade. The state did not hesitate to use coercive force to deal with them. At Estevan, Saskatchewan, in 1931, poor wages, lousy living conditions, and unsympathetic management led to a confrontation between striking mine workers and police in which three strikers were killed, eleven more injured, and five policemen sent to hospital (Berton, 1991: 126–27).

As the Depression continued, governments took steps to curtail political unrest. One such step involved the setting up of work camps in remote rural areas. Before being shut down in 1936, Canada's relief camps housed 170 248 men and provided 10 201 103 worker-days of relief (Howard, 1999: 2408). But the food was poor and monotonous, the clothing of army issue and distinctly prison-like, and camp control was authoritarian and punitive (Berton, 1991: 176). The camps became breeding grounds of hopelessness and anger.

In June 1935, 1500 young men of different racial and ethnic backgrounds, refugees from the British Columbia camps, set off from the Vancouver waterfront by train, headed for Ottawa, picking up supporters along the way. They were forcibly halted at Regina, however, on Dominion Day. Under orders from Prime Minister Bennett, the RCMP and local police moved into an unsuspecting crowd of 1500 people on Regina's Market Square to arrest the trek leaders. A panic ensued. By the time it was over, 12 trekkers and five Regina citizens were hospitalized for gunshot wounds, 39 RCMP officers had been hospitalized for injuries (none from gunfire), and one plainclothes detective lay dead. Over a hundred people were arrested. Twenty-eight went to trial; eight were eventually convicted and sent to jail (see Berton, 1991).

In the main, unrest in Canada during the Depression paled in comparison with other countries where strikes, protests, civil violence, and state repression were daily news. Still, it was a time of serious political unrest. Both communism and fascism gained converts in Canada. Communists, or those suspected of being communists, were treated by the authorities far more harshly than fascist sympathizers, who garnered at least tacit support from some members of Canada's business and religious elite (see Robin, 1991; Berton, 1991: 22).

Two less politically extreme alternatives to communism and fascism arose in western Canada. Like the agrarian parties of the early 1920s, both of these were **populist** parties, that is, *parties built around mass political movements, mobilized around symbols and traditions congruent with the popular culture, which express a group's sense of threat, arising from powerful "outside" elements and directed at the group's perceived "peoplehood."*

In Saskatchewan, the Co-operative Commonwealth Federation (CCF), built around a broad coalition of farmers, labourers, religious activists (mainly Protestant), and university-trained intellectuals (mainly economists), melded traditional Prairie populism with democratic socialism. Its leader was J.S. Woodsworth, a former Methodist minister, social activist, and devout pacifist who had been among those arrested in the Winnipeg Strike and later elected as a National Progressive in 1921. In 1944, another minister, Tommy Douglas, led the CCF to success in Saskatchewan, bringing to power the first socialist government elected in North America. In 1961, the CCF became the New Democratic Party (Lipset, 1968a; also Conway, 1994) (see Chapter Eight).

In Alberta, Rev. William Aberhart, a radio evangelist, adopted the economic ideas of a British engineer, Colonel Douglas, in founding the Social Credit Party. In 1935, Aberhart's party was elected, defeating the tired and scandal-ridden United Farmers of Alberta. Broadly supported by farmers and workers alike (Bell, 1993), the party at first mixed populist rhetoric and evangelical zeal, demanding protection against bankruptcy, while supporting unemployment insurance and public health care. Following a series of legislative setbacks, Aberhart's death in 1943, and the discovery of oil in the late 1940s, however, Social Credit became a fairly conventional conservative party opposed to government intervention in the economy (Finkel, 1989).

Government policies in Canada in the 1930s were shaped by events in the United States. In 1932, Franklin Delano Roosevelt became president. Soon, Canadians as well as Americans were hearing Roosevelt over the still-new medium of radio. Canadians liked what they heard. Like Canada, the United States was faced with massive unemployment, civil unrest, and populist agitation. Unlike Bennett, Roosevelt offered solutions to the crisis, embarking on a series of economic and social reforms between 1933 and 1938 that protected farmers, regulated banking, gave relief to the unemployed, and extended labour rights (Langer, 1948: 1053–56; Hofstadter et al., 1957: 650–75; Zinn, 1995: 382–84).

Facing political pressures, Bennett's government in 1934 launched its own version of Roosevelt's "New Deal": unemployment insurance, minimum wages and legislation dealing with hours of work, marketing legislation, and laws against price-fixing (Langer, 1948: 1060; Morton, 1997: 205–06). The reforms came too late, however, to save Bennett's government from defeat in 1935 at the hands of William Lyon Mackenzie King's Liberals.

Under King, as under Bennett, the state's role in building Canada grew stronger. The Canadian Radio and Broadcast Commission became the Canadian Broadcasting Corporation, and government-owned Trans-Canada Airlines was launched (Morton, 1997: 207). The economy, however, continued to languish. After a short period of recovery, both Canada and the United States entered recessions again in 1937. Labour and civil unrest continued. A strike in 1937 by General Motors workers in Oshawa, Ontario, over poor wages and union recognition led to violence. Meanwhile, ties to the United States grew, symbolized by the signing of a limited reciprocity agreement in 1935, King's almost fawning relationship with Roosevelt, and the latter's comments at Queen's University in 1938 pledging American support in the event of war (Martin, 1982).

CANADA AND THE SECOND WORLD WAR

On September 1, 1939, what English poet W.H. Auden referred to as a "low, dishonest decade" ended as Germany invaded Poland. Within days, much of the world (except the United States and Russia) was at war.

Recent estimates suggest nearly 15 million people were killed and 26 million more were wounded during the Second World War (*Time*, 1999: 399). Hobsbawm (1995: 43) notes, however, that the "losses are literally incalculable" because many of those killed were civilians and "much of the worst killing took place in regions, or at times, when nobody was in a position to count...."

More than a million Canadian men and women (out of a total population of only 11 million people) joined the army, navy, or air force during the Second World War. Of these, 42 042 were killed and 53 145 were wounded (*Time*, 1999: 399). Canada's financial expenditures rose from $118 million in 1939–40 to $4.5 billion in 1943–44 (Stacey and Hillmer, 1999: 2552). Public debt rose from $5 billion in 1939 to $18 billion by 1945 (Norrie and Owram, 1996: 378), resulting in a net federal public debt of nearly 107 percent of GNP in 1946–47 (Chorney, 1989: 43).

Journalist Blair Fraser (1967: 14) later wrote, "The most that could be said was that World War II had done less damage to the fabric of the nation than World War I did." The lasting effects of the conscription crisis of the Second World War were less—no "gaping wound," merely "a bruise." There were "no jobless veterans begging or rioting in the streets," no "counterpart of the Winnipeg General strike"—though a strike at Windsor in 1945 proved significant for labour relations. Canada's liberal self-image, however, did take a beating for its treatment of ethnic minorities, notably the expulsion and internment of men, women, and children of Japanese extraction.

Yet, there had been positive gains, especially for the Canadian economy. The war dragged Canada and the world out of the Depression and set off Canada's third great period of economic growth, a period that continued into the early 1960s (Aitken, 1959). Enormous investments in economic infrastructure had turned Canada into a gigantic armaments factory, producing thousands of aircraft, tanks, anti-aircraft guns, tracked vehicles, and machine guns (James, 1997: 509). These plants were soon refitted to meet peacetime consumer demand. Likewise, Canada ended the war with a huge and disciplined navy and the world's fourth largest merchant marine, important to export trade. At the same time, however, Canada's military and economy were more integrated than ever into the American orbit.

CONCLUSION

Within a few short decades of Confederation, the world of 1867 had ceased to exist except in memory and old photographs. The basic contours of Canadian society in the second half of the twentieth century were forged by events during this period; the after-effects continue into the twenty-first century.

First, the United States clearly arose as successor to the British Empire, both internationally and in its influence upon Canada. In the words of Innis (1956), Canada had gone from colony to nation to colony. In this context, new notions of English-Canadian nationalism arose with consequences seen 20 years later (Chapter Eight).

Second, English Canada's culture changed during this period, largely as a result of mass immigration. Thus was set in motion a further decline of English dominance, the distinctive pattern of ethnicity that marks Canadian provinces, and the enactment of Canada's policy of multiculturalism.

Third, corporate capitalism largely replaced petite bourgeois capitalism. No elements of Canadian society, from family size to social values to urban growth, were left unmarked by this event. By the end of the Second World War, the vast majority of Canadians, including large numbers of women, had become part of the paid labour force.

Fourth, the state gradually came to play a larger role in the lives of Canadians. The crumbling of traditional society and its institutions, accelerated by the wars and the Depression, resulted in a deepening and centralizing of state policies. State and civil society, more than ever, became inseparable.

Canada in 1945 seemed a land of promise. On its outskirts, however, lay new perils to Canadian identity, harmony, sovereignty, and peace. The next chapter examines Canada's efforts to wend its way through the postwar world's uncertain waters.

KEY TERMS

American system
Anglo-conformity
British system
Canadian imperialists (a.k.a. imperial nationalists)
corporate capitalism (a.k.a. monopoly capitalism)
direct investment
European system
populist
portfolio investment
racism
scientific management
unemployment rate
xenophobia

chapter eight

Postwar Canada and English-Canadian Nationalism

You know, it seems ridiculous. We both speak the same language. We think alike. We behave the same. Don't you think you would be better off as the 49th state?
—U.S. President Dwight D. Eisenhower to Canadian diplomat Lionel Chevrier, 1956

The impossibility of conservatism in our era is the impossibility of Canada.
—George Grant, 1965

Living with you is in some ways like sleeping with an elephant. No matter how friendly or temperate the beast, one is affected by every twitch and grunt.
—Prime Minister Trudeau, speaking to the National Press Club in Washington, 1969

INTRODUCTION

The end of the Second World War stimulated in Canada an unprecedented, albeit uneven, period of economic expansion and social and political transformation. Increased demands for skilled labour were ultimately met by immigration and the increased workforce presence of women. Birth rates soared, before resuming in 1956 a longer trend of decline (Li, 1996: 70), and family forms changed. The welfare state evolved, underpinning a compromise between labour and capital. And, on April 1, 1949,

Newfoundland joined Confederation (though some Newfoundlanders to this day claim they annexed Canada).

Meanwhile, abroad, the hot menace of fascism was replaced by the Cold War. Anti-communist hysteria gripped the United States and soon found its way across the border. At the Bretton Woods conference held in 1944, western countries (led by the United States) designed an economic regime meant to rebuild and stabilize the postwar world. Not incidentally, it paved the way for orderly capitalist expansion. Key institutions of this plan included the International Monetary Fund (IMF) and the World Bank (also known as the International Bank for Reconstruction and Development). The General Agreement on Tariffs and Trade (GATT), formed to negotiate tariff reductions and the removal of other trade barriers, joined these institutions in the early 1950s (Lairson and Skidmore, 1997). Politically, the international postwar era saw also the creation of the United Nations, successor to the failed pre-war League of Nations.

Consumption flourished throughout the next decade, underpinned by continued strong economic growth. Suburban Canada was born, aided by the ubiquitous presence of automobiles. Television invaded family living rooms and bedrooms.

The prosperous 1950s gave way in Canada in the early 1960s to renewed concerns of American control. In the context of growing American defeats abroad and social discord at home, and in contraposition to Quebec's demands for sovereignty, a new nationalism arose in English-speaking Canada. In the 1970s, English-Canadian nationalism paved the way for a further expansion of state involvement in the economy and society, referred to as "Canadianization." By the 1980s, however, debt and internal divisions hobbled the Canadian state, setting the stage for adoption of a new developmental paradigm.

This chapter traces the key events and changes that occurred in Canadian society between the end of the Second World War and the Canadian election of 1984, and the state's role in those changes.

CANADA AND THE UNITED STATES IN THE COLD WAR ERA

In 1945, Canada's 12 million people seemed enviably blessed. The country had a large public debt but also ample resources much in world demand: steel, timber, wheat, and oil, for example. It also had an established industrial and state infrastructure. Abroad, Canada's chief economic competitors lay in ruins. Reconstruction in Europe under the Marshall Plan and the subsequent Korean conflict (1950–53) fuelled demand for Canadian resources. Meanwhile, at home, a large reservoir of consumer power was ready to be unleashed (Norrie and Owram. 1996). The result was generally high economic growth throughout the 1950s. Yet, the new prosperity also hid real political, economic, and cultural dangers.

To the north and across the Arctic waters lay the Soviet Union. The Soviet Union only months before had been a staunch ally. Now it was suddenly the enemy. The period was highlighted by the case of Igor Gouzenko, a Soviet embassy clerk who in September 1945 defected with documents revealing Soviet espionage in Canada (Finkel, 1997). As in the United States, anti-communist hysteria soon became a staple of Canadian political and cultural life.

To the south lay a more subtle threat, however. The United States ended the Second World War as the globe's lone superpower, possessor of the world's strongest economy and a large battle-hardened military. The United States alone also had the atomic bomb, a fact quickly interpreted by several American politicians and religious figures as symbolizing America's divinely chosen status among countries (Ungar, 1991).

More than ever, Canada in 1945 fell under America's sway. Following a secret meeting between Prime Minister King and President Roosevelt at Ogdensburg in 1942, the two countries' militaries became strategically linked. These links became more formal in 1949, when Canada became part of the newly formed North Atlantic Treaty Organization (NATO), an anti-communist self-defence bloc headed by the United States. In the 1960s, Canada also became the United States' northern partner in a continental defence pact, the North American Air Defense Command (NORAD).

Economically, wartime production had stimulated Canada's growth but also increased links with the United States. After the war, American companies began buying up Canada's redundant war factories and retooling them for civilian use. Much the same occurred regarding Canadian resources. In 1952, President Harry Truman released the Paley Report (Roberts, 1998). The report, issued as the Cold War heated up, suggested Canada's resource wealth made it a potential economic rival to the United States. The report argued further that the American government should do everything in its power to secure Canadian raw materials, especially uranium, in the service of defending the United States.

America's cultural presence in Canada also grew during and after the war through cinema and radio, and increased again in the 1950s with the rise of television. The fact that a disproportionate number of Canadians found employment in movies and television, both in front of the camera (for example, Deanna Durbin and Raymond Massey) and behind the scenes as writers, technicians, and directors, did not change the impact. The productions were generically American, meant to be sold first to Americans, then resold abroad to foreigners, including Canadians, who were increasingly entranced by that empire's technology, power, and wealth.

But the American presence in Canada was also increasingly demographic and social. Construction of the Alaska Highway during the Second World War (see Chapter Eleven) was completed almost entirely with American labour and investment, and the development of large-scale oil production in Alberta after 1947 resulted in a further influx of American money, personnel, and expertise (House, 1978; Richards and Pratt, 1979). Calgary quickly became the Houston of the North, and an ethos of rugged individualism slowly replaced the settler traditions of cooperation and community. In the long term, the development of Alberta's oil industry set the stage for interprovincial rivalry and federal-provincial hostility, while furthering a continental approach to development at odds with the tenets of the old National Policy.

Internationally, the immediate postwar period saw the start of the divvying up of the world between state communism, represented by the Soviet Union, and corporate capitalism, represented by the United States. During the early period, the final dismantling of colonialism provided opportunities for both superpowers to expand into new territories, notably the Middle East, Africa, and—especially following the French retreat from Vietnam in the late 1950s—Asia. Both the Soviet Union and the United States took measures to secure their borders and expand their influence throughout this period and after. The Soviet Union invaded Hungary in 1956, Czechoslovakia in 1968, and Afghanistan in 1979. Similarly, the United States, acting on the Monroe Doctrine (Chapter Six), continued a long policy after the 1950s of threatening, destabilizing, and sometimes invading sovereign countries throughout the Americas. Occasionally, as during the Cuban Missile Crisis in 1963, the boundaries of interest intersected, nearly resulting in nuclear conflagration. For Canada, finding its way in this bipolar world was a task not easily accomplished.

There was one notable similarity, however, between communist and capitalist countries: the continued growth of the state. This was no less true in the case of Canada.

FROM STATE TO "WELFARE" STATE

Far from being a nation-state or even a multi-national state, Canada may best be described as a state-nation (see Chapter One). That is, the state often came first, and then set about constructing the institutions of nationhood. In the course of this construction, Canadian society was also changed in particular ways.

The Hudson's Bay Company was a kind of prototype for early Canadian development, with other corporations following (for example, the CPR). From building railroads and canals to building defensive fortifications, to the pacification of the West by the North West Mounted Police to pave the way for immigrants, the Canadian state (including, to a lesser degree, the provinces) acted as chief architect, administrator, and banker. Until the 1930s, much of this involvement was minimalist and remained tied directly or indirectly to furthering private capital accumulation. Slowly, however, the state's involvement in Canadian society entered broader areas of nation-building (such as CBC radio) and social concern.

To a degree, the state's initially minimalist role in Canadian society in 1867 is understandable given that Canada was a small, still largely pre-capitalist and pre-industrial country. Thereafter, however, the Canadian state and society expanded together. Four periods marked this expansion and transformation (see Rice and Prince, 2000; Johnson and Stritch, 1997). The first period occurred between 1867 and 1914, during Canada's initial industrialization and expansion. The second period occurred between the start of the First World War and the end of the postwar boom, 1914–1929, during which corporate capitalism took hold and Canada urbanized (see Li, 1996). The third period, 1929–1945, began with the Depression and ended with the closing of the Second World War. The fourth period, with which we are primarily concerned here, began in 1945 and continued until the mid-1980s, when changes brought on by neo-liberal globalization (see Chapter Nine) further altered the relationship of state and society and the role of government.

Each period saw a gradual shift in government functions in areas of social policy. Rice and Prince (2000) note that responsibility for social welfare changed over time in five important ways. First, responsibility shifted from the private to the state sector. Second, responsibility shifted from lower to higher levels (that is, from municipalities to the provinces or the federal government). Third, the administration and provision of services became more centralized and under the auspices of professional authorities. And fourth, there was a move in policy approaches from remedial to preventive policies.

A fifth related but gradual change saw a shift from particularistic to more universal policies. The Pension Act of 1919 was Canada's first universal program in the sense that it was provided to all returning soldiers without resort to a means test. A further move to standardization and universality occurred with the federal government's introduction of the Old Age Pensions Act in 1927.

In Canada, as elsewhere in the industrialized West, the greatest public expansion into social programs, however, occurred after the Second World War (see Turner, 1981; Rice and Prince, 2000). Underpinning this expansion were the ideas of influential British economist John Maynard Keynes, who argued that the state had a role in ensuring economic and, hence, political stability (Lekachman, 1966). With full employment as the goal, counter-cyclical measures, to ward off market fluctuations, became a standard feature of postwar government planning. In the context of the Cold War, such interventions also proved useful in showing that capitalism could be responsive not only to market demands but also to human needs.

As in other countries, the war enlarged, centralized, and strengthened the Canadian state, increasing its capacity to act. By 1945, the Canadian government also had several sources of new ideas. Important models were provided by Roosevelt's New Deal (Chapter Seven) and Britain's Beveridge Report (1942). Within Canada, the recommendations of the Royal Commission on Dominion-Provincial Relations (Rowell-Sirois Commission) in 1940 and the Federal Government's Advisory Committee on Post-War Reconstruction (the Marsh Report) in 1943 provided similar blueprints for reshaping Canada's system of social security.

Pressures for political change came from a variety of sources, particularly unions, social activists, progressive think-tanks (such as the League for Social Reconstruction), and the CCF (see Chapter Seven). These pressures resulted in 1940 in King's government bringing in Canada's first Unemployment Insurance Act. This was followed in 1944 with introduction of the Family Allowances Act, a universal program that (at the time) substantially assisted young families in raising their children and, not unintentionally, also encouraged Canada's birth rate.

These tentative steps at reshaping Canada's social security system were nothing compared with what followed, however. Health care provides a specific example of this process of state expansion.

The postwar period saw the Canadian federal government set up a system of national health grants (1948). This was followed in the 1950s by the Old Age Security Act (1951), the expansion of government assistance under the Unemployment Insurance Act (1956), and the passing of the Hospital Insurance and Diagnostic Act (1957), which introduced federal cost-sharing to pay for provincial hospital insurance. In 1965, the compulsory Canada Pension Plan and Quebec Pension Plan were introduced. The following year, the Guaranteed Income Supplement Plan and Canada Assistance Plan were created, and medicare was introduced with the passage of the Medical Care Act (see Li, 1996: 84–85). (Medicare was modelled on a program implemented in Saskatchewan by the CCF government of Premier Tommy Douglas.)

Together, programs such as health care, education, unemployment insurance, social allowance, and others make up what is often referred to as the Canadian "welfare state." It is a term used frequently, but what exactly does it mean? What does a welfare state do?

Briefly, the term **welfare state**—sometimes referred to as the Keynesian welfare state (KWS) after John Maynard Keynes, refers to *a system of state provision of people's social needs outside private markets.* Unlike regular commodities that are bought and sold, social needs are **de-commodified** and provided as a right of citizenship (Esping-Andersen, 1990).

In practical terms, the postwar years saw the KWS result in what is sometimes termed "the Great Compromise" between capital and labour. Labour accepted the right of owners to a profit and to make decisions regarding company matters. In return, capital (that is, owners and managers) accepted the right of labour to organize and to bargain. The state, meanwhile, provided the legal, political, and often financial underpinning for this compromise. During the Depression and the Second World War, for example, Canada experienced a series of bitter strikes (Roberts, 1998: 7). In 1944, however, the Canadian government passed legislation granting private sector workers the right to organize, to bargain collectively, and to strike (Panitch and Swartz, 1988). This and similar labour legislation and decisions (such as unemployment insurance and the Rand Formula), introduced a period of relative harmony to labour relations. In effect, the state set the rules for Canada's postwar form of capital accumulation. But, in doing so, the state also shaped more broadly the contours of Canadian society.

The state's greater role in Canadian society after the Second World War was not restricted, however, to areas of health and social security. The late 1960s also saw the state—both federal and provincial—finance a rapid expansion of post-secondary education (Wanner, 1999). Between 1971 and 2001, the percentage of Canadians 15 years of age and older with some post-secondary education rose from 17.1 to 35.6, while the percentage of those with university education climbed from 4.8 to 15.4 (look ahead to Table 13.2). In 2000, Canada sported the highest percentage of college and university educated people, aged 25 to 64, among the 30 countries belonging to the Organization of Economic Cooperation and Development: 41 percent, followed by the United States at 37 percent (Statistics Canada, 2003b: 26 and 32).

The state also became more concerned with issues of nation-building and social inequality. Especially worth noting in regard to these are the Royal Commission on Bilingualism and Biculturalism, also known as the Dunton-Laurendeau Commission (Chapter Three); the Hawthorn-Tremblay Report into Canada's indigenous peoples (see Chapter Twelve); and the Royal Commission on the Status of Women in Canada, also known as the Bird Commission. Echoing President Lyndon Johnson's war on poverty in the United States, similar efforts were made in Canada, highlighted by a massive government study (1973–1980) into the efficacy of a Guaranteed Annual Income (see Hum, 1983), in which many sociologists played a major role.

THE CANADIAN WELFARE STATE IN PERSPECTIVE

In the 1960s, many theorists went so far as to argue that the KWS represented a form of social organization toward which all modern industrial societies, including the Soviet Union, would in time converge (Bell, 1961; Kerr et al., 1964; Galbraith, 1969; Wilensky, 1975). From the beginning, however, no two welfare states were alike. Esping-Andersen (1990) describes three broad types of welfare states: **conservative welfare states**, such as Austria, France, Germany, and Italy; **social-democratic welfare states**, such as Sweden, Norway, and Denmark; and **liberal democratic welfare states**, such as the United States and Australia (see also Baker, 1996; Olsen, 2002). Of these, social-democratic welfare states exhibit high taxes, but also extensive and universal social programs, while liberal democratic welfare states have low taxes, few social programs, and programs that are means-tested, that is, not available to all. Conservative welfare states fall somewhere in-between, with moderate to high taxes and fairly extensive programs, but ones that often are designed to maintain traditional class and gender hierarchies. Finally, until the 1990s, Japan, with a corporatist feudal structure in which workers exchanged loyalty for lifetime security in the employ of large companies, constituted a fourth system of providing welfare services (outside the formal state). Since then, however, a prolonged recession has been unravelling this bargain as companies have laid off workers.

Canada's form of welfare state is a kind of hybrid. It best fits the liberal-democratic model, with its emphasis upon means-testing, modest levels of social transfers, belief in individualism, faith in markets, and protection of private profits (Li, 1996). At the same time, however, Canada's welfare state also embraces some conservative elements (for example, an emphasis upon maintaining traditional gender roles) and social democratic elements (elements related to social equality and universality, for instance) (see Baker, 1996; Finkel, 1997; Rice and Prince, 2000). Finally, we should note the criticisms of many feminist theorists that none of the existing models adequately deal with the problem of poverty for many women, insofar as their situation results from barriers to full participation in the labour force. That is, de-commodification *per se* is not unimportant to issues of equality, but it does not address the real inequalities resulting from a stratified labour market (see Olsen, 2002).

By European standards, Canada's welfare state programs historically have been far from generous or extensive (see Finkel, 1997; Olsen, 2002). In 1993, for example, Canada spent 19.7 percent of its GDP on social expenditures (including health, education, and social services). Compare this with Austria (25.8 percent), Belgium (27 percent), Denmark (31 percent), Finland (35.4 percent), France (28.7 percent), Germany (28.3 percent), Italy (25 percent), the Netherlands (30.2 percent), Norway (29.3 percent), Sweden (38 percent), Switzerland (20.6 percent), and the United Kingdom (23.4 percent) (see Olsen, 1999: 244–245).

But compared with that of the United States, the Canadian welfare state that developed after the 1960s was generally more extensive, generous, and universal (for instance, through public health care). In 1993, for example, only 15.6 percent of America's GDP went toward social expenditures (Olsen, 1999: 244–245). Of course, whether they live in the United States, Canada, or Sweden, people still require many of the same services. The difference lies in whether these services are publicly provided, requiring larger tax revenues, or paid for by individuals out of their own pocket, in which case state taxes may be reduced. Among G-7 countries in 1995, the United States had the lowest rate of taxes per gross domestic product, 27.6 percent, compared (for example) with Canada at 36.1 percent, Germany at 39.1 percent, Italy at 41.8 percent, and France at 44.5 percent (OECD, 1997).

Why the relative differences between Canada and the United States in regard to the social welfare state? **Cultural theory** points to the greater sense of collective responsibility and a greater historical acceptance of state activism in Canada than in the more individualistic and socially fragmented United States. By contrast, **power resources theory** points to the role and capacity of social actors (such as unions or women's organizations) in mobilizing and pushing for political reforms. Since the 1970s, for example, the strength of Canadian unions (especially public sector unions) has grown while that of American unions has declined (see Russell, 1990: 262). Finally, **polity-centred/neo-institutional theory** points to differences in the political and institutional structures of the two countries as the causes of welfare state differences (Olsen, 2002).

By the late 1980s, however, Canada faced increased pressure to lower corporate and personal taxes and to accept the minimalist welfare state model of its American counterpart (Li, 1996) (see Chapter Nine). Though distinct in some areas (such as medicare), Canada moved closer throughout the 1990s to the American welfare state model (Olsen, 2002). Closely tied to the "rise and fall" of Canada's welfare state during the postwar years were also material, cultural, and ideological changes in the role of women.

WOMEN IN THE CHANGING CANADIAN SOCIETY

As the Second World War began, women at last had formal political power, but little actual political, economic, or social power. The war began the process of changing this.

Economically, while many women remained to work the farms deserted by men fighting overseas, many others were pressed into non-traditional occupations in the wartime factories, such as welding. Yet others moved out of the clerical ranks to take on higher administrative roles in the growing public service. Fears that the end of war would see mass unemployment proved unwarranted. Indeed, the demand for skilled labour increased (see below) and women now ably filled it.

Of course, some women did return to the home and to unpaid labour to raise families; the postwar baby boom was about to start. But a large number of women remained in the workplace—though sometimes casually and often shunted to the service end of the labour market—attracted both by the social and economic opportunities. Moreover, the period after 1945 saw an intensification of consumerism that could be met only by families with one-and-a-half (if not two) salaries.

To a degree, women's increasing participation in Canada's labour force mirrored that of other countries. Participation was more intense in Canada, however, and increased even more after 1960. Between 1960 and 1975, female labour force participation rose from 28 percent to 41 percent, increasing again over the next two decades to nearly 60 percent in 2000 (Krahn and Lowe, 2002: 49). In turn, these changes in the female participation rate set off a series of unintended consequences for fertility rates, family structures, gender roles, and family and individual finances. After 1975, for example, dual income families, rather than single income families, became the Canadian norm.

Other interrelated factors besides labour economics and increased consumerism were changing the situation of women, however. The idea of greater individual freedom took hold in Canadian society as elsewhere. Likewise, the 1950s saw a loosening of cultural prescriptions for male and female gender roles and behaviours, as sometimes—and sometimes not—reflected in Hollywood films. Technological advances in the early 1960s, notably the contraceptive pill, further changed sexual behaviours and gender relationships. In turn, and over time, these things also began changing family structures. Divorce rates rose while, despite the incidence of the baby boom, the average family size declined.

Underlying the changing status of women in Canada (and elsewhere) was also a transformative change in ideology led by a second wave of feminism (see Chapter One). **First wave feminism**, beginning in the mid-nineteenth century, sought to gain for women equal property rights and the right to vote. These rights were gradually obtained, but significant inequalities remained (Macionis et al., 2002: 247). The 1960s brought **second wave feminism**, inspired by writers such as Simone de Beauvoir, Kate Millett, and Germaine Greer. Whereas the attention of first wave feminists had been upon political institutions, second wave feminists, many of whom had been involved in student protest movements, concentrated on establishing women's organizations from below, in civil society (Brym, 2001: 490). (By the 1990s, some scholars noted the onset of **third wave feminism**, launched by women belonging to ethnic minorities and questioning the dominance within the feminist movement of middle-class white women [Morrow, 1994: 18].)

As in the previous century, those in dominant positions—but also many in Canada at large, including some women—often opposed feminist demands for greater equality. In the mid-1970s, a backlash against the gains made by women began building, finding its political champions in the 1980s and 1990s in a series of New Right political parties. Often, the complaints of these parties and their supporters were economic. One might argue, however, that the conflict also was, and is, cultural; that women's demands (and gains) upset what Hiller (1987) termed the **symbolic order**, that is, *the set of values, beliefs, and behaviours that lend predictability to our everyday surroundings*. More often than not after the 1970s, these fears were focused not only on the feminist movement but also on Canada's changing ethnic and racial profile.

LABOUR MARKETS, IMMIGRATION, AND MULTICULTURALISM

Canada's KWS, like that of other countries, was predicated on a prosperous national economy and full employment, since employed workers could pay taxes and would not draw upon social security. At the macro level, Canada's finances to pay for these expanded programs remained particularly dependent, however, upon the export of raw resources. Meanwhile, Canada's economy after the Second World War also underwent a substantial transformation.

Most especially, Canada experienced a gradual change in its labour market as jobs shifted from the **primary sector** (for example, resource extraction industries such as agriculture and forestry) to the **secondary sector** (manufacturing, construction, and the like) and the **tertiary (or service) sector**, where the commodities exchanged have no tangible form (as in health and education, retail trade, restaurant services, and finance). In 1891, for example, 49 percent of Canada's labour force worked in primary industry, compared with 20 percent in secondary industry, and 31 percent in the service sector. By 1951, however, 31 percent of Canada's labour force worked in the secondary sector, of which the auto industry was key, while 47 percent were employed in services (Krahn and Lowe, 2002: 56–57).

The following decades saw a further growth in Canada's service industries, while the other sectors declined in relative importance to the economy. At the same time, however, the service sector itself became bifurcated between jobs in an **upper tier** (employing well-paid and well-educated people, often "symbolic analysts" able to manipulate information) and a **lower tier** (employing often the young or very old, often marginalized, at low wages in such things as the fast food, retail, and hostelry industries). Between 1988 and 1998, for example, the number of workers employed in professional, scientific, and technical occupations rose from 526 000 to 897 000, while similarly the number of people in accommodation and food services rose from 751 000 in 1988 to 916 000 in 1998 (*CGA*, 1999: 232–233).

At least immediately after the Second World War, however, Canada experienced a heightened demand for labour, especially skilled labour. Some of this demand was met by returning veterans, whom the government retrained under generous financial terms. Especially in the growing service industries, women (as noted above) played also a particularly large role in filling demand (Lowe, 1987; Li, 1996: 149). Canadian industry's demand for labour after the Second World War was inexhaustible, however. Immigration to Canada had virtually ceased during the Depression and subsequent war years (see Table 7.1). Now the Canadian government once more opened up the immigration tap to let in new workers.

At first glance, Canada's postwar immigration policy seems remarkably similar to that during earlier periods of economic expansion (see Chapter Seven), especially in favouring immigrants from Britain and western Europe (ECC, 1991). But there were important differences. While British immigrants at first remained favoured, there were fewer people wishing to come from that country. Also, Canada faced increased competition from Australia and the United States throughout the 1950s for a shrinking pool of labour, especially skilled labour. Thus, Canadian policy gradually stretched to allow more immigrants from non-traditional source countries, first eastern and southern Europeans (especially those escaping communism), and later people from Asia, Africa, and the Caribbean. Changes in the Immigration Act of 1967, which saw the introduction of a point system, furthered this transition. Before this time, race and ethnicity were explicit criteria for entry. After this time, immigration and labour market needs became more closely aligned. The criteria for entry shifted first to educational qualifications, then (by the 1980s) to financial and class (that is, business) qualifications (Harrison, 1996). Table 8.1 compares the birthplaces of immigrants before 1961 with those of later arrivals. Note the dramatic shift away from Europe, especially western and northern Europe, toward immigrants from Asia, in particular.

While earlier immigration reflected largely the state's need to populate new territories, immigration after the 1970s was influenced by broader social changes. Cultural changes, including the introduction of the birth control pill in the early 1960s, brought about a rapid decline in Canada's birth rate. By the 1970s, some policy-makers feared Canada's working-age population might one day be insufficient to pay for the expanding services required of an aging population. Immigration thus became tied not only directly to economic needs but also to the growing fiscal requirements of the welfare state (see Li, 1996).

The changes to Canada's immigration policy were particularly noticeable in some major cities (Toronto, Montreal, Vancouver), where sizable ethnic communities arose. As in the past, however, the settlement of new immigrants was not uniformly spread across Canada. These early settlement patterns continue in the ethnic makeup of Canada's provinces today. As Table 8.2 shows, British ancestry tends to predominate on the East Coast and decline generally as we move west, while French ancestry dominates Quebec (see Part One). By contrast, a large proportion of the Prairie provinces' population traces its ancestry to middle and eastern Europe, while the West Coast features a large number of people of Asian ancestry.

Note also, however, the increasingly mixed nature of ethnic identifications in Canada. While a larger proportion of Canadians have either British or French ancestry, these are not exclusive in many instances of other heritages.

Finally, at the political level, these changes resulted in 1971 in Canada's adoption of a policy of **multiculturalism**. Two years earlier, Canada had adopted the policy of official bilingualism in response to the rise of Quebec nationalism (Chapter Three). Many people accepted (albeit some grudgingly) the need for two official languages to bind the country together and address the demands of Quebec's sizable francophone population. Fewer, especially visible minorities and Canada's Native peoples, accepted the notion of two official cultures, however.

Multiculturalism today is an official mainstay of Canadian identity. Supporters of the policy contend that Canada is leading the way in becoming a postmodern society, and that the country's ability to manage cultural differences adds to its strength, economically, culturally, and politically. The policy also has critics, however. In the eyes of some, multiculturalism merely hides the continuing reality of an ethnic hierarchy in Canada. Others see it as an expensive and destructive policy that encourages people to retain past identities and

TABLE 8.1   Immigrant Status and Period of Immigration and Place of Birth, 2001 (total and percent)

Ethnic Origin	Total Immigrant Population*	Before 1961	%	1961-2001	%
Americas	837 055	47 835	5.3	789 220	17.3
North America	238 350	34 945	3.9	203 405	4.5
Central America	108 085	1595	0.2	106 490	2.3
Caribbean and Bermuda	294 050	6985	0.8	287 065	6.3
South America	196 560	4310	0.5	192 250	4.2
Europe	2 287 555	809 325	90.5	1 478 230	32.5
Western Europe	423 805	215 135	24.1	208 670	4.6
Eastern Europe	471 365	135 425	15.1	335 940	7.4
Northern Europe	677 015	250 875	28.0	426 140	9.4
Southern Europe	715 370	207 900	23.2	507 470	11.1
Africa	282 600	4635	0.5	277 965	6.1
Western Africa	32 885	75	—	32 810	0.7
Eastern Africa	108 035	535	—	107 500	2.4
Northern Africa	93 165	2595	0.3	90 570	2.0
Central Africa	12 920	125	—	12 795	0.3
Southern Africa	35 595	1305	0.1	34 290	0.8
Asia	1 989 180	28 850	3.2	1 960 330	43.0
West Central Asia and the Middle East	285 585	4445	0.5	281 140	6.2
Eastern Asia	730 595	18 325	2.0	712 270	15.6
Southeast Asia	469 110	2240	0.3	466 870	10.2
Southern Asia	503 895	3845	0.4	500 050	11.0
Oceania	47 935	3020	0.3	44 915	1.0
Other	4160	795	0.1	3365	0.1
Total	**5 448 480**	**894 465**	**100.0**	**4 554 015**	**100.0**

Source: Adapted from Statistics Canada Web site at www.12.statcan.ca/english/census01/products/standard/themes/RetreiveProductTable.cfm.

* Total population does not include non-permanent residents. Discrepancies in percentages are due to rounding.

TABLE 8.2	Canadian Population, by Ethnic Origin and Province, 1996 (in percent)[1]												
Ethnic Origin	CANADA	Nfld	PEI	NS	NB	Que	Ont	Man	Sask	Alta	BC	Yuk	NWT
British[2]	17.1	57.7	42.8	33.0	25.0	3.0	21.1	15.7	14.3	16.5	21.5	17.1	9.5
French[3]	9.4	1.3	6.4	4.3	17.0	29.3	2.9	3.1	1.9	1.2	1.3	2.3	1.4
British and French	3.0	3.3	10.6	7.2	7.3	2.4	3.3	2.2	1.9	2.3	2.3	3.0	1.6
British and/or French & Other[4]	21.3	13.4	23.3	26.7	22.5	11.4	22.6	25.6	30.2	29.3	26.1	31.3	17.5
Canadian[5]	20.7	21.5	13.6	20.8	24.7	39.0	14.2	11.5	13.7	15.9	12.1	18.2	8.9
Aboriginal	1.2	1.4	0.3	0.9	0.9	0.8	0.7	7.3	7.4	2.4	2.1	11.8	51.1
European	13.1	0.6	1.8	4.0	1.5	6.4	17.9	20.8	19.7	16.2	13.1	8.5	3.6
Western	3.9	0.2	1.3	2.7	0.9	0.7	4.1	9.1	10.4	7.5	5.6	4.6	1.6
Northern	0.6	0.1	0.1	0.2	0.2	—	0.4	1.0	1.8	1.3	1.4	1.0	0.4
Eastern	3.0	0.1	0.2	0.4	0.2	0.9	3.7	7.7	6.9	5.4	3.1	2.1	1.0
Southern	4.8	0.2	0.2	0.5	0.2	4.0	8.6	2.1	0.6	1.8	2.7	0.7	0.5
Other European	0.7	—	—	0.1	—	0.9	1.1	0.8	—	0.3	0.3	0.2	0.1
Asian, Arab and African	8.4	0.5	0.7	1.7	0.6	3.8	11.1	5.0	2.0	7.6	15.1	1.9	1.8
Arab and West Asian	1.4	—	0.3	0.5	0.2	1.5	1.3	0.2	0.2	.7	0.6	0.2	0.2
South Asian	2.1	0.1	—	0.3	0.1	0.6	3.2	0.9	0.3	1.7	3.8	0.5	0.3
East and Southern Asian	4.4	0.2	0.3	0.4	0.3	1.5	5.5	3.6	1.3	4.9	10.4	1.1	1.2
African	0.5	—	—	0.4	0.1	0.3	0.9	0.3	0.2	0.3	0.2	—	0.1
Pacific Islanders	—	—	—	—	—	—	—	—	—	—	0.1	—	—
Latin, Central, and South American	0.4	—	—	—	—	0.6	0.5	0.2	0.1	0.4	0.3	0.1	0.1
Caribbean	1.1	—	—	0.1	—	1.2	1.9	0.4	0.1	0.3	0.1	—	0.1
Other Single and Multiple Origins	4.1	0.3	0.5	1.4	0.4	2.1	4.2	8.2	8.7	7.0	5.4	5.8	4.4
Total	100.0	100.0	100.0	100.0	100.0	100.0	100.0	100.0	100.0	100.0	100.0	100.0	100.0

Source: Calculated from the Statistics Canada Web site *Nation Tables*, Census 1996, at www.statcan.ca/english/Pgdb/demo28a.htm.

1. Total population includes non-permanent residents.
2. Includes British single responses and the British-only multiple.
3. Includes French single responses and the French-only multiple.
4. Includes British Isles and Canadian; British Isles and other; British Isles, Canadian, and other; French and Canadian; French Canadian, and other; British Isles, French, and Canadian; British Isles, French, and other; and British Isles, French, Canadian, and other.
5. Includes Canadian single responses and Canadian and other. Discrepancies in percentages are due to rounding.

live in ethnic quarters of Canadian cities rather than forge together a common sense of being Canadian (Bissoondath, 1994).

The impact of the "new ethnics" upon Canadian identity was not particularly evident in the 1960s. Nonetheless, a new sense of identity already was emerging in English-speaking Canada.

THE RISE OF ENGLISH-CANADIAN NATIONALISM

After the Second World War, English-speaking Canada remained very British. It was not until the Canadian Citizenship Act of 1946, for example, that the designation of "Canadian citizen" was created. Before that time, Canadians were British subjects, and many—at least those outside Quebec—were quite content to hold British passports.

Into the mid-1960s, Canadian culture outside Quebec also remained decidedly British. At a time when there were only two television channels (CBC and CTV), a large number of British programs filled the airwaves. Comedians like Eric Sykes, Sidney James, and Tony Hancock set the stage for the *Monty Python* invasion later in the decade, while such English adventure shows as *Robin Hood*, *Danger Man*, *The Prisoner*, and *The Avengers* were standard viewing for many English-speaking Canadians growing up.

Beneath the surface, however, Canada's British ties were weakening. Economically, bilateral trade between Canada and Britain declined sharply after the Second World War, replaced by trade with the United States (see Marchildon, 1995; Norrie and Owram, 1996). Politically, Canada's ties to the throne also were eroding. In 1951, for example, Britain's Privy Council was replaced as Canada's last court of appeal by Canada's Supreme Court, setting the stage for Canada's later dropping of other British symbols.

Britain's declining role in Canadian life reflected in part a growing pride and confidence among Canadians themselves. Success in the war caused English Canadians as a whole to become less parochial and to slough off some of their colonial anxieties. Many wanted Canada to take a greater, and more independent, role among the victorious states. Thus, Canada after 1945 proudly took out membership in the United Nations, NATO, and other international organizations. Likewise, it participated in the Korean conflict (1950–1953) and took a leading role in settling the 1956 Suez conflict (for which Lester Pearson won the Nobel Peace Prize). Unfortunately, each of these paths also led to policy convergence with the United States. Thus, as Canada drew away from Britain's embrace, it also found itself increasingly under America's blanket. The arrival of new immigrants from non-traditional cultures did not immediately remedy the problem; indeed, it added to considerable anxiety.

In short, English-speaking Canada by the late 1950s was seeking a new vision of itself, an identity. The result was the rise of English-Canadian nationalism. English-Canadian nationalism was not supported by all elements. Business generally disliked, or feared, nationalism in any form. Francophones viewed English-Canadian nationalism as merely a new variation on assimilation. Regional elements often feared Ottawa as much as nationalists feared America (Finkel, 1997: 157). Nonetheless, a sizable portion of people in English Canada favoured the heightened nationalism of the time.

The new nationalism was not of one type, however. Some forms of nationalism expressed nostalgia over the loss of things British (especially the adoption of the Maple Leaf flag over the Union Jack in 1965). Some variations were defensive, a response to the rise of

Quebec nationalism or to the increased influence of the United States. Others were frankly imperialist, as when John Diefenbaker in the election of 1958 invoked his vision of the Canadian North (see Chapter Eleven). The forms came in different political and ideological variations, defying simple description. In general, however, English-Canadian nationalism manifested itself in three specific ways: politically, culturally, and economically.

Politically, English-Canadian nationalism can be divided into formal and popular politics. At the formal level, Canadian prime ministers after 1950 found themselves in a series of delicate skirmishes with their American counterparts. Until Roosevelt, most American presidents had ignored Canada. Canada was viewed as an extension of the United States, a place of eccentric country cousins. In the context of the Cold War, however, the United States demanded particular obedience from its allies, beginning with Canada. Thus, efforts by the Diefenbaker administration (1957–1963) at an independent defence policy, not to mention encouraging trade with Castro's Cuba and Communist China, aroused particular antagonism. President Kennedy called Diefenbaker an "SOB" and in the 1963 Canadian election gave encouragement and strategic support to successful Liberal efforts to unseat him. Relations between Prime Minister Lester Pearson (1963–1968) and President Lyndon Johnson (following Kennedy's assassination) proved no better, however. Quickly, Canada found itself at odds with the United States over the war in Vietnam and trade policy, especially the 1965 Auto Pact (see Martin, 1982; Norrie and Owram, 1996). Pearson, like Diefenbaker before and Trudeau after, learned the truth of the axiom that states do not have friends, they have interests. Increasingly, the interests of Canada and the United States were diverging.

English-Canadian nationalism also manifested itself politically at the popular level. In keeping with the times internationally, many of these expressions were anti-American and directed at American imperialism in Vietnam and elsewhere. But there was also widespread revulsion directed at "the American way of life" in general, as reflected nightly on American television. Race riots and the killings of civil rights workers and politicians provided an ample "negative model" for Canadians (and for between 70 000 and 125 000 American draft dodgers and deserters [Finkel, 1997: 154]) who wanted to build a better society in North America.

Even more than politically, however, English-Canadian nationalism was cultural. In 1951, the Massey Commission appointed by Prime Minister Louis St. Laurent (1948–1957) outlined the need for Canada to develop its own cultural institutions and distinctly Canadian voice. The commission's report focused on high culture and drew little initial response, official or otherwise (see Morton, 1997). Eventually, however, such institutions as the Canada Council, the National Film Board, and Telefilm Canada were formed to encourage Canadian culture. Whether these institutions were responsible for the spread of cultural nationalism or not is debatable. Nonetheless, except in the area of television and film that remained largely overwhelmed by American capital and technology, a distinctively Canadian cultural industry slowly emerged in English Canada. In the area of literature, the 1950s and 1960s saw the rise to prominence of a host of writers, including Pierre Berton, Leonard Cohen, Robertson Davies, Timothy Findley, Margaret Laurence, and Irving Layton. (A few intellectuals, notably Marshall McLuhan, even became international cultural icons.) Other writers, often women (such as Margaret Atwood, Alice Munro, and Carol Shields), followed in the 1970s, and were joined later by Michael Ondaatje and Rohinton Mistry. (These latter two examples also point to the increasingly multicultural nature of Canada over time.)

There had long been a Canadian popular music scene, stretching from jazz to pop to country. Except at the local and regional level, however, much of it was derivative of American music. Canada's climb aboard the rock 'n' roll bandwagon of the 1950s continued this trend. But the late 1960s saw Canadian music also take a nationalistic turn. Bands such as The Band (headed by Robbie Robertson) and Blood, Sweat and Tears (David Clayton-Thomas) became internationally known, as did individual artists such as Neil Young, Joni Mitchell, and Ann Murray. More importantly, each also remained distinctly Canadian, as often evidenced in their lyrics, setting the stage for bands such as The Tragically Hip in the 1990s. In keeping with the times, the music of this period sometimes took on an overtly anti-American tenor, as in the words to The Guess Who's "American Woman" and Gordon Lightfoot's "Black Day in July" (about the Detroit riots).

ECONOMIC NATIONALISM: THEORY AND PRACTICE

Among the subgenres of nationalism, however, economic nationalism was arguably the most influential. After years of growth, the Canadian economy in the late 1950s entered a recession (Norrie and Owram, 1996). In this context, a number of influential Canadians—led by political economist Melville Watkins (1963), conservative philosopher George Grant (1965), and Liberal finance minister Walter Gordon (1966)—asked (each in his own way) why Canada continued to be "the world's richest underdeveloped country" (Levitt, 1970: 25). In particular, many noted that Canada's declining economic performance coincided with increased foreign, mainly American, control of the economy. Were the two events related? For economic nationalists, the answer was a definite *yes*.

The British economist John Maynard Keynes once remarked that there is nothing so practical as a good theory. But good theory must first arise out of the need to examine real issues. The economic nationalism of the 1960s arose out of genuine concerns over Canada's future; in turn it provided impetus for a renaissance of investigation into the roots of Canada's economic, political, and social development (see Laxer, 1991), a renaissance that, in some instances, had practical impacts upon Canadian policy.

At least initially, these studies took their inspiration from the work of political economist Harold Innis. Years before, Innis had developed **staples theory** to describe Canada's particular course of economic and social development. For him, Canada's founding as a hinterland producer of raw exports for world markets, over which it had no control, had curtailed normal economic and political development. The result was Canada's being caught in a **staples trap**. The nature of the trap was that, while staple products—cod, furs, trees, and wheat—were often profitable, they were inherently unstable commodities, subject to boom and bust. An economy built upon raw resources alone did not develop the forward and backward linkages and social structure characteristic of a fully developed economy (see Innis, 1995).

Innis's staples theory, based on the historical relationship between the metropolis and the hinterland, bears some relationship to **dependency theory**, which *emphasizes the unequal relationship between the core and periphery in the world capitalist system set in motion by early colonialism* (see Frank, 1975), though the latter utilizes a Marxian class analysis absent in Innis. Dependency theory did not fit the Canadian situation well, however. After all, many parts of Canada by the 1960s were heavily industrialized, while residing uneasily with pockets of underdevelopment. Moreover, the benefits of industrialization were—as now—unevenly distributed by gender, race, ethnicity, and region (see Panitch, 1977; Laxer, 1991; Clement, 1997). Hence, the years following the late 1960s saw a "new" tradition of political economy that took analyses of Canadian dependency in different explanatory directions.

Some used **elite theory** to explain Canada's development. Naylor (1975), for example, went back in history to argue that merchants concentrated in export industries (especially the fur trade) had conspired against industrial capitalists to hinder economic development (the **merchants against industry thesis**). Clement (1975) meanwhile argued that a troika of elites continued to dominate the Canadian economy: a **parasite elite** (foreign owners and managers), an **indigenous elite** (Canadian owners and managers), and a **comprador elite** (Canadians managing companies in Canada for foreign firms).

Others, however, used **class theory** to explain the trajectory of Canadian development. Panitch (1981), for example, argued that, ironically, the relative power of Canada's proletariat during the country's initial stage of industrialization development (1870–1910) hindered capitalism's accumulation of surplus. By contrast, Laxer (1989) argued that Canada had been a successful late industrializing country but had fallen back into dependency. The cause of this retraction was, claimed Laxer, the political weakness of Canada's agrarian class during this period that prevented Canada from adopting the kind of policies (low taxes, easy credit, the targeted construction of railroads, and a robust defence policy) that worked successfully in similar countries, notably Sweden.

Many of these studies focused particularly on the impact of the National Policy in Canada's economic development. You will recall the National Policy's use of tariffs was meant to encourage manufacturing within Canada (Chapter Seven), making it more expensive to purchase imported products, a policy referred to as **import substitution**. As intended, the result had been the building of a number of American branch plants in Canada, beginning in the early part of the twentieth century, to feed the Canadian market and also to gain preferential entry at that time into other Commonwealth countries, especially Britain. In the short term, the economy boomed. Employment in new industries soared, out-migration decreased, banks made profits. The long-term impacts, however, were less rosy.

According to the economic nationalists, several problems accompanied the building of these branch plants (see Laxer 1991). First, company profits were unavailable for further domestic investment. Finkel (1997: 161) notes that, in the 1960s, dividends to American owners exceeded American investment in Canada. Alternatively, the profits were often used to buy up more Canadian companies. Second, branch plants tended to obtain materials and personnel in the home country. Thus, Canada lost the backward and forward linkages, or "multiplier effects," necessary to develop the economy fully. Third, the branch plants were not sources of innovation. Statistics showed Canadian companies invested little in research and development. Instead, Canadian branch plants produced copies of American (or other foreign) products for the local market, a pattern known as the **miniature replica effect** (Finkel, 1997: 163; Levitt, 1970).

Ultimately, however, economic nationalists also saw the issue in broadly political terms. American Secretary of State John Foster Dulles had once opined there are two ways to conquer a country: by force of arms or by taking over its economy (Laxer, 1995: 229). The economic nationalists took Dulles at his word, arguing no country could for long remain politically sovereign with an economy controlled by a foreign power.

George Grant (1965) stated the case eloquently. A conservative professor of philosophy and a grandson of George Monro Grant and Francis Parkin (see Chapter Seven), Grant argued that the creeping continentalism practised by Liberal governments and the country's business class since the Second World War could only mean the end of Canada.

But Grant also traced Canada's problems to important changes in Canada's dominant ideology, to which we now turn.

POLITICAL IDEOLOGY IN CANADA

We have previously examined the notion of ideology in relation to the development of modern Quebec (Chapter Three). Here we want to ask, What is Canada's dominant political ideology as a whole, and how does it compare with that of the United States? The most famous thesis answering these questions belongs to an American political sociologist, Seymour Martin Lipset (1968b; 1986; 1990; 1996). Lipset has long argued that Canadian political values fall between those of the United States and Great Britain. He argues that Canadians stress conformity and obedience while Americans value liberty, egalitarianism, individualism, populism, and laissez-faire (Lipset, 1996).

Lipset's thesis is contentious. Many would argue that even if such depictions were once correct, they are not today. Canadians today are far from deferential, for example (see Newman, 1995; Nevitte, 1996; Adams, 1998; also Chapter Nine). Others suggest that even the historical evidence does not support Lipset. Grabb et al. (1999; 2000) contend that the American revolutionary leaders were republican individualists, not the liberal individualists identified by Lipset, and that the colonial masses believed in "local communalism," not rugged non-conformity. More broadly, it seems the beliefs of most early Americans were like those of the Loyalists who came to Canada.

Thereafter it seems likely, however, that the war of 1812 and the failed rebellions of 1837–38 reinforced conservative elements in Canada. Meanwhile, the United States experienced (among other things) a civil war followed by rapid industrialization. There, myths of rugged individualism took hold, reflected in the rise in the late nineteenth century of self-made "robber barons" and the arrival on bookshelves of Dale Carnegie's famous tome on the power of positive thinking.

In Canada, by this time, conservatism was the dominant ideology, both inside and outside Quebec. The nineteenth-century form of English-Canadian conservatism was of a particular type, however. It was what is referred to as **Toryism**.

Like its British counterpart, English-Canadian Toryism was monarchist. Likewise, it lauded tradition and order, and believed in a natural order of things that extended across class, race, religion, and gender. Finally, Canadian Toryism's belief in a natural social hierarchy was also (in its better moments, at least) balanced by a deep sense of *noblesse oblige* toward those less fortunate.

But certain characteristics also distinguished Canadian Toryism from its British forebear. First, for historical, political, and geographic reasons, Canadian Toryism was staunchly anti-American; thus, the Tory party's opposition to free trade in both 1891 and 1911. Second, for similar practical reasons, the Canadian Tory tradition also espoused a particularly strong belief in a positive role for the state both in the economy and in society at large; hence, Macdonald's formulation of the National Policy (Chapter Seven) and, later, R.B. Bennett's founding of the CBC.

By the 1960s, however, the Tory tradition in English-speaking Canada was in decline. Its decline was only partly due to Britain's fading presence in Canadian life. More fundamental were two other factors: the dominance of both the Liberal Party and of liberal ideals in Canada (and much of the world) throughout the twentieth century, and the growing influence of the United States upon Canada, culturally and economically.

This is perhaps the key point of Grant's (1965) *Lament for a Nation*. He argues fundamentally that Toryism had been an ideological bulwark against Canada's absorption into the American empire, supporting a strong role for the state in the economy. By contrast, liberalism, with its faith in free markets and support of continentalism, could only result in Canada's demise. Canadian liberalism was entirely compatible with, and submersible in, the American version of conservatism, "republicanism":

> The Americans who call themselves "Conservatives" have the right to the title only in a particular sense. In fact, they are old-fashioned liberals. They stand for the freedom of the individual to use his property as he wishes, and for a limited government which must keep out of the marketplace. Their concentration on freedom from governmental interference has more to do with nineteenth-century liberalism than with traditional conservatism, which asserts the right of the community to restrain freedom in the name of the common good....Their "right-wing" and "left-wing" are just different species of liberalism (Grant, 1965: 64–65).

Grant's arguments regarding the fate of Toryism are sometimes viewed as romantic more than empirical, though Horowitz (1966) later supported Grant's contention that Toryism wedded to socialism had played an important role in creating Canada. The point is that Grant—along with Gordon, Watkins, and even Diefenbaker in his "One Canada" speeches—held a particular ideal of Canada that invariably challenged the dominant ideology of liberalism and continentalism.

But it clashed also with Quebec nationalist aims (Chapter Three) and the regional realities of Canadian development. Years before, in 1938, Innis (1995) had argued that Canada's failure to construct a genuinely national economic policy would result over time in a strengthening of federal-provincial and inter-provincial conflict. Given the historic roots of its founding, it was perhaps inevitable that the centre of much of this conflict was the emergent new West, especially the province of Alberta, where ideological beliefs about rugged individualism and the efficacy of free markets were particularly strong and where the oil industry was about to take off.

THE NEW WEST

No part of Canada changed more after 1945 than the West. The changes were particularly apparent in Alberta and British Columbia, which experienced enormous population growth and industrialization. But all the western provinces changed in important ways, and influenced Canada as they did.

In 1941, Saskatchewan still had the largest population in western Canada: 896 000 people, compared with Manitoba's 777 000, Alberta's 796 000, and British Columbia's 818 000 (see Table 1.1). Twenty years later, British Columbia's population had doubled, to 1 629 000, while that of Alberta and Manitoba had risen to 1 332 000 and 922 000, respectively. Saskatchewan's population, after declining in the 1950s, had risen to 925 000. Thereafter, population growth continued to tilt toward the westernmost provinces. By

1998, more than four million people resided in British Columbia, nearly three million in Alberta. By contrast, Manitoba's population had stabilized at around 1.1 million, and Saskatchewan's at just over a million (*CGA*, 1999: 42).

These population changes do not tell the whole story. Like the rest of the country after the war, western Canada experienced rapid urbanization (Macionis et al., 1999: 547; also Driedger, 1991; *CGA*, 1999: 55). This occurred even in Manitoba and Saskatchewan. Winnipeg, for example, grew from 412 000 people in 1956 to 667 000 in 1996. During the same period, Regina's population went from nearly 90 000 to 193 000, while Saskatoon's population increased from 73 000 to 219 000. The greatest urban growth, however, occurred in British Columbia and Alberta. Between 1956 and 1996, Vancouver's population nearly trebled, from 665 000 to more than 1.8 million people. Victoria's population also increased rapidly, from 134 000 to 303 000. In Alberta during this period, Edmonton's population expanded from nearly 255 000 to 862 000, while Calgary's population climbed from 201 000 to nearly 822 000. These figures alone do not tell the tale, however, for many smaller cities and suburbs of larger cities were also spawned during this period. In consequence, the urban centres within areas such as the Vancouver mainland and that between Edmonton and Calgary became largely contiguous. Distinctions between rural and urban blurred.

Western Canada's population changed in other ways. Settled by massive immigration in the early twentieth century, the West had always been culturally, religiously, and ethnically diverse. But this diversity was often suppressed in the name of Anglo-conformity (Chapter Seven). After the 1970s, however, as multiculturalism became Canadian government policy, the West allowed its diversity to emerge more fully (see above).

Underlying these population shifts were fundamental economic changes. The Prairie provinces were originally opened up for agricultural development (Chapter Seven). Changes in the farm economy throughout the twentieth century resulted in a reduction in the agricultural labour force. In 1951, 15.6 percent of Canada's workforce as a whole was employed in agriculture. By 1971, this had fallen to 5.6 percent. By 1991, the proportion of the Canadian workforce employed in agriculture had dropped to 3.6 percent (Li, 1996: 45), dropping to 2.5 percent in 1996. Even then, however, more than nine percent of the workforces of Manitoba and Saskatchewan remained employed in agriculture (Krahn and Lowe, 2002: 60 and 71).

The continuing importance of agriculture to the Saskatchewan economy underpins much of the cultural life of that province, but it also reflects a problem of economic diversity that resulted in a steady out-migration of young workers throughout the twentieth century. By contrast, Manitoba experienced a less drastic fate. The province's—in particular Winnipeg's—heyday came just after the First World War. The Winnipeg General Strike of 1919 (Chapter Seven) was a seminal event in many ways. Thereafter, declines in agriculture resulted in a similar decline in the fortunes of the Winnipeg grain exchange and the city in general. Still, Manitoba's economy is stable and, compared with that of Saskatchewan, relatively diverse, involving agriculture, mixed farming, mining, hydroelectricity, manufacturing, and services.

Meanwhile, Alberta experienced a post-Second World War boom, beginning with the discovery of oil at Leduc in 1947. Alberta's fortunes did not change all at once, or for everyone. Indeed, Alberta technically remained a "have-not" province within Confederation until the late 1960s. Meanwhile, British Columbia also experienced rapid growth, based on a similar exploitation of its raw resources and that province's geographic location on the Pacific Rim.

Economic growth, large or small, in all the western provinces shared certain characteristics. First, it was invariably government-led. Local capital was often scarce, while private, exogenous capital was reluctant to invest in what often seemed tenuous opportunities for profit. Thus, eastern and (more often) foreign capital and expertise were welcomed in under favourable conditions set by the provincial governments. The 1970s, in particular, saw every western government, of every political stripe, engage in what was termed **province-building**: *an activist approach to economic development on the part of provincial governments.*

Second, economic growth in all the western provinces focused on megaprojects, especially in the North (see Chapter Eleven). Hydroelectricity in Manitoba, potash and uranium in Saskatchewan, tar sands in Alberta, hydroelectricity and forestry in British Columbia: these became the hallmarks of economic development in the West. In classically liberal and typically Canadian fashion, the belief was that these projects would create the capital necessary to diversify the economy and break the cycle of boom and bust so common to the West. Often, however, it meant putting the provinces' eggs in one or two baskets. Too frequently, when the world price of the particular commodity collapsed, individuals and governments, who had backstopped the projects with huge amounts of public capital, were left holding the empty bag. People either sat out the downturn or moved on. No region in Canada fit better Harold Innis's description of a "staples trap" than did the West (Watkins, 1963; Drache, 1995).

Third, and finally, economic development in the West also shared another characteristic: in every case it meant movement into, and exploitation of, each province's northern region. Flin Flon in Manitoba, Uranium City in Saskatchewan, and Fort McMurray in Alberta are but a few examples. The result sometimes was the building of temporary resource towns that disappeared in time (such as Uranium City, and also Cassiar and Tumbler Ridge in British Columbia). But the impacts of the changes were always permanent, especially for the indigenous people living in the areas. In Canada, as elsewhere around the world, the forces of modernity and capitalism displaced the old ways of living (see Chapter Eleven).

Population shifts and economic growth brought other political and social changes. In the mid-1960s, Porter (1965) noted that Canada's elite were largely British, represented "old money," were highly interrelated through business, political, school, and even marital ties, and were located primarily in central Canada. His findings were generally validated a few years later by Clement (1975), who traced the corporate interlocks underlying the power of this insular elite.

The emergent power of the new West challenged this elite structure (Richards and Pratt, 1979). Throughout the West, but particularly in Alberta, a new regional elite arose, demanding its say in how Confederation should be run. The shift of Sun Life from Montreal to Calgary in the 1970s, followed by the establishment of other financial institutions and corporate head offices in that city, was not merely symbolic. It represented a genuine shift in power within Canada.

The changes in Canada's West did not come without problems. As the provinces diverged, and their governments became more individually powerful, some argued regional identification gradually was being replaced with provincial identification (Gibbins, 1979; see also Chapter Nine). Increased cultural and ethnic diversity created tensions in some communities. Expansion into the North disrupted Aboriginal communities (in particular) and created social problems (see Chapter Eleven). At the same time, economic development did not always lead to security. From the 1970s on, the West's economy continued to experience waves of boom and bust.

Finally, the changes also heightened traditional tensions between western Canada and the other provinces and the federal government over the structure of Confederation. By the 1970s, many in the West, like others in the past, were coming to view the Canadian government as alien and unsympathetic to their views. They resented the "imposition," as they saw it, of policies such as bilingualism and metrification. They believed Canadian institutions had an eastern bias, and "national" policies, in general, meant central Canadian policies. Thus, the late 1970s and early 1980s saw the rise throughout western Canada, but especially in Alberta, of a number of western separatist movements (Pratt and Stevenson, 1981). Later, in 1987, regional alienation combined with right-wing populism to underpin the founding of the Reform Party (Harrison, 1995) and then, at the cusp of the new millennium, its offspring, the Canadian Alliance Party (Harrison, 2002). In short, the re-emergence of regional alienation, as much a staple of western Canada as wheat, became a central feature of Canadian society in the years following the 1970s (see Box 8.1).

THE ECONOMIC CRISIS OF THE CANADIAN STATE

Taken as a whole, the period from 1945 until the 1990s was a time of spectacular economic growth for Canada. Canada's GDP (gross domestic product) in 1947, for example, was $91.7 billion (constant dollars). By 1992, GDP had grown to $560 billion. Even accounting for the impact of population growth on GDP, the average Canadian in 1992 was three times better off economically than in 1947 (Norrie and Owram, 1996: 398).

These figures are misleading, however. For Canada, the period can be broken into two halves, the first signalling the prosperous times of an economic "long wave," the second a

---

BOX 8.1 | What is a Region?

A **region** is *a territory defined physiologically, geographically, climatically, culturally, politically, or economically*. This definition is not as straightforward as it seems, however. Even using the same definition, two people may recognize different regional boundaries. Thus, regions do not exist as physical things. Rather, they are "read into" the landscape, socially constructed (as symbolic-interactionists might say), then reified (Chapter One).

The concept of **regional differences** refers to *observable variations between two or more regions*. The West Coast is wet, while the Prairie provinces are dry. Likewise, Newfoundland is a "have-not" province; Alberta is a "have" province.

Regionalism refers to *an individual's personal identification with a region*. In this sense, regionalism provides a sense of who we are, much as nationalism does.

Regional alienation refers to *a sense of grievance based on the belief that regional differences are not "natural" but result from the actions of individuals or groups residing outside the region*.

Sources: Brodie (1990); Westfall (1993); Wonders (1993).

period of economic decline (Watkins, 1997). But the recession of the early 1970s was not Canada's alone. Every country in the Western industrial world experienced rising unemployment and increased government debt during this period. In Canada after the early 1970s, personal and corporate bankruptcies skyrocketed, while the annual unemployment rate (see Chapter Seven) rose steadily, changing also from a temporary or occasional situation to one more long-term and chronic (see Table 8.3). In this context of rising demands but falling revenues, federal and provincial government deficits and debt also spiked. Canada's massive federal debt per gross domestic product following the Second World War had declined steadily during the prosperous years, hitting 11.24 percent in 1975. Thereafter, however, it began rising alarmingly during the 1980s and early 1990s, with interest payments on the debt eating up a growing proportion of revenues (Li, 1996: 89).

What led during this period to the fiscal crisis faced by Western governments and the Canadian government in particular? First, new technologies were beginning to displace workers; hence the rising unemployment that lowered demand for goods and services, while also reducing tax revenues just as state expenditures increased for unemployment insurance and welfare. For Canada, these new technologies cut into jobs in both the primary and secondary sectors. Second, in a preview of globalization, transnational corporations began shifting finance capital and production to low-wage countries, at the same time avoiding taxation or pressuring governments to lower corporate taxes. In Canada, corporate taxes fell from a postwar high of 31.02 percent of all federal tax revenues in 1953 to 23.84 percent in 1970 to 18.47 percent in 1980. By contrast, personal income taxes in Canada rose from 29.51 percent to 37.29 percent to 44.66 percent of all federal tax revenues (Li, 1996: 156–157). In all countries, these factors combined to weaken the full employment policies upon which the Keynesian welfare state relied.

Also exacerbating the economic recession of the early 1970s, however, were the economic circumstances surrounding a single commodity, oil. Since the beginning of the second industrial revolution, and particularly with the advent of the automobile, oil and natural gas had increased in prominence and power as commodities. Their worldwide importance became quite apparent in 1973 when, following the Yom Kippur War, the Organization of Petroleum Exporting Countries (OPEC) announced it was limiting supply and increasing the price of oil. The OPEC Crisis, as it became known, awakened Americans to the fact their country was no longer capable of ensuring a stable and low-priced oil supply. Hence, discussions began on exploration in previously untapped areas under American control (such as Alaska) and means of securing stable supplies from reliable sources (such as Canada).

On the surface, the crisis should have provided a unique opportunity for Canadian development. With large untapped reserves of oil and natural gas, Canada would seem to have been in an ideal position to take advantage of the escalating market price. But Canada was not.

First, 75 percent of Canada's petroleum and natural gas in 1973 was under foreign control, 58 percent under American control (Li, 1996: 24–25; also, Fossum, 1997). Canada might be the home of large oil and gas reserves, but Canadians had no right of first call on them. Second, while the governments of producing provinces could do quite well from rising prices that translated into increased royalties, non-producing provinces faced only rising costs. The crisis thus pitted the oil-producing provinces, especially Alberta, against the manufacturing provinces of central Canada, with the federal government caught in the

TABLE 8.3 Key Indicators of the Canadian Economy, 1970–2001

	1970	1975	1980	1985	1990	1995	2000	2001
Unemployment Rate	5.7	6.9	7.5	10.5	8.1	9.5	6.8	7.2
Bankruptcies (Personal)	2732	8335	21 035	19 752	42 782	65 432	75 137*	79 453
Bankruptcies (Business)	2927	2958	6595	8 63	11 642	13 258	10 055*	10 405
Gross Domestic Product (in billions of dollars)[1]	351.4	445.8	535.0	612.4	705.5	769.1	1012.3	1027.5
Federal Government Expenditures (in billions of dollars)[1]	15.3	35.8	62.0	114.4	154.6	177.1	184.8	191.0
Net Federal Debt (NFD) (in billions of dollars)[2]	16.9	19.3	72.2	199.1	357.8	545.7	561.7	545.3
NFD per capita[2]	796	849	2857	7911	13 484	18 435	18 242	17 528
NFD as percent GDP[3]	19.01	11.24	26.10	46.40	55.10	67.61	55.48	53.07

Sources: Adapted from the Statistics Canada publication *Canadian Economic Observer–Historical Statistical Supplement,* Catalogue 11-210, July 2002, the Statistics Canada CANSIM database at http://cansim2.statcan.ca/cgi-win/CNSMCLEXE, Tables 379-0004, 282-0022, 385-0014, 380-0002 and with the permission of the Office of the Superintendent of Bankruptcy, Industry Canada (2002), *Economic Indicators–Annual Bankruptcies in Canada, 1966–2001,* at http://strategis.ic.gc.ca/SSG/br01011e.html. Reproduced with the permission of the Minister of Public Works and Government Services.

1. Constant 1992 dollars. 2. Nominal dollars. 3. Percentages calculated by the author.

middle. But the problem was not merely political. In Canada, as elsewhere, rising oil prices provoked a worldwide phenomenon known as **stagflation**, *the simultaneous occurrence of a declining economy and increasing unemployment with rising inflation.*

Finally, Canada's fiscal crisis beginning in the 1970s was particularized by its relationship to the United States. In the late 1960s, facing increased competition from the rebuilt economies of Japan and Germany, and in the midst of the widely unpopular Vietnam War, the United States found itself suffering a negative balance of trade with most countries, including Canada. As economic times worsened, the United States government resorted to a time-worn measure: it adopted a series of protectionist measures to buffer American workers, consumers, and companies against the outside world. In 1972, President Nixon came to Canada bearing news that while the two countries might be good friends, there was no special relationship between them. The United States was going to pursue its own agenda, and Canada should feel free to do the same (Martin, 1982).

As an exporting country, with the United States its major market, Canada was rightly concerned about American protectionism. In 1968, 24 percent of Canada's GDP resulted from exports, a figure six times larger than in the United States. Moreover, 60 percent of Canada's trade was with its southern neighbour (Finkel, 1997: 159–160). Given the American actions and the country's own declining economic prospects, what was the Canadian government to do?

THE RISE AND FALL OF CANADIANIZATION, 1972-1982

In the early 1970s, in the context of Quebec separatism, the federal Liberal government of Pierre Trudeau began taking steps to increase the role of central government, politically and symbolically, in the lives of Canadians (Chapter Four). The economic crisis of the same period, in conjunction with the federal election of 1972, which saw the Liberals reduced to a minority government propped up by the left-wing New Democratic party (Appendix 1), likewise gave the federal government impetus to strengthen its role in the economy. For the Liberal Party, it was a remarkable turnaround. Over the years, the Liberals had developed a solid reputation as pro-business, pro-free-trade, and pro-continentalist. Yet, over the next decade (1972–1982), Pierre Trudeau's government instituted a series of measures designed both to increase the role of government in the economy and to patriate the economy in much the same way that the Constitution was brought home from Britain in 1982. The name given to these measures is **Canadianization**.

Specific manifestations of Canadianization included creation of the Foreign Investment Review Agency (FIRA), designed to oversee foreign takeovers of Canadian companies, and the strengthening of cultural institutions such as the Canadian Radio and Television Commission. Given the specific nature of the economic crisis, however, the heart of Canadianization was a series of measures dealing with oil and gas.

One of these measures was the creation of Petro-Canada. Today, Petro-Canada is a large private company with retail outlets spread across the country. Its original mandate was very different. Petro-Canada was originally created by the federal government in 1975 as a Crown corporation for the purpose of exploring and developing oil reserves, mapping out the number of existing reserves in Canada, and generally providing the government with a window on the oil industry.

In many ways, Canadianization can be seen as an extension of the wave of English-Canadian nationalism that swept the country in the 1960s. Certainly, many of the actions taken by the federal Liberals had considerable public support, though this varied from region to region. People in Ontario were the most supportive, while most opposed were people in Quebec and the western provinces, especially Alberta. Many Quebecers, separatist or not, viewed the strengthening of the federal government as threatening their "national" interests. Equally, many in western Canada viewed with suspicion the efforts of the federal Liberals, who had little parliamentary representation in their region. More broadly, many westerners saw this Canadian nationalism as a veil disguising central Canadian interests opposed to their own.

The federal Liberals were defeated in the spring 1979 federal election by the Progressive Conservatives of Joe Clark. Within a matter of months, however, Clark's minority government lost a key parliamentary vote, which resulted in another election being held (Clarkson and McCall, 1990). This time, the Liberals won, and quickly the resurrected government of Pierre Trudeau set about efforts to rebuild the central powers of the Canadian state. Thus, a new constitution was enacted in 1982. Meanwhile, on the economic front, and in the wake of the Iranian Revolution in 1979, which sparked a second major world oil crisis, the Liberals introduced the National Energy Program (NEP) (Fossum, 1997).

The NEP had four purposes. First, it was intended through a series of taxes on the oil industry to increase federal revenues with which in turn to deal with the growing debt. Second, the NEP was meant to keep Canadian energy prices below world levels, smoothing out the impact of rising prices—$13.34 (U.S.) in January 1979, $26 in January 1980, $32 in January 1981 (Fossum, 1997: 106)—between producing and consuming provinces. (At the same time, it also placed a floor on prices should they suddenly drop, thereby protecting producing provinces.) Third, the NEP was designed to foster Canadian ownership of oil and gas through a series of monetary incentives. Fourth, the program was meant to encourage exploration in the Canada Lands (such as in the North, particularly the Beaufort Sea), therefore increasing energy self-sufficiency. Finally, the NEP also was explicitly meant to promote energy conservation (Finkel, 1997: 306; Fossum, 1997).

The National Energy Program represented the pinnacle of Canadianization. In retrospect, many of its goals (such as its restrictions on foreign ownership and efforts at self-sufficiency) seem modest, the measures it proposed standard elsewhere. But its implementation and timing were poor, and it ran up against powerful enemies. By 1982, the NEP was dead, though not formally buried until 1986 by the subsequent Progressive Conservative government of Brian Mulroney (see Chapter Nine). Why did the NEP fail?

First, the NEP was based on pricing projections that failed to materialize (Fossum, 1997). As members of the OPEC cartel began cheating on oil production, the price rapidly declined, throwing economies once more into turmoil and ruining the revenue hopes of both the federal government and the oil-producing provinces.

Second, the NEP and Canadianization in general ran afoul of the newly elected Reagan administration in the United States. Reagan's electoral campaign was based on a promise to the American people to make that country "strong" again. Politically, Reagan promised to confront the threat of the "Evil Empire" (the Soviet Union). Economically, he promised to make the United States self-sufficient and, further, to use the power of the state to open doors for American free enterprise and business. Implementation of the NEP resulted in a series of hostile letters to the Canadian government written by high-level individuals in the Reagan administration, warning of retaliation for Canadian actions that harmed American business interests (Clarkson, 1985).

Third, competing interests and internal fractures within Canada itself undermined Canadianization. These conflicts were not limited to the federal-provincial or inter-provincial level, although these were important. For obvious reasons, American-owned businesses in Canada, including many in western Canada's oil and gas industry, opposed Canadianization. But large private corporations in general opposed Canadianization both on theoretical grounds (opposing government regulation in general) and because increasingly they favoured open borders for capital. These interests lobbied hard to forestall state intervention in the economy, including encouraging the Reagan administration in its threats toward the Canadian government.

Today, the NEP remains controversial; in Alberta, it is mythic. From the point of view of its detractors, the NEP was an unconstitutional intrusion on provincial jurisdiction that stole millions of dollars from the Alberta treasury and led to a subsequent recession (1981–82). NEP supporters, however, argue that the program was a legitimate effort by the Canadian government to carve out an economic policy independent of the United States, and they suggest that the policy is unfairly blamed for a downturn that hit all oil-producing regions, including Texas and Oklahoma.

No matter the relative merits of these arguments, the fact is that the failure of Canadianization, politically and economically, left the Liberal government and the Canadian state more broadly without an economic blueprint for managing the country. Sir John A. Macdonald's National Policy (Chapter Seven) of a hundred years earlier had led to Canada's industrialization. Its modern equivalent, Canadianization, had attempted to resurrect the role of activist government in shaping the country for the late twentieth century. The policy was now in tatters. What path should Canada now take?

CONCLUSION

In the early 1980s, Canada was one of the world's most prosperous and envied countries, a "peaceful kingdom" sporting a high standard of living and a range of quality public services. Dark clouds were on the horizon, however. Economically, public deficits were rising, debts were accumulating, and productivity was in decline. Politically, regional alienation and Quebec separatism remained active. Socially, demands for greater equality and inclusiveness were increasing. Culturally, English-speaking Canada in particular was straining to find its own identity in the wake of changes in immigration policy and the onslaught of modern technologies.

Internationally, a new regime had been installed in the United States. The Reagan administration had two interrelated goals. First, Reagan wanted to roll back "the Red Menace." Second, Reagan wanted to expand opportunities for free market capitalism and (specifically) American corporations. Few realized it then, but the Cold War was about to end, replaced by a new era marked by American dominance, an era of neo-liberal globalization.

KEY TERMS

- Canadianization
- class theory
- comprador elite
- conservative welfare states
- cultural theory
- de-commodified
- dependency theory
- elite theory
- first wave feminism
- import substitution
- indigenous elite
- liberal democratic welfare states
- lower tier service sector
- merchants against industry thesis
- miniature replica effect
- multiculturalism
- parasite elite
- polity-centred/neo-institutional theory
- power resources theory
- primary sector
- province-building
- region
- regional alienation
- regional differences
- regionalism
- second wave feminism
- secondary sector
- social-democratic welfare states
- stagflation
- staples theory
- staples trap
- symbolic order
- tertiary (or service) sector
- third wave feminism
- Toryism
- upper tier service sector
- welfare state (a.k.a. Keynesian welfare state)

chapter nine

Canada in the Age of the American Empire

There are two ways to conquer a country—one is by force of arms; the other is by taking control of its economy.
—American secretary of state John Foster Dulles in the 1950s

"New World Order"
—term used by U.S. president George Bush, Sr., on the occasion of the signing of the North American Free Trade Agreement, 1993

Our overriding purpose from the beginning right through to the present day, has been world domination—that is, to build and maintain the capacity to coerce everybody else on planet: nonviolently, if possible; and violently if necessary....[T]he purpose is to facilitate our exploitation of resources. And insofar as any people or states get in the way of our domination, they must be eliminated—or, at the very least, shown the error of their ways.
—former U.S. attorney general Ramsay Clark, November 2000

INTRODUCTION

Postwar Canada was built upon an expanding and prosperous economy. The welfare state was an integral part of this expansion, underpinning the social adjustments necessary to such an economy. A distinctive English-Canadian identity in turn arose around the notion of creating a "better" country on the North American continent.

The fiscal crisis beginning in the mid-1970s challenged this vision of Canada. Canadianization was a response to this crisis. Indeed, in many ways, Canadianization was an attempt to create a modern-day National Policy. These efforts crashed, however, against internal, regional divisions and pressures exerted by the United States and its business allies. The failure of Canadianization left Canadian politicians and policy-makers without a clear direction for the Canadian economy.

This chapter examines Canada's subsequent search for a new economic policy, resulting in the embrace of free trade in 1988. The chapter further traces political, economic, social, and ideological changes in Canada since that event. More broadly, the chapter examines Canada in the age of neo-liberalism, globalization, and—since the collapse of the Soviet Union in 1990—unchallenged American dominance. It concludes with a look at the issues facing Canada in the wake of the terrorist attacks on the United States in the fall of 2001.

ADOPTING FREE TRADE

The Conservative government of Brian Mulroney was elected in 1984, replacing the tired and discredited Liberals, now led by John Turner (see Appendices 1 and 2). Two items headed the Tories' policy agenda: a new constitutional arrangement with Quebec (Chapter Four) and a new economic policy for Canada. In seeking the latter, Mulroney had to look no further than a study recently commissioned by the departing Liberals.

In the wake of the failure of Canadianization, the Liberal Party in late 1982 set up the Royal Commission on the Economic Union and Development Prospects for Canada. Also called the Macdonald Commission after its chair, Donald Macdonald, the commission over the next two years garnered a host of submissions from academics, bureaucrats, social activists, and businesspeople on the topic of the future direction Canada should take. Many of the submissions advocated a strengthening of government in the economy, including an expansion of Canada's social programs to alleviate poverty (Finkel, 1997: 309).

The commission's final report, published in 1985, took a different view, however. The report concluded that the Canadian economy needed less government involvement, that businesses and workers in Canada were insufficiently competitive, and that the only solution was greater reliance upon market forces. The report advocated a policy of free trade with the United States.

To understand fully the significance of this recommendation, one has to go back into Canadian history. The option of free trade with the United States had always been there; indeed, the Reciprocity Agreement of 1854–66 (see Chapter Six) was a form of managed free trade (Norrie and Owram, 1996). After 1867 and particularly after the formulation of the National Policy in 1879, however, Canadian economic, political, and social development had been nurtured along an east-west grid. The idea of free trade with the United States persisted, pursued by the Liberal Party and certain supporters, especially western farmers, but it was a minority position. In the elections of both 1891 and 1911, Sir Wilfrid Laurier's Liberals campaigned on a platform of unrestricted trade with the United States, losing on both occasions to the Tories, the first time to Sir John A. Macdonald, the second time to Sir Robert Borden (Appendix 1). Thereafter, the topic of free trade largely disappeared from sight. Free trade was the ideological plaything of a few academics and "continentalists," those who saw Canada's future within a greater North American whole. The vast majority of Canadians viewed free trade, however, as a potential threat to Canadian sovereignty. Why then did the notion of free trade receive support in 1988?

There were several reasons (see Doern and Tomlin, 1991). First, the idea of free trade garnered important support from Canadian business. Many Canadian businesses were in fact American branch plants headed by American CEOs, or "compradors" (Clement, 1975; see Chapter Eight), and did not view the border between the two countries as real. But even within Canada's "indigenous" business class there was support for free trade as a means of assuring Canadian access to American markets for export goods and investment capital, and as a safeguard against the kind of protectionist policies favoured by former president Richard Nixon in the early 1970s. For all these reasons, big business, represented by the Business Council on National Issues (BCNI), heavily favoured free trade in 1988.

Second, several provinces also supported free trade. These included Quebec, whose separatist government believed free trade would loosen that province's dependence upon the rest of Canada and pave the way for sovereignty (see Chapter Four). Likewise, the Alberta government supported free trade as a means of preventing the imposition in future of another National Energy Program (Chapter Eight).

Third, Canada faced enormous political and ideological pressures from outside its borders. These pressures were the result of the worldwide rise throughout the 1980s of a set of ideological beliefs favourable to minimal government intervention and the pursuit of free trade.

These ideas gained their first major victory with the election of Margaret Thatcher's Conservative government in Britain in 1979. Thatcher's government privatized services, deregulated business, downsized government, and broke the back of Britain's trade unions. When called upon, Thatcher's government was also staunchly imperial, going to war (for example) over the Falkland Islands. But Thatcher's conservatism also was different from traditional British Toryism in its denunciation of some aspects of privilege, its espousal of economic individualism, and its implied rejection of the common good. Margaret Thatcher expressed this best when she said, "There is no such thing as society." Ideologically, such beliefs are sometimes termed **neo-liberal** because they emphasize Adam Smith's notions of laissez-faire economics and David Ricardo's notions of free trade and comparative advantage (Merritt, 1996).

The election in 1980 of Ronald Reagan as American president provided the idea of free trade with its second major victory. Reagan, like Thatcher, proclaimed the values of individual free enterprise and capitalism, while reaching out also to moral conservatives. (This merging of liberal economics and moral conservatism is sometimes termed **neo-conservatism**.) In the United States, there were fewer public services to privatize and fewer unions to attack, but Reagan did fire several thousand striking air-traffic controllers as an object lesson. He also lowered taxes, deregulated business, stepped up military production, and intensified the Cold War (see Parenti, 1995). (Ironically, in responding to these actions, and in becoming engaged in a debilitating war in Afghanistan, the Soviet Union over-stretched its own economic resources, speeding up its collapse in 1990.) Finally, in an important move for Canada, Reagan pressured Canada to abandon its policy of Canadianization (Chapter Eight) in favour of more liberalized trade. The Reagan administration's pursuit of open markets found an echo in the new Mulroney government.

Mulroney, like Thatcher, was not a traditional Tory conservative (see Chapter Eight). He was a social liberal, strong on individual rights, for example. Moreover, his personal background—he grew up in a resource-based town dominated by an American employer and later became CEO for an American branch plant—predisposed him to view without threat greater continental integration (McQuaig, 1991; Sawatsky, 1991). Understanding this helps explain why it was that a Conservative government brought in free trade, historically a liberal policy.

Finally, the adoption of free trade as a policy was in part based on purely political considerations. Free trade put the Liberal Party on the defensive because, after all, it was that party's historic policy. In fighting against free trade in the 1988 election that followed, Liberal denunciations always rang hollow.

The 1988 election was highly polarized, comparable only to the conscription election of 1917 (Chapter Three). In the end, though by a narrow margin (only 43 percent of Canadians voted for the PCs), Mulroney's Tories won a majority of seats (see Appendix 1). The free trade agreement was ratified. Almost immediately, the newly elected administration of George Bush, Sr., in Washington began pushing for a broader continental agreement that would include Mexico. The United States—militarily, politically, and economically powerful, but resource poor—was poised to access the resources of its two closest neighbours. In the world of the late twentieth century, North America quickly emerged as one large trading block, with its headquarters in the United States, to compete against other trading blocks that began emerging in Europe and Asia.

Nor was the move to closer ties reversed with the election in 1993 of a new Canadian government. That year, the Tory party was defeated in dramatic fashion. The Meech Lake debacle, hatred of the Goods and Services Tax (GST), and personal animus toward Brian Mulroney culminated in the Tories' winning only two seats (see Chapter Four). (Mulroney was no longer Tory leader, having stepped down in favour of Kim Campbell, Canada's first female prime minister, but his shadow nonetheless remained.) The victorious Liberal Party, which only five years earlier had denounced free trade, under new leader Jean Chrétien signed on to the NAFTA Accord. The years that followed saw Canada pursue closer economic ties with the United States, while that country spearheaded efforts for global free trade through agreements such as the Multilateral Agreement on Investments. For Canadians, the tepid economic nationalism of the Trudeau era was quickly swept away under the aegis of globalization.

ASSESSING THE LONG-TERM IMPACT OF FREE TRADE

Free trade remains controversial today (Hurtig, 1992; Orchard, 1998; Jackson, 1999; Lipsey, 2000). Assessing free trade's impact is not easy for at least two reasons. First, it is hard to isolate the independent effects of free trade from those resulting from other factors, such as the recession that occurred shortly after the FTA was signed (Martin, 1993a) and broader changes in the macro-economy—such as the shift of jobs in the primary and secondary sectors to the service sector—that had already been occurring for decades (Krahn and Lowe, 2002) (see Chapter Eight). Second, different measurement instruments—employment figures, trade figures, the value of the Canadian dollar—give different results.

Canadians themselves remain unconvinced of free trade's benefits. A *Maclean's*-CBC poll, conducted in December 1999, showed 63 percent of Canadians believed the United States gained more from free trade than did Canada. Beyond this subjective appraisal, it remains difficult to accurately assess free trade's impact. One way is to examine the contentions made by free trade's supporters and opponents at the time and to assess their accuracy since.

Assessing Pro-Free Trade Arguments

In 1988, free trade supporters said the agreement would increase Canadian exports (and cross-border trade in general); result in more and better-paying Canadian jobs; secure access to American markets; and encourage efficiency, making the Canadian economy better able to compete in world markets. Have these things occurred?

Exports and Imports. Canadian exports in general have increased under free trade, from 25 percent of GDP to 40 percent of GDP during the first decade (Lipsey, 2000). Nearly all of this increased export activity has been to the United States, jumping by 169 percent. During the same period, imports—mainly from the United States—also rose by 149 percent (*Edmonton Journal*, 1999f: A3). Today, 87 percent of Canada's exports go to the United States. At the same time, only 25 percent of U.S. exports go to Canada (Grunwald, 2002). Altogether, cross-border flows between Canada and the United States are worth over $1 billion per day (Pearlstein, 2000).

Job Growth and Income. Free trade opponents note that Canada in the first few years after 1989 lost one-fifth of its manufacturing jobs (Jackson, 1999), as many as 300 000 jobs in Ontario alone (Morton, 1997: 326), amidst rising levels of business and personal bankruptcies and unemployment rates generally higher before 1988 (see Jackson, 1999) (see Table 8.3 in previous chapter). Free trade supporters, however, argue that, even if some of these job losses resulted from economic restructuring due to the agreement (which is uncertain), a large number of jobs have since been created in Canada (Lipsey, 2000). Indeed, employment in Canada grew at a faster pace than in the United States throughout the period 2000–2002 (Bowlby and Usalcas, 2003; Stanford, 2003), while unemployment levels steadily declined.

Opponents, however, argue that the decline in unemployment figures is in fact a consequence of changes in Canada's Unemployment Insurance program (renamed Employment Insurance) that compel workers to take poorer jobs (Morton, 1997)—changes reflecting opponents' original concern that Canada under free trade would have to harmonize its social programs with those of the United States. Opponents further ask, What kinds of jobs has free trade produced? They suggest that far too many of these have been part-time, insecure, and low paying—part of a trend toward non-standard employment (Krahn and Lowe, 2002).

What of income? A Statistics Canada study shows that, in constant dollars, the median income of the two-parent working family in 1999 was lower than it had been in 1990 ($54 100, versus $55 174) and that most Canadians were actually working longer hours in 1999 than they had a decade before (*National Post*, 2001a). Similarly, a recent study for the Canadian Centre for Policy Alternatives, using Statistics Canada data, shows a growing gap in wealth between rich and poor in Canada (Kerstetter, 2002). But the same study also shows that this trend has been occurring since at least 1977, that is, before free trade, and that it is particularly the middle class that is being "hollowed out." In short, the evidence suggests free trade may be partially to blame for the declining economic circumstances of many Canadians, but it is not the only or perhaps even the prime contributor.

Secure Access to American Markets. Threats of American protectionist policies being launched against Canada were a chief argument for the FTA in 1988. The

Mulroney government insisted the FTA's dispute settlement mechanism would protect Canadian businesses from arbitrary barriers being erected by the American state. Economist Richard Lipsey (2000) argues that the dispute resolution mechanism has worked well and that Canada would have been much worse off during the economically turbulent 1990s without it.

Critics, however, point out the United States did not give up under the FTA (or NAFTA) its right to make laws restricting trade with Canada. (American trade negotiators in 1988 emphasized the same point.) American trade restrictions on softwood lumber, which have crippled British Columbia's forest industry, provide only the most striking example of this fact, but it is not singular. Since free trade, the United States has continued to invoke trade restrictions on a host of things, such as uranium, beer, magnesium, steel, pigs, sugar, peanut butter, tobacco, milk, and paper (Dyck, 1998: 92–93). In early 2002, American government officials suggested they were prepared to take "dead aim" at the Canadian Wheat Board (CWB), forcing it to drop its "monopoly practices"—despite the fact that the United States heavily subsidizes its own large corporate agricultural producers and the World Trade Organization (WTO) has repeatedly found the CWB to be in compliance with trade practices.

Efficiency and Global Competitiveness. Free trade supporters argued in 1988 that the agreement would prepare Canadians to compete in the emerging global economy. Canadian businesses would have to become more entrepreneurial and efficient; workers would be forced to become more productive. In time, Canada might at last break out of its staples dependency (see Chapter Eight).

Free trade supporters today argue the agreement has had just these results (Lipsey, 2000). Gross Domestic Product (GDP) provides one measure for assessing Canada's increased productivity. In 1986, calculated in constant 1992 dollars, per capita GDP was $24 082. In 1998, it was $27 665 (calculated from CGA, 1999: 42 and 197).

GDP is a controversial measure, however. Because it is a measurement of the total value of goods and services produced in a country during a given period, GDP typically goes up not only during good times but also during wars or immediately after a natural disaster, such as an earthquake, as rebuilding starts. In this sense, GDP says nothing about the quality of life being lived.

Moreover, opponents dispute the economic efficiency arguments of free trade supporters. Jackson (1999) argues that the productivity gap between Canadian and American workers is actually wider today than before free trade; that is, compared with American workers, Canadian workers appear less productive than before 1988. He further argues that free trade has not brought the investments in research and development that might prepare Canada for the new knowledge economy. Finally, opponents note that, far from being a global player, Canada is less "globalized" today than before free trade, with nearly its entire economy dependent upon exports to American markets.

Assessing Anti-Free Trade Arguments

Besides countering the claims of free trade supporters, free trade opponents in 1988 argued several other points against the agreement. These arguments included the identification of a series of interrelated threats posed by free trade to Canada's social programs, democracy and sovereignty, national unity, and cultural identity. Have these fears been proven correct?

Social programs. Free trade opponents argued the agreement would require over time the systematic harmonization of Canada's social programs with those of the United States and that, since the latter is the larger partner, the direction of harmonization would generally tend toward the lower levels of that country. Rice and Prince (2000) and Olsen (2002) suggest this has been the case. They note, for example, that after free trade Canada's family allowance program (begun in 1945) was eliminated (1992), the eligibility qualifications and benefits for unemployment insurance (renamed employment insurance) were made more stringent, and medicare—arguably, the capstone of Canada's welfare state—came under increased pressure to move away from public administration and universality toward the private American model.

Free trade supporters, however, argue that the changes to Canada's welfare state programs were made necessary not by free trade but by the country's rising debt load in the 1990s. They contend that the kinds of programs that will emerge in future will be more durable in helping Canada and Canadians adjust to changing economic and social conditions.

Democracy and sovereignty. It is clear that the intent of free trade was to remove political control over the economy, placing decisions instead in the hands of the market. For many conservatives and businesspeople, this was a chief benefit of free trade. Opponents, however, argue that free trade removes democratic control of the economy from citizens, placing important decisions in the hands of companies, investment dealers, and shareholders who may in fact not be Canadian citizens. A good example is energy policy.

Energy is necessary for survival, especially in a climate as cold and potentially inhospitable as Canada's. The perceived need to ensure supplies for Canadians was behind many of the federal government's Canadianization policies in the early 1970s (see Chapter Eight). In consequence of these policies, foreign control of Canada's petroleum and natural gas industries declined from 75 percent to 35 percent between 1968 and 1987. American control, specifically, during this period declined from 61 percent to 25 percent (Li, 1996: 22). Since free trade, however, this trend has been reversed. Today, nearly 50 percent of Canada's energy sector is once more foreign—mainly American—owned (see *Edmonton Journal* 2001a; 2001b). The takeovers that brought this rise in foreign ownership were made easier by the sliding value of the Canadian dollar against its American counterpart during the 1990s. Looked at another way, American direct investment in Canada in 2001 was nearly $14.5 billion (U.S.). Of this, more than $8 billion (or 56 percent) was in petroleum (*Time*, 2002: 646). A headline in the *Edmonton Journal* of September 27, 2001, asked the question, "Whose oil is it, anyway?" The answer (approved by those who believe that markets must be allowed to trump politics) is simple: the owners are those with the money to buy it (Pratt, 2001).

Foreign ownership does not end with oil and gas, however. Indeed, free trade critics argue that free trade agreements are really a Trojan Horse for demands on other Canadian resources desired by the United States since at least the 1950s (see Chapter Eight), especially fresh water. The result, according to journalist Peter C. Newman (1999: 51), responding to a spate of American takeovers during the 1990s—Seagram's, Nortel, Nova Corps, Canadian National Railways—means that Canadians are quickly becoming "squatters on our own land." A *Maclean's* December 1999 poll shows many Canadians share concern with growing American control of the Canadian economy. A later *Maclean's* poll (2002) shows that 57 percent of Canadians are specifically concerned that the country is losing its independence from the United States.

From the point of view of free trade supporters, however, questions of ownership and of a loss of political sovereignty are red herrings. They argue that markets are neutral and that companies naturally respond to consumer demand. The "invisible hand" of the marketplace, it is argued, provides a more economical and fair means of distributing scarce resources than would result from government interventions. Governments can still do what they want. Free trade merely ensures they treat companies—foreign or domestic—equally and respect the rights of private property.

National unity. Free trade opponents argued that the agreement would loosen Canada's east-west system of political, economic, and cultural exchanges, while weakening the role of the federal state. In turn, regional divisions (see Chapter Eight) would be increased, and perhaps also the desire to join the United States.

There is no doubt that north-south economic exchanges have increased since 1988, while those in an east-west direction have decreased. Take three examples: Quebec, western Canada, and Ontario. Between 1981 and 1995, Quebec's exports to the rest of Canada grew by 67 percent, but to the rest of the world (mainly the United States) by 208 percent (Ip, 1996: D1). Exports from western Canada, especially Alberta (oil and gas), to the U.S. have also increased markedly since 1989 (Canada West Foundation, 2001). In Ontario, foreign trade (most of it with the United States) in 1989 made up about 30 percent of Ontario's GDP. Ten years later, however, the figure had jumped to 54 percent, most of the increase representing trade with the U.S. (see Courchene, 1998; Ibbitson, 2001).

This change has potentially important impacts on Canadian national policy. Under the old system of economic exchanges, money flowed back and forth east and west, but remained largely in Canada. Money from transfer payments, for example, might go from richer to poorer provinces, but would flow back again to the "have" provinces through the purchase of goods and services, thus stimulating their economies. Free trade (it is argued) has broken this "virtuous cycle," however. Today, money transferred across Canada is more likely than in the past to then flow south, with no tangible benefit to the original lender. Perhaps in consequence, in recent years an increasing volume of complaints from wealthy provinces have been directed at federal programs that equalize opportunities for Canadians in the "have-not" provinces.

The Canadian elections of 1993, 1997, and 2000 provide, on the surface at least, further proof of growing regional fragmentation since the implementation of free trade (Appendix 1). In each of these elections, the Bloc Québécois prevailed in Quebec, the Reform (later Alliance) Party in much of western Canada, the Tories and New Democrats in the Atlantic region, and the Liberals in Ontario. But do these election results really point out vast regional differences, or do they reflect the peculiar characteristics of Canada's "first past the post" electoral system?

How do Canadians in general feel about Canada's future? To what extent is there an increased belief since 1988 that Canada should throw in its lot with the United States?

A World Values Survey conducted in 1990, after the FTA went into effect, asked the following question: "All things considered, do you think that we should do away with the border between Canada and the United States?" In response, 46 percent of Americans and 24 percent of Canadians answered yes (Nevitte, 1996: 140–141). Similarly, according to a *Maclean's* poll in 1999, 32 percent of Canadians and 19 percent of Americans said they thought union would occur within 25 years, though only 19 percent of Canadians (compared with 34 percent of Americans) thought this a good idea.

Cultural identity. The same 1999 *Maclean's* poll shows more than 90 percent of Canadians (ranging from a low of 84 percent in Quebec to a high of 93 percent in the Prairies and Atlantic Canada) believe Canada has a unique identity. And 77 percent (ranging from 73 percent in Quebec to 85 percent in Atlantic Canada) argue that this identity is based on "a strong sense of our own history, rather than simply a desire not to be Americans." Are these self-appraisals accurate? While Canadians and Americans are probably more alike than unlike, evidence suggests there are some very large differences as well, differences that underlie the notion that Canada does indeed constitute a distinct North American society (see Box 9.1). Moreover, contrary to the concerns of anti–free traders, these differences appear to be strengthening over time, perhaps as a result of something psychologists refer to as a "reaction formation." That is, faced with the crucible of cultural and perhaps political absorption, it may be that many people in Canada are forging a new sense of what it means to be Canadian.

The cultural industries are an area of specific concern. During the 1988 election, Canadians were told culture was not "on the table." But the United States, home to Hollywood production and many of the world's largest music and magazine industries, has since pressured Canada to drop "protectionist" policies toward its cultural industries. For the American government, culture is just another commodity—though some argue it is also a vehicle for American imperialism and, in the specific case of some Hollywood movies, even state propaganda (Gardner, 2002). For many Canadians, however, culture is an essential element of identity that must be nurtured and protected or it will be lost.

BOX 9.1 — Canadian and American Values Compared

We noted earlier (Chapter Eight) some historical theories explaining the differences between Canadians and Americans. Though some studies (including Baer et al., 1993) suggest growing value convergence, with North America now defined by three cultural regions—Quebec, the old American South, and the rest—other recent surveys conclude that some, often surprising, differences remain between Canadians and Americans. Studies by Nevitte (1996) and Adams (1998), for example, suggest Canadians compared with their American counterparts are:

- less deferential to authority
- less conformist
- less formally religious
- less characterized by a traditional work ethic
- less accepting of violence
- more desirous of personal autonomy
- more individualistic
- more hedonistic
- more relaxed
- more suspicious of big business

At the same time, however, it should be noted that 50 percent of Canadians polled by *Maclean's* in 1999 believed Canadians were becoming more like Americans, while only 18 percent believed they were becoming less like Americans.

Sources: Nevitte (1996: 10-18); Adams (1998); *Maclean's* (1999).

Critics of that point of view charge that Canadian government regulations (such as those enforced by the Canadian Radio and Television Commission) restrict choice and really protect mediocrity. They also argue that public radio and television force people to pay for things for which there is no market demand and otherwise compete unfairly with private business. The counter-argument is that organizations such as the CBC and the National Film Board and cultural subsidies actually provide the means for a greater variety of "voices" that otherwise would be suppressed by a cacophony of mass-market sound coming from the United States (see Gordon, 2002).

We have noted the potential divisiveness for Canadian unity of Canada's regional nature. Pevere and Dymond (1996) present an alternative argument, however. They suggest the essence of Canadian culture arises precisely from its regions. Canada's proximity to the United States allows many of its artists to mirror American culture and therefore to do very well in that marketplace. Shania Twain and Nickelback provide only two examples. They can "pass" as generically American. By contrast, regional artists (Great Big Sea) and films (*Margaret's Museum* or *Atanarjuat* [*The Fast Runner*]) or those artists whose content remain too resolutely Canadian (The Tragically Hip) are not as easily sold in the United States. They are "too Canadian."

Ultimately, the evidence for the impact of free trade upon Canada is mixed. It may be, however, that, in the words of Martin (1993a: 195), the real significance of the free trade agreement lay in the fact that it represented "the final crossing of the psychological divide—from thoughts of Britain and third options, to home continent." In other words, Canada's thoughts now focused on its relationship with its alter ego, the United States.

CANADIAN SOCIAL STRATIFICATION AND INEQUALITY

Questions of social stratification and inequality are central to all societies. Stratification systems may elicit general consensus or may be terrains of social conflict. We have previously examined social stratification in early Canada (Chapter Two). What is the nature of Canada's social stratification system today? To what extent are the life chances of Canadian citizens relatively equal? To what extent are they becoming more or less equal?

There are generally two ways of examining social stratification and inequality in society. The first employs the neo-Marxist notion of class, updated to reflect the complexity of modern labour markets and especially the rise since Marx's time of managers and technical experts. The second method, termed a measure of **socio-economic status**, or SES, combines education, occupation, and income in a composite index (see Box 9.2).

There are similarities between Marxian class and SES measures of class. Occupation as measured in the SES model, for example, is a reasonable proxy for class in the Marxian sense. But there also are clear theoretical and ideological differences in the manner in which each describes systems of social stratification in modern, capitalist societies. First, there is a structural relationship between Marxist classes, especially between (as Marx saw it) the two chief antagonists, the capitalist class (or bourgeoisie) and the workers (or proletariat). There is no such relationship between any of the strata described in the SES model. These are merely continuous statistical categories. Second, and related to the first point, people move through life in the Marxist model as members of a group, with the potential of becoming conscious of this affiliation (that is, **social class**), and acting politically upon this knowledge. The people in the SES model are by contrast individuals placed in a category on the basis of their

> BOX 9.2 **Neo-Marxist and Socio-Economic (SES) Models of Class**
>
> | Neo-Marxist* | SES Model** |
> |---|---|
> | Capitalist Classes | Upper Upper |
> | Grande bourgeoisie | Lower Upper |
> | Small employers | Upper Middle |
> | Petite bourgeoisie | Lower Middle |
> | New Middle Classes | Upper Lower |
> | Managers and supervisors | Lower Lower |
> | Expert and semi-credentialed workers | |
> | Proletarians | |
> | Underclass | |
>
> *Source*: Adopted from Wright (1985); Knuttila (2002).
>
> * Capitalists own the means of production (in varying degrees), but may or may not purchase labour. The managerial and supervisory members of the new middle class may have discretionary control over capital and command labour. All members of this class exercise some degree of job autonomy. The proletarians neither own nor control the means of production, do not command labour, and have no assets in the labour market but their labour.
>
> ** There is no necessary correspondence between the two classification schemes. While the grande bourgeoisie might roughly approximate the upper upper strata, the linkage is far more tenuous for other groups.

individual credentials, a fact that suggests the essentially liberal basis of this model and its further congruence with functionalist explanations of social inequality (see Chapter One). Third, whereas the Marxian model implies a relatively closed and static society, based on the class position to which one is born, the SES model implies a far more open and fluid social structure in which individuals either rise on the basis of merit or fall for lack thereof.

On this latter point of **social mobility**—*the upward or downward movement of individuals or groups from one position in the social stratification system to another position*—both models are probably in error with regard to Canadian society. At least at the top end, and also at the very bottom, social mobility in Canada is relatively low, contrary to the implications of the SES model. At the same time, opportunities for members of the working class and new middle class to rise higher in their individual lifetimes, referred to as **intra-generational social mobility**, or for children to rise higher than their parents, known as **inter-generational social mobility**, are greater than envisioned by the Marxist model.

Fourth, the SES model explicitly ignores **wealth**, *the total amount of money and other financial assets owned by individuals or families*, in favour of **income**, *money earned through the sale of labour or through investments*. By contrast, the Marxist model concerns all sources of wealth, particularly those that arise out of the ownership of the means of production, for this is also a source of major political power.

With these considerations in mind, what does Canada's social stratification system look like today? How large are social inequalities in Canada today? Tables 9.1 and 9.2 provide

TABLE 9.1	Distribution of Personal Wealth in Canada, All Family Units, 1999			
	Aggregate wealth	Distribution of wealth	Average wealth	Median wealth
All family units	$2 439 025 000 000	100.0%	$199 664	$81 000
Poorest 10%	–$8 693 000 000	–0.4%	–$7110	–$2050
Second	$4 207 000 000	0.2%	$3445	$3137
Third	$17 981 000 000	0.7%	$14 728	$14 000
Fourth	$44 455 000 000	1.8%	$36 387	$35 525
Fifth	$79 350 000 000	3.3%	$64 919	$64 678
Sixth	$24 589 000 000	5.1%	$102 050	$101 540
Seventh	$187 469 000 000	7.7%	$153 471	$152 550
Eighth	$272 464 000 000	11.2%	$223 116	$220 760
Ninth	$423 493 000 000	17.4%	$346 581	$338 051
Tenth	$1 293 710 000 000	53.0%	$1 059 423	$703 500

Source: Adapted from Statistics Canada, *Distribution of Net Worth by Deciles, All Family Units, Canada, Regions and Alberta,* special data tabulations; Kerstetter (2002), *Rags and Riches,* Canadian Centre for Policy Alternatives, Request 14275-Part 1, at **www.policyalternatives.ca**.

TABLE 9.2	Percentage Distribution of Wealth in Canada, All Family Units, Selected Years, 1970-1999			
	1970	1977	1984	1999
All family units	100.0%	100.0%	100.0%	100.0%
Poorest 10%	–1.0%	–0.6%	–0.5%	–0.6%
Second	0.0%	0.1%	0.1%	0.0%
Third	0.3%	0.5%	0.5%	0.4%
Fourth	1.3%	1.6%	1.7%	1.3%
Fifth	3.0%	3.5%	3.5%	2.8%
Sixth	5.4%	5.9%	5.6%	4.7%
Seventh	8.3%	8.6%	8.2%	7.4%
Eighth	11.8%	12.1%	11.5%	11.0%
Ninth	17.6%	17.6%	17.5%	17.4%
Tenth	53.3%	50.7%	51.8%	55.7%

Source: Adapted from the Statistics Canada publication *Changes in the distribution of wealth in Canada, 1970-1984,* Catalogue 13-588, April 1989; Kerstetter (2002), *Rags and Riches,* Canadian Centre for Policy Alternatives, at **www.policyalternatives.ca**.

some answers. Table 9.1 shows the enormous gap between the richest ten percent of Canadians and the poorest. Note that the poorest ten percent of Canadian families are in fact in deficit circumstances; that is, their debts are larger than their assets. Table 9.1 suggests that the gap between rich and poor has been growing steadily since 1984. The greatest decliners, in this instance, are middle-income families. Meanwhile, the assets of the country's top ten percent of families have risen to nearly 56 percent of all the wealth in Canada.

Who are the people in these various classes and strata? The very wealthiest of Canadians are fairly easy to identify. Many are household names. Table 9.3 lists the names of Canada's 15 billionaires in 2002, as identified by *Forbes Magazine*. This number of billionaires was up from nine in 1999 (Kerstetter, 2002: 65).

By contrast, those at the bottom are, in the eyes of many Canadians, generally faceless or caricatures. Most exist outside the labour market, and so are not easily fit within the standard descriptions of Canada's stratification system (above). The cuts made to Canada's social safety net during the 1990s to tackle the country's deficits and debt had a particularly strong impact on those individuals who relied upon non-market sources of income (Laxer and Harrison, 1995; Ralph et al., 1997) (see Table 8.3). The result has been a steady increase in the use of food banks throughout Canada. A report prepared for the Canadian Association of Food Banks shows that the number of people using food banks rose by 90

TABLE 9.3	Canadian Billionaires, 2003		
Name	Primary Source of Wealth	Estimated Wealth in billions (U.S. dollars)	Ranking Among World's Billionaires
Thomson, Kenneth & family	media, legal, and financial	14.0	13
Weston, Galen & family	groceries	6.2	43
Irving, James, Arthur, and John	oil refining	3.5	94
Skoll, Jeffrey S.	founder and president of eBay	2.8	123
Bronfman, Charles	liquor, entertainment	2.2	177
Pattison, Jim	various industries	2.2	177
Sherman, Bernard (Barry)	uncertain	2.2	177
McCain, Wallace	frozen food	1.8	222
Desmarais, Paul & family	chair and co-CEO of Power Corporation	1.7	236
McCain, Harrison	frozen food	1.5	278
Katz, Daryl A.	pharmaceuticals	1.5	278
Lee-Chin, Michael	financial investments	1.4	303
Melnyk, Eugene	pharmaceuticals	1.4	303
Coutu, Jean	retail drugstore chain	1.3	329
Emanuele, (Lino) Saputo & family	dairy processing	1.2	348

Sources: Ugbor (1993); *Forbes* (2003), www.forbes.com; Kerstetter (2002).

percent between March 1989 and March 2001, to 718 334 people (Wilson and Tsoa, 2001). Similarly, homelessness has become a feature of Canadian urban life, so much so that Statistics Canada in 2001 began for the first time trying to count the number of people in such circumstances.

Finally, it must be noted that when it comes to great poverty, great wealth, and positions in-between, not all people are treated equally (Grabb et al., 1999). While the average income of women in the labour market is nearing that of men in similar occupations, women in 2000 still earned overall 64 cents for every dollar earned by men, though for women aged 25 to 29, working full-year, full-time, this amount is 81 cents (Statistics Canada, 2003a). The gap has closed since the 1980s for several reasons. More women are working and working longer. Many are more highly educated and trained than in the past, resulting in their qualifying for better jobs. Finally, during the 1990s, the gap closed as men's wages actually declined due to job restructuring.

Still, the highest-paid professions remain dominated by men, while women often remain located in fairly specific job ghettos (Krahn and Lowe, 2002). Additionally, women do not often control large corporate enterprises—the source of wealth (note the gender of Canada's billionaires in Table 9.3)—but do disproportionately count among Canada's poor, especially those on some form of welfare. The fact that women are disproportionately represented among the poor has led some policy-makers to speak of the **feminization of poverty**.

Likewise, Canada's system of social stratification continues to reflect differences based on ethnicity and race. The influence of ethnicity and race is not as stark as when John Porter published his seminal tome, *The Vertical Mosaic*, in 1965 (see Nakhaie, 1997; Lian and Matthews, 1998). But ethnicity and race still play a part, most particularly in the case of Aboriginal people (Part Three).

Other factors also continue to shape Canada's stratification system. These include regional disparities (see previous Table 5.1), physical and mental disabilities and, increasingly, the impact of age, often involving elderly women left widowed (Curtis et al., 1999). A recent study produced for Statistics Canada is instructive (Morissette and Zhang, 2001). It shows that persons in lower-income circumstances over long periods tend disproportionately to be women, unattached, or lone parents.

Issues of inequality are fundamental to societal cohesion. It should be noted, however, that since the late 1980s, the gap between rich and poor evidenced in Canada has been replicated in many other Western countries, none more strongly, however, than the United States.

CANADA AND THE UNITED STATES: A COMPARISON

Canadians could compare their country with Australia, with which it shares a similar cultural background as one of Britain's "white" dominions, as well as size and history of economic development. Canadians could also compare their country with Argentina, a country of similar size and resources residing in South America beside a larger, wealthier country, Brazil. Finally, Canadians might profitably compare their country with Sweden, a country of similar geography and climate, even reindeer, as well as a history as a "late developer" (Black and Myles, 1986; Laxer, 1989). Instead, Canadians spend much of their time and energy asking how their country stacks up against the United States.

It should be noted that Americans rarely ever compare themselves with Canadians or anyone else. Indeed, while Canadians know a great deal about the United States, Canada is largely unknown to Americans. (A survey conducted in 2000 by Canada's Department of Foreign Affairs found that Americans are familiar with Canadian singers, comedians, and beer, but believe that furs remain Canada's fourth-largest trading commodity, behind lumber and paper, wheat, and fish [*Edmonton Journal*, 2000c]).

How does Canada compare with the United States? For starters, Canada's population today is 31 413 990 versus 280 562 489 in the United States (Statistics Canada, 2003c; *Time*, 2002: 885). Canada, however, is more than 350 000 square kilometres larger than the United States. In theory, this means that Canada has 3.14 people per square kilometre versus 28.6 per square kilometre in the U.S., but in actuality much of Canada more than 100 miles north of the border is sparsely populated. Nonetheless, large distances and a small population present challenges and opportunities for Canadians that differ from those faced by Americans and their governments.

In terms of the economy, Canada's GDP in 2000 was (in U.S. dollars) $774.7 billion (per capita, $24 800), compared with $9.963 trillion (per capita $36 200) in the U.S. (*Time*, 2002: 743, 885). Canada's exports that year amounted to $272.3 billion (U.S), while imports were $238.2 billion (*Time*, 2002: 743). By comparison, the United States in 2000 had total exports of $776 billion (U.S.) and imports of $1.223 trillion (*Time*, 2002: 885–86).

In general, official unemployment rates in the United States in recent years have been lower than in Canada. In 1996, for example, the U.S. unemployment rate was 5.4 percent, compared with 9.7 percent in Canada (Riddell and Sharpe, 1998: S36). In 2000, it was 4.0 percent in the United States, compared with 6.8 percent in Canada in December of that year (*Time*, 2002: 743, 885). But the end of 2002 saw the U.S. rate at 6.0 versus 7.5 in Canada. Even more interesting perhaps, the **employment rate**, *the percentage of employed people as a share of the working-age population*, was higher in Canada than in the United States (Stanford, 2003).

What of income? As noted above, per capita incomes in Canada (in U.S. dollars) in 2000 were more than $10 000 lower than American incomes. The difference reflects the lower value of the Canadian dollar against American currency. This gap may not be as large as it seems, however, as the Canadian dollar's purchasing power in Canada is higher than its trade value against the U.S. dollar. In 1999, for example, its purchasing power in Canada was 84 cents, nearly 25 percent higher than its trade value (Kesselman, 2001: 88).

What of wealth? There is little doubt the United States, home of many of the world's largest corporations, is also home to many of the world's wealthiest individuals and their families (including the Walton family of Wal-Mart fame, Warren Buffett, and Bill Gates). Only a small handful of individuals make it on *Forbes Magazine*'s list, even fewer of whom are Canadians (see Table 9.3 above).

The diminished presence of a capitalist elite in Canada means that gaps between the rich and poor in Canada are less pronounced that in the United States. Statistics Canada figures show that, in 1997, lower-income Canadians were better off than lower income Americans, at the same time that the gap between rich and poor was exploding in the United States (*Edmonton Journal*, 2000d). Another Statistics Canada study (Wolfson and Murphy, 2000) tells a similar story. In 1997, people with incomes of less than $25 000 (Canadian) paid the same or lower taxes in Canada than in the United States, while those earning $150 000 or more pay more tax than those in the United States. In short, Canada has a more egalitarian social structure than does the United States. Nonetheless, there are clear signs, as we have noted, that the gap between rich and poor is also growing in Canada (Kerstetter, 2002).

If Canada is less economically prosperous (though more equal) than the United States, Canadian society comes off better when considered according to several quality-of-life measures. Infant death rates in Canada are 5.0 per 1000 live births; in the U.S. the number is 6.71. Canadian life expectancy is 79.7 years versus 77.4 years in the United States (*Time*, 2002: 714). Canadian crime rates also are lower than American rates, although the differences on certain crimes (burglary, car thefts) are small, and even the significant differences between robbery and murder rates in the two countries are greatly reduced when regional and metropolitan effects are controlled (Quimet, 1999).

The two nations can also be compared in a series of other policy realms. The United States has one of the most punitive, expensive, and arguably ineffective justice systems in the world. It imprisons far more people per capita than any other Western industrialized country—in 1995, 600 per 100 000 people (compared with Canada, in second place with 115 per 100 000 people)—and is the only one of these countries with the death penalty.

The United States has by far the world's largest military budget, $396.1 billion (U.S.) in 2001 alone, compared with Russia, in second place, at $60 billion (figures for 2000). Canada spent $7.7 billion (U.S.) on its military in 2001 (*Time*, 2002: 716). The U.S. also spends far more money than Canada (or any other Western state) on health care: in 1997, 13.6 percent of GDP versus 9.3 percent of GDP in Canada (Government of Alberta, 2002: 11), but more of these expenditures are "private." Ironically, despite its high cost, the American health care system has generally poorer health outcomes, while leaving over 40 million people (roughly 14 percent of the population in 2000) without affordable health care. By contrast, Canada's publicly funded health care system is universal, covering everyone as a right of citizenship.

In the end, societies are the product of choices. But, as conflict theorists and feminists theorists argue, not everyone has an equal voice in making these choices. Rather, the choices manifested are the result of real struggles, conducted between and amidst groups defined by class, gender, race, and ethnicity (among other factors), for control over the instruments of the state. Canada tends in a host of areas—education, health, and (to an albeit shrinking degree) social welfare—to invest a substantial amount of money in public services compared with the United States, and this fact reflects a different history of struggles and resultant choices. At the start of the twenty-first century, one of the questions facing Canadians is whether they have the will to continue to make choices for themselves in the face of increasing global and American pressures.

THE GLOBAL CONTEXT

Free trade was only part of broader efforts begun in the 1980s by governments (led by the United States), academics, and business leaders to open up opportunities for expanded trade. The heyday of what has become known as globalization started with the Canada-U.S. free trade agreement that came into effect in 1989 and ended (roughly) in 1997 with a global monetary crisis that set off a global recession lasting two years. Though efforts at neo-liberal globalization continue through organizations such as the World Trade Organization, the World Bank, and the International Monetary Fund (IMF), these efforts have slowed in recent years due to a series of events: several state bankruptcies (especially in Latin America) followed by in some cases the election of new governments espousing policies of de-globalization, the rise internationally of a counter-globalization movement, a host of corporate scandals that shook faith in business and markets and, finally, the onset of global insecurity brought on by terrorism and the threat of war (see below). In this context, even some of its former cheerleaders—among them, George Soros, a multi-millionaire currency speculator, and Joseph Stiglitz, a former senior economist with the World Bank—have denounced globalization as a source of political and economic instability and growing international poverty.

Proponents of economic globalization make three assertions. First, they claim that everyone (over time) benefits from free and open trade. More jobs are created, consumers have access to a wider variety of goods and services, and resources are used in a more efficient manner than would otherwise occur under protectionist policies. Second, proponents argue that economic freedom is necessary for political freedom and an expansion of human rights. Third, proponents argue that, in any case, global economic integration is inevitable, part of the natural history of progress.

Opponents of economic globalization dispute each of these assertions. They note that the world's wealthiest countries got that way not through free trade but through protectionist policies (see Chapter Seven). They further note that, while the economic situation of many countries has actually declined over the past decade, the wealthiest have more than prospered. For example, in 1995, 51 of the world's 100 wealthiest economies were in fact corporations, up from 49 in 1991 (Robbins, 1999: 137). A United Nations report released in 2000 shows that the combined wealth of the world's 200 richest people is over $1 trillion, while the combined incomes of the 582 million people living in the 43 least-developed countries is $146 billion (*Edmonton Journal*, 2000e).

Indeed, from the point of view of its opponents, globalization is merely an updated name for a pattern of global exploitation that began with mercantilism (Chapter Two), then became colonialism, and now holds countries hostage through trade agreements and debt (Sassan, 2001) rather than military force (though the latter is still often used). The richest countries of 200 years ago remain rich; the poorest of that time generally remain poor. Moreover, even those countries that in recent years have strictly followed neo-liberal policies have suffered. Argentina provides a case example.

In the early 1990s, under pressure from the United States and the IMF, and investors in general, Argentina abandoned protectionist policies in favour of neo-liberal solutions for economic development. Many of its public enterprises were privatized and bought up immediately by foreign corporations. As elsewhere, this flood of direct foreign investment fuelled rapid and immediate growth. Argentina briefly became a poster child for neo-liberal policies.

Within five years, however, growth plummeted and Argentina entered a prolonged recession. Unemployment rose, wages stagnated, and foreign debt grew. The IMF told Argentina's government it had to cut deeper into its public spending to pay off its foreign debt of $155 billion (U.S.). The country's public health system, once a source of pride like Canada's, was gutted, and other social programs similarly cut, to no avail. Political turmoil ensued. In early 2002, the straitened middle classes of Buenos Aires took to the streets demanding reforms and protection from losing their houses. Within days, four successive Argentine presidents were toppled. Argentina soon defaulted on its foreign debt, much as Russia had done a few years earlier.

Like Argentina, Canada embarked on similar policies in the late 1980s and early 1990s, being also warned at one point by the IMF to cut its cumulating debt. Deregulation, downsizing, privatization, and cost cutting occurred at all government levels, implemented by parties of different political stripes (see Laxer and Harrison, 1995; Ralph, 1997; Rice and Prince, 2000).

Gradually, the deficit and debt "crisis" was controlled, but pro-market policies tend still to dominate Canada's economic and political decision-making. The result has been, in the eyes of many, an object lesson in how external organizations and forces can exert control over domestic policies. But globalization also binds countries in patterns of functional interdependence and political conflict, as became starkly apparent in the fall of 2001.

THE AMERICAN WAR ON TERRORISM

For years, theorists have suggested that globalization not only connects people in positive ways but also increases tensions in ways that might heighten conflict, especially along cultural and religious lines (Barber, 1996; Huntington, 1996; Sassan, 2001). On September 11, 2001, terrorists aligned with an extreme Islamic fundamentalist group known as Al-Qaeda rammed two passenger planes into New York's World Trade Center, killing roughly 2800 people. Another plane was flown into the Pentagon in Washington, with the loss of nearly 200 more lives. The numbers killed were by some measures relatively small, far less, for example, than the number murdered in the United States every year (12 943 in 2000) or killed in motor vehicle accidents (43 501 in 2000) (*Time*, 2002: 134, 361).

Nonetheless, it is clear the attacks have already entered into American history and mythology alongside Pearl Harbor. As the perpetrators no doubt planned, the attacks pierced the American myth of invincibility. They shocked the American psyche and brought home to some the fact that in the twenty-first century terrorism also had gone global (Keohane, 2001), though some might argue that it had long been so (Parenti, 1995).

There was understandable sorrow, bewilderment, and anger throughout the United States (Gitlin, 2001). A wave of flag-waving patriotism, mixed with jingoist rhetoric from President George Bush, Jr., suggested that the United States was prepared to launch a war in perpetuity and without limits or borders against suspected terrorists. American military spending again increased to fight what was dubbed the War on Terrorism, though the term *war* was clearly inappropriate to describe the situation. (Wars occur between states. In this case, there is no clearly identified enemy and no certainty of what *victory* might mean.) Dissent and critical discussion of the causes underlying the attacks (see Johnson, 2001; Chomsky, 2001) all but disappeared in America. Incidents of students, professors, and media being silenced took on McCarthyite tones (see Gonzalez, 2001).

A few weeks after the attacks, the United States and its allies invaded Afghanistan, where many members of the terrorist group and its leadership resided, and toppled the Taliban regime governing that country. That conflict quickly ended with the Taliban defeated and the Al-Qaeda terrorists dead, imprisoned, or on the run. Afghanistan, an underdeveloped country already ruined by over 20 years of war, began a slow fade from the world's television screens.

In early 2002, the War on Terrorism took an abrupt detour. In his State of the Union address, President Bush identified an "axis of evil": Iraq, Iran, and North Korea, which he alleged were supporting international terrorism. Over the next few months, the United

States increased pressure upon Iraq to account for "weapons of mass destruction" unaccounted for since the 1991 Gulf War. The fall of 2002 saw United Nations' weapons inspectors embark on a series of missions to discover whether Iraq had any nuclear, biological, or chemical weapons. Over the months that followed, none were located.

Meanwhile, in September 2002, the Bush administration released its new National Security Strategy (Government of the United States, 2002). The document, popularly called the **Bush Doctrine**, argues that the attacks of September 11, 2001, had made the principle of launching war purely in retaliation (that is, for defensive purposes) inoperative. Instead, the document states that the United States will in future attack in pre-emptive fashion any country that it believes may possess, or may seek to possess, weapons dangerous to the U.S. The Bush Doctrine further argues that, because the threat to American interests is now worldwide, the United States is justified in taking military actions anywhere. For this reason, some see the Bush Doctrine as an extension of the Monroe Doctrine (Chapter Six). Finally, the Bush Doctrine argues that no country in future will be allowed to compete militarily with the United States.

After months of debate at the United Nations, which attempted collectively to implement a peaceful way of disarming Iraq, the United States, Britain, and a handful of smaller countries broke with the UN and (in March 2003) launched a twenty-first-century war against Iraq, designed not only to ensure its disarmament but also to replace its leadership. The United States claimed the United Nations, by failing to support its military action, was proving itself irrelevant to deal with world problems. Opponents, however, argued that the United Nations was in fact proving its relevance in a multinational, globalized world and that the United States by its actions was acting as though it were now ruler of the world.

REFLECTIONS ON STATE AND EMPIRE: THE CASE OF THE UNITED STATES

This text began its exploration of Canadian society with a discussion of the concept of the state (Chapter One). To refresh your memory, and save your returning to the early pages, we defined the **state** as *a set of institutions successfully claiming a monopoly over political rule-making and the legitimate use of violence and coercion within a given territory, i.e. a country*. Note that this definition is entirely neutral. States are neither good nor bad. They are merely instruments for achieving certain ends. The specific character of each state arises out of the class, gender, ethnic, ideological (etc.) configuration of those who have their hands on the controls, and the historical period and circumstances of its formation. States come in many forms: feudal, capitalist, fascist, social-democratic, communist— even welfare states and warfare states. Every modern society has some form of state because, as you also will recall, states and societies have arisen together.

The United States began as a republic. It is sometimes referred to as a product of the Enlightenment because of its belief in individual freedom, social equality, and democracy. For much of their history, the American people have been isolationist, unwilling to become entangled in affairs outside their borders.

At the same time, however, since the mid-nineteenth century the American state has increasingly advanced its interests and those of its capitalist class abroad. In 1853, U.S. Commodore Matthew Perry and four American warships arrived in Japan and forced the Japanese government to sign a series of treaties opening that country up to foreign trade

(Balaam and Veseth, 1996: 262). Throughout the remainder of the nineteenth century, the United States continued to acquire territory and military bases overseas. The end of the First World War saw the U.S. viewed by many as Britain's natural imperial successor.

Americans traditionally do not like to think of themselves as imperialists. For obvious political reasons, American politicians also shy away from describing their country in terms of empire. Increasingly, however, this reluctance is giving way (see Johnson, 2000). Ignatieff (2003) in fact has argued that, given the events of September 11, 2001, the United States should now embrace its transition from republic to empire in the interests of ensuring a Pax Americana. But is the United States an empire?

Analytically, empires have the following attributes. First, empires have overseas possessions. The United States does not formally have a lot of these any more, but it does have a few, such as Puerto Rico (see *Time*, 2002: 102). Second, empires have military bases in other countries. The United States today has numerous bases strewn around the globe, from the Americas, to the Philippines and Japan, to the many Gulf states, to Africa and Europe. Third, empires have client states or "vassals." Again, the United States has these in abundance, exerting financial and political control through such institutions as the International Monetary Fund and the World Bank. (Many of the countries supporting the U.S.-led war in Iraq in 2003 were financial dependencies.)

Fourth, empires act independently in their own interests, without regard for others—**unilateralism**—in part because they have the power to do so, but in part also because empires are by nature blind to others. Since the end of the Cold War, and especially in recent years, the United States has rejected coordination of its policies with other countries on a number of issues of common concern—**multilateralism**. Even before the attacks on New York and Washington, for example, the U.S. refused to sign a treaty banning land mines and the Kyoto treaty curtailing the worldwide emission of greenhouse gases. Just before September 2001, the United States also ended its 1972 Anti-Ballistic Missile Treaty with Russia and has since made known its intentions to militarize outer space. Furthermore, the U.S. has refused to recognize the jurisdiction of the world criminal court, set up to try war criminals, and an international convention on torture, in both cases because it did not want to subject American citizens, laws, or practices to an international body.

Fifth, empires *do* attempt to impose their laws on others, what is referred to as **extraterritoriality**. The United States' decades-old embargo on trade and commerce with Cuba is a good example. American-owned firms based in Canada that trade with Cuba are subject under American law to prosecution. Likewise, Americans who travel to that country on holidays, if caught, can be taken before the courts. But recent American efforts, through trade agreements, to impose American patent law on other countries are also typical of an empire.

Sixth, empires are generally possessed of a quasi-religious sense of mission that provides a moral, and thus social-psychological, justification for expansion. Alexander the Great, for example, believed in his personal mission to spread Hellenic culture. Likewise, the British saw themselves as civilizing the "lesser breeds before the law," while the French under Napoleon believed they were liberating Europe and spreading the trinity of "liberty, fraternity, equality."

We noted in Chapter Six that the United States' political culture, from its infancy, has held a series of beliefs congruent with an empire's sense of mission, that the United States is not "just another country" but rather one with the divine task of promoting freedom and American liberal democracy. These beliefs remain alive in the U.S. today. In February 1998, for example, Secretary of State Madeleine Albright referred to the United States as the world's "only indispensable nation" (Johnson, 2000: 217). President Bush's use of religious imagery to describe the War on Terrorism (and on Iraq) as one between "Good" and "Evil" is one with great resonance for many Americans who see the United States as a liberator and are confused that much of the world sees the actions of the American state far less positively (Richburg, 2001). (In the case of Iraq, the worldwide view, held also by many academics, is that control over oil, and not the welfare of the Iraqi people, lies at the heart of American intervention [Roberts, 2003].)

Seventh, more than those of most societies and states, an empire's societal parts function in a way enhancing the empire's continued expansion. C.W. Mills (1956) noted in the mid-1950s the mutually reinforcing relationships between the United States' political, business, and military establishments. A few years later, in 1961, as he resigned the American presidency, Dwight D. Eisenhower warned of the rise of a "military-industrial complex" (Kurth, 1993). Today, one might add a fourth leg to America's corporate-dominated state: the media.

The terrorist attacks of September 11, 2001, have only increased the fear, sense of mission, and obedience of the American people to their country, their flag, and the empire. But will efforts by the United States to create a Pax Americana resolve the short-term problem of terrorism and the long-term problem of global governance? There are reasons to believe not. The United States may find itself suffering from imperial over-stretch, isolated, and beset by internal conflicts, as occurred during the Vietnam war years.

WAR, THE BUSH DOCTRINE, AND ITS CONSEQUENCES FOR CANADA

Unlike the Gulf War of 1991, Canada did not join the American-led coalition in the Iraq war of 2003. As a small country, Canada has always relied upon multilateral relationships as a counterweight to the power of great nations, whether Britain, the United States, or the former Soviet Union. When the United States failed to gain United Nations approval for military action, Canada announced it would not join the war effort.

Given its geographic proximity to the United States and the high level of integration between the two countries (see above), Canada faced some potentially serious consequences for its decision. Indeed, many political leaders in Canada and most of the country's big business community argued that Canada *had* to side with the American government or face economic reprisals. In short, Canada's exercise of sovereignty was seen by at least some as a purchasable commodity.

Beyond the immediate question of the Iraq war, the United States has made a series of specific demands upon Canada since September 2001 (see Clarkson, 2002a; 2002b). Militarily, these demands include the creation of a military zone around North America under American command and control. (In Afghanistan after the successful war to overthrow that country's Taliban regime, Canadian soldiers found themselves under the control, though not the command, of the American army. In late 2002, the Canadian government signed an agreement allowing Canadian and American troops to enter the other's territory.) Politically, American demands include Canada's adoption of American immigration policies and common security practices. (Within months of September 11, American and Canadian immigration officials began working side by side at the border.) Economically, these demands (from business as well as political leaders) include, besides calls for greater border security, further integration of North American resources (especially oil) in order to break American dependence upon "unstable regions" for resources (American Natural Resource Defense Council, 2002; see also *National Post*, 2001b). Early 2003 saw some business leaders and right-wing think tanks, such as the C.D. Howe Institute, suggest it was time to eliminate altogether the economic border and move to full economic (if not political) integration.

Taken together, these demands amount to the creation of a single economic, political, and social entity—a United States of North America—in all but name. Canada might continue to exist as a territory on world maps, but the possibility of its people charting, in any meaningful sense, an independent course would be ended.

But, as became quickly apparent in the months leading up to the Iraq war, world events also pose opportunities and threats of another sort for Canadian sovereignty and national identity. Canadians by and large agreed with their government in not supporting the United States' unilateral actions in Iraq. And, in the aftermath of the war's beginning, Canadian cities—like cities throughout much of the world, including cities in the United States—were often scenes of massive protests against the war.

But, many Canadians also felt torn, wanting to support their American neighbours. And some believed Canada should join in the war effort, a few because they believed in the U.S. cause, others because they feared American economic and political retaliation against Canada for not joining.

Given strong opposition among francophone Quebecers to the war, the support for war among some in English-speaking Canada could have threatened Canadian unity, as occurred during previous world conflicts (see Chapter Three). At the same time, however, recent wars, notably the war in Vietnam, coincided with a resurgence of Canadian nationalism as the American model became less appealing to many Canadians. Might Canada experience a similar wave of nationalism again?

CONCLUSION

Years ago, Harold Innis wryly amended the title of Arthur Lower's book *From Colony to Nation* to suggest Canada had then reverted again quickly to a colony, this time of the United States. Canadians have always faced the task of carving out an existence and an identity on the margins of the world economy and a series of empires. Today, the fight for Canadians to remain a sovereign people with their own distinct society has taken on a new urgency. Canada's fate lies not in the stars, however, or in the inexorable workings of some imaginary manifest destiny imposed by others: it lies rather in the will of its people to find or create new reasons to continue as a society, a country, and a different kind of nation. In this quest, they might look no further for answers than among Canada's Aboriginal people who, earlier than most, faced the onslaught of global imperial forces.

KEY TERMS

Bush Doctrine
employment rate
extraterritoriality
feminization of poverty
income
inter-generational social mobility
intra-generational social mobility
multilateralism
neo-conservatism
neo-liberalism
social class
social mobility
socio-economic status
state
unilateralism
wealth

part three

Canada and the Aboriginal Nations

For 11 weeks in the summer of 1990, Canadians watched transfixed as a confrontation over development of a golf course in Quebec threatened a bloodbath between Aboriginals and the Canadian military. The Oka Crisis was a watershed in Aboriginal relations with Canadian society. On the one hand, many Canadians felt some sympathy for Aboriginal demands. As during the FLQ Crisis in 1970, a few Canadians also were appalled by the use of the military in the name of "law and order." On the other hand, a large portion of Canadians feared the new Aboriginal militancy.

The Oka Crisis sparked renewed efforts by government (at all levels) to come to a new arrangement with Aboriginal communities. But it also unleashed fierce resistance to change, in both communities.

In Part One, we examined Canada's French and English "solitudes." But Aboriginal and non-Aboriginal people in Canada constitute another pair of solitudes, separated by history, culture, class, and experience. This separation continues despite the fact that Aboriginals, especially in western Canada, are increasingly part of the urban landscape. Instead, relationships between the two groups are too often mediated by state institutions, particularly Indian Affairs, children's service agencies, welfare agencies, and the courts. In this context, the knowledge that non-Aboriginals possess about Aboriginals is largely abstract or anecdotal, often stereotypical.

Part Three of this book explores the history of relations between Aboriginals and non-Aboriginals in Canada. As in the previous two sections, the first chapter of Part Three provides a historical overview. Chapter Eleven then examines a part of Canada not yet discussed here in detail: the North, a place where Aboriginal people still predominate and yet one which is, for many non-Aboriginals, a prime source of what it means to be Canadian. Chapter Twelve examines the genesis of recent Aboriginal demands and growing militancy. Finally, Chapter Thirteen concludes with a portrait of Aboriginal peoples today in Canada, an examination of the major issues still to be resolved in this area, and a discussion of the profound impact that Aboriginals may have in shaping Canadian society in future.

QUESTIONS

- What part did Aboriginal peoples play in the early history of Canada?
- What is the nature of relations between Aboriginals and non-Aboriginals in Canada today?
- Why do individual Aboriginals and their communities lag behind other Canadians, on average, in social development, while leading in such things as suicide, imprisonment, and unemployment rates?
- What issues lay behind the Oka Crisis in 1990?
- Why have land claims and treaty negotiations suddenly become prominent in Canadian news?
- What factors are pushing or pulling Aboriginal Canadians into Canadian cities?
- How do Aboriginal cultural values differ from those of mainstream Canadian society?
- What lessons might non-Aboriginal society learn from Aboriginal society in meeting the challenges of this century?

chapter ten

When Cultural Worlds Collide

We had a cross made thirty feet high, which was put together in the presence of a number of the Indians on the point at the entrance to this harbour, under the cross-bar of which we fixed a shield with three *fleurs-de-lys* in relief, and above it a wooden board, engraved in large Gothic characters, where was written, LONG LIVE THE KING OF FRANCE. We erected this cross on the point in their presence and they watched it being put together and set up.

—Jacques Cartier, *Diary*, 1534

But the face of the red man is now no longer seen. All traces of his footsteps are fast being obliterated from his once favourite haunts, and those who would see the aborigines of this country in their original state, or seek to study their native manners and customs, must travel far through the pathless forest to find them.

—artist Paul Kane, 1859

[T]oday it is popular to be an Indian. Within a decade it may be a necessity. People are not going to want to take the blame for the sorry state of the nation, and claiming allegiance with the most helpless racial minority may well be the only way to escape accusation.

—Oglala Sioux elder and scholar Vine Deloria, Jr., 1995

INTRODUCTION

The Aboriginal peoples of Canada are much in the news these days. Stories about treaty rights, land claims, residential school litigations, and the Indian Act regularly dot the pages of daily papers and newsmagazines. In a real sense, much of the fallout from the original culture clash between incoming Europeans and the First Nations is only now being felt.

When the first Europeans arrived in North America, they encountered peoples with an entirely different view of social organization and government, who lived by an allegiance to high spiritual powers and the universe. The newcomers ignored these differences. Armed with a strong sense of **ethnocentrism**—*the tendency of people to see the world only from their own cultural perspective*—they "boldly went where no man [sic] had gone before."

This chapter examines the cultural world of Canada's Aboriginal peoples before and after the arrival of Europeans, including the political economy of the two peoples' early relations. The chapter further shows how the dominant-subordinate relationship between the non-Aboriginal and Aboriginal peoples became institutionalized, with consequences for both parties and for Canadian society as a whole.

PRE-CONTACT LIFESTYLE

Accounts penned by archaeologists inform us that the indigenous peoples of North America have been on this continent for 10 000 to 12 000 years, but the truth is that no one really knows when the first Aboriginal peoples arrived. Some evidence points to an arrival as long as 30 000 to 50 000 years ago (Dickason, 2002: 6). In fact, as their oral tradition testifies, they may well have originated on this continent. American comedian Will Rogers, himself of Cherokee extraction, once remarked, "I suppose I am not as American as those who came over on the Mayflower, but we met them at the dock when they landed."

Historians for years insisted that the First Nations peoples arrived in North America thousands of years ago via an ice bridge that temporarily linked Asia to this continent. This was known as the Bering Strait theory. There is little scientific evidence to support the theory, however. Deloria (1995: 81) wryly suggests that one day someone, lamenting the lack of explanation for the origins of the Aboriginal peoples of the Americas, simply invented the Bering Strait theory, and said, "I don't know, but it sounds good and no one will check it out." Recent evidence suggests they may have arrived by various routes.

Initial encounters between the Europeans and indigenous North Americans were limited to south and central regions of the continent. Northern contact occurred much later. The first Europeans arriving often failed to make distinctions, but in fact the peoples they encountered represented a variety of different civilizations and cultures.

In what is today Canada, five distinct cultural areas could then be identified among the First Peoples: the Northwest Coast, the Plateau, the Plains, the Mackenzie District and the Eastern Woodlands. Authorities differ regarding the linguistic varieties, but today language groups comprise most First Nation language families (Wilson and Urion, 1995: 32). The first of the three major linguistic groups is Algonquian, which includes most Canadian Aboriginals and the vast majority in southern Canada east of the Rockies. Two Algonquian groups, Cree and Ojibway, are closely related, implying recent separation. The Blackfoot also appear to be distantly related.

The second major language family in Canada is Athapaskan, with the majority of speakers occupying much of northwestern Canada and Alaska. Because of the limited diversity that exists among this language group, linguists believe this area was more recently occupied. The greatest Athapaskan diversity is found on the southeast coast of Alaska, although linguists believe numerous migrations from that location may have occurred to such regions as the Alaskan interior and eastward into northern Canada. Considerable similarity between the Athapaskan languages and those of the Navajo and the Apache suggests further that some groups moved to the American southwest.

The third language family is Eskimo-Aleut, represented in Canada by Inupik (Inuktitut), is identified only in the northern regions from northern Alaska across to eastern Greenland. Apart from any archaeological evidence, this seems to imply that the region has only recently been occupied (see Chapter Eleven).

Addicted as we are to the magic of the technological age, it is sometimes hard to realize the dramatic cultural changes that have occurred these last several centuries in Canada. The impact on Aboriginal cultures has been considerable, and while many First Nations have successfully adjusted to elements of the technological revolution, others are still determining how they can best participate in this transition. Consider, for example, that only a few short centuries ago, most of Canada was occupied by people who worked with Mother Nature rather than seeking to subdue her. Up till 1877, the southern third of the province of Alberta was controlled entirely by members of the Blackfoot Confederacy (Blood, Peigan, and Siksika).

Cultures may differ materially and non-materially (through their particular languages, values, beliefs, norms, and behaviours) in ways passed on from one generation to the next (Macionis and Gerber, 1999: 60). From a functionalist perspective, however, all cultures, Aboriginal or other, possess certain elements (Durkheim, 1978; Wissler, 1923). These elements include (1) language; (2) artifacts (that is, physical objects) that serve functional purposes; (3) social organization; (4) authority and decision-making arrangements; (5) underlying spiritual or religious beliefs and structures; (6) forms of welfare arrangements whereby the aged, the sick, and the young are taken care of; (7) arts and music; (8) forms of property ownership or usage; and (9) a means of educating the young to assure perpetuation of the system.

Pre-contact Aboriginal lifestyles represented a very present-oriented way of life. Use of the term "survival culture" in this context is inappropriate, however, because these were "living cultures." The people did not merely survive; they enjoyed their lives and took time to live. Unlike their twenty-first century counterparts, they were never in a hurry to get somewhere else: they were already where they needed to be. They did not have the luxury of placing things in a freezer to save for another day, though they had ways of preserving some foods. Nor did they make use of such future-oriented facilities as savings accounts, pension plans, or registered retirement savings plans; they relied instead on the people and environment around them. Primary to all considerations was their relationship to nature, the elements—sun, earth, water, wind, fire—and the cycle of natural growth and change.

Their awe of nature did not hinder the First Nations from developing elaborate metaphysical belief systems or developing complex forms of food gathering, food preparation, art, and weaponry. Often these cultural elements were related. Food gathering and religion, for example, are highly related activities in nearly all pre-technological societies. All in all, it was a satisfying way of life. As the late Chief Walking Buffalo (Tatanga Mani) of the Stoney (Nakoda Sioux) Nation put it:

> We were on pretty good terms with the Great Spirit and Ruler of all....We saw the Great Spirit's work in almost everything: sun, moon, trees, wind and mountains. Sometimes we approached Him through these things. Was that so bad? Indians living close to nature and nature's Ruler are not living in darkness (Friesen, 1998: 30).

The primary unit of traditional social structure among indigenous peoples was the band, often considered a subunit of a tribe (now called "First Nation"). The chiefs who headed the bands often possessed valuable talents, with varying gifts for leadership in hunting or war, or in other contexts. Chiefs were mentors or servants of the people rather than managers or rulers (Snow, 1977). But real authority within the bands or tribe might reside with the elders: those perceived as having wisdom or medicinal knowledge gathered through years of living (Meili, 1991). This diffuse power structure confused the Europeans, who were used to their own rigid and hierarchical authority structures.

Bands were often formed on the basis of numbers; if a band got too large to set up or shut down camp easily, the people might divide into two units. Hunting and gathering bands tended to be small. By contrast, bands engaging in horticulture could accommodate larger populations. Other factors might also lead to the division of a band. Disagreements or the emergence of a charismatic leader, questioning the way things were being done, might lead to a group's splitting off to form a new band. The nomadic bands of western Canada would sometimes meet during the summer months to renew acquaintances, socialize, or celebrate the sun dance.

First Peoples of the West Coast and Eastern Woodlands developed elaborate clan systems of social organization. The clans were exogamous and bore animal names such as Bear or Turtle. They were subdivided on a matrilineal basis, and clan mothers were guardians of clan traditions and sacred practices. Clan mothers alone had the right to select and depose chiefs and councils, and had primary authority in such matters as land allotment, supervision of field labour, care of the treasury, the ordering of feasts, and dispute settlement (Johnston, 1964). Clans played an important role at the village level since all dwellers in a particular village belonged to the same clan. Clan subdivisions often had their own chiefs who managed internal affairs and represented their clan on village, tribal or confederacy councils. Chieftainships were not primarily hereditary along patrilineal lines, so a man might pass on his office to his sister's son, the latter not being a member of his clan (Trigger, 1969).

FIRST CONTACT

As yet unsubstantiated stories of Asian voyages to the West Coast aside (see Menzies, 2002), the initial meetings between First Nations outside civilizations probably occurred in the eastern Arctic, likely on Baffin Island (Dickason, 2002). The parties involved were Dorset and Beothuk peoples (both since mysteriously vanished) and incoming Norsemen (see Chapter Eleven). Then, beginning in the fifteenth century, a series of European visitors reached North America. They represented a host of states and nationalities. For example, Christopher Columbus sailed from Spain (in 1492); the Italians John and Sebastian Cabot from England (in 1498); Cortereal from Portugal (in 1517); and Baron de Léry (in

1518), Giovanni da Verrazano (in 1524), Jacques Cartier (in 1534) and Samuel de Champlain (in 1603) from France (see Tracy, 1908). Other names that could be added to this Hall of Fame (or Infamy) include John Davis, Martin Frobisher, Henry Hudson, Antonio Pigafetta, and Amerigo Vespucci.

Of these, Cartier and Champlain are probably the most important figures in early Canadian history because of their role in fostering further explorations of the New World. When Cartier returned to France with descriptions of the new land and its inhabitants, the whole of France attended him with extraordinary interest. As proof of his feats, Cartier even kidnapped two young Aboriginals, the sons of Iroquoi chief Donnacona, and brought them back to France with him. Later he returned and endured a most severe winter, barely surviving an onslaught of scurvy, thanks in large part to assistance from the Aboriginals. This could have dampened the enthusiasm he displayed in his first evaluation of the potential of the new country, but explorations continued. Champlain, following Cartier's lead, made friends with the Iroquois and established colonies in Acadia and New France (Chapter Two).

Nearly a century later, in 1610, the English built their first colony in the New World. It was established in Newfoundland under the governorship of John Guy. Further settlements followed along the eastern coast and along the St. Lawrence, heightening contact, competition, and conflict between the French and English and their Aboriginal allies.

Cook (1995: 22) suggests it was not immediately obvious that contacts between Aboriginal peoples and the Europeans, beginning in the late fifteenth century, would prove disastrous to the former. Aboriginals remained central economic actors during the period of the fur trade (see below). They were also instrumental politically during both the European wars for dominance of that fur trade in North America and the post-revolutionary wars, as the United States attempted to take over Canada. However, "the long-term advantages... lay with the Europeans: a growing economy, an increasingly complex technology, an expanding population, and a centralized political system supported by military power" (Cook, 1995: 22).

In Newfoundland, the Europeans (mainly English, Portuguese, and French) encountered the Beothuk. The Beothuk practice of colouring everything in red ochre—clothing, belongings, weapons, burial goods, and so on—resulted in the phrase "Red Indian" (Friesen, 1997: 49). Contact between the two cultures was marked by conflict, to say the least. By the early nineteenth century, the last Beothuks had died, though there is disagreement whether this resulted from intentional **genocide** —*an organized attempt by one society to eradicate another society or subgroup, often, but not always, violently* (see Dickason, 1984; Cook, 1995). By contrast, European contact with the Micmac, a neighbouring tribe to the Beothuk, by all accounts was mutually beneficial. The invaders were quite impressed with the Micmac way of life, particularly their well-built homes (mamateeks), their methods of procuring food from both the land and the sea, and their sociopolitical structures.

Among the Europeans, the French proved the most inclined to merge culturally and biologically with the Aboriginals, a fact that secured their interests in the fur trade (below). In general, however, attempts to meld the European and Aboriginal peoples did not succeed. As Dickason (1984: 147) notes, "the policy of creating one race was doomed to failure in New France as elsewhere—Amerindians and French were still distinct entities at the end of the French Regime in 1760."

THE FUR TRADE

Early twentieth-century writings on the fur trade tend to portray Aboriginal peoples as victims of the fur trade. More recent writings provide a more complex view. Cook (1995: 28) stresses three points concerning the fur trade. First, trade among Aboriginals in North America preceded the coming of the Europeans and was occasionally accompanied by conflict. The arrival of the Europeans only intensified the level of both. Second, insofar as eastern and coastal tribes had more immediate contact with Europeans than did the more western and inland tribes, the latter were able for a longer period to preserve their cultures and base of power. Third, Aboriginal people were not passive participants in the fur trade, but willing and motivated, and—in the early period—frequently did very well in bargaining.

Central to the fur trade was, of course, the beaver. Beaver pelts could be "felted" and used for making what became the treasured beaver pelt hat. The popularity of this unique item persisted in the seventeenth and eighteenth centuries, and became a badge of social status (Innis, 1962). Everyone in Europe with pretensions to "respectability" wanted a beaver hat, and when the hats began to age they were refurbished and shipped to South America to grace less particular heads. As Lower (1977: 99) puts it:

> So close was the relationship between the fur trade and the beaver hat that when early in the eighteenth century fashion in Europe decreed that brims should be a little narrower, a crisis ensued in the backwoods of Canada.

When the first Europeans settled along the eastern coast of North America, the First Nations brought them furs in exchange for European goods. Almost immediately, some Aboriginal people became intermediary traders between their counterparts further inland and the newcomers. Very soon, this established pattern had to be altered as the heavy European demand for furs resulted in a scarcity of pelts that drove the fur traders further inland. As Innis (1962) later observed, the search for staples—in this case, furs—led to Canada's economic development.

The Europeans quickly learned the value of Aboriginal people and their culture in procuring the desired furs. Aboriginal people not only trapped and transported the pelts but, more importantly, knew how to survive in the New World. Their means of cross-country transport, the canoe and snowshoe, were superior to anything possessed by the Europeans. They knew the habits of the sought-after animals, which plants were suitable as food and medicine, and the best routes to take (Cook, 1995: 27–28). Aboriginal women, in particular, also proved adept as translators and trade negotiators, not to mention valued companions to the European traders (van Kirk, 1999). For these reasons, it was to the advantage of Europeans in Canada, unlike the Spanish invaders to the far south, to develop harmonious relations with the Aboriginal peoples (Conrad et al., 1993).

In this context, the early years of the fur trade were beneficial in some respects to both sides. In fact, some of the new colonists in New France found trading more profitable than farming and turned their energies in that direction. Meanwhile, members of local tribes made annual trips to trading ports in hope of obtaining the kinds of agricultural supplies and other products—notably guns, but also such items as steel traps, axes, pots, and other domestic items—upon which they soon became dependent. But the fur trade also carried dangerous consequences for the Aboriginal peoples.

Intensified conflict, both with the Europeans and each other, was one obvious consequence. The introduction of guns raised conflict to new levels and changed the balance of power between Aboriginal nations. No less lethal were the recurrent epidemics unleashed by the Europeans. In 1634, smallpox or measles killed large numbers of Montagnais and Algonquins. Similarly, between 1636 and 1639, a series of epidemics reduced the Huron population from 25 000 to around 10 000 (Dickinson and Young, 1993: 19). Like the influenza epidemic that swept the world in 1919, the devastation experienced by Aboriginal people in these instances was unintentional, a result of contact. Not every instance was unplanned, however. During the Seven Years War (1756–1763), General Amherst achieved the dubious distinction of being the first person to utilize germ warfare when he ordered blankets contaminated by smallpox to be distributed among France's Aboriginal allies.

Liquor was another danger. Motivated by economic desires, the fur traders used virtually any available means to accumulate their bounty. The exchange of goods between First Nations and Europeans was not necessarily always fair exchange, particularly from the standpoint of the fur trading countries. With the high demand for furs back home, the traders did whatever it took to obtain furs. Various items were traded or even given as gifts, but easily the most damaging was liquor. Cheap goods accompanied its supply, and the records are full of French complaints about the poor quality of English goods offered to Aboriginal people, though this may be a case of one business simply "slamming" its competitor.

In liquor the English traded rum and the French relied on brandy. Not familiar with either commodity, the Aboriginals did not differentiate between the liquids, which made the traders quite happy, particularly since the two were equally effective as trade items. The long-term effects of the dispersal of this commodity meant that old and salutary habits of life were abandoned, independence and character were lost, and the structure of tribal life broke down. War, disease, and liquor quickly threatened the First Nations with a peril unmatched in their history.

As the fur trade flourished, the traders sought out various means to maintain the flow of furs, notably gift-giving. Although the exchange of gifts was initially instigated to affirm friendship between participating parties, European traders also used the arrangement to enhance the status of tribal leaders in the eyes of their people and to reward them for their efforts on behalf of the trading companies (Ray, 1974). In effect, the European traders attempted to co-opt the Aboriginal leaders. If a band later failed to obtain a sufficient quantity of furs or provisions to pay off its debts, the leader was denied these symbols of office. If, on the other hand the crop was ample or abundant, Aboriginal leaders were paid in more generous terms. Thus, one consequence of the fur trade was the undermining of traditional Aboriginal authority structures.

In the latter years of the sixteenth century, France attempted to form a monopoly on trade. The attempt failed. Over the next two centuries, France and England went repeatedly to war, until the former was finally defeated in the Seven Years War (1756–1763) (Chapter Two). The end of war saw the British government pass the Royal Proclamation. Fully one-third of the Royal Proclamation was devoted to matters pertaining to First Nations (Johnston, 1989). The practice of signing treaties was already deeply entrenched between the Aboriginal peoples and government, but the Royal Proclamation went further. It implied that the Aboriginal peoples and their lands needed further legal protection and, indeed, gave negotiating powers to the Crown. In effect, Aboriginal title henceforth could only be extinguished by a bilateral agreement. This became the model for signing treaties and the basis of subsequent government dealings with the First Nations (Scott-Brown, 1991: 97f).

The end of war and France's defeat did not immediately change the contours of the fur trade. The French merchants were soon replaced in Montreal by a new organization of American and British merchants and French-Canadian voyageurs. The North West Company, as it was called, challenged the Hudson's Bay Company for supremacy in the fur trade, especially in the West.

Nonetheless, the fur trade was in trouble. By the early nineteenth century, over-harvesting, changes in European fashion, and the impact of settlement upon habitat were taking their toll (Innis, 1962). After a long and sometimes bloody struggle (including the Seven Oaks Massacre in 1816) to gain control of the fur trade, the Hudson's Bay Company and the North West Company merged in 1821. While the merger ended the bitter rivalry between the two companies, it did not end the fur trade's decline. Thus, the company's new governor, George (later Sir George) Simpson made several policy changes. To increase profits, he ordered that cheaper goods be traded for furs, reduced the use of alcohol as a trade item, and forbade the use of steel traps. He also tried to dissuade Aboriginals from trapping endangered species and taking furs out of season. This sat poorly with the First Nations trappers, whose way of life now revolved around the fur economy and who reasonably insisted they had no choice but to keep on trapping in areas where food was in short supply.

THE INDIGENOUS PEOPLE'S RESPONSE

Unaccustomed to long-range planning, the attitudes of the Cree and Ojibway toward conservation, territoriality, and trespassing were particularly negative. Simpson fought back, requesting the British government place the First Nations on permanent, well-defined territories as a means of better implementing his policies. In time, Simpson took even more extreme measures, closing the redundant trading posts. By the middle of the nineteenth century the fur trade labour force was cut back by as much as two-thirds (Ray, 1974: 205).

The Simpson incident is reminiscent of other Aboriginal expressions of opposition to European actions. Aboriginal bitterness over land-grabbing had been growing since 1760, when Pontiac, an Ottawa chief, organized a pan-Aboriginal confederacy to oppose British policy. Unlike the French, who celebrated a policy of "gift diplomacy," the British preferred making treaties or "purchasing" lands outright. (The European meanings of "property" and "ownership" were alien to Aboriginals.) "Pontiac's Rebellion"—as white historians named it—ended when he was captured and the Aboriginals discovered that their allies, the French, had been defeated (Francis et al., 1988: 166).

A later event depicting the strength of Aboriginal resistance to mistreatment occurred in 1811, when Shawnee chief Tecumseh and his brother (and spiritual adviser) The Prophet assembled an Aboriginal confederacy of some 30 nations. Tecumseh challenged the cessions of territory, particularly those in Indiana, and conducted a series of raids, many of them financed by the British, leading in part to the War of 1812 (Chapter Six). Tecumseh was killed in the war and today is widely viewed as a Canadian hero for helping to save the fledgling country. He did not succeed, however, in gaining for his people the autonomous homeland he believed had been promised by Sir Isaac Brock as a reward for his fighting against the Americans.

Meanwhile, there was also Aboriginal resistance on another front. One of the unexpected results of the cultural clash between European fur traders and First Nations was the birth of the Metis people. There was a shortage of women when New France was first being settled, so many European men took Aboriginal wives. Children of those unions were commonly called "half-breeds" or Metis, meaning "mixed." Eventually, there were enough Metis people to be identified as a separate cultural group. Morton (1970: 46) has described the Metis as hunters, trappers, fishermen, voyageurs, horsemen, and farmers, but above all, soldiers. Between 1820 and 1869, the Metis settlement at Red River in what became Manitoba was one of the most populated settlements in the West (Sprague, 1988: ix). The Metis represented the chief labour force of the western fur trade and were hit particularly hard by that trade's demise.

The end of the fur trade can be dated to December 1, 1869, when the Hudson's Bay Company formally transferred its western lands to Canada. The move, part of the Macdonald government's efforts at nation-building (Chapter Seven), took place with no consideration for Metis concerns or the Aboriginal way of life. Canada's west was to be opened up for agriculture. Hunting and gathering were to be shunted to the margins.

The Metis resented previous British indifference to their fate and worried Canada would do no better. To protect themselves, the charismatic Metis leader Louis Riel and his colleagues set up a provisional government and took control of the Red River region. Riel today remains a controversial figure. Was he a traitor or a hero? Was he insane or not (Flanagan, 1977)? Was he tried fairly, or was he railroaded (Thomas, 1977)?

In the end, this first act of Aboriginal resistance in western Canada ended more or less peacefully with Manitoba's entry into Confederation (1870), though Riel fled to the United States. The second act played out 15 years later at Batoche (near Prince Albert), with Riel and his followers defeated and Riel hanged.

Metis resistance has often been portrayed in derogatory terms such as rebellion, insurrection, or defiance, but a strong argument can be made that the Metis were simply defending their native lands. Moreover, the Metis have a unique place in Canadian history, being the only charter group in the country with a history of national political independence before joining Confederation. The charter of the Province of Manitoba was formulated by the Metis under Riel's leadership (Friesen, 1996). Despite this, it was only in 1972 that the Canadian federal government acknowledged the Metis as a separate national entity. Since then they have worked hard to attain additional historical and cultural recognition through political action.

THE INTRODUCTION OF AGRICULTURE

The first 100 years after Confederation saw an estimated nine million newcomers enter Canada (Chapter Seven). Although many of them left Canada after a trial run at making a living in the cold climate (see McKie, 1994), many of them stayed, obviously impressed by the availability of land in Canada. For the next century, the landed immigrants dominated the population growth of the country. The relatively small populations of Aboriginal bands who occupied the country were pushed aside in the interests of economic development and to whet the appetites of the immigrants for land. Beginning in 1871, ten major treaties were signed across the country with First Nations, thus limiting their ownership of inherited lands and opening up seized territories for the newcomers. An 11th treaty was signed in the Northwest Territories in 1921.

The terms offered in the western treaties essentially followed the conditions outlined in eastern negotiations. The government agreed to provide a grant of land, a measure of military protection, a small per capita annuity, instruction in the basics of farming, and some form of education (Buckley, 1993: 34). Some chiefs objected to the amounts of land prescribed for them and voiced their objections. The chiefs rejected the terms of Treaty Six three times before signing it. (The negotiations ended with a fourfold increase in assigned lands.)

As the conditions brought about by the treaties gradually became reality, the Aboriginal people were informed that they would soon become sedentary farmers instead of nomadic hunters. Father Albert Lacombe, missionary to the Blackfoot, urged Chief Crowfoot to lead his people to a way of life that would eventually provide them with a new kind of prosperity. Chief Starblanket of Saskatchewan optimistically stated, "... we Indians can learn the ways of living that made the white man strong" (Buckley, 1993: 34).

Scholars are divided in their views on the degree of enthusiasm with which Aboriginal farmers in the West took up an agrarian lifestyle. The situation in the East was quite different because many Woodland First Nations were already solidly entrenched in agriculture (growing corn, beans and squash) when the first Europeans arrived. Historian G.F.G. Stanley (1975) in 1936 fostered the view, later promoted by Hanks and Hanks (1950) in their study of the Blackfoot Reserve in Alberta, that Aboriginal warriors and hunters looked upon farming with disdain. According to this view, most Aboriginal peoples shunned the concepts of steady work and acquisitiveness promoted by the dominant Euro-Canadian society, though some chiefs changed their minds about farming when they saw the rewards that could be theirs, such as axes, blankets and beads.

Carter (1993: 9–10) argues that the view promoted by Stanley and others is based on a dualism theory that recognizes two distinct and largely independent thinking patterns, modern and traditional. In this view, the modern perspective is characterized by high productivity and a market orientation, and is quite receptive to change. It pursues rational and maximizing aims. By contrast, the more traditional (Aboriginal) perspective is regarded as pre-capitalist, subsistence-oriented, primitive, and small-scale. It is depicted as resistant to change and affected by incentives quite different from the modern model. Instead of saving or building for the future, the traditional perspective emphasizes an orientation to the present.

First Nations have consistently been regarded as adherents to the traditional way of thinking and thus (presumably) opposed to taking up farming. Carter notes, however, that East Coast Natives were long involved in horticulture and cites also studies by Tobias (1977) and Carlson (1981) as proof that many Plains First Nations in the West were actually quite anxious to take up farming. The Crees, for example, adopted farming, and much of the political activity of their leaders was taken up with a concern about the lack of promised assistance rendered to them in that regard. Likewise, the Dakota of Manitoba initially showed great enthusiasm about farming until environmental setbacks and government restrictions brought about a period of stagnation (Laviolette, 1991).

Loss of the buffalo was the catalyst making farming a legitimate option for many Aboriginals. The demise of the "supermarket of the plains"—as the buffalo has been called—occurred a mere decade after treaty signing began. Many Aboriginal leaders could not fathom what was happening to their way of life. As the number of bison on the plains thinned out, competition for the animals among First Nations grew. Many former warriors who were now expected to become agriculturalists resisted the task of digging in the ground with a stick. Others grasped at spiritual straws: when their religious leaders reported revelations in which the Great Spirit was critical of mankind for replacing hunting with plowing, the people eagerly believed them. Some prophets even predicted the eventual return of the animal, perhaps in some other form. (A spokesman for the Smallboy Band of Cree in Alberta recently declared the buffalo were now coming back out of the ground in the form of oil and gas.)

COLONIZATION

With the collapse of the fur trade, its replacement by an agricultural and industrial economy, and the easing of tensions with the Americans, the British government in 1830 transferred management of Aboriginal affairs in Canada from military to civil authority. An abrupt change occurred in the way First Peoples were viewed by civil authorities who immediately sought to "take care of" (dominate) the Aboriginals. This was the real beginning of colonialism in Canada.

Colonialism is *a complex national system of racial, cultural, and political domination that produces privileges beyond the surplus value generated by capitalism* (Adams, 1999: 7). As a process, colonialism shapes the culture and life of both the colonizer and the colonized, with the important difference (of course) that the former assumes a superior position and assigns the latter an inferior status. Frideres and Gadacz (2001: 4–7) delineate the process of colonization in terms of seven characteristics.

The first characteristic is the invasion by a colonizing group of a geographic territory occupied by an indigenous group. This is usually undertaken by force, with the invaders acting only in their own best interests. The second characteristic is a campaign of deliberate destruction aimed at the indigenous group's social and cultural structures. In Canada, formal programs to carry out destructive policies were enacted between 1830 and 1875 (Surtees, 1969), particularly involving religious denominations and the provision of education designed to assimilate the Aboriginal peoples to European values and norms (see below).

The third and fourth dimensions of colonialism are the interrelated processes of exerting external control while encouraging economic dependency among the conquered people. Typically, the invading nation sends out tetrarchs to run things in the newly acquired territory, rather than assigning such responsibilities to leaders of the colonized peoples. In Canada the federally appointed "Indian agent" filled this role, often admirably, frequently becoming a most despised foreign despot among the Aboriginals whose lives he made miserable (Halliday, 1935). Nearly every activity on a reserve had to be approved by the Indian agent, including requests for seed, farm implements, or livestock, or even to ask permission to leave the reserve on a temporary basis. Eventually, such practices led to complete economic dependence on the part of Aboriginal people on the Canadian federal government and its managers.

The fifth attribute of colonialism is the provision of low-quality social services including health, education, and welfare. The negative statistics resulting from this policy have been evident in First Nations communities since the day the Canadian government took over control of Aboriginal matters. Reduced life expectancy, high mortality rates, poverty, inadequate education, high incidence of infectious diseases such as tuberculosis, poor housing, and heavy reliance on social assistance are among the characteristic features of such policy. Alcohol and substance abuse have further led to such unfortunate practices as suicide, rape and child abuse, as well as family deterioration.

The last two characteristics of colonialism are the practice of racism and the establishment of a "colour line." Analytically, racism may be defined as the perspective which tends to stress the real or alleged features of race and supports the use of them as grounds for group and inter-group action (Fairchild, 1967: 246). In practice this means that some people simply believe one racial category is innately superior or inferior to another. If the practice of **endogamy** (*marriage within one's own group*) is any indication, the enforcement of a colour line has certainly worked in Canada; Aboriginal people have the highest rate of marriage within their own ranks: almost 94 percent (Frideres and Gadacz, 2001: 7).

The total population of North and South America, at the time Columbus arrived, was about 57 million people, 4.5 million of whom lived north of Mexico (Cook, 1995: 33). Of these, about 500 000 lived in what is today Canada. Shortly after Confederation, however, Canada's Aboriginal population had sunk to 102 000 (Ponting, 1997a: 68). This number did not rise again until the 1940s, but steady growth since has raised the population of "status Indians" in Canada to nearly 700 000, while more than a million people today claim Aboriginal origins (CGA, 1999: 48) (see Table 10.1, below). However, living conditions in First Nations communities have not greatly improved even as we enter the twenty-first century. Why is this the case?

The answer is complex. Some observers suggest, however, that subtle forms of colonialism still exist in the form of **internal colonialism**, *the process of continuing settler control and domination of indigenous peoples*. Box 10.1 outlines eight indicators of internal colonialism still plaguing Aboriginal peoples in Canada as exercised by the Department of Indian Affairs over its Aboriginal clientele. Arguably, the worst nightmare of the Department of Indian Affairs would be a united front in Aboriginal country.

BOX 10.1 | Empirical, Micro-level Indicators of Internal Colonialism

1. Inadequate preparation and/or resourcing for bands administering their own affairs; e.g., inadequate funds for training in modern skills of administration.

2. Economic underdevelopment; e.g., inadequate resourcing of bands' economic development; refusal to relinquish control over economic development.

3. An intemperate orientation toward risk; e.g., excessive risk aversion to the point of over-protectiveness; irresponsible exposure of bands to excessive risk.

4. Flow of information; e.g., manipulation of information as a form of social control; excessive secrecy or over-burdening Aboriginals with information; overly rigid (or frequent) accountability requirements; inadequate consultation with bands.

5. Decision-making and control over allocation of scarce resources; e.g., excluding bands from decision-making; depriving bands of control over allocation of resources.

6. Obstructionism—vs. facilitation.

7. Socio-fiscal control; e.g., manipulation of discretionary funds; withholding of funds.

8. Divide and rule tactics—vs. promotion of co-operation among bands.

Source: Ponting (1986: 86).

TABLE 10.1 Aboriginal Population and Status Indian Population of Canada, by Provinces and Territories

	Aboriginal Population (1991)				Status Indian Population (2001)[1]			
	Aboriginal Origins	North American Indian	Metis	Inuit	Total	On Reserve	Off Reserve	Crown Land
Canada	1 002 675	783 980	21 650	49 255	690 101	373 121	293 413	23 567
Nfld.	13 110	5845	605	6460				
PEI	1880	1665	185	75				
NS	21 885	19 950	1590	770				
NB	12 815	11 835	975	450				
Atl. Prov. (Total)	—	—	—	—	26 991	17 390	9579	22
Que.	137 615	112 590	19 480	8480	64 404	43 569	19 547	1288
Ont.	243 550	220 135	26 905	5250	157 062	78 170	77 392	1500
Man.	116 200	76 370	45 575	900	109 788	67 960	40 099	1729
Sask.	96 580	69 385	32 840	540	108 801	53 501	53 461	1839
Alta.	148 220	99 650	56 310	2825	87 703	55 361	29 657	2685
BC	169 035	149 570	22 295	1990	112 305	56 455	55 410	440
Yukon	6390	5870	565	170	7751	476	3843	3432
NWT	35 390	11 100	4310	21 355	15 296	239	4425	10 632

Sources: Data adapted in part from the Statistics Canada publication *Profile of Canada's Aboriginal Population* (1991 data), Catalogue 94-325, December 1994, and from Statistics Canada's Web site at www.statcan.ca/Daily/English/980113/d980113.htm#ART2; Canada, Indian and Northern Affairs Canada, *Registered Indian population by sex and residence, 2001*, Ottawa: The Dept., 2002 (also available on the Web at www.ainc-inac.gc.ca/pr/sts/rip/rip_e.pdf. Reproduced with the permission of the Minister of Public Works and Government Services Canada, 2002; and the *Canadian Global Almanac 2000* (1999: 48), "Native Population in Canada" (as taken from Statistics Canada, Census of Canada), reprinted with permission from Macmillan Canada, an imprint of John Wiley & Sons Canada, Ltd.

1. Status Indians are those individuals registered with the Department of Indian and Northern Affairs under the Indian Act. 2. The 1991 census question on ethnic or cultural origins gathered information on the number of people who reported North American Indian, Metis, or Inuit origin as either a single response of in combination with other origins.

There is little doubt that during the period following the cultural clash of incoming Europeans and resident First Nations, some of the latter group's cultural and spiritual traditions were altered or even lost. Recent evidence, however, suggests the problem is not as severe as first judged. Indeed, many sacred practices that were frowned upon were simply carried on in secret. Now, bolstered by the strong cultural and spiritual renaissance evident in most Aboriginal communities (Lincoln, 1985; McGaa, 1990), it is simply too pessimistic to imply, as do McCrackan and Dyck (1972: 4), that "most of the sacred practices have become virtually lost beyond recall." Indeed, it is likely the resolution of present and future challenges facing the Aboriginal community will be undertaken with a strong spiritual base, enabling both cultural and educational development and economic empowerment.

Adams (1999), however, insists that colonialism is alive and well in the form of neo-colonialism fostered by Aboriginal organizations themselves. As recipients of government grants, Adams alleges leaders in these organizations often manipulate funds in ways to benefit themselves and do no good for the membership. In turn, this arrangement works well for government: by using Aboriginal reactionary regimes, governments can hide their own colonial support. Thus, neo-colonialism allows a corrupt minority of Aboriginals to benefit at the expense of the membership. In the end, the state succeeds in crushing Aboriginal efforts toward self-sufficiency by dispersing and disorganizing the Aboriginal population.

Boldt (1993) echoes Adams's concerns, cautioning First Nations people that they must carefully monitor their own leaders if they are to attain justice. Evidence suggests that when blind faith is placed in Aboriginal leadership for the development of economic conditions or the resolution of problematic situations, "these individuals often manifest the same degree of paternalism, authoritarianism, self-interest and self-aggrandizement in their leadership as their non-Aboriginal counterparts" (Boldt, 1993: 141). A corollary to this concern is the matter of accountability. Flanagan (2000: 197) argues that Aboriginal leaders will never be held accountable by their people as long as the money they spend comes from the public treasury, and that a new definition of Indian self-government is needed. Self-government, however, requires some degree of economic self-sufficiency. This is something Canada's reserve system was not set up to provide.

THE RESERVE SYSTEM

One of the 1990s' enduring moments was the final collapse of apartheid in South Africa. Few Canadians realize the setting up of "homelands" under that system, beginning in the late 1940s, was modelled on Canada's system of Aboriginal reserves.

The original Canadian reserves were established following the negotiation of the treaties between representatives of Queen Victoria in the late nineteenth century and the various Aboriginal chiefs. Wuttunee (1971: 111) argues that reserves were designed to take First Nations people away from their natural habitat and segregate them on small parcels of land so that the surrounding areas would be safe for incoming settlers. The government then assigned Indian agents to supervise Aboriginals' adjustment to the land. Melling (1967: 37f) supports this argument. He notes, for example, that no reserves were created in areas where settlers did not migrate, such as the Yukon, Labrador, or the Northwest Territories. But it also could be argued that reserves were at least partially designed for the administrative convenience of government. It was a lot easier to deal with Aboriginal "problems" if they were all located on a specific plot of land rather than trying to minister to the needs of a group of nomadic wanderers.

Whatever the underlying reason, it is clear much of the land reserved for Aboriginals was unsuitable for farming. Thus, the period after the treaty signings saw Canada prosper, while the First Nations people remained behind. The reserve inhabitants suffered quietly from malnutrition and disease in primeval silence, often far from the hurly-burly of mainstream Canadian life and thus unseen, in semi-permanent havens from the modern world.

In time, many reserves became centres of shiftlessness and inertia (Melling, 1967: 38). Alcoholism proliferated. Unemployment and suicide rates soared. The reserve system killed any incentive among Aboriginal people, transforming them into a great family of wards, dependent on government for direction and subsistence. Schools, about whose operation the Aboriginals had no say, were provided by religious organizations that forbade the practice of traditional sacred ceremonies.

The first generation of reserve dwellers often reminisced about the glory days of hunting, trapping, and fishing. The second generation only listened to the stories of the past as they watched the old ones die. The third and fourth generations could only dimly picture the glorious past, but upon their shoulders fell the onus of preserving a dying culture amidst their struggles with a strange, unsympathetic, and domineering society.

Until the 1960s, there was practically no economic development on Aboriginal reserves. Far from markets, often situated on marginal land, and with little capital for investment, reserves lacked an economic base. Were it not for government transfer payments such as relief, family allowance, youth allowances, blind and disabled persons' allowances and old age assistance, few Aboriginal people would have survived. In 1959, the average income of Aboriginals in Saskatchewan was $200 per year. That same year, the average Saskatchewan citizen was making $1245. In monetary terms, Aboriginal people were making only one-sixth the income of their non-Aboriginal counterparts.

In contrast to their western counterparts, the Algonkian and Iroquois nations did quite well. The Iroquois, for example, had received land grants on the Grand River in Upper Canada. Although surrounded by settlers, their success in farming was easily comparable to that of their neighbours. Unlike the situation in the West, no great gulf emerged between Aboriginal farmers and the incoming Europeans.

There was also another difference between the two regions. Aboriginal males in eastern Canada who had previously been successful voyageurs now became river pilots and guided boats and barges loaded with supplies through the rapids to the port in Montreal. When the Grand Trunk Railroad began building the Victoria Bridge, some of these river men learned the skills of the high-steel workers, from which many Iroquois today are still making a living from. In short, eastern Aboriginals had built up over time a repertoire of skills usable in the changing economy. By contrast, when the railway cut through the western plains, Aboriginals were not approached with prospective employment. The reserve system, so heavily concentrated in the West, promoted the public's view that Aboriginals constituted at best an alien and dying society, at worst an obstacle to progress (Buckley, 1993: 60).

In 1967, Canada celebrated 100 years as a nation. It was also a time of civil unrest and many questions about relationships between people and institutions, including the state. The role of the United States in the Vietnam War was under scrutiny, city parks were laden with "earth people" (hippies), universities were sites of "sit-ins," and marches protesting all sorts of things were frequent. In this context, a new form of literary effort stirred the markets. From the Aboriginal sector emerged such books as Harold Cardinal's *The Unjust Society* (1969) and Waubageshig's *The Only Good Indian* (1970). These and other Aboriginal authors pointed out the evils wrought upon their people by an uncaring and insensitive government and presented a plea to their fellow citizens to put things right. By the 1950s, a number of Aboriginal organizations were emerging that collectively would draw attention to a wider sphere of concerns than those of individual First Nations (Frideres and Gadacz, 2001). This move catapulted the economic and educational conditions in many Aboriginal communities into the public limelight, forcing governments to take a harder look at a society too long ignored.

ABORIGINAL EDUCATION

Colonialism is not merely economic or political. It also is cultural. Where colonial systems have been most successful, they have entered into the psychology of the colonized. The truly colonized individual "apes" the language, beliefs, and behaviours of the colonizer, while denigrating his or her own cultural heritage (Fanon, 1968). Schools have always played a key role in this process.

The campaign to colonize Aboriginal culture via schooling has a long history in Canada. Mission schools were tried in early New France but soon proved unsuccessful due to low attendance. An alternative plan saw young Aboriginal boys and girls sent directly to France, where they could be "properly educated" and later returned as teachers to their own people. But, again, the results were not favourable; more often than not the young Aboriginals returned as misfits, unable to function in either society. A few died. By 1639, scarcely a dozen had returned to the colony to assist the missionaries. The practice was ended (Cornish, 1881; Hawthorn, 1966/67; Jaenen, 1986).

The Hudson's Bay Company operated Canada's first schools that educated Aboriginal children. The company built and operated them primarily for the children of their employees, but a few Aboriginal children were enrolled. But it was mainly representatives of the religious orders that operated schools for Aboriginal students. The first of these was probably Sister Marguerite Bourgeoys, who arrived in New France in 1653 in response to a call by Montreal's governor to start a school. Five years later, Sister Bourgeoys (who later founded the Ursulines) opened a school for French girls in a converted stable, where eventually Aboriginal children also were enrolled (Chalmers, 1974).

By the middle of the seventeenth century, the Jesuits developed day schools in permanent settlements in New France and tried to lure Aboriginal students with a view to teaching them the Catholic faith and French culture. The curriculum consisted of religious studies, agriculture and manual trades. The Aboriginal children adapted to the French diet, manner of dress, and other aspects of the French lifestyle, but were never very successful in agriculture or manual trades (Brookes, 1991). Simultaneously the Ursulines instructed Aboriginal girls in French manners and customs, household duties, reading and writing and religion; later they also added knitting and spinning. Indicative of the serious intent of the program developers, and notably contrary to normal colonizing practice, was their attempt to provide instruction in these courses in Aboriginal languages.

A number of church denominations in Canada by the middle of the nineteenth century were involved in Aboriginal education with the double-edged objective of spreading the gospel and "culturally rehabilitating the Indian." During the period from 1833, when missionary Peter Jones petitioned the Methodist church to build a residential school among the Ojibway people of Ontario, to 1988, when the last residential school in Canada closed (the McKay Residential School in Dauphin, Manitoba), 80 such schools were in operation.

It was the Catholic Oblates, however, who, following their founding in the 1840s, virtually dominated the early stages of missionary education in Canada. The Grey Nuns (Sisters of Charity), who were responsible for the education of Aboriginal girls, established their first school, St. Joseph's Academy, in St. Boniface in 1845. Further west, a host of well-known individuals, Catholic and non-Catholic alike, laboured for the same cause. These included James Evans, Robert Rundle, Father Albert Lacombe, Henry Steinhauer (a Aboriginal missionary), and others. Typical of the educational philosophy of the time, Methodist missionaries George McDougall and his son John strove to "Christianize, educate and civilize" the Aboriginals, in their case the Woodland Crees and the Stoneys (McDougall, 1903: 71).

When the success rate of the campaign to make farmers of Aboriginal youth via day schooling indicated "low returns," the priests turned their attention to the establishment of "seminaries" or boarding (residential) schools. Aboriginal parents were naturally reluctant to part with their children for lengthy periods of time and the missionaries often had to bribe them into letting their children go. A special aspect of this program was to enroll some French children in Aboriginal schools as a means of encouraging Aboriginal pupils to take on French cultural ways. Aboriginal parents objected to this deliberate socialization plan, wanting instead to teach their children their ancestral beliefs and culture.

Industrial schools represented a short-lived experiment in Aboriginal education (Titley, 1992). These were begun shortly after 1830 when the civil branch of government took over Aboriginal matters from the military. The objective of these schools was to prepare Aboriginal youth for a new way of life. The fur trade was over, and to assist Aboriginal people in warding off destruction and ruin, their children would need to learn skills required in the New World. The boys were taught such gender-specific manual trades as shoemaking, carpentry, blacksmithing, and tailoring. The girls learned sewing, knitting, washing and cooking.

Like the missionary schools, the industrial schools failed. After a few years of operation it became evident that few of the students were applying the skills they learned in everyday life. Some of the factors that led to this dismal result included late enrollment for many students, parental prejudice against the schools, short periods of attendance, and lack of funds to establish graduates when they completed their term of studies. Aboriginal parents resented residential industrial schools. They did not like their children being taken away from them, often very far away. They also disliked the deliberate attempts to convert and "civilize" their children, whom they wanted to retain their cultural heritage. They also resented the restrictions on the use of Aboriginal languages and the teaching of "women's chores" to young men. Parents who did consent to having their children educated in these institutions often did so because they thought they were being taught how to read and write (Miller, 1987: 3f). They objected to the work component of the industrial schools, believing that their offspring were being shortchanged. After all, they were being sent to school to learn literary skills, not to become unpaid apprentices with full-time jobs.

A dramatic shift in policy occurred in 1830 with a scheme to assimilate the Aboriginal people. The plan was to establish the First Nations in permanent settlements and commence instruction so that an agricultural form of lifestyle would be possible. Missionaries and schoolmasters were brought in to instruct the children and to teach them to pray, read the Scriptures, and pursue "moral lives" (Friesen, 1991: 14). In 1857, legislation to design education for Aboriginals was passed, entitled An Act for the Gradual Civilization of the Indian. This was followed by the Civilization and Enfranchisement Act in 1858.

Confederation in 1867 saw responsibility for educating Aboriginal youth fall to the federal government. The treaties signed shortly thereafter likewise specified the provision of schooling for Aboriginal children. But the quality and mode was not specifically spelled out. "Her Majesty" might agree "to maintain schools for instruction in such reserves" (Brookes, 1991: 168), but given governmental assumptions that the Aboriginal culture was dying, why bother providing a first-class education? And, since the missionaries were already involved in the enterprise, why not continue to finance the residential schools a few more years until they were no longer required? Naturally, the churches concurred with the arrangement and even competed with one another for students.

Despite Aboriginal protests, the push to have residential schools for Aboriginal children continued, and by the end of the nineteenth century every region of the nation had boarding schools for Aboriginal children. Promoted by Egerton Ryerson, who in 1844 became the first superintendent of schools in English-speaking Canada, government financed these schools, while churches provided spiritual guidance and management. Ryerson suggested that Aboriginals could not accomplish civilization without a "religious feeling," and thus "the animating and controlling spirit of each residential school should be a religious one" (Brookes, 1991: 20). The Province of Canada endorsed Ryerson's plan, acknowledging "the superiority of the European culture and the need to raise them [the Aboriginals] to the level of the whites" (Haig-Brown, 1993: 29).

The best efforts of residential school educators to assimilate Aboriginals were rarely successful, however. Aboriginal and non-Aboriginal societies continued largely to operate independently of one another. Aboriginal students who endured the system until their time of leaving in most cases still found it impossible to adjust to the outside social order. Moreover, they were often poorly equipped to deal with their own communities when they returned to them. In order to survive they formulated an artificial "self" to deal with both worlds simultaneously.

By the 1940s, it was clear to federal authorities that residential schools were not accomplishing what they were designed to do. The shift in policy was signalled in 1947 in a paper entitled (with admirable honesty), A Plan to Liquidate Canada's Indian Problem in Twenty-Five years (Pauls, 1984: 33). The scheme outlined a plan to transfer the authority for the operation of Aboriginal schools from federal to provincial governments, a stance later reiterated in the White Paper of 1969 (see Chapter Twelve). Integration, rather than assimilation, was to be the basis of the new policy. (Given that "integration" was still to be one-way, it seemed a distinction without a difference.) Aboriginal students would interact with their non-Aboriginal peers, thereby slowing absorbing the values of the dominant European culture (Allison, 1983: 119). The "Indian problem" remained unresolved, however, and the economic gap between Aboriginal peoples and other Canadians continued to exist. Before another line of attack was devised, plans were made to turn over the administration of residential schools directly into the hands of government bureaucrats instead of religious leaders. The process of transforming administration of residential schools to secular control began in 1949. That year a Special Joint Committee of the Senate and the House of Commons recommended that, wherever possible, Aboriginal children should be educated in association with other children (Friesen, 1983: 48). Despite considerable input from Aboriginal leaders, education according to the traditional European format was still perceived as a vehicle for assimilating First Nations (Hawthorn, 1966/67).

LIFE IN A RESIDENTIAL SCHOOL

Many Aboriginals remember with deep pain the experiences they suffered during their sojourn at the ill-famed residential schools (Friesen, 1999: 251f). Life in that institution meant participating in an entirely different cultural milieu, replete with such alien features as corporal punishment, strict discipline, hard work, loneliness and, worst of all, confinement. Students living in residential schools had to cope with a highly structured institution. Church-employed staff constituted the power structure and the ideological ethos of the school. Since their identity was derived theologically, it was inevitable their view was regarded as having more authority than that of parents or students. In turn, the status of school administrators was regarded superior to that of hired teachers, since they made the rules.

There was frequent disagreement about how children should be treated and how schools should be run. As King pointed out (1967: 58), many teachers who worked in residential schools were ill-qualified to do so. Many teachers were minimally educated and came from lower socio-economic backgrounds. Often they had only recently immigrated to Canada and did not fully understand Canada's history or value system. More importantly, they knew little or nothing about the First Nations way of life. They were, however, armed with a strong sense of mission. If teachers found this mission frustrated in any sense (sometimes by inflexible and unmovable upper administrations), children made an easy target upon which to vent aggression.

Indeed, the entire power structure of residential schools was coercive and authoritarian. Students saw adults, correctly, as controllers of their fate. Because they often did not know the precise rules—and there were rules about *everything*—children were uncertain and easily directed. Such socialization into passivity and deference in turn greatly affected students' decision-making abilities in later life.

Grant (1996: 89) argues that residential school education was never intended to fully educate Aboriginal youngsters, because if they were too well-prepared they would become a threat to dominant society. Similarly, Barman (1986) suggests white Canadians never wanted young Aboriginals entering their socio-economic order, even at the bottom rung, because they feared the Aboriginals might be successful. If Aboriginal youth triumphed by surviving the residential schools, further obstacles and discrimination awaited them ahead. The bottom line is that Aboriginal children were imprisoned on the pretext of educating them, while in reality their potential to develop fully as members of either Aboriginal or non-Aboriginal society was impeded.

Daily activities in a residential school were quite crude and very public. Initially the huge brick buildings built on the factory model had sealed windows. Often, the buildings produced a foul smell and a rank odour, contributing no doubt toward the spread of diseases, notably tuberculosis, which took a fearful toll on Aboriginal youth. Grant (1996: 123) cites one school in which 26 of the boys wet their beds. When it was discovered that fresh air might be a solution to this situation, the other extreme was practised and the windows were left open at night. Thus the children often slept in what seemed like freezer compartments because of frigid air invading their rooms. Bathing was a group activity, with the younger students bathing first. The water was often too hot when they started the ritual, but by the time the older students got their turn the water was cold and dirty.

When the children arrived at boarding school they were often given Christian names to replace their own. (The children's first assigned task was often to select a white individual's name from a list on the blackboard by pointing to it with a pointer. Even these names were sometimes ignored, however, as students in a few schools were referred to only by assigned numbers.) They were also given stiff uniforms in place of their Aboriginal clothing, and a haircut. As if cutting the hair was not a sufficient form of insult to a culture that revered long hair, students who ran away had their hair completely shorn.

The quality of residential food was poor, the quantity scanty, and today former residents frequently recall long periods of hunger. In most schools, the staff ate better food than did the children, though there were exceptions. Students sometimes would wolf down their food as fast as possible in hope of getting an additional helping. (Later on parents were often aghast when they discovered the undisciplined eating habits of their offspring.) Students sometimes stole bread from the kitchen, but if they were caught the punishment was severe. Thus, stealing food became a complex operation involving a number of participants (including thieves, lookouts, and distributors of the goods), resulting, some have argued, in the development of a particular institutionalized subculture (Haig-Brown, 1993: 99).

Once downed, the food was seldom allowed to digest naturally, so the condition of the children's bowels was another staff concern. Part of the daily routine was to administer a laxative to the children, many of whom really did not need it. Often the number of toilet pails provided was insufficient for the need. At times students would dare to use a nearby staff bathroom only to run the risk of being caught and severely punished.

Even more than in white schools of the period, the curriculum of the residential schools was primarily based on the three Rs—readin', 'ritin', and 'rithmetic—plus a fourth staple: large doses of religion. Perley (1993: 123) notes the latter was indubitably the most important of the four components. There were also specialized subjects such as farming and trades for boys and housekeeping, mending, and knitting for girls. Learning was by rote. Discipline and obedience were the real lessons learned. Punishments could be harsh.

The use of Aboriginal languages was discouraged in residential schools and students were severely punished if they were caught speaking in their mother tongues. There were never references made to the history or cultures of First Nations. These were completely ignored. Music and songs taught reflected only the themes of English and French societies, and later on those of the new dominant society. Academic achievement was low, based partially on the fact that the teachers had low expectations of students. When students later transferred to provincial schools for high school training they were often ashamed of their poor records. In short, the system was inadequate, demeaning, and dehumanizing. Small wonder that less than three percent of those children attending residential schools ever graduated from high school.

It is true that residential schools did provide some training in the communication arts imported from Europe, and today many Aboriginal leaders can trace their literary beginnings to the years they spent in residential schools. This in no way justifies the existence of that form of teaching and learning, but it offers some measure of consolation. In addition to mastering the basic forms of communication required to negotiate effectively with governments, many students formed lasting friendships with their peers that have endured to this day. In some ways these bonds may have served to partially alleviate painful memories of the cruelties and hardships endured in residential schools.

Surprisingly, some individuals claim actually to have enjoyed their residential school experience. They are few in number, however. It is interesting, though not necessarily reassuring, to note that the majority of First Nations leaders today are products of residential schools. On a parallel note, it should be mentioned that the non-Aboriginal contemporaries of these residential inmates were also educated under harsh conditions; such was the order of the day in North America. Non-Aboriginal students, however, did not have to undergo the painful and demeaning experience of constantly having to listen to lectures and innuendoes about the negative (and evil) components of their heritage.

Grant (1996) catalogues the negative personal results of having been educated in a residential school. These include an inability to express feelings; apathy and unwillingness to work; values confusion and culture shock; anti-religious attitudes; and a long-term negative impact on succeeding generations. Many former residential school dwellers have had to work very hard to overcome the psychological, spiritual, physical, and sexual abuses they suffered. Wax et al. (1964: 46) observed that the overwhelming majority of complaints by Aboriginal children were directed against other Aboriginal children, rather than against teachers or school conditions. In turn, those abused in residential schools often became abusers themselves (O'Hara, 2000: 18). The cycle continued with many former inmates' transmission of the unhappy tendencies they witnessed and experienced at the hands of the staff and teachers onto their own children.

Why did Aboriginal parents enroll their children in such dreadful environments? The answer has many sides. First, residential school conditions were not well known. Second, parents had no real choice. Members of the Royal Canadian Mounted Police came to the homes of Aboriginal parents and took their children away. Some parents who were having a difficult time supporting their families because of changing economic conditions grudgingly released their children with hopes they would have a better chance because of the promised enhanced skills they would learn in school (Furniss, 1995). Others gave up their children to gain approval from the local Indian agent; by coming on side with his recommendations they hoped to be more favourably treated in terms of needed supplies.

Sadly, when the residential system ended, it was not because the system failed. That should have been the reason, but instead its end came about because of increased government intervention motivated by citizen concern (King, 1967: 87). As a first step toward liquidation, schools run by missionaries were taken over by government bureaucrats in the 1950s, but this stage was brief. Aboriginal parents, some of them educated in residential schools themselves, grew increasingly involved in the education of their children. In 1970, the residential school at St. Paul, Alberta, was turned over to local control after nearly 300 Aboriginal people conducted a sit-in at the school. Reluctantly, the government gave in to the demands of the promoters of the three-month-long event, and the first locally controlled school in Canada came to be (Persson, 1986). Fifteen years later, two-thirds of reserve schools in the nation were either partly or completely managed by Aboriginal school boards.

The closed residential schools were turned over to other purposes. Some were managed for a time by committees established by First Nations themselves. In 1995, for example, six residential schools in Saskatchewan were operating under Aboriginal management. Several former residential schools became cultural centres, adult learning centres, or private schools. Many were simply torn down. When the administration of these schools was transferred to Aboriginal control, the influence of Aboriginal input was quickly evident. Gradually, First Nations influence won over past religious domination. It is more than symbolic that, when the final closing exercises of several residential schools transpired in the 1980s (for instance, at Qu'Appelle Indian Residential School in Saskatchewan), Aboriginal dancing and social events often took precedence over denominational activities (Gresko, 1986: 89).

Today, traditional culture and spirituality have become an integral part of Aboriginal education. Reclaiming their culture may not be important solely for Aboriginals, however. Boldt (1993) suggests the time has come for Aboriginal cultures to "open up" to outsiders so that the inherent wisdom of Aboriginal ways can become more commonplace. Couture (1991: 54) suggests that this process is already occurring. Till recently, he contends, elders have been reticent and most discreet about sharing and teaching their knowledge. However, those same elders now point to an unfolding prophecy that states that "the time has come to share secrets." Are non-Aboriginals ready to listen?

CONCLUSION

Contact between Aboriginals and non-Aboriginals in North America occurred in several stages. During the first stage, Aboriginal peoples had a degree of control over the relationship. The outsiders wanted a valuable commodity: furs. The Aboriginals were pleased to supply them in return for various products. But the fur trade also carried hidden dangers, such as disease and war (including conflict between the Aboriginal tribes). In the long term, the fur trade also eroded Aboriginal culture.

By the time the fur trade collapsed in the early nineteenth century, the relationship between Aboriginals and non-Aboriginals was no longer that of equals. Aboriginals were excluded from the agricultural and industrial economies that followed, while Canadian expansion westward exacerbated the decline of Aboriginal culture. Viewed by successive governments as a dying people, Aboriginal people gradually vanished from the Canadian landscape into places of physical and psychological retreat. Modernity passed them by.

Like the trains that brought western settlement, Canada's economic development proceeded, seemingly unstoppable. On the West Coast in 1896, eyes turned suddenly northward in search of gold. Southern Canada was about to discover its north.

KEY TERMS

colonialism
endogamy
ethnocentrism
genocide
internal colonialism

chapter eleven

Keepers of the North

[T]hey were the healthiest and finest looking Indians I have ever seen in the northern country.
—Charles Shelden, American sportsman, 1905

The North is the only place, where Nature can still claim to rule, the only place as yet but little vexed by man. All over the globe there spread his noisy failures; the North alone is silent and at peace. Give man time and he will spoil that too.
—Canadian humorist and historian Stephen Leacock, *Reflections on the North*, 1936

One Canada, one Canada, where Canadians will have preserved to them the control of their own economic and political destiny. Sir John A. Macdonald gave his life to this party. He opened the west. He saw Canada from east to west. I see a new Canada—a Canada of the North!
—Prime Minister John Diefenbaker, 1958

INTRODUCTION

Canada is said to be a northern country, and indeed much of Canadians' sense of identity is built around vague images of the northern frontier. Today, Canada's North is also growing more important to Canadians economically, as a source of oil and gas reserves, not to mention diamonds and other minerals. In future, it is likely to play an even larger role in Canadian society. Yet most Canadians know little about the North, and few have ever travelled there. In fact, about 90 percent of all Canadians live within 160 kilometres of the American border, and when they travel, many head south, not north.

Throughout much of the North, Aboriginal peoples are predominant (see Table 10.1). They constitute a majority in the Northwest Territories and Nunavut. They also make up a sizable proportion of the population in Yukon and in the northern regions of the four western provinces as well as Ontario, Quebec, and Labrador. These are their lands, and they are its guardians.

For several centuries the northern regions of Canada remained relatively untouched by outside influences. Generations of northern peoples carried on their lives in much the same fashion as their ancestors. True, European explorers undertook a number of historic explorations into the northern regions, but it was not until the turn of the eighteenth century, when the Hudson's Bay Company pushed northward, that the Inuit and Dene peoples experienced any significant outside influence. This expansion brought the northern inland First Nations into direct contact with fur traders and transferred the role of trade intermediaries from the Cree to the Chipewyan tribes. Thus began the North's colonization.

A PORTRAIT OF THE NORTH

Outsiders to the Far North are amazed anyone could enjoy life in an environment almost entirely void of trees, surrounded by great amounts of snow and ice. For about eight months of the year, most of the Arctic is covered with snow and extensive portions of its seas are frozen. The Subarctic seems only slightly more hospitable, a place of pesky black flies in summer and cold winter twilight. To those raised in the North, however, life in the crowded, fast-paced urban centres of the South seems equally strange and even tantamount to suicide. Besides, the long summer days in Inuit country balance the long, bleak winter.

Canada's North consists of arctic and subarctic regions and stretches "north of 60" to the North Pole. The Arctic comprises three million square kilometres of ice, water, and tundra, while the Subarctic includes over 4.5 million square kilometres of land. Combined, these regions amount to nearly 80 percent of the land and water mass of Canada, an area populated by nearly 1.5 million people. While these areas together comprise the largest geographic region in Canada, they have by far the smallest economy and population.

Increasingly, the region is a resource frontier for both Canada and the world, with energy and mineral products accounting for most of the North's output. But the cold environment of the Arctic and Subarctic also greatly limits economic development and settlement (Bone, 2000: 440).

The Arctic's unique physical environment is primarily a result of the sun's relative absence. The tilt of the earth on its axis keeps the northern area facing away from the sun throughout the winter months and facing toward the sun throughout the summer months. For as long as four consecutive months, from mid-October to mid-February, the Arctic is plunged into darkness. During the summer, it becomes the Land of the Midnight Sun, experiencing constant daylight for a few short months.

During the very short Arctic summers, snow melts, plants grow and the midnight sun shines over most of the land area. Spring and fall are virtually non-existent in the area.

Most Arctic regions experience January temperatures as cold as 40 or 50 degrees below zero with a mean temperature of only 10 degrees above zero during the warmest months. The 200 varieties of vegetation in the Arctic (shrubs, scrub trees, herbs, and lichen), are well suited. They are low to the ground, growing away from the wind, and they thrive on a brief and intense growing period.

The Arctic Ocean and surrounding lakes and rivers begin to freeze over in October and remain frozen until May in most areas. The frozen ocean extends the Arctic coastline by hundreds of kilometres, but the ice is not always safe to travel on, and in recent years has been growing thinner. Strong winds often drive vast floating fields of ice across the waterways. Often these islands of ice crash into one another, creating upheavals. A sudden spring breakup can create ice floes that may carry off unsuspecting hunting parties or migrating families (Osborn, 1990: 27–28).

Traditionally, the peoples of the Arctic relied on a variety of game and birds for food supply. This included the Arctic hare, the Arctic fox, the muskox, and a variety of birds such as rock ptarmigans, sandpipers, plovers, eider ducks, red-throated loons, and ruddy turnstones. Little-appreciated life forms included a variety of obnoxious insects such as small flies, mosquitoes, and bumblebees.

An obvious "tree line" separates the Subarctic from the Arctic and consists of four distinct zones: the wooded tundra, the lichen woodland, the closed boreal forest and the forest parkland. The wooded tundra forms the transition zone. This wooded area contains sporadic patches of spruce and larch trees, and the lichen woodland has a few stands of spruce and pine. The closed boreal forest offers a denser stand of fir, spruce, and pine, while the forest parkland combines elements of forest and grass milieu (Bone, 1992: 21). Wildlife in the Subarctic region is more plentiful and includes some 50 species of birds and 600 species of plants.

Over time, climate and geography resulted in the development by people indigenous to each region of cultures and technologies suitable for living as hunters and gatherers. As Bone (1992: 27) points out, the North's fragile physical environment poses unique challenges for modern times. For example, its cold climate and slow rate of natural growth means it takes longer to recover from modern industrial accidents such as oil spills. Unfortunately, considerations of the environment and the people have not always influenced the North's development.

THE PEOPLE

Until the 1960s, the North for most Canadians was akin to the thirteenth-century mariners' maps that described large uncharted areas with the words, "There be dragons." Even today, few Canadians know the northern region's old and fascinating history or its current reality. Slowly, however, this oversight is being corrected (Abel, 1993).

Contrary to widespread belief, Canada's northern cultures have not been static. Like those in the more southern regions, they have been subject to constant change. Over time, even the names of tribes and nations have changed. This has happened partly as an adjustment to social perceptions, and partly because certain First Nations have wished to return to more traditional forms of nomenclature. The latter is the case with the Inuit of Northern Canada (see below), who have chosen that name (meaning "the people") in preference to the name once given them by Europeans: Eskimo (meaning "eaters of raw flesh").

The North's indigenous people can be separated into three primary groups: the Inuit of the Arctic, the Algonquian-speaking people of the eastern Subarctic, and the Athapascan-speaking people (the Dene) located in the western Subarctic (Brody, 1987: 29). The latter two groups also span the northern portions of several provinces, including Quebec and Labrador, as well as the western provinces.

The Inuit

McGhee (1978) speculates that occupation of the Arctic by humans occurred between 12 000 and 7000 years ago. Contact between northern Aboriginal peoples and Europeans (the Vikings) dates back several centuries and begins with those who are now referred to as the Dorset people (1000 BC–1000 AD) (see also Crowe, 1974: 15f).

Before the Dorset people were the Denbigh people. Living in the Far North on Ellesmere Island around 2500 BC, the Denbigh had a unique cultural repertoire probably including the use of dogs, skin-covered boats, bows and arrows, stone lamps, and sewing needles (made of fox or bird bones). They lived in oval houses, partly sunk in the ground, with a complex form of social organization comprising small nomadic groups. Around 1000 BC, the climate warmed and the Denbigh moved south. This was the beginning of Dorset culture, so named for their place of settlement, Cape Dorset on Baffin Island.

Dorset culture spread rapidly across the Arctic region, aided by a series of tools that helped them adjust to the otherwise unfriendly climate and geography. The Dorset made snow knives of bone, igloos from packed snow, and crampons of ivory for walking on ice. They lived in partly de-elevated houses with turf walls and skin roofs, heated by open fires and oil lamps. As the climate gradually warmed, new immigrants to the region arrived and the Dorset people, like the Denbigh before them, vanished.

What happened to the Dorset people? Stories told by the Inuit until today tell of the Dorset being invaded and taken over by another group, the Thule Inuit. The Thule had sprung up in the Bering Strait region centuries before, developing elaborate technologies suitable to that area. They domesticated dogs to haul sleds or carry packs and built sea-going boats called umiaks and kayaks. Around 900 AD, they also developed a successful whale-hunting technique. Gradually, the Thule spread from the northern coast of Alaska to the Mackenzie delta and then finally into the area occupied by the Dorset people, the last of whom died out—it is speculated—sometime in the early twentieth century (Purich, 1992: 30). Most historians and archaeologists today believe the contemporary Inuit are descendants of the Thule people (Crowe, 1974; Wilson, 1976).

Linguistically, the Inuit language is unique, with no discernible relationship to that of any New World First Nations people. Some scholars believe Inuit language to be akin to the Uralic languages of Eurasia. The Inuit language probably descended from Aleut, from which it diverged about 6000 years ago, and thereafter evolved into two distinctive sub-family units, Yupik and Inupik. This includes all dialects between western Alaska and Greenland (Jennings, 1978).

The land of the Inuit is divided into a western portion, which includes the Aleut on the Aleutian Islands as well as the Inuit of Alaska, and a central and eastern region, which embraces all the Inuit from the Mackenzie River Delta east to Greenland. The groups broadly identified as Inuit include: Mackenzie, Copper, Netsilik, Sadliq, Caribou, Iglulik, South Baffin Island, Ungava, and Labrador (Crowe, 1974; Brody, 1987).

At the time of first contact with Europeans, some 22 000 Inuit lived in the North. There is evidence of a fairly widespread exchange of various minerals among the tribes before the arrival of Europeans, including such items as soapstone, iron, and copper, and products made from raw materials like ivory (Crowe, 1974).

Essentially an ocean-oriented culture, the Inuit obtained most of their food supply from the sea. Indeed, water was a major influence on virtually every aspect of Inuit life, from food to technology, domesticity, and the arts. In many ways, the Inuit had a sophisticated culture, fitted to the materials and circumstances of their climate and geography. The Alaskan Inuit and Aleuts, for example, developed the two-holed kayak and, in place of the toggling harpoons used for large sea mammals by other Inuit, a multi-barbed harpoon dart head (Dumond, 1977). Likewise, housing construction, from portable summer tents made of sealskin or caribou skin to winter homes of the classic igloo type (Baldwin, 1967), to (in the south) rectangular, semi-subterranean, turf-covered houses of logs, reflected a firm grasp of such things as ventilation and insulation.

No usable material was wasted. The blubber of sea mammals was used in lamps and for cooking. Utensils were fashioned from pottery or soapstone. The Arctic Inuit used antlers and bone, particularly ivory, to make harpoons and arrows, ice-chisels, sled-shoes, toggles, thimbles, thimble-holders, and decorative items in human or animal forms, a commercial trade that continues today.

The Inuit were probably unique among First Nations of Canada in functioning with a non-complex social system, unencumbered by elaborate hierarchical forms of governing individuals or bodies. They had no chiefs among them. Contrary to the western dichotomy of individualism versus collectivism, the Inuit way of life was a form of **individual egalitarianism**. When food was scarce, supplies were stretched out as far as possible and a spirit of goodwill prevailed. Age and gender determined one's status, though the sexes were more equal than in European countries of the day. In hunting, for example, women acted as assistants to their husbands, often driving animals into an ambush. Still, women had the chief role in raising children and preparing food (Giffen, 1930). Long before it became trendy, Inuit clothing was "unisex," with both sexes wearing loose-fitting fur trousers and shirts, usually made of caribou hide, but sometimes of polar bear or other animal fur. The main difference was that women cut their clothing a little larger than men to accommodate their babies beneath their clothing (Josephy, 1968).

Polygyny, *the marriage of one man to more than one woman*, was not uncommon. Since the Inuit practised female infanticide, however, there was often a scarcity of women. This being the case, on occasion a man might lend the use of his wife to a friend on a short-term basis. The "wife swap," as Europeans termed it, elicited both sensationalist intrigue and condemnation among outsiders, who understood neither its cultural underpinnings, nor the intricate rules that surrounded the practice, nor the woman's say in the matter (Mowat, 1952; Balikci, 1970; McMillan, 1995). Like the sundance of the Prairies and the potlatch of the West Coast, the Europeans, especially the missionaries, viewed wife sharing as something to be eradicated.

The Inuit believed in a large host of generally harmless supernatural beings. By European standards they had quite vague concepts of life in the hereafter. Their religious festivities revolved around the seasons and food supply, with celebrations beginning and ending the whale hunt season, and the busy summer months surrendering to slow winters and time for visiting, songfests, games, and storytelling.

Storytelling, along with everyday modelling, were means of transmitting valued Inuit cultural beliefs and values to the young. In some tribes storytellers were designated, while in others both men and women of respect could relate stories. Among the Labrador Inuit each village had a designated storyteller, and in Alaska certain old men monopolized this art (Giffen, 1930).

Seals and other sea mammals were a chief source of food, though in the summer months fishing and caribou hunting supplemented the Inuit diet. Taylor (1974) describes a typical annual cycle utilized by the Netsilik around the turn of the twentieth century. The sea began to freeze around October, the caribou herds departed for the south, and the building of snow houses commenced. Char continued to be taken from the sea until the middle of November and the women were busy making winter clothes. During December and January the people remained at home, relying on provisions laid up during the previous summer and fall. The breathing-hole seal hunting began in February when the snow was deep on the ice, and by April and May other hunting techniques were employed. These included sneaking up on the seal or catching new pups at the breathing holes. A few stray caribou showed up, and in June when the snow houses caved in from the hot sun, the people moved into tents. Kayaks were prepared for caribou hunting, which continued until the herd disappeared south again.

The Dene

The Subarctic is inhabited by two primary groups of Aboriginal peoples. One of these groups includes peoples of the Algonquian language community: the Cree, the Naskapi, and the Montagnais, with those located in Labrador referred to as Innu. The second, and largest, group comprises what are now referred to as the Dene people (Brody, 1987: 29).

The Dene (sometimes spelled "Dinneh") speak a dialect of the Athapaskan language (Chapter Ten). They share this language family with the Apache and the Navajo of the American Southwest. Abel (1993) suggests these northern people traditionally used the word *Dinneh* to identify the larger population and distinguished separate groups by adding the name of a river or lake associated with their particular hunting grounds. Thus, it is possible to identify a large number of tribes as Dene. Irwin (1994) provides the most comprehensive list of Dene tribes. The list includes the Chipewyan, of the Canadian interior (not to be confused with the Chippewa-Ojibway of Lake Superior); the Dogrib, between Great Slave lake and Great Bear Lake; the Beaver, along the lower Peace River in Northern Alberta; the Slavey, along the southern shore of Great Slave Lake; the Hare, northwest of Great Bear Lake; the Klaska or Nahani, west of the headwaters of the Mackenzie River; the Sekani, in central British Columbia; the Carrier (named for their widows' custom of carrying the charred bones of their dead husbands on their backs); the Chilcotin, south of Carrier lands; the Tahlan, on the upper Stikine River in northwestern British Columbia; and the Tuchone in southern Yukon Territory (see also Crowe, 1974; Ryan, 1995; Massey and Shields, 1995). An official document issued by the Dene of the Northwest Territories (1975) cites the Chipewyans, Dogribs, Slaveys, and Loucheux as member groups of the larger Dene community.

Like the Inuit, the Dene people were primarily hunters and trappers. Huge herds of caribou and moose were vital components of the Dene diet and culture, supplemented by the fish of lakes and rivers. Predictability of supply was important. Any change could spell disaster for a band. The Chipewyan people, for example, followed the migration patterns of the caribou, and if there was even a slight shift in their migration paths the band's food supply was affected. In fall these animals were slaughtered by waiting hunters as they passed a certain point, and the meat was cut into strips, dried in the sun and pounded into pemmican for the winter food supply (McMillan, 1995). Like the Plains Indians to the south, who trapped the buffalo in a similar fashion, Chipewyan people used the pound—driving the caribou into a natural trap where they could be speared or shot at will. Winters in the North posed the greatest threat of starvation and the fear of having to yield to the elements. Still, at times the people were grateful for the cold winter that would put an end to the beastly miseries of swarming hordes of flies and mosquitoes. The caribou provided pelts used as lodge covers as well as clothing thick enough for individuals to endure the harsh winters. The bones of the animal were used for tools and domestic instruments.

It was customary among the Dene to function as groups of friendly neighbours. Each tribe adapted to its immediate terrain. For example, the Hare, so named for their use of rabbit skins for clothing and shelter, lived in small extended families in ego-centred **bilateral kindreds**. Cross-cousin marriage divided relatives into two opposing groups, although actual cross-cousin marriages were rare. Cross-relatives were in-laws, while parallel relatives were akin to parents, siblings, or one's own children (Ives, 1990). A similar situation prevailed in Slavey country where the people identified two kinds of relatives, kinsmen and in-laws.

Among the early Beaver and Slavey tribes, marriage patterns represented what Ives (1990) has termed "a polygynous gerontocracy of senior men." Older men often married younger women, leaving a shortage of mates for younger men, as well as a significant number of widows as the husbands died. But family practices were also quite diverse.

The Dene had quite explicit social rules (Ryan, 1995). These rules covered three specific areas: natural resources, families, and governance or decision-making. In turn, these rules were intertwined with the Dene's holistic view of the universe. Rule-breakers were punished in various ways. For minor offences, an elder might deal verbally with the guilty party. Individuals committing more serious offences were often made the subject of a gathering requiring an admission of guilt and restitution, followed by a process of reconciliation. If this failed, shunning was possible. Finally, for particularly severe infractions, there was the death penalty, though this would seem to have been rarely used.

A nineteenth-century visitor to Dene country, Father Petitot, noted that Dene beliefs were reflected in daily practices but not formalized (Savoie, 1970). A series of lunar beings were worshipped as deities: the midnight sun, for example, was a real national and tutelary god, supremely recognized and worshipped. At the same time, Petitot described the Dene as having a primordial knowledge of a Good Being who was placed above all other beings and possessed a multitude of names, the most usual one being Bettsen-nu-unli (he by whom the earth exists). The Hareskin and Loucheux peoples saw this supreme being as a triad made up of father, mother, and son. Frequently, spirit beings would personify themselves in the form of birds, such as the eagle; the male spirit brought the day and the female spirit brought the night (Savoie, 1970). As in the South, the trickster was recognized (in the form of a raven) as a creator, culture hero, and miracle worker (Merkur, 1991: 215). Finally, the Dene also believed their departed souls could become celestial beings, such as the northern lights (Savoie, 1970).

The Roman Catholic priests who later arrived in Dene territory introduced concepts that blended well with traditional Dene beliefs: love your spouse, be kind to your neighbours, take good care of your children and raise them well, and stay together forever (Ryan, 1995). The formal European style of marriage was not practised when the missionaries first arrived. Locals often lived together in traditional style and had several children before they appeared before a priest for a formal European-style marriage. In many instances, priests became viewed as emissaries from God possessing spiritual power and authority, and served also as elders, providing advice and direction, resolving disputes, and meting out disapproval for acts of violation. In effect, priests supplanted traditional shamans—understandable enough, given the apparent failure of the latter to ward off the mysterious evils that befell Aboriginal peoples after the Europeans arrived.

At the same time, Christianity's capacity to fully transform Aboriginal culture was not total; indeed, its influence was in some ways superficial (Brody, 1987: 205). Often, Christianity merged with Aboriginal beliefs—in a process known as **syncretism**—in ways the missionaries did not recognize. This does not mean Christianity did not have important effects on Aboriginal culture. Aboriginal people took what they wanted from the new religion, while retaining many of their old beliefs and values.

In summary, the Aboriginal peoples of the North before the arrival of Europeans had developed cultures and technologies appropriate to their climate and surroundings. As nomadic or semi-nomadic peoples, they lived in small groups, hunting, fishing, and gathering by season. Their belief systems and social structures were entirely congruent with this existence. Beginning in the late fifteenth century, however, their lifestyle slowly began to change.

THE COMING OF THE EUROPEANS

Initial contacts between the northern people and Europeans in the tenth century were not friendly. Erik the Red, a Norwegian who explored Greenland, and whose son Leif later returned to establish a colony in Newfoundland, viewed the locals as quite primitive, "little people" who had no iron and used missiles made of walrus tusks and sharp stones for knives (Osborn, 1990: 77). It was a pattern of contact repeated several centuries later with the arrival of a new band of explorers.

Among these early explorers were John Cabot (in 1497 and 1498), Martin Frobisher (in 1576, 1577, and 1598), John Knight (in 1606), and Henry Hudson (in 1610). Why did they come? In part, they were searching for precious metals, especially copper and gold. But they also had a larger quest: a Northwest Passage to the Orient (see Box 11.1, below).

European exploration beginning in the fifteenth century with Cabot was inextricably linked to mercantilism (Chapter Two). In the modern context, we can see this period as an early expression of globalization, with its search for new products and markets and the expansion of trade. While considerable trade occurred overland between Europe and Asia, it also occurred by sea. But a ship sailing to the Orient from Europe, either eastwards around the Cape of Africa or westwards around South America might journey more than a year. By contrast, a passage more directly westwards would save time and money; hence, the search for what Berton (1988) termed "the Arctic Grail."

Ultimately, a Northwest Passage was found. It was not mastered, however, until the Norwegian Roald Amundsen sailed his sloop, the *Gjoa*, through the ice in 1905 (see Berton, 1988). By then, the North had claimed a host of explorers and their ships. Among these was Hudson, who steered a course into a strait that later bore his name and became icebound, whereupon his crew mutinied and set him and a few loyal crewmen adrift in a small boat, never to be seen again. Hudson's lurid fate and that of other disastrous expeditions that followed—from Jens Munk in 1619 to Sir John Franklin in 1845–48 (see Beattie and Geiger, 1987)—did not dissuade outsiders, however. Far from it. The North became transformed into a place both mystical and mythical. (Note that Mary Shelley's monster in *Frankenstein*, published in 1819, dies on an Arctic ice floe.) And where mystery's allure failed to attract, Europeans came nonetheless in search of profit.

And profit there was. In 1665, two disgruntled fur traders from New France, Pierre-Esprit Radisson and Médard Chouart, sieur des Groseilliers, went to London to meet King Charles II and local merchants. Radisson and Groseilliers believed that the Hudson Bay region offered enormous opportunities in the fur trade, but the two had been turned down by the French, who feared opening up the northern route would harm industry along the St. Lawrence. The English were more responsive, and shortly thereafter, in 1670, Charles II issued the Hudson's Bay Company charter, granting the company rights to all lands whose waters drained into the Hudson and James bays. The Hudson's Bay Company (HBC) thus became the "the vastest empire any private company ever controlled" (Morton, 1997: 75; also Newman, 1998: 54–61).

The company did not immediately thrive. Over the next decades, the French several times captured HBC forts and burned them to the ground, only to see them rebuilt. Gradually, however, the Hudson's Bay Company grew. Defeat of the French in 1763 and amalgamation with the rival North West Company in 1821 left the company unassailable in the North. For roughly the next 50 years, the HBC represented a kind of quasi-government, making rules and regulations, enforcing order, and even providing social services, such as education. Well into the twentieth century, the company continued to provide unique services in the North. HBC radio stations, for example, provided—until eclipsed by the CBC—an important means of linking northern communities.

With the advent of the fur trade and the arrival of missionaries, the lifestyle and political economy of the northern indigenous peoples changed dramatically. Some Aboriginal people initially did quite well with the arrangement. For a people living primarily as hunters, rifles and ammunition were a real gain. Likewise, certain tribes also did initially well, notably the Cree, who quickly became "middlemen" and spread westwards across Canada. But, as we have noted (Chapter Ten), the fur trade also brought negative consequences. In the words of Brody (1987: 199), the "fur trade was built upon the economics of dependency." Trade with the forts became habitual. Hunters became trappers and changed their lifestyles accordingly. The role of women also changed, as they now had to clean and tan additional furs for market. As in the south, disease and alcoholism also took their toll, causing many tribes to break up and perish.

Not all the North, especially the Arctic, was brought into the world economy all at once. Beginning in the seventeenth and eighteenth centuries, some tribes in the Subarctic had initial contact with fur traders pushing north from the St. Lawrence and whalers arriving from the North Atlantic. Others, however, experienced their first contact only in the nineteenth century. At that time, European ships began regular trips to the Arctic to garner whale oil, baleen (whalebone, used in making corsets), and walrus ivory. In the 1850s, the ships began to winter over, and contact between Europeans and Inuit intensified. The establishment of whaling stations upset the seasonal economic cycle of the settlements, which became handout stations soon known as places where "weekly biscuits were handed out" (Wilson, 1976: 85).

This increased contact brought other material and cultural changes. By the time commercial whaling came to an end (around 1912), "hunters were using rifles, telescopes, sheath knives, jack-knives, hatchets, saws, drills, awls, steels and files. Women cooked in metal pots and kettles, and used steel needles, cotton thread and metal scissors in sewing" (Brody, 1987: 193). Clothing materials and styles also changed, as did music and dancing.

The changes were not all positive, however. Over-hunting depleted the whale herds and led to starvation in some instances. Alcoholism, suicide, and disease also took their toll. As early as 1887, Father Emile Petitot quoted a chief of the Chiglit Eskimos on the terrible living conditions among the Inuit: "We are all dying....[W]e are getting snuffed out day by day and nobody cares about us. No one looks after our sick or pities our misfortunes" (Petitot, 1999: 15). In 1912, Captain Henry Toke Munn described the Inuit of Baffin Island as a "passing race" destined to extinction because of the coming blight of complex European civilization, without whose influence he felt they would be better off. Brody (1987: 193) notes that around this same period the Inuvialuit of the Mackenzie delta were reduced from a community of 2000 to about 30. Finnie (1940) later made a similar observation regarding the high death rate of the Copper Eskimos in Coronation Gulf.

The Aboriginal people further west survived better for a time, outside the thrust of European contact. In 1905, an American sportsman, Charles Sheldon, met some members of the Dene Nahanni tribe who had never made contact with any of the European newcomers, and described them as follows:

> [T]hey were the healthiest and finest looking Indians I have ever seen in the northern country. Most of the men were fine specimens, and also the women, who bore children abundantly and reared them in health and vigour. They were absolutely honest and lived a primitive Indian life (Finnie, 1948: 40).

The life of northern peoples was changing quickly, however. As so often in the past history of the Americas, the impetus for these changes stemmed from a single source: gold.

THE YUKON GOLD RUSH

The California gold rush of 1849 begat the British Columbia gold rush of 1858, followed in 1896 by the discovery of gold on a tributary of the Klondike River by George Washington Carmack and his two Aboriginal brothers-in-law, Skookum Jim and Tagish Charley. This was not the first "discovery of gold" in the North. Robert Campbell, a trader with the Hudson's Bay Company, found gold in the gravel near his trading post at the junction of the Yukon and Pelly rivers in the early 1850s. An Anglican missionary, Robert McDonald, reported traces of gold in Birth Creek near the Yukon-Alaska border in the 1870s (Cruikshank, 1998: 434). This time, however, the world caught gold fever.

News of the strike was slow reaching the outside world. By the summer of 1897, however, hordes of men were swarming over the area, some arriving by water, many taking the arduous journey over the White Pass and Chilcoot Pass, then down the Yukon River by a colourful assortment of handmade boats and rafts. By 1898, a total of 30 000 people lived in the Klondike region, of whom about 16 000 resided in Dawson City, which became Yukon's capital. Most of the newcomers knew only three things about the Yukon: it was cold, it was remote, and gold nuggets were available for the picking. The men who arrived were relatively young and well-educated, and they outnumbered women by a ratio of five to one. While many of the fortune seekers sought female companionship among the locals, few of these relationships lasted very long. Most of the men soon drifted back to the South, many leaving children behind them. Those who stayed and struck it rich were few. Success more often came through parallel business ventures as traders, hoteliers, or providers of goods and services considered essential on the frontier (Cruikshank, 1998: 451; Berton, 1958). Most of those who remained ended up working for wages, their stay occasioned by either a love of the North or dreams still nursed of becoming wealthy (Fried, 1969).

Sadly, the 1896 gold rush ended quickly. The "boom and bust" pattern of Canadian development, so familiar to the south, was replicated in the North. Dawson City's fortunes and population experienced a steep decline. For all the wealth generated, little remained to be invested locally. By contrast, between 1902 and 1903 alone, $12 million left the northern territories. Observers blamed an uninterested government and lack of local control for this loss of revenue. Almost overnight, the gold rush ended. Its impact, however, was long-term.

First, the gold rush augured the North's full integration into the world capitalist economy. It was a slow process. The fur economy remained strong throughout the 1920s, bringing considerable wealth to the Yukon and the Northwest Territories. Fur towns like Aklavik sprang up, and a few local families got rich, but prosperity was again short-lived. For many people, however, tied only tangentially to the labour market, the downturn was not critical. Meanwhile, companies were increasingly entering the region, searching for exploitable resources. Gold remained in high demand, leading to the foundation of towns at Noranda, Quebec; Kirkland Lake, Ontario; and Flin Flon, Manitoba. Increasingly, also, other minerals were mined, such as radium and uranium, in places like Great Bear Lake, high in the Northwest Territories (Careless, 1970: 353). And then there was oil.

It had long been known the North possessed rich pockets of oil. Writing in his diary in the eighteenth century, Peter Pond recounts seeing the thick pitch along the banks of the Athabasca River in what is today northern Alberta. In 1907, Alfred von Hammerstein, known as "the Count," acquired surface and mineral rights to 12 000 acres of freehold land downstream of where Fort McMurray stands today, and set about drilling wells. He was unsuccessful. A few years later, however, in 1920, the Imperial Oil Company announced the discovery of large amounts of oil at Norman Wells. The announcement temporarily spurred the Canadian government to seek a treaty with the local Dene to pave the way for development. Fortunately perhaps for the Dene, the oil find soon proved significantly smaller than anticipated, and the government dropped its plans to settle the Dene on specified plots of land. Nonetheless, the discovery proved a harbinger of events to come in the North.

Second, while the North's economy as a whole was being transformed, local indigenous people were frequently left on the margins of these changes. The pattern began with the gold rush, when Aboriginals became bearers for the invading southerners, but rarely staked claims themselves. Similarly, the 1920s and 1930s saw an influx of white southerners seeking their fortunes at a time when jobs "back home" were growing scarce (Brody, 1987). Thus, at a time when the North's indigenous peoples found themselves increasingly pressed for work in the old economy, jobs in the new economy (mining, oil, the government bureaucracies) often went to outsiders with the education, skills, and connections to participate.

Third, the gold rush signalled the growing involvement of the Canadian government and state in the lives of northerners. Canada had gained jurisdiction over the West, Rupert's Land, and the Northwest Territories in 1870. In 1880, the British government ceded responsibility over the Arctic Islands to Canada, in large part to thwart American and other efforts to claim Baffin Island (Purich, 1992: 31). Canada's failure to enforce jurisdiction, however, subsequently resulted in claims pressed by other countries. Thus, the late nineteenth century saw a host of countries—particularly Britain, the United States, and Norway—sending polar expeditions, ostensibly in the name of exploration, but also to "plant the flag."

Following the Yukon gold rush, Canada responded to these threats in various ways. In the name of law and order, the Canadian government quickly dispatched the North West Mounted Police to the Yukon. By 1903, there were three NWMP posts in the Arctic, introducing western European notions of property rights and legal justice. In 1897, the Canadian government also sent a reconnaissance mission to Hudson Bay and Baffin Island, where Captain William Wakeham declared Canada's sovereignty over that and surrounding islands. Similar missions followed, leading up the First World War. Between 1913 and 1918, the Canadian government also funded the research of Vilhjalmur Stefansson, whose work quickly popularized for Canadians "their" northern heritage. Finally, beginning in 1922, the Canadian government also instituted a yearly patrol of the Eastern Arctic to enforce its claims to sovereignty over the North (Purich, 1992: 32–33; also, Brody, 1987).

The Royal Canadian Mounted Police—expanded and changed in 1920 from the North West Mounted Police—played an important role in this enforcement. In 1903, the NWMP had established three police posts in the Arctic. These were now increased throughout the North. From these posts, the RCMP performed a multitude of functions and roles. Besides being police officers, the RCMP over the next decades also became the North's administrators, social workers, and, perhaps most importantly, explorers. In 1940–42, the RCMP vessel the *St. Roch*—a kind of floating detachment—travelled the Northwest Passage from west to east, then in 1944, from east to west, becoming the first ship to navigate the passage in both directions.

Within less than 50 years, Canada's North had been transformed from a peripheral and even exotic appendage to a politically, economically, culturally, and administratively integrated colony of the South. In 1939, the North also began being militarily integrated into the modern world.

THE SECOND WORLD WAR AND THE POSTWAR NORTH

The Second World War and the subsequent Cold War brought renewed interest in the North, this time not only for its resources but more immediately for strategic reasons. A major supply route for oil and other military supplies for Alaska moved down the Mackenzie River along a new highway. Local centres like Fort Smith and Whitehorse suddenly burgeoned with population, and Frobisher Bay became a vast military complex. A former ghost town, Churchill, Manitoba, became a military base with a satellite town of skilled and unskilled workers and a large number of unemployed Aboriginal "squatters." War's end saw the economic situation of many of these towns immediately deteriorate, and many people were left financially stranded.

Nonetheless, the Second World War saw a number of large-scale construction projects launched in the North. These included the construction of a series of landing fields, a military base at Goose Bay, the expansion of oil production at Norman Wells, the building of a pipeline from Norman Wells to Whitehorse, and the construction of the Alaska Highway. Both Goose Bay and Gander became strategic links in the North American chain of defence, between the two of them supplying over 900 warplanes to the United Kingdom (Bone, 1988; 1992).

Construction of the Alaska Highway was a particularly monumental task for its time. Originally proposed in the 1930s, construction began finally in the 1940s, partially motivated by the Japanese bombing of Pearl Harbor in December 1941. The road was built both to supply Russians with needed materials to fight the Nazi invasion of their country and as a safeguard against a Japanese invasion of North America. The road was over 2500 kilometres in length, built over muskeg and unstable fields of tundra, and took 11 000 men, including U.S. Army engineers and civilians, to complete the job. Although 80 percent of the highway was built on Canadian soil, the United States government paid the entire cost of $133 million, while Canada absorbed the costs of upkeep. The road had two long-term impacts outlasting the war. First, it stimulated oil and gas exploration in the North. Second, the road's construction had the effect of reinforcing American influence in western Canada, especially Alberta (see Chapter Eight).

As important as was the military intrusion into the North, more crucial in bringing about change was the role of the Canadian government (Vallee, 1971). We have seen how the presence of the state in the North increased during the gold rush. This presence increased markedly after 1945, with the government taking over direct responsibility for economic and social affairs (and, in consequence, the withdrawal of Hudson's Bay Company support services, as the company no longer felt obligated to buffer Aboriginals from economic swings in the marketplace).

Soon, government facilities existed for services that touched on every aspect of Aboriginal life. To some extent this intervention improved the local way of life. Housing standards were raised, and famine became virtually a thing of the past. Instead of hunting and trapping, new sources of income were generated including wages, the sale of handicrafts, family allowances, various pensions, and social assistance.

Education was a key area of increased government involvement. As in the South, missionary schools had long existed in the North. Mission schools were opened as early as 1867 at Fort Providence on Great Slave Lake and 1874 at Fort Chipewyan on Lake Athabasca (Fisher, 1981). Others followed, with a spate of residential schools set up by missionaries for Arctic and Subarctic children in the 1940s and 1950s (Brody, 1987: 143). As elsewhere, the missionary teachers were armed with an irrelevant curriculum and otherworldly allegiances. The purpose of their "education" was acculturation and assimilation (see also Chapter Ten). Thus, local language training was downplayed, and religious practices related to Aboriginal spirituality were discouraged. Many parents felt attendance at school provided children with less opportunity to observe and participate in traditional Aboriginal life. Boys no longer hunted or trapped with their fathers and girls were removed from situations where they could take up domestic responsibilities (Cline, 1975: 173).

Prior to the Second World War, direct federal investments in health and educational facilities were virtually non-existent in northern regions (Rea, 1968: 184). After the 1950s, however, government intervention increased, in the form of social and educational assistance, as a means of integrating Aboriginal people into the body of national life.

For government and bureaucrats, the North's increased integration seemed a necessity. In the 1930s and 1940s, the fur economy was still a mainstay of northern families. After 1947, however, the price of furs collapsed and remained low until the 1960s. Many Canadian officials viewed trapping as a dying way of life and were determined to drag the North and its residents into the "modern world." Education and economic development were seen as key elements of this process.

Understandably, the Dene and other peoples of the North viewed government actions, including game laws, with suspicion. Too often, government policies ignored traditional obligations, including land claims. In the eyes of Aboriginals, their traditional hunting lands were being cleared to make way for corporate development.

Increasingly, the Dene and Inuit found themselves backed into a corner by the realities of a shrinking resource base, their own geography, and the forces of international markets (Abel, 1993: 268). In the 1950s, settlements based on the fur industry declined. Meanwhile, especially in the Subarctic, planned resource towns like Thompson, Manitoba, became major producers of minerals and attracted sizable populations. Sometimes, and by deliberate plan, Aboriginal people found employment in these towns. Too often, however, they did not (Bone, 1992: 69).

NORTHERN VISIONS

In the late 1950s, English-speaking Canada was beginning to discover (or, rather, make) itself. Having broken with Britain over the period of the two world wars, Canada was also in the early stages of trying to separate itself from the United States. In part, these efforts were economic. Thus, Conservative leader John Diefenbaker in the elections of 1957 and 1958 spoke out regarding the need for Canada to diversify trade by seeking out new markets in Asia and reviving those in Britain. But Diefenbaker also lit a fire in many Canadians' imaginations with visions of opening up the North in much the same way that Sir John A. Macdonald had opened up the West in the nineteenth century. Concerned about growing dependence on social assistance in the North, and addressing increasing demands for forest products, minerals, and energy, the Diefenbaker government decided to turn things around for northerners. The plan was to transform the fur-trading economy of the North into a resource-based, urban-like economy.

Under Diefenbaker's leadership, Canadian Aboriginals garnered unconditional federal voting rights. Before 1960, they had had to surrender their Indian status, a process known as enfranchisement, if they wanted to vote as Canadian citizens. During the Diefenbaker years, assimilation as an official government policy toward First Nations also was downplayed. For these and other liberating manoeuvres, some observers have jokingly referred to Diefenbaker as "The Lincoln of the North" (McMillan, 1995: 314).

By the late 1950s, Diefenbaker's "northern vision" had growing cultural support. Years before, Vilhjalmur Stefansson's book *The Friendly Arctic* (1921) and subsequent speeches, and Robert Flaherty's *Nanook of the North* (1922)—the world's first full-length documentary film—had popularized the North among Canadians and non-Canadians alike (Brody, 1987; Srebrnik, 1998). The harrowing tales of bush pilots in the years after, followed by the popular writings of people like Farley Mowat and Pierre Berton in the 1950s, added further lustre to the North's reputation and role in Canadian identity.

From the beginning, however, development of the North has faced economic challenges unlike those of any other area of the country. First, the terrain (largely muskeg or rock) is unwieldy. Second, the North's summer season, when outside work is most feasible, is very short. Third, a lack of skilled labour means bringing in people from the outside. (Even today, many indigenous northerners over the age of 40 have little or no formal schooling and are functionally illiterate.) Fourth, the North is far from markets and supplies, resulting in high transportation costs in both directions. Finally, under all these circumstances, economic development in the North requires a lot of capital. In the past, this has often been supplied by the state, either directly or through loans, or by private, often foreign, investors. But private investors often demand generous terms or conditions that relegate the environment and local job creation and training to a distant second place.

Beyond these purely economic factors, there are also significant political, social, and environmental considerations. Many of these began coming to the fore in the 1970s. On the one hand, Aboriginal peoples increasingly developed the political organizations and skills to press their demands for a greater role in economic development and the use of their lands (see Chapters Twelve and Thirteen). On the other hand, the period 1965–1975 also witnessed a renewed interest in the North on the part of many provincial governments driven by beliefs in activist government and a spirit of province-building (Chapter Eight). Megaprojects became a feature of the north part of nearly every province: forestry in British Columbia, the tar sands in Alberta, potash and uranium in Saskatchewan, hydroelectricity and mining in Manitoba and Quebec, mining in Ontario. These projects introduced modern kinds of employment, a case in point being the hydroelectric project at James Bay.

In the early 1960s, the Quebec government began searching for a northern supply of power (see Chapter Three). These ideas were finally realized in 1971 with Premier Robert Bourassa's announcement of a land agreement between the Cree First Nation at James Bay and the Quebec government that would allow construction of a dam (see Chapter Thirteen). A key part of the agreement was Aboriginal employment in the project. And by 1981, service industries employed 35 percent of the local Aboriginal population. There followed an announcement in 1991 of another stage of the project. In the beginning, many viewed the agreement as a model, and there was considerable praise for its impact on the Aboriginal community. More recently, however, there have been criticisms the project involved massive unforeseen social and environmental costs borne largely by the Cree people (Clerici, 1999; also Frideres and Gadacz, 2001).

Similar stories arise from other projects, such as the Churchill Nelson River Hydroelectric Project at Pike Lake, Manitoba, and the Dryden Chemicals Plant at Kenora, Ontario. When the Pike Lake project began, local Aboriginal people were told tremendous benefits would accrue from the project. The end result, however, was that little job training took place and instead outside labour was brought in. At Dryden, the plant flushed its waste of chlorine and other chemicals directly into the Wabigoon River, creating a relatively high level of mercury. Eventually, the mercury worked its way up the local food chain, severely damaging the mental and physical health of people in the local Aboriginal communities who ate the contaminated fish (Bone, 1992: 167).

These instances highlight a further aspect of changes in Canadian society with implications for northern development: increased recognition of environmental considerations. The pressures for economic development upon a poor region with rising unemployment and a diminishing "old industry," such as furs, are enormous. It becomes difficult to imagine why people in such a region might turn down the chance, at any price, to jump aboard the development train.

In the 1970s, however, the people of the North did just that. The oil crises of that decade suddenly made financially feasible the possibility of shipping northern oil and gas to southern markets via an overland pipeline crossing Yukon and the Northwest Territories. Large companies were eager to exploit the moment. Federal government approval was required, however, and though technically able to make decisions for the northern territories, which lack the status of provinces, the federal government was increasingly sensitive to concerns expressed by northern residents. The government struck a commission of inquiry.

The Mackenzie Valley Pipeline Inquiry (better known as the Berger Inquiry, after its chair, Justice Thomas Berger) went on for three years (1974–1977) and may properly be described as the first significant public study of the environmental and social effects of economic development ever conducted in Canada. Altogether, a thousand people, including 300 experts in 35 communities, testified at the hearings, resulting in 204 volumes of relevant data. Berger's final recommendation was blunt. He rejected outright the pipeline proposal, based on the threat of damage to the local ecosystem, and recommended an alternative route through the Mackenzie Valley after a wait of ten years. Today, in the midst of renewed fears about energy shortages, the idea of a northern pipeline is being revisited. It is garnering more support from northern people, especially Aboriginals, this time around, however. They have had years to plan, to build the social infrastructure, and to develop the kind of local skills they hope will assist them in taking advantage of the opportunity.

The importance of the Berger Inquiry rests not only on its conclusion, however. For the first time, the wishes of local northerners themselves became central to decision-making. The North was gaining a voice. But the inquiry also had the effect of informing many Canadians elsewhere about the North and about environmental issues generally. In this sense, the North played a role in shaping Canadians' growing concern, reflected in subsequent years, regarding environmental matters.

Arguably, these concerns have not translated into firm actions. Today, global warming has become an issue everywhere, with its own specific impacts upon the North and perhaps political as well as environmental consequences (see Box 11.1). Cohen (1997) speculates, for example, that changing weather conditions could cause more frequent landslides due to permafrost thaw, lower minimum annual water levels on rivers and lakes, more for-

BOX 11.1 Will Canada Lose Control of the Northwest Passage?

In the next decade global warming may result in the opening up of the Northwest Passage to year-round shipping. For Canada, the consequences of such an occurrence are important.

Few Canadians realize that the country's jurisdiction over the region, especially its waterways, is disputed. Many countries, including the United States, argue that the passage is international and not territorial water. Should the waterway become ice-free all year round, foreign fleets may seek to use it freely.

Just as they were hundreds of years ago, the commercial attractions of a northern route are obvious, shortening significantly the time needed to ship goods east and west. An open water corridor would also facilitate exploitation of northern oil and gas, as well as valuable minerals such as diamonds. Because the waters are disputed, the North might also face intensified militarization.

For Canada, the stakes of such events would be high, with economic and environmental considerations on the line, not to mention Canadian national identity. As too often in the past, however, the real losers might well be the people of the North themselves.

Sources: Nickerson (2000); Bueckert (2002); and Starnes (2002).

est fires, and lower yields from softwoods. These impacts could offset potential benefits from a longer growing and ice-free season.

CONCLUSION

Today, the North is nearly fully integrated into the rest of Canada and the world economy. Gradually, the number of indigenous people working in the old economy and living in the old ways has decreased. Meanwhile, a few have also found their way into the new economy, with jobs in the hydrocarbon industries (including diamonds), government bureaucracies, tourism, and the manufacture of cultural products (such as narwhal carvings and beadwork).

To an extent, cultural integration also is happening. Most northern peoples today live in permanent settlements. The pickup truck and the snowmobile have replaced the dog team, and the same stores, schools, churches, hospitals, sports arenas, and other institutions found in many small Canadian towns in the South can be seen (Condon, 1987).

To be sure, there also remain thriving vestiges of the old culture. Many families continue to live off the land, living in fishing camps in the summer and organizing hunting parties in the winter (Massey and Shields, 1995). They are part of what Stabler (1989) has identified as a **dual economy**, *a livelihood earned by both traditional and modern means*. In 1989, for example, while one-third of family breadwinners in the Northwest Territories made a living by modern technological means, two-thirds still hunted and trapped.

Moreover, Aboriginal languages and cultures are no longer being explicitly attacked (though they continue to face enormous cultural pressures) but instead are encouraged (Brody, 1987: 163). The training of Aboriginal teachers has been undertaken and curriculums have been amended to reflect local themes.

Still, problems remain. In schools, high rates of absenteeism and dropout are still a concern (Tompkins, 1998: 47). Unemployment remains stubbornly high. Alcoholism, solvent abuse (especially among the young), and murder and suicide rates have increased. The North has also experienced a high incidence of new diseases, such as diabetes and, since the 1990s, AIDS, as well as the return of an old nemesis, tuberculosis.

By the 1980s, it was clear southern Canada's aims in the North could not be achieved without consideration of the people living there. Calls for resolution of land claims and self-government increased. They were calls echoed by First Nations peoples everywhere.

KEY TERMS

bilateral kindreds
dual economy

individual egalitarianism
polygyny

syncretism

chapter twelve

The Road to Oka

There is but one law for all, namely that law which governs all law, the law of our Creator, the law of humanity, justice, equality—the law of nature, and of nations.
—philosopher Edmund Burke, 1794

All men were made by the same Great Spirit Chief. They are all brothers. The earth is the mother of all people, and all people should have equal rights upon it.
—Chief Joseph, Nez Perce Nation, 1877

After the outcome of the events at Oka, I am tempted to say that justice no longer exists for the cause of the Native North Americans, there is only fate.
—Helene Sevigny, Montreal lawyer and co-author of *Lasagna*, 1994

INTRODUCTION

For several weeks in the summer of 1990, Canadians watched their televisions in horror as a dispute over a golf course outside Montreal escalated into a Canadian version of Third World political violence. The Oka Crisis set the scene for a series of confrontations between Canada's largely white establishment and Aboriginal peoples, from the Atlantic to the Pacific shores, from rural reserves to parks to previously quiet residential suburbs. Emotions ran deep and, as always, dire predictions of more violence and "the end of Canada" were heard. In the end, the Oka Crisis was resolved (sort of), and baby steps were begun toward resolving problems facing Aboriginal–non-Aboriginal relations in Canada.

This chapter examines the events and actions leading up to the Oka Crisis and the meaning of that crisis itself. The chapter begins with a discussion of the legal basis of Aboriginal–non-Aboriginal relations. It is important to understand that, some significant breaches aside, much of what has been done to Canada's Aboriginal people since first contact has occurred within the rule of law. That these laws, from the time of Jacques Cartier's arrival, were made by outsiders is, of course, fundamentally important. Legality and justice are not always the same, and those with the power to define laws are frequently not the subjects of their implementation. The search into the legal basis of Aboriginal–non-Aboriginal relations begins with a document we have seen before (in Chapter Two), the Royal Proclamation Act.

THE ROYAL PROCLAMATION ACT

The Royal Proclamation Act of 1763 is the founding document of all written negotiations between First Nations and the federal government of Canada. Some critics argue that the Royal Proclamation was intended to dispossess First Nations of both their sovereignty and lands. According to Boldt (1993: 3), the document was based on the "self-serving, villainous doctrine which held that, by right of 'first discovery', a Christian nation was Divinely mandated to exercise dominion over conquered 'non-Christian primitives'."

One component of the Royal Proclamation decreed that Aboriginals would be allowed to live unmolested on their traditional lands at the Crown's pleasure. By this means the British government set itself up as protector of those Aboriginal lands, which "have not been ceded or purchased by us." Specifically, the proclamation declared first that Aboriginal peoples had certain legal rights to the lands they traditionally used and occupied. Second, it declared that incoming settlers could take over Aboriginal lands and use them for their own purposes only after these legal rights had been surrendered by formal agreements such as treaties. Third, it also declared that only the British government (and later by extension the federal government of Canada) had the authority to negotiate such agreements (Angus, 1991: 67).

Boldt (1993: 4) suggests further that the Royal Proclamation set forth five important principles. First, the Crown legally held title to all Aboriginal lands. Second, the Crown allowed Aboriginal peoples **usufructuary rights** (that is, rights of possession) to their traditional lands. Third, possession of these lands could be surrendered only to the Crown. Fourth, the Crown could extinguish Aboriginal rights of possession at its discretion, subject to reasonable compensation. And fifth, selected lands described as reserves would be set aside for Aboriginal domicile. None of these conditions included the entrenchment of Aboriginal rights as a principle of justice for First Nations.

In short, the Royal Proclamation established a framework for treaty-making as a means of dispossessing Aboriginals of their lands, while also achieving political order in the (now) British colonies by eliminating the possibility that private persons might try to purchase Aboriginal lands. By this means, the British government became a kind of real estate agent, able to transfer title to surrendered Aboriginal lands to either provinces or corporations, such as the Hudson's Bay Company.

The legal principles established by the Royal Proclamation were the motivating factor behind treaty negotiations in Upper Canada prior to Confederation as well as those conducted across the Prairies following 1871. What changed after Confederation was the emphasis placed on these principles. Until Confederation, protection of First Nations and their lands had been the paramount goal. The notion that Aboriginals needed to become civilized gained in importance but assimilation was regarded as a gradual and long-term process. In 1869 the goals of civilization and assimilation were officially added to government objectives with the passing of the Act for the Gradual Enfranchisement of Indians (Tobias, 1983: 43).

All Aboriginal land claims in the twenty-first century will likely be negotiated on the basis of the principles in the Royal Proclamation. Aboriginal proprietorship of ancestral lands will not be recognized, and negotiations will be restricted to small areas of selected lands. Aboriginal leaders, who have insistently laid claim to ancestral lands, will likely deem any compensation paid to them by government as only an initial instalment.

How do Aboriginal peoples view the Royal Proclamation? A document prepared by the Union of Ontario Indians (UOI) in 1970 gives us some insight. The document reads, in part:

> As Indian people we will always see our special status and our legal rights as flowing from the original sovereignty of our nations. The colonial legal system to a large extent denied that sovereignty, but they never denied the existence of rights based on the aboriginal possession of tribal territories. It was the unauthorized violation of these rights that led to the unrest which [sic] promoted the Royal Proclamation (quoted in Plain, 1988).

That document, the first constitutional document for British North America, recognized the existence of Aboriginal peoples' rights, and established legal procedures for the surrender of land (Plain, 1988: 31).

The UOI document notes further that there are many lands in Canada never ceded or purchased by the colonial power. When and if negotiations occur for such lands, no doubt the procedures established by the Royal Proclamation will be applied for the ceding of Aboriginal lands.

CONFEDERATION

The British North America (BNA) Act, later renamed the Constitution Act of 1867, was in fact only one act of British parliament. It formalized previous acts, notably the Act of Union (1841), while not repealing any previous acts relating to the colonies; indeed, many of these continued in force until the Statute of Westminster of 1931 (Lower, 1977: 332).

The BNA Act makes reference to Aboriginal rights as follows: Section 91(24) gives the federal government exclusive jurisdiction to make laws in relation to Aboriginal tenure and rights in lands reserved for Aboriginals. No constitutional authority exists for provincial jurisdictions to make laws concerning lands reserved for Aboriginals.

Section 35(1) of the Constitutional Act of 1982 declares: "The existing aboriginal and treaty rights of the Aboriginal peoples of Canada are hereby recognized and affirmed." Section 35 "does all it can to guarantee the rights and freedoms of the Aboriginal Peoples of Canada by making them part of the constitution 'so that they cannot be diminished or reduced'" (Battiste and Henderson, 2000: 206–207). Some Aboriginal observers contend that the United Kingdom's intent was to delegate the rights of its one-time treaty allies to Canada. It was the British position that no parliament should do anything to lessen the worth of these guarantees.

The foregoing sections formed the basis for the new government's actions towards First Nations. Tennant (1988: 323) identifies four major elements evident in the making of subsequent Canadian Aboriginal policy. These four elements are 1) the conversion of Aboriginals to Christianity with the help of various religious denominations; 2) the signing of treaties and confinement of Aboriginals to reserves; 3) the enforcement of compulsory schooling, often in residential schools run by church denominations; and 4) the inducement of Natives to adopt government structures and procedures derived from the British model.

These elements were particularly prominent in western Canada, where the new Dominion quickly set about creating its own colony. As previously noted (Chapters Seven and Ten), the West gradually was opened up for agricultural settlement. This process required the displacement of the indigenous people of the region. In counterpoise to the American experience, where a century of warfare and forced internment cleared the way for settlement, Canada (with the notable exception of 1885) resorted to the use of treaties.

THE NUMBERED TREATIES

By the nineteenth century, treaty-making in Canada was well established. Treaties had been signed between the Aboriginal peoples and the Europeans going back more than two centuries. The form and intent of these treaties, however, changed over time. The first treaties between Aboriginals and Europeans were conducted on the stated basis of "friendship and peace." The later pre-Confederation treaties carried out in the Maritimes generally dealt with military and political arrangements involving land transfers, annuities, or compensation for rights that were given up (Frideres and Gadacz, 2001: 169). By contrast, the post-Confederation treaties, conducted in the West, dealt explicitly with the transfer of land from Aboriginal peoples to the Canadian government. But these latter treaties also went further. Whereas previous treaties implied an agreement between equals, the so-called "numbered treaties" imposed the will of the new colonial government. Thus, Aboriginals were enjoined to divide themselves into bands and elect chiefs and councillors to govern themselves. Likewise, status Indians who wanted to have a vote in Canada or even leave a reserve and go to a bar would have to disavow their "Indian-ness," a practice known as **disenfranchisement**. It is not an exaggeration to suggest these treaties determined virtually every aspect of Aboriginal people's everyday lives.

Treaty No. 1, signed in 1871, involved the Ojibway people on the Peguis Reserve in Manitoba. By 1877, Treaties 1 to 7 had been signed; by 1899, the remaining treaties (8–10) were signed. Generally speaking, the components of these numbered treaties included surrender of Aboriginal rights and title to traditional lands, and the creation of reserves not to exceed one square mile (1.6 square kilometres) per family of five. The location of each reserve was determined after consultation with First Nations by someone sent by the chief superintendent of the Indian Affairs Branch (IAB) of the Department of Indian Affairs and Northern Development. Other terms included a ban on intoxicating beverages, a guarantee of hunting and fishing rights, the provision of a school, and the annual award of a few dollars per individual. In Treaty No. 6, for example, the amount was $12 per year. In addition, the government would make provisions of implements, twine, and farm animals so that the reserve residents could take up agriculture.

The Penner Commission, formed in 1983 to study Aboriginal self-government, argued that the writing of these treaties was based on the principles of the Royal Proclamation of

1763. However, the commission also argued that the treaties did everything the Royal Proclamation said not to do (Krotz, 1990: 166). Indeed, the treaties imposed the will of the new colonial government on First Nations, mandating that this was the way to do things, often irrespective of the Royal Proclamation.

How do Aboriginal peoples view the meaning of these treaties? Perhaps surprisingly, there is little agreement, even among Aboriginal peoples, as to their exact meaning. Likewise, there is little agreement with the view, held by Chief John Snow (1988) for example, that contemporary governments must negotiate the intent of the treaties. Snow regards the treaties as sacred deals made between trusting parties. In a speech two months before the First Ministers' meeting held in Ottawa on March 15 and 16, 1983, he stated:

> The Indian treaties with the Crown are real, and we must see to it that the terms of those treaties and related documents are fully included with the new constitution. Without our treaties we would be in the same unfortunate situation as the non-status and non-treaty Indians. I remind all treaty and registered Indians that the treaties are sacred covenants; they are binding documents and they must not be altered unilaterally by the government of Canada (Snow, 1988: 42).

There is evidence that some of the treaties were formulated by government agents and simply presented to Aboriginals who did not know what they were signing. There is evidence also, suggest Frideres and Gadacz (2001: 173), that hard-won oral promises gained by Aboriginals in many cases during treaty-signing have never been recognized or honoured by government. On the one hand, Aboriginal activist and Metis leader Howard Adams (1989) suggests the treaties are worthless because they primarily served to further the process of colonization. On the other hand, a former president of the Indian Association of Alberta, Harold Cardinal (1969), labels them an Aboriginal "Magna Carta" because they were entered into with faith and with hope for a better life with honour.

Research (via the oral tradition) into Treaty No. 7 suggests reasons for some of the problems we have today in deciphering the original meaning of these treaties (Treaty Seven Elders et al., 1996). This research reveals many elders understood signing the treaty did not mean giving up the land. A treaty was viewed by the original Aboriginal signers as an agreement to share the land to the benefit of both sides. Their position is that the Aboriginals who signed Treaty 7 obviously did not understand the government's intent, which was based on European notions of ownership.

It should be noted that this view of the treaties is not universally held. Some academics argue that, far from being weak or passive victims of the process, Aboriginals made the best of an admittedly difficult situation. Friesen (1986), for example, argues that some Aboriginal leaders discussed the terms of the agreements handed to them, and when necessary, manoeuvred, stalled, appeased, and compared offers to get the best deal.

What is clear, however, is the enormous difficulties of adjusting to reserve life after treaty-signing. Farming had no long history on the open plains and innovations that would make it possible, such as better agricultural implements, summer fallowing, and early ripening wheat, had yet to emerge. Many first harvests were lost to frost and want of animal power and implements to get the crops in. To the impediments of nature and technology were added the actions of Indian Affairs officials, who in some instances prohibited Aboriginals from acquiring new equipment. They would be better off, it was suggested, if they learned first the benefits of hard, manual labour before moving too quickly into the machine age (Carter, 1993). When the Second World War ended, most Prairie farmers bought bigger and better machines and changed the whole scale of Prairie farming, while the reserve farmers remained behind, thereby becoming an insufficient economic base for social and political development. By the 1960s, Aboriginals began to discover wage work as a replacement for poor success in farming and many fled to the cities. There, because of racism, fear of the unknown, and lack of education and technical skills, many were forced to turn to social assistance (Buckley, 1993).

WHITE PAPER, RED PAPER

The Trudeau administration that came to power in Ottawa in 1968 was modernist to a fault (see Chapter Three); that is, it believed firmly in the role of the state in society and (at the same time) the values of liberal individualism and economic progress. In this vein, the Liberal government decided to adopt a new Aboriginal policy, the intent of which was to resolve Aboriginal land claims and to eliminate distinctions between Aboriginal peoples and other Canadians. Aboriginal peoples were to be made individually self-reliant. Indian status was to disappear as a meaningful term in law (Boldt, 1993: 18).

The government's deliberations on Aboriginal policy occurred against the backdrop of one of the most important studies ever conducted in Canada. In 1963, the federal government asked University of British Columbia anthropologist Harry Hawthorn to survey the living conditions of Canada's Aboriginal peoples. This was at a time when Canada was rapidly becoming urbanized and Aboriginals—rural and confined to the reserves—made little impression on the Canadian radar screen. Hawthorn's subsequent study (1966–1967) stunned everyone, including government leaders. Few knew, or took time to know, of the devastating conditions under which most Canadian Aboriginals were living. The Hawthorn Report catalogued the plight of Aboriginals from high rates of unemployment and poverty to health problems, including malnutrition, and a resultant life expectancy dismally below that of other Canadians. It made clear that Aboriginal housing was substandard and education was inadequate. Finally, the report made an important plea that Aboriginal people *both* be extended the same rights as other citizens *and* be assured that their legal status as Aboriginals be honoured as well. This observation later gave rise to the term **citizens plus**.

The Hawthorn Report was delivered in the context of a great deal of discussion of human rights and fundamental freedoms. The American civil rights movement spilled over into Canada and forced attention to neglected minorities. The Red Power movement and Vietnam War demonstrations in the U.S. threatened many Canadians who feared that similar protests might occur in this country—fears that were amplified by the armed occupation of Anicinabe Park in Kenora, Ontario, and a near riot on Parliament Hill (Purich, 1986: 188). Fear alone does not explain the majority reaction, however. The 1960s in Canada, as elsewhere, reflected a sincere if paternalistic belief in providing opportunities for neglected communities to "join" the rest of society. Unfortunately, these efforts implied that all responsibility for accommodation lay within the minority camp. These efforts further assumed that education and good teaching were the chief vehicles for equalizing opportunity and minimizing differences (Friesen, 1993: 7).

Against this background, Pierre Trudeau's Liberal government in 1969 made public in a White Paper its new Aboriginal policy. The White Paper (1969) included the following proposed government actions:

1. Abolish the Department of Indian Affairs and Northern Development.
2. Repeal the Indian Act.

3. Transfer all responsibility for Indian programs to provincial administration. Provide economic assistance to those reserves that are furthest behind.
4. Formulate a policy to end treaties.
5. Appoint an Indian Claims Commissioner.
6. Recognize the contributions that Indian people have made to Canadian society.

Many Aboriginal leaders immediately and vigorously denounced the government's White Paper and were joined in their repudiation by a number of non-Aboriginal social and political organizations. Contrasting the White Paper with Pierre Trudeau's vision of a "Just Society," for example, a prominent young Aboriginal leader, Harold Cardinal, called the White Paper "a programme which offers nothing better than cultural genocide" (1969: 1).

The first official reaction to the White Paper came in the form of the Red Paper in 1970. Authorized by the Indian Chiefs of Alberta, the Red Paper heavily criticized the White Paper, claiming that it was a document of despair, not hope. The framers of the Red Paper contended that, if the proposals of the White Paper were implemented, within a generation or two Aboriginals would be left with no land and the threat of complete assimilation. (Indeed, the White Paper made clear the government did not accept the notion of Aboriginal rights.)

But the Red Paper itself was also strongly criticized, notably by Cree lawyer William Wuttunee in his book *Ruffled Feathers* (1971). Wuttenee accused the Red Paper's authors of fostering a treaty mentality and supporting a buckskin and feather culture. It soon became public that the Red Paper was actually prepared by M & M Systems Research of Alberta, an organization established by former Social Credit premier Ernest Manning and his son. In light of their bias, Wuttunee suggested that the report might be better labelled "The Socred Paper" (Wuttunee, 1971: 58).

A second major paper critical of the White Paper emanated from the Union of British Columbia Indian Chiefs and became known as the Brown Paper. The Brown Paper argued that the special relationship between Aboriginals and the federal government, developed through the years, should not be negated. Indeed, the framers of the Brown Paper insisted that this relationship carried immense moral and legal force and should constitute the foundation for future co-operative policy-making. The Brown Paper also made reference to the principle of self-determination and suggested that bands take over aspects of reserve administration at local levels. In this, the authors of the Brown Paper joined with other Aboriginal organizations in asking the Indian Affairs Branch to provide the necessary financial resources to develop their plans, programs, and budgets toward that end.

The federal government was surprised and dismayed by the response of Aboriginals to its White Paper. The surprise of government officials was not related solely to the forcefulness of the response. They were surprised also by the articulate and organized nature of Aboriginal response to the White Paper. Faced with such opposition, in 1970 the federal government decided not to proceed with implementing the White Paper (Purich, 1986: 187).

Nonetheless, the White Paper and the ensuing controversy had several important impacts. First, was the sudden bursting on the Canadian scene of a number of new Aboriginal organizations. In the past, such bodies had been impeded by lack of funds and active discouragement by the federal government. Members of such organizations were prevented from meeting by a pass system that forbade individuals to leave their reserves without permission of the Indian agent. Likewise, Section 141 of the Indian Act, introduced in 1927, made it an offence to raise money for the purpose of advancing Aboriginal claims (Purich, 1986: 185).

Despite these impediments, a few Aboriginal organizations did emerge in Canada during the 1930s and 1940s. These included the Native Brotherhood of British Columbia, the Indian Association of Alberta, and—with the encouragement of that province's CCF government—the Union of Saskatchewan Indians. The federal government's decision in the 1960s to fund Aboriginal organizations meant that when the White Paper was made public there were many existing political avenues through which Aboriginal peoples could express their dismay at the proposals. The National Indian Brotherhood (NIB) was formed in 1968 when the National Indian Council split into two factions, the NIB and the Canadian Metis Society. These and other, newer Aboriginal organizations experienced some success through lobbying, organizing, and protesting.

A second impact of the White Paper controversy was a change in government land claims policy. This change began with the appointment of an Indian Claims Commissioner. Such an appointment had been one of the few recommendations of the White Paper acceptable to most Aboriginals and resulted, in 1969, in Dr. Lloyd Barber taking the post, which he held until 1977. In August 1973, the federal government announced a comprehensive land claims policy recognizing two broad categories of claims: comprehensive claims based on Aboriginal rights, and specific claims based on specific legal commitments. Funding for pursuit of these claims was made possible through a newly established Office of Native Claims. In 1975, the Dene of the Northwest Territories became one of the first Aboriginal groups to claim First Nation status. The following year the Inuit Tapirisat proposed a land claim settlement that eventually gave birth to the territory of Nunavut on April 1, 1999 (Geddes, 2000) (see Chapter Thirteen).

The third impact is harder to measure, but no less important. The debate surrounding the White Paper and Aboriginal response to it educated many in the non-Aboriginal community about the issues facing Aboriginal people. It was knowledge reinforced on many occasions over the next 30 years through commission reports, constitutional meetings, and conflict.

ABORIGINALS AND THE 1982 CONSTITUTION

In February 1980, Pierre Trudeau's Liberals regained power after a brief interlude led by Joe Clark's Conservatives (Appendix 1), and Trudeau strongly declared his intentions to "bring home" Canada's Constitution. Trudeau's central aim was to deal with the threat of Quebec separation by strengthening the role of the federal government (Chapter Four). Immediately, however, a number of Aboriginal organizations began lobbying both the federal government and the British parliament to include Aboriginal rights in the process of patriation. The lobbying worked, for Minister of Justice Jean Chrétien in January 1981 introduced an amendment to the proposed constitution that would "recognize and affirm" the Aboriginal and treaty rights of Canada's Aboriginal peoples. The amendment included in its recognition the existence of Indian, Inuit, and Metis people. Chrétien also proposed that a conference to define Aboriginal rights be held within two years of the date when the patriation process would be complete.

Almost immediately, these amendments ran into problems. On November 5, 1981, all provinces except Quebec agreed to repatriation, but this incomplete consensus was achieved by dropping Aboriginal rights from the Constitution. Then, the first ministers reversed their position, agreeing—led by Alberta's premier, Peter Lougheed—to the inclusion of these rights on condition that the word *existing* be added. This meant that Aboriginals could expect no new rights and that only the rights they already possessed would be endorsed by the Constitution. Many feared that this condition would hinder the development of Aboriginal self-government. As the record shows, perhaps these concerns were somewhat justified; progress toward Aboriginal **self-government** has certainly been slow.

Angus (1991: 32) states that, whatever its form, if Aboriginal self-government is ever realized, it will have to fulfill three specific criteria. First, the federal government will have to recognize Aboriginal authority in specific areas of jurisdiction. Second, there will have to be a recognized structure for exercising that authority. And third, there will have to be sufficient economic resources to make that structure work. To date, governments have seemed willing only to fulfill the first criterion, by transferring certain responsibilities to Aboriginal bands and councils. The federal government has been careful to control the process by which such transfers have occurred in order to assure its objectives. At the same time, the Department of Indian Affairs and Northern Development (DIAND) in Ottawa legally and constitutionally controls the self-government process. The nature and extent to which Ottawa chooses to offer that right to Aboriginal peoples will determine exactly the kind of self-government they will ultimately achieve.

The federal government so far has denied First Nations the right to self-government on three fronts. First, this denial has occurred at the constitutional level. Aboriginal peoples have the right to negotiate for self-government, but its form has not been specifically spelled out either in the Constitution or by government in any adjoining document. All that has been offered is the *right* to negotiate for self-government. Second, Ottawa has left the door open for the negotiation of self-government in the Dene-Metis and Yukon claims, but only on the condition that this kind of right does not receive the same constitutional protection accorded the rest of the settlements. Essentially, this means that any constitutional recognition of the Aboriginal right to self-government, gained by the Dene-Metis constituency, cannot be used as a precedent in any other sector of the Aboriginal community. Third, it is clearly the intent of Ottawa to control the process of self-government. The DIAND will decide at what rate each band may proceed toward complete self-government (which as yet remains undefined). Indian Affairs bureaucrats in Ottawa will decide which bands are at a sufficiently advanced stage to be ready to move on toward increased responsibility (Angus 1991: 33).

On April 17, 1982, Canadians could finally say that they had their own constitution. Problems remained, to be sure, notably Quebec's refusal to sign the document (Chapter Four). Insofar as Aboriginal peoples were concerned, however, the new constitution represented an important step. It affirmed existing Aboriginal rights in broad terms and thus opened the door for making land claims (Chapter Thirteen). For the first time, the Metis, along with the Inuit, garnered specific mention in Canada's constitution. Furthermore, the document set out a process of ongoing constitutional conferences aimed at defining Aboriginal rights and giving Aboriginal people opportunity to present their views. Finally, the Canadian Charter of Rights and Freedoms not only recognized and affirmed Aboriginal treaty rights, it also put a spotlight on what some observers saw as the Indian Act's discriminatory provisions.

Since the establishment of the Indian Act in 1876, legislation governing Aboriginals had defined who was an Aboriginal in a way that discriminated against women. To begin with, on "the day that the government counted the Indians," or enfranchised them, all who "stood in line" became status Indian by law. This afforded them the privilege of having matters pertaining to health, education, and welfare delivered directly through federal auspices. Children born to status Indians were added to the Indian Register.

But what happened if a status Indian woman married a non-status male (either Aboriginal or non-Aboriginal)? In these cases, she lost her status rights. Likewise, any children born to her also were deprived of status. This was not true for males, however. In fact, if a status Indian man married a non-status woman (either Aboriginal or non-Aboriginal), that woman became a status Indian. This gender discrimination bothered many people, particularly since the 1973 Lavell case that upheld this discriminatory provision of the Indian Act. The terms of the Charter of Rights and Freedoms may have been influenced by the 1975 case of Sandra Lovelace, who took her complaint of gender discrimination to the Human Rights Committee of the United Nations. In 1981, this committee decided that her case was one of "an unjustifiable denial of her rights under the United Nations' Covenant on Civil and Political Rights" (Miller, 2000: 357–358).

The issue of how Aboriginals viewed women's rights was complex. Aboriginal women were not unanimous in endorsing the equal-rights amendment that would end status women's loss of their rights through marriage to non-status males. Some argued that women who married "outside" knew very well what they were doing. Insofar as Aboriginals believe tribal spirituality is mainly transferred through women, who alone have the power to give life, marrying outside was viewed by some Aboriginals, male and female alike, as disregarding the spiritual welfare of the band. Hence, some believed women doing so deserved to lose their status.

Such arguments were decidedly out of step with Canadian society and with many in the Aboriginal community, however. Thus, in 1985, Bill C-31 was passed, eliminating sexual discrimination, abolishing the concept of enfranchisement, and providing for those who had lost their Aboriginal status to gain partial reinstatement. The Bill had the almost immediate effect of greatly enlarging Canada's Aboriginal population. By 2001, more than 105 000 people had regained Indian status under Bill C-31 (Frideres and Gadacz, 2001: 35).

The conferences specified in the Constitution began with one held March 15–16, 1983. This first conference was followed by three additional conferences. From the beginning, at least one practical problem beset these conferences: that of representation. Through tradition and the Indian Act, status Indians had a recognized seat at the gatherings. This was not the case, however, for Metis people and non-status Indians. In the past, the Native Council of Canada (NCC) had spoken for Metis people. But the Metis disagreed with the NCC's definition of Metis (anyone of mixed blood) and wanted a more explicit definition including the origins and domicile of the Metis in the Red River area. Similarly, non-status Indians demanded equal rights with status Indians. By contrast, the Metis were not requesting status rights; they simply wanted to be recognized as a distinct Aboriginal group.

In the end, Prime Minister Trudeau asked the NCC to represent Metis interests, a move that caused a further split in the Aboriginal community. A new organization, the Metis Nation Council, was then formed by a group of dissidents who launched a court case to demand that their interests also be represented at constitutional conferences. When the first conference was over it was agreed that no constitutional changes affecting Aboriginal rights would be made without a constitutional conference for that explicit purpose, to which Aboriginal representatives would be invited (Schwartz, 1986: 127). It was further agreed that future land claims would include a definition of "existing rights" and that sexual equality would be guaranteed; hence, the later passing of Bill C-31.

THE PENNER REPORT AND THE NOTION OF SELF-GOVERNMENT

In 1983, the federal government released a report prepared by the Special Committee on Indian Self-Government in Canada (also known as the Penner Report). The Penner Report dismissed the terms and intent of the Indian Act as out of date and ineffective for contemporary negotiations. Instead, the report made several recommendations calling for government to establish a new kind of relationship with Aboriginal people based on the notion of Aboriginal self-government. Among specific recommendations, the report suggested that Aboriginal governments be made accountable to their own people. The report also recommended that bilateral federal-Aboriginal agreements govern respective jurisdictions, with the federal government ceding all areas of competence required for Aboriginal First Nations to govern themselves effectively and ensuring that provincial laws would not apply to Aboriginal land except with Aboriginal consent. The report further recommended that complete control be given First Nations over their lands and resources, with financial backing through federal grants and settlements of land claims. The report also originated the concept of a third order of government with respect to Aboriginal self-government, with Aboriginal governments functioning in six major areas: source, purpose, power, autonomy, base, and structure (Tennant, 1988: 329).

The notion of self-government is important to First Nations people for two fundamental reasons. First, it is a natural desire on the part of any cultural group to manage their own affairs in order to preserve elements of their unique way of life. It was this kind of desire that fuelled the decolonization of much of the Third World after the Second World War. Second, Aboriginal people have seen the damage that years of government control have done to their standard of living, languages, and lifestyle. For them, self-government is a means of redressing these damages and ensuring they are not inflicted again (Buckley, 1993).

The federal government's response to the Penner Report was to try to entrench Aboriginal self-government for status Indians at a First Ministers' meeting in 1984. At that meeting, Prime Minister Pierre Trudeau followed the initiative of the report but found little agreement among the premiers. Brian Mulroney made similar proposals in 1985 and 1987, when his government was in office, but again consensus was lacking. Without a full definition of costs and terms, the governments of Alberta, British Columbia, Newfoundland, and Saskatchewan (in particular) were reluctant to support federal proposals for Aboriginal self-government (Miller, 1988: 304). But it is likewise true that some Aboriginal organizations also found the self-government proposals inadequate. For its part, the federal government—while supporting self-governing institutions—wanted the actual power of those institutions to be a matter for negotiation. Often, the image of self-government that the government had in mind approximated that of Canadian municipalities. By contrast, Aboriginal organizations wanted assurances that their actual institutions would be protected in the Constitution and that such self-governing institutions would be on (more or less) the level of provincial counterparts.

THE MEECH LAKE AND CHARLOTTETOWN ACCORDS

In the spring of 1987, Canada's first ministers met at Meech Lake in the Gatineau Hills of Quebec and quickly agreed to a package of proposals that would lead Quebec to sign the

Constitution "with honour and enthusiasm" (Miller, 2000: 375). As we have seen (in Chapter Four), the Accord fell apart over the next three years, leading to acrimony, the creation or legitimation of two political parties, and fears of the country's breakup. Something that has not been assessed above is the significant role Aboriginals played in the Accord's failure.

From the beginning, Aboriginal groups opposed the Meech Lake Accord. They opposed it practically, fearing that its provisions recognizing Quebec's specificity would lead to a similar delegation of powers to the other provinces, including jurisdiction over Aboriginal affairs. But, symbolically, the phrase respecting Quebec as a "distinct society" also rankled Aboriginals. For them, the Accord completely overlooked the historical traditions of the Aboriginal peoples; indeed, it identified Quebec as the "foremost distinct society" in Canada, implicitly building on the notion of "two founding races" (French and English) while ignoring the pre-existence of Aboriginal people on the continent. Further upsetting Canada's Aboriginals was that the country's first ministers had long rejected the entrenchment of Aboriginal rights on the grounds that the concept was too vague and undefined, yet suddenly they were quite willing to grant similar rights to the province of Quebec (York, 1989: 266).

In the end, the Meech Lake Accord died. Technically, due to the time difference, it died first on the East Coast, when the Newfoundland legislature failed to vote on the Accord. In fact, however, the Accord's final defeat can be attributed to the actions of one lone individual, Elijah Harper, an Aboriginal NDP member of the opposition in the Manitoba legislature. By the spring of 1990, the House of Commons and most provinces had given the Accord approval. Newfoundland and Manitoba had not, however, and time was running out. Procedure required that for the Manitoba legislature to vote on the Accord, and thus to make the deadline, there had to be unanimous approval by the members. When the proposal to cut debate short was put forward, however, Elijah Harper stood alone in refusing approval. Without this approval, the Accord could not be passed in time. Newfoundland's government knew this outcome already on the day it refused also to vote on the Accord.

Quebecers' reaction to the Meech Lake failure is well-known. The newly founded Bloc Québécois and the cause of Quebec separatism were both given a boost, leading ultimately to near success in the 1995 sovereignty referendum. But the Accord's failure also had profound consequences for Aboriginal–non-Aboriginal relations. Henceforth, Aboriginal issues took on a greater status in constitutional negotiations. Witness the invitation given by Prime Minister Mulroney in 1992 to Aboriginal leaders to participate in the all-Canada round of deliberations in Charlottetown, which led to the Charlottetown Accord in that same year. To be sure, this invitation came only after intense lobbying on the part of Grand Chief Ovide Mercredi and others representing the Assembly of First Nations (AFN). Likewise, though Aboriginal rights were recognized at the gathering, limits were placed on them, such that "Aboriginal legislation should not be inconsistent with those laws which are essential to the preservation of peace, order and good government in Canada" (Miller, 2000: 378). Still, Aboriginals at least had a place at the table.

Like the Meech Lake Accord, the Charlottetown Accord also died, this time at the hands of a national referendum held in October 1992. The Charlottetown Accord died, as we have seen (Chapter Four) for numerous reasons, faring poorly also among Aboriginal people. About 50 000 First Nations people voted on the Accord, representing only about eight percent of the Aboriginal population in Canada. (This reflects voting patterns among Aboriginal people in other instances.) Of those who voted, 62.1 percent rejected the terms of the Accord, while 37.9 percent favoured the Accord. There were some notable splits within the Aboriginal community, however, pointing out the fact, too often ignored by outsiders, that Aboriginals are no more homogeneous than their non-Aboriginal counterparts. Most Aboriginals in the Yukon favoured the proposal while almost all of those in Alberta rejected it, and leaders of the various Aboriginal organizations also found themselves on opposite sides. Ovide Mercredi of the AFN stated:

> We had an opportunity here to end dominance in the lives of the people I represent and we blew it....Something went seriously wrong. We allowed our prejudices, our biases to dominate (quoted in Smith, 1993: 231).

In between the twin failures of the Meech Lake Accord and the Charlottetown Accord, however, was a more violent conflict, one that, for many people, exposed the darkest side of Canadian society.

THE OKA CRISIS

As a budding sociologist, you may have discovered that the apparent connections between events may be merely coincidental, while seemingly unrelated events may be related in indirect and very complex ways. Sorting these connections out is part of the fun of being a sociologist. The failure of the Meech Lake Accord and the onset of the Oka Crisis during nearly the same period make a case in point. In strictly empirical terms, the two events were unrelated. Yet, in symbolic and emotional terms, the two events take on a deeper sociological meaning and resonance.

As noted, the Meech Lake Accord was already in trouble in the spring of 1990. Around this same period, a long-standing land claim was about to hit the front pages. Cross and Sevigny (1994: 80) describe the events:

> Everything began on a nice day in March 1990, when the Municipal Council of the Village of Oka [outside Montreal] adopted the proposal to expand the area's golf course. In one stroke, Oka's Pines and Mohawk cemetery at Kanehsatake were threatened. To protect their land and the graves of their ancestors, the Mohawks erected a barricade to make the Whites understand that they intended to protect their land against all invaders.

The conflict's roots were much older, however. In fact, the conflict dated back to 1717, when King Louis XV of France granted the land in question to the Seminary of St. Sulpice to set up a mission for the resident Aboriginals, mainly Huron, Algonquin, and Iroquois. By French law (which never recognized Aboriginal land title) and as confirmed later by British and Canadian legal successors, the lands of Kanesatake (Oka) did not legally belong to the Aboriginal inhabitants. To the Aboriginals themselves, however, this was their land (Dickason, 2002: 343–46). Indeed, for many Mohawks and their supporters, such legal decisions merely reinforced the notion that law and justice are often strangers and that the Canadian legal system is simply another tool of oppression.

The crisis escalated to violence when the Quebec police decided to capture and take down the barricades. A fight ensued amidst Oka's pines. Shots rang out and a police officer was killed, though no one to this day is certain whether the bullet that killed him was from a Mohawk shooter or the result of "friendly fire." Quickly, the conflict over a few square kilometres of pine forest became a crisis. As in the FLQ Crisis of 1970, 2500 Canadian soldiers were called in. Meanwhile, the Mohawk cause was strengthened by khaki-clad "warriors" bearing automatic rifles, and sympathy barricades erected elsewhere, notably at the nearby Kahnewake reserve. The crisis lasted 11 weeks, during which many Canadians, Aboriginal and non-Aboriginal alike, feared a horrible bloodbath (Alfred, 1995: 100). Thankfully, this did not occur. On September 26, the crisis ended and the last few holdouts walked out from behind the barricade. Only a few dozen Mohawk warriors were tried in court.

In the short and medium term, the incident left many non-Aboriginal Quebecers upset and angry. They had always prided themselves on their relations with Aboriginal people being better than those in the rest of the country. Already angry over the failure of Meech Lake, francophones felt betrayed by the province's Aboriginal minority, particularly as some in the rest of Canada took glee in Quebec's "Indian problem."

As it turned out, however, any such glee was short-lived. One consequence of Oka was a series of "copy-cat" confrontations between Aboriginals and non-Aboriginal authorities in various parts of Canada: Ipperwash in Ontario, the Old Man Dam in Alberta, and Gustafson Lake in British Columbia. In the Canada of the late-twentieth century, those who lacked formal channels of redressing wrongs were quickly finding other means. Aboriginals were in the forefront. Regrettably, in some quarters, racism and prejudice once more reared their heads in response to the challenge.

In the longer term, the Oka Crisis and the coincident angst surrounding the Meech Lake Accord's failure spurred serious efforts to deal with Aboriginal issues. British Columbia, for example, suddenly reversed its position and decided to negotiate Aboriginal land claims. The government of Saskatchewan did much the same regarding the category of specific claims known as "treaty land entitlement" (Miller, 2000: 384).

Today, the Mohawks of Oka have discounted the idea of seceding from Quebec. There remains a great deal of mistrust between Mohawks and the Quebec government over the province's drive for increased power within the Canadian federation, and between Mohawks and the surrounding non-Aboriginal community. But there also are fractures within the Mohawk community between "moderates" and hard-line sovereigntists, worsened since 1990 by the emergence of criminal gangs thriving on gambling and smuggling.

As for the disputed land, the Kanesatake Mohawk Band in June 2000 signed a deal with Ottawa gaining control (but not legal title). The Mohawk band council also gained the right to establish bylaws, zoning regulations, and a process for resolving disputes on those lands. Minister of Indian Affairs Robert Nault described the event as marking the beginning of a form of self-government for the Mohawks.

CONCLUSION

The Oka Crisis stunned many Canadians, both Aboriginal and non-Aboriginal. The sight of Canadian soldiers and Mohawk warriors squaring off against one another revealed the depth of the divide between Canada's other "two solitudes" and the possible dangers if that gulf was not addressed. For 20 years, Canada-Quebec issues had dominated the political agenda. In the context of the failures of the Meech Lake and Charlottetown accords, and in the aftermath of Oka, Aboriginal–non-Aboriginal issues came to be seen as parallel to Canada-Quebec issues. They became better known to the general public and gained support, albeit sometimes grudgingly. Within government circles, a heightened sense of urgency over such things as treaties and the Aboriginal right to self-government also emerged (Mercredi and Turpel, 1993: 209–210).

The movement of Aboriginal peoples from Canada's back stage to front stage raised broad political, economic, and cultural issues for Canadian society, however. Would self-governing Aboriginal communities be on a par with provincial governments? Would they be sovereign? How would self-government be financed? Who owns the land? Given the difficulty of accommodating the Quebec nation into Canada, how might the multifarious Aboriginal nations be fitted in? Equally, how does Canada fit into Aboriginal identity? These are but some of the difficult questions Chapter Thirteen explores.

KEY TERMS

citizens plus
disenfranchisement
self-government
usufructuary rights

chapter thirteen

The Search for New Learning Paths

The day will come when Indians will not be concerned with struggling for their basic rights only, but for the basic rights of all.
—Cree lawyer William Wuttunee, 1971

Canada is a test case for a grand notion—the notion that dissimilar peoples can share lands, resources, power, and dreams while respecting and sustaining their differences.
—Indian and Northern Affairs Canada, 1996

The governments of the day...do not want to discuss ways of transforming legal or political institutions to include indigenous peoples in nation-states. They do not want to end their national fantasies and myths about our nations. They do not want to expose the injustices that have informed the construction of state institutions and practices.
—Marie Battiste and James (Sákéj) Youngblood Henderson, 2000

INTRODUCTION

The Hawthorn Report of the 1960s (see Chapter Twelve) suggested that the impact of Aboriginal people on federal and political systems in Canada would always be marginal, as their population was small. The early 1990s proved the errant nature of this prediction. The

Aboriginal role in the failure of the Meech Lake Accord, and no less the Oka Crisis, awakened Canadians and their governments to the seriousness of Aboriginal issues and demands. Identifying these issues and prescribing solutions are two different things, however. This concluding chapter of Part Three examines some of the key recommendations of the recent Royal Commission on Aboriginal Peoples and several specific issues: land claims, treaties, the notion of self-government, and resolution of lawsuits stemming from residential abuse. The chapter further explores the backlash arising from efforts to resolve these issues. Finally, the chapter examines how Aboriginal values might fit into a modern Canada, that is, how Canadian society may in future benefit from rediscovering its Aboriginal roots. The chapter begins, however, with an empirical look at the situation of Aboriginal peoples in Canada today.

PORTRAIT OF THE ABORIGINAL PEOPLES TODAY

Today, there are nearly 700 000 status Indians in Canada, though more than one million Canadians can lay claim to Aboriginal ancestry (see Table 10.1). In recent decades, the number and proportion of Aboriginals has been rapidly increasing. There are two reasons for this. First, Aboriginal birth rates, though declining, remain high above the Canadian average. In 1993, for example, Aboriginal women had 2.7 children compared with the Canadian average of 1.67 (Frideres and Gadacz, 2001: 64). One consequence of this continued explosion of Aboriginal births is that Canada's Aboriginal population, compared with the general population, is on average very young. Second, the passage of Bill C-31 in 1985 allowed for Aboriginal peoples to regain their status previously lost for various reasons. More than 105 000 individuals have regained their status since 1985 (Frideres and Gadacz, 2001: 35).

Roughly a quarter of Canada's status Indians live in Ontario, with another 16 percent residing in Saskatchewan and British Columbia. Their numbers are increasing especially rapidly in the Prairie region, where birth rates are among the highest in Canada.

Across Canada, 58 percent of Canada's status Indians live on one of 2284 reserves (Frideres and Gadacz, 2001: 56). These reserves vary in size, the largest (at 900 square kilometres) being that of the Blood (Kainai) Nation in southern Alberta.

The term **band** referred originally to *small cultural and linguistic groups living together, or coming together at various seasons and times, as part of a larger Aboriginal society*, such as the Cree or Inuit. Today, the term describes *a local unit of administration, operating under the Indian Act* (see below). Currently, there are 621 bands in Canada (Frideres and Gadacz, 2001: 56). Most bands consist of about 500 members. A few bands, however, such as the Six Nations Band in Ontario with nearly 20 000 members (*CGA*, 1999: 48), are very large.

Many Aboriginal people continue to live in rural areas, in the northern parts of Canada's provinces, and in the territories. Increasingly, however, Aboriginal people, status and non-status, are moving to Canada's cities and towns. This is especially the case in western Canada. Aboriginal people today make up seven percent of the populations of Saskatoon, Regina, and Winnipeg, six percent in Thunder Bay, and four percent in Edmonton (Statistics Canada, 2001; 2003d). One related and recent phenomenon has been the emergence of **urban reserves**.

Baron and Garcea (1999) suggest three reasons for the growth of urban reserves. First, they are in some instances directly tied to treaties and treaty land entitlements. In Saskatchewan, for example, almost 30 bands were short-changed when land entitlements for reserves were negotiated. The provincial government has since settled with the bands, offering them compensatory funds with which to buy real estate. Second, the creation of urban reserves is tied to the desire of First Nations people to develop and diversify economic opportunities. The federal government transferred land to Aboriginal ownership in Saskatoon, for example, resulting in the creation of an urban reserve. Third, the creation of urban reserves is a territorial expression of First Nations' demands for self-government. Aboriginals want to be full players in society, but not assimilated. Urban reserves function as an extension of a band's national land patrimony and authority to make decisions about their own lives. The increased physical presence of Aboriginal peoples within urban areas has resulted in heightened tensions between Aboriginals and non-Aboriginals but also greater awareness and concern about Aboriginal issues within the broader society.

Many on-reserve Aboriginals live in conditions comparable to those found in the world's least-developed countries. On-reserve housing is generally substandard and often poorly ventilated. The homes are too hot in summer and too cold in winter. Running water is frequently a luxury. In consequence, the infant mortality rate among Aboriginal people remains substantially above that of Canadian infants in general (13 per thousand live births versus eight). Likewise, male and female life expectancy among Aboriginals is below that of the Canadian population. In 1995, status Indian men lived an average of 69 years compared with 75 years among Canadian men as a whole, while status Indian women lived 76 years compared with 82 years for Canadian women as a whole (Frideres and Gadacz, 2001: 66–67).

Illness and poor health are some of the causes of this early mortality. Tuberculosis is less a threat than in the recent past but has been replaced by the scourges of diabetes, AIDS, and drug and alcohol abuse. The fact is that for a substantial number of Aboriginal people, on and off the reserves, life is fraught with danger and hopelessness. Suicide rates, especially among young Aboriginals (15 to 34 years), eclipses Canadian averages. Likewise, interpersonal violence within Aboriginal communities plays a part. Thus, a disproportionate number of inmates within correctional institutions, especially in western Canada, are Aboriginals, many of them convicted of manslaughter and assault (Statistics Canada, 2001).

While on-reserve conditions are generally poor, the situation of Aboriginals migrating to urban areas is often not much better. While cities may provide some Aboriginals with increased opportunities and bring services closer to them, many Aboriginal people also find they have to contend with a myriad of other challenges not experienced on the reserve, such as cultural alienation and racism (Buckley, 1993: Fox and Long, 2000).

Lack of education and training, discrimination, and systematic exclusion over the years from occupational opportunities is reflected in the poor economic circumstances faced by many Aboriginals. Since 1971, the proportion of Aboriginal people in the labour force has steadily increased, though it still trails that of other Canadians. In 1991, the participation rate for Aboriginal people in Canada was 57 percent, compared with 67.9 percent for all Canadians. The proportion of Aboriginals in the labour force varies significantly, however, according to whether they remain on reserve or not. On-reserve Aboriginals are less likely than off-reserve Aboriginals to enter the labour force, for very good reason: there are fewer jobs to be had. But the situation of off-reserve Aboriginals seeking employment is often not much better, with a rate of 17 percent unemployment at any given time (Frideres and Gadacz, 2001: 95–97).

Nonetheless, today about 43 percent of Aboriginal people are employed (Frideres and Gadacz, 2001: 97). We should keep in mind that the economic circumstances of Aboriginals are not uniform. These circumstances vary by region, band, and gender, for example. Within Aboriginal bands also there is marked stratification, with the gradual emergence of small-business owners and a middle class. Finally, there are marked differences in income among the various Aboriginal peoples. Table 13.1, taken from recent work by Maxim et al. (2001), compares the average income (from all sources) of Aboriginals and non-Aboriginals in 1995.

The table reveals at least three significant things. First, it confirms what many Canadians already know, that the average income of Aboriginals is far behind that of Canadians as a whole. Second, however, Table 13.1 reveals significant differences within the Aboriginal community. Third, the table also confirms previous studies showing that a disproportionate amount of total income obtained by Aboriginal peoples comes from social assistance or welfare payments. Frideres and Gadacz (2001: 120), for example, state that over half of the Aboriginal population in 1991 received social assistance or welfare, and that 90 percent of Aboriginals during their lifetime have received assistance or welfare.

Education is a key to occupational attainment and economic prosperity in Canada. Traditionally, Aboriginal educational levels have lagged behind those of other Canadians. In recent years, educational attainment levels for Aboriginal Canadians have improved. Today, far more Aboriginals than ever go to university. The increase is particularly sharp for Aboriginal women, but the educational level of Aboriginal men also is increasing (see Table 13.2).

Disturbingly, however, comparisons with other Canadians reveal a continuing gap. For example, in 2001, 9.4 percent of Aboriginal identifiers had attained university and 18.5 percent had attained college, up substantially from 1991. In that same year, however, 22.6 percent of all Canadians had also attained university while 20.7 percent had attained college, and these percentages have also increased since 1991. The gap in educational levels between Aboriginal people and all Canadians actually increased during the period 1981–1991 (Frideres and Gadacz (2001: 111) and appears not to be closing since.

Altogether, these and similar statistics suggest a people remaining largely outside the opportunities experienced by other Canadians. In the early 1990s, the circumstances of Aboriginal Canadians provided the context for a rise in Aboriginal–non-Aboriginal troubles, which led to subsequent efforts by Canadian governments and society at large to come to terms with the issues. A starting point for this new resolve was the Royal Commission on Aboriginal Peoples.

TABLE 13.1	Average Income, Aboriginal and Non-Aboriginal People, 1995				
	Aboriginal				Non-Aboriginal
	Registered	Non-Registered	Metis	Inuit	
Mean Income—Those Reporting salary/wages	$16 863	$20 835	$19 529	$17 537	$27 188
Mean Income—All Persons	$9747	$13 161	$12 956	$12 089	$19 843
Percent Not Reporting Income	42	37	34	31	27

Source: Adapted with the permission of the *Canadian Review of Sociology and Anthropology* from Maxim et al. (2001: 470).

TABLE 13.2 | Population Aged 25 to 64, by Level of Educational Attainment and Sex, Canadian Population as a Whole and Individuals Reporting Aboriginal Identity, Canada, 2001

	All Canadians						Aboriginal Identifiers					
	Both	%	Men	%	Women	%	Both	%	Men	%	Women	%
Less than high school	4 573 120	22.7	1 874 785	23.4	1 823 455	22.0	171 725	38.7	86 495	41.3	85 225	36.4
High school	3 898 400	23.9	1 796 465	22.5	2 101 940	25.4	101 365	22.9	45 770	21.8	55 575	23.8
Trades	2 097 145	12.9	1 323 705	16.5	773 450	9.3	69 265	15.6	41 340	19.7	27 940	11.9
College	2 917 890	17.9	1 201 225	15.0	1 716 670	20.7	66 805	15.1	23 580	11.2	43 225	18.5
University	3 676 620	22.6	1 804 240	22.6	1 872 390	22.6	34 465	7.8	12 440	5.9	22 015	9.4
Total	14 539 600	100.0	8 000 420	100.0	8 287 905	100.0	443 625	100.0	209 625	100.0	233 980	100.0

Source: Adapted from Statistics Canada Web site at www.statcan.ca/english/census01/products/analytic/companion/educ/contents.cfm.

THE ROYAL COMMISSION ON ABORIGINAL PEOPLES

In 1991, the federal government established the Royal Commission on Aboriginal Peoples (RCAP). As clearly stated in the final report's preamble, the commission arose out of "anger and upheaval," "concern and distress," and "hope." Oka was clearly on the authors' minds, but in fact the commission was a direct result of the Meech Lake debacle (Chapter Four). Creation of the RCAP followed from an offer made by Prime Minister Brian Mulroney to Elijah Harper and his supporters in June 1990 in the lead-up to the Accord's slow death in the Manitoba legislature. The Meech Lake Accord died, of course, but the Royal Commission lived on, despite considerable skepticism among Aboriginal peoples as it began its hearings.

Chaired by former AFN chief George Erasmus and Quebec judge René Dussault, the commission included seven members, four of them Aboriginal and three of them non-Aboriginal. A number of public meetings were held, transcripts were analyzed, and a great deal of research was undertaken. It was clear, however, both from the structure of the report and from the public hearings, that the commissioners regarded their task as an exercise in public education as well as a government investigation (Miller, 2000: 385).

Altogether, the Commission cost $50 million. Its final report in 1996 consisted of five volumes, over 3500 pages, and 400 recommendations. The report's main findings were contained in five sections.

In essence, the report recommended a major reconstruction of Canadian society so that justice and equality would be better assured for Aboriginal Canadians. Two specific and urgent concerns of the report had to do with the high suicide rates in Aboriginal communities and the high incidence of Aboriginal people in jail, especially in the Prairie provinces, which raised issues regarding the fairness of Canada's criminal justice system. The commission recommended swift action in these areas, starting with a meeting of the various bars, law societies, and lawyers' associations. It urged increased government expenditures in preventive programs.

More broadly, the RCAP also recommended a rewriting of the principles of the Royal Proclamation to reflect the new nation-to-nation concept of negotiation as well as a new constitutional foundation by which to perceive the past treaty-making process. In the words of Ponting (1997b: 470), the report recommended at its core "the re-balancing of political and economic power between Aboriginal nations and the Canadian governments." Among its many recommendations was the formation of an Aboriginal parliament with an advisory but no law-making authority. This was seen as a first step toward creating a House of First Peoples as the third chamber of the Parliament of Canada. The commission also recommended the abolition of the Department of Indian Affairs and Northern Development and its replacement by two departments: the Department of Aboriginal Relations and the Department of Indian and Inuit Services.

A number of other structures were also recommended by the RCAP. These included an Aboriginal Peoples' International University along with Aboriginal student unions and Aboriginal residential colleges. An Aboriginal Languages Foundation would parallel the work of the international university and supplement its efforts to maintain Aboriginal languages and culture.

What was the government's response to the report's recommendations? In 1998, the Liberal government set up a special healing fund in the amount of $350 million to be used over a four-year period, as a token of the government's apology for the treatment of Aboriginals in residential schools. In addition, the government approved an increase of $250 million in their next year's budget as a means of supporting the Aboriginal cause.

The report had critics, however. While Phil Fontaine, grand chief of the AFN, generally approved of the recommendations, suggesting that they were the best one could hope for at the time, most Metis, Inuit, and non-status Indians were critical of it (and subsequent government actions) as favouring status Indians. Others noted the report's lack of emphasis on the situation of urban Aboriginals, privileging reserve life and cultural persistence over solving socio-economic problems across the board (Allan Cairns, cited in Miller, 2000: 385). This is particularly important, since more than one-third of Canada's Aboriginals now live in urban centres.

Likewise, the report also met with strong criticism in the non-Aboriginal community. There was widespread concern regarding the commission's handling of Aboriginal complaints regarding treatment in residential schools (Chapter Ten). The report called for a public inquiry into the matter, but some critics countered that this task was already part of the commission's mandate, while others feared the legal consequences (subsequently justified) of such an inquiry.

One of the report's harshest critics is political scientist Thomas Flanagan (2000). Flanagan disagrees with the assumption that first habitation gives Aboriginals any particular rights over later arrivals, pointing out that Aboriginal peoples arrived in North America in three different migrations. Regarding territorial claims, he further argues that, before the European invasion of North America, Aboriginal peoples were in almost constant motion and in perpetual competition with one another for land, and therefore did not constitute a continuous community. Finally, Flanagan also contests First Nations claims to original sovereignty, statehood, or nationhood. From Flanagan's perspective, Aboriginal peoples cannot be considered nations; rather, they are subordinate communities within the nation of Canada with no legitimate basis for claims to self-government.

Flanagan acknowledges the current plight of Aboriginal peoples and their communities. However, he denies that the solution lies in collective (racially based) claims for political status and Aboriginal property rights. Instead, Flanagan argues for a "realistic" interpretation of the ongoing relationship between Aboriginals and non-Aboriginals, including a full integration of Aboriginal peoples into the modern economy. This implies a willingness to leave the reserves, if necessary, and to relocate to where there are jobs and investment opportunities (Flanagan, 2000: 7).

What can we make of Flanagan's criticisms? Essentially, his call (like that of many before him) is for Aboriginals to integrate into the dominant society, to—as it were—"get with modernity's program." Specifically, Flanagan's arguments point to the wide cultural gap remaining between non-Aboriginal understandings of such things as social relationships, individualism, private property, capitalism, and notions of state and nation, and understandings possessed by many Aboriginals. In contrast to dominant non-Aboriginal assumptions, Aboriginal societies more broadly present a question worth consideration: What is the world we have lost?

We will return to this question. For now, it is clear that the Royal Commission's Report has set Canadian society on a new path in dealing with several Aboriginal issues. These issues include dealing with residential claims, revising or eliminating the Indian Act, defining and implementing self-government, settling existing land claims, and signing modern treaties.

HEALING THE PAST: DEALING WITH RESIDENTIAL CLAIMS

As we have seen, residential schools played an important role in the colonization of Aboriginal peoples (Chapter Ten). The impact of these schools is not of merely historical interest, however. For one thing, the last of them was closed only recently, in the 1980s. For another, many Aboriginal adults alive today are products of these schools, some of them carrying emotional and psychological scars which are often visited upon their offspring.

Not all Aboriginals are products of residential schools. In fact, only about 20 percent of Aboriginal children ever attended residential schools. And not all had horrible experiences. Indeed, compared with life on some reserves, the experience for some may on balance have been preferred. Nonetheless, many Aboriginals and their descendants today claim the effects of sexual or physical abuse or cultural loss as a result of residential school experiences. The evidence for these claims is not seriously challenged. The ramifications, in turn, are enormous.

By April 1, 2000, there were a staggering 6324 cases before the courts, many of them naming church denominations as well as governments in their litigations. The Anglican, Presbyterian, Roman Catholic, and United Churches now face significant costs which could bankrupt them if the Aboriginals are successful (O'Hara, 2000).

The Anglican Church has been hit hardest by the legal costs arising from these residential school claims. Total costs to date for nine dioceses for legal fees alone have exceeded five million dollars. In a particularly well-known instance, the Diocese of Cariboo in southeastern British Columbia recently declared bankruptcy and officially closed at the end of 2001 (*Edmonton Journal*, 2001c).

Ironically, little of the money won through litigation seems to have gone to the plaintiffs. For example, on July 12, 2001, the Supreme Court of British Columbia found the United Church of Canada 25 percent responsible and the federal government 75 percent responsible for damages suffered by six Aboriginal plaintiffs, and awarded them half a million dollars. The group originally had asked for five million dollars, but after lawyers deducted 40 percent for their expenses, and when court costs were calculated, there was little money remaining (*Calgary Herald*, 2001a).

In addition to laying claim to settlement funds for physical and sexual abuse, some Aboriginal peoples are asking for damages pertaining to loss of language and culture. The government seems reluctant to bargain in that area, choosing to define the issues in narrow terms. If interpreted on a wider scale, such losses go well beyond the parameters of residential school cases.

THE INDIAN ACT

A second issue needing redress is the Indian Act. The Indian Act originated in 1876 and has not been substantially changed since. In recent decades, the federal government has suggested either revising or even abandoning the act, most notably in the White Paper of 1969. Most Aboriginals and their organizations quickly rebuffed these suggestions. But recent court rulings in such areas as reserve elections and matrimonial and property rights for Native women have greatly reinforced the idea that the act is outdated and given renewed impetus to calls for its revision. In the fall of 1999, the federal government once more threatened to do away with the act, "at least in its present form" (*Edmonton Journal*, 1999g).

As in the past, Aboriginal responses to the idea of changing the Indian Act have been mixed. While some Aboriginal leaders view the act as protecting their rights, others view it as hindering efforts to get ahead. Others, such as Matthew Coon Come, grand chief of the Assembly of First Nations (AFN), support changing the Indian Act, but dislike the federal government's process for making changes, especially efforts at speaking over the head of the AFN leadership to the Aboriginal grassroots directly. Instead, Coon Come and others want the government to work through the AFN, representing about half of Canada's Aboriginal people. Additionally, they want the talks to concentrate on Aboriginal self-government, treaty rights, and social and economic concerns, and they have threatened to launch campaigns to barricade highways and engage in other disruptions, similar to that at Oka (Chapter Twelve).

It is clear that the federal government is prepared to enact changes in the Indian Act and that it has considerable support in the non-Aboriginal community to do so. Typical of these supporters is Walter Robinson, federal director of the Canadian Taxpayers Federation. Robinson argues that the total federal and provincial bill for Aboriginal health, education, and welfare is $10 billion annually, yet the conditions on Aboriginal reserves remain poor. Moreover, while many Aboriginal bands are run well, the number of bands in financial receivership or under third-party management is mounting (*Calgary Herald*, 2001b). Like many inside and outside the Aboriginal community, Robinson calls for changes to the Indian Act that would ensure greater accountability and transparency for the money spent.

In this context, in May 2001 Robert Nault, federal minister of Indian Affairs and Northern Development, also proposed changes. In a letter to his Aboriginal constituents Nault wrote:

> You and your leaders have told me that you want legislation that offers your council more freedom and responsibility with respect to the day to day operations of your communities. You have to decide what the right mechanisms are to ensure you have access to your government, and that your government is effective and accountable to you. Our collective challenge is to come up with an approach that works for everybody.
>
> **Source**: Indian and Northern Affairs Canada. Reproduced with the permission of the Minister of Public Works and Government Services Canada, 2003.

Nault's letter was accompanied by a questionnaire and packet of materials entitled Communities First: First Nations Governance under the Indian Act (2001). A discussion paper included in the packet highlighted three key issues to be addressed: 1) legal standing and capacity; 2) leadership selection and voting rights; and, 3) accountability to First Nation members.

Regarding the first issue, the discussion paper noted that the Indian Act does not make clear the powers of chief and council. The act further does not set out the legal standing and capacity for Aboriginal bands and band councils in such areas as the capacity to sue, to contract, to borrow, and so on. The result is that it is difficult for band councils to conduct the day-to-day business of their bands.

Regarding the second issue, leadership selection and voting rights, there are currently two systems in place. Some bands follow the procedure outlined in the Indian Act for the election of chiefs and councils. Others continue to follow a hereditary system of appointment. The government has no power under the Indian Act to interfere in the latter procedures. Although the Indian Act now allows off-reserve Aboriginals to vote in band elections, they cannot run for the office of councillor. This does not apply to the office of chief. In fact, one does not have to live on a reserve or even be a band member to run for that office. The federal government believes many First Nations people want these requirements to change.

Regarding the third issue, accountability, the Indian Act says almost nothing about rules ensuring that First Nations communities are run in a fair and equitable manner. Many First Nations bands have in place their own system of accountability, but these vary in structure and function. As it is, many Aboriginal band members have virtually no say in such matters as band management of funds or incurred debt load. Band council recommendations, for example, can be made without giving notice to band members, and the same goes for bylaws, annual reports, accounting, and band budgeting. Often local members have no idea what goes on in band council meetings. The federal government wants to change this.

Legislation to replace the Indian Act continues winding its way through Parliament. The government has set aside a budget of $13 million for the project.

ABORIGINAL SELF-GOVERNMENT AND SELF-DETERMINATION

We have previously examined the issue of self-government and its growing place on the political agenda since 1982 (see Chapter Twelve). It is necessary here to revisit the concept of self-government and the problems and criticisms that it faces.

Essentially, Aboriginal people have been asking for independence and self-determination within Canada, but a workable application of that concept remains unclear. In language reminiscent of the Lesage Liberals in Quebec in the early 1960s (Chapter Three), the Union of British Columbia Indian Chiefs, for example, has defined its position on self-government in this way:

> We must be masters in our own house, in order to survive as Indian people. There is no basis in the laws of Canada to restrict the recovery of Aboriginal rights because we have never given up our rights to control our own lives and means to live (Wall, 2000: 144).

This statement seems clear enough, but putting teeth into the concept is another matter. First, the relationship of Aboriginal people under self-government to the provincial and federal governments remains unclear. Would self-government reduce the status of First Nations' governments to that of glorified municipal governments with very limited powers, as suggested in the Penner Report of 1983? Or would it mean something more akin to political sovereignty, as suggested in the quote above?

Second, if the latter, then how does one square the notion of Aboriginal citizenship, and all the rights and privileges that entails, with that of Canadian citizenship? Flanagan (2000) argues that Aboriginal militants tend to define self-government in racial terms. He warns that a third order of government based on race would represent a special privilege for a very small number of people and further would invite other ethnic minority groups to request similar status (Flanagan, 2000: 194).

Third, the idea of Aboriginal self-government is complicated by the fact that a significant (and increasing) number of Aboriginal people live in urban areas, some on urban reserves (see Baron and Garcea, 1999), integrated territorially into Canadian society as a whole. The concept of self-government is clear enough if determined geographically. It is more problematic when different institutions and rules govern different groups of people within the same space.

Fourth, the concept of Aboriginal self-government inevitably runs up against economic limits. Many of Canada's reserves do not have a strong economic base and cannot support the people who live there. For this reason, large numbers of Aboriginals have moved and are moving to Canadian cities in search of jobs and other opportunities. Many of them have integrated into the dominant society. Many of those remaining on the reserves are supported by government social assistance and welfare (see above). How can a people be termed self-governing if they are dependent upon financial support from "external" governments (Miller, 2000: 347)? Boldt (1993: 261) argues the point well:

> Any proposal that Indian political autonomy and culture should be financed by another government makes a mockery of Indian nationhood. It is a manifestation of the "culture of dependence" in the political sphere. Such an arrangement is a design for continued subordination and paternalism.

Finally, Flanagan (2000) and others (see Adams, 1999; Cairns, 2000; Friesen, 1995a: 128) caution that the idea of Aboriginal self-government, embedded in broader notions of Aboriginal self-determination, contributes to cultural exclusiveness and a host of other problems, such as the entrenchment of a Aboriginal elite. Flanagan (2000: 195) argues that Aboriginal self-government on "traditional lands," with "Aboriginal economies," is the wrong direction to go economically. He suggests further that it will only enable the political and professional elites to do well for themselves at the expense of the majority. This belief is shared by Adams (1999: 54), who argues that cultural exclusivity has been used by a small, privileged minority of Aboriginals, many of them educated in Aboriginal studies departments at universities, to control and pacify their unsuspecting peers, a role previously held by government bureaucrats.

It is argued, moreover, that assertions of cultural, political, and legal separateness may have unanticipated and negative consequences. While such an arrangement might satisfy some, it might also encourage Canadians to absolve themselves of any further responsibility for Aboriginal welfare. Cairns (2000) opines, for example, that the notion "we are not you" (Denis, 1997), if carried too far, may give non-Aboriginals a convenient excuse for withdrawing responsibility, financial or otherwise, for the condition of Aboriginal peoples.

Such fears may be unwarranted. Frideres and Gadacz (2001: 251) suggest that First Nations will never gain the rights of self-determination and status of self-government envisioned by their more radical members. Governments will see to it that any arrangement for Aboriginal self-government will harmonize with existing Canadian laws, including the Charter of Rights and Freedoms. Indeed, it seems likely that self-government, when it is finally defined and implemented, will approach something of the status of municipalities. But this is not certain.

In the meantime, efforts toward self-government continue. Few observers are optimistic about fast results. Henderson (2000: 167) accuses legal bureaucrats of unreflectively asserting colonial privileges and power when dealing with the issue of self-government, but others are a bit more optimistic. Hylton (1999) observes that some progress toward Aboriginal self-government has been made, in terms of both federal attitude and experiences reported by some Aboriginal bands. He notes:

Aboriginal people in Canada are increasingly engaged in the practice of self-government....[A] number of Aboriginal nations have already negotiated far-reaching self-government agreements....[T]he federal government appears more ready than previous administrations to enter into new arrangements with Aboriginal people (Hylton, 1999: 432).

Still others, however, suggest that the debate over self-government actually obscures debate over the more important notion of self-determination. In the words of McDonnell and Depew (1999: 353), "The processes associated with self-government are so powerfully unilateral in their focus that they have all but displaced considerations relating to self-determination." Boldt (1993) similarly argues that, beyond self-government, the survival of Aboriginal cultures requires development by Aboriginal peoples of a clear vision and consensus about their future. Aboriginal peoples must assess the damage that colonialism has inflicted on them in the past (and which continues to this day) and invent ways to stop the processes of assimilation and acculturation. They must further critically evaluate what must be done and mobilize their people in an effort to make that identity a reality. "Such a process of cultural revitalization will necessitate a purge of corrupting colonial institutions, and of traits derived from the culture of dependence and from Euro-Western acculturation" (Boldt, 1993: 219). Self-government alone will not do these things.

LAND CLAIMS AND MODERN TREATIES

We have previously examined the historical development of treaties in Canada (Chapter Twelve), noting differences between the early pre-Confederation treaties and the later "numbered treaties" signed with the Canadian government. Additionally, beginning with the Manitoba Act of 1870, Metis people in that province were allocated land or money in the form of scrip, basically a certificate granting the individual holder future payments. During the subsequent years 1885–1923, a related series of scrip agreements were made with Metis in the remaining Prairie provinces and the Northwest Territories, amounting to over one million hectares of land and $3.6 million (Frideres and Gadacz, 2001: 180). Current claims by Aboriginal peoples, under negotiation with the federal government, frequently involve *promises not fulfilled or interpretations of what was promised by either the treaties or scrip*. For this reason, these are often referred to as **specific claims**.

A second type of claim exists, however, in large areas of Canada, especially in British Columbia and the North, where treaties were never signed. These **comprehensive claims** *involve modern treaties meant to deal with lands that Aboriginal peoples have never legally surrendered*.

The need to deal with both specific and comprehensive claims has intensified in recent decades for two reasons. First, as Canadian economic development has shifted northward, governments and companies have wanted to ensure jurisdiction. Failure to make agreements in the NWT and Yukon, for example, where Aboriginal land claims have been based on the customary principle of Aboriginal rights (see Wittington, 1985), is currently holding up the transfer of Crown lands and the consequent construction of pipelines.

Second, Aboriginal peoples themselves have become more politically aware and adept in pressing their claims (Chapter Twelve). An example of this is a recent pact formed between four Blackfoot nations in southern Alberta and Montana. All are members of the once mighty Blackfoot Confederacy. Before Treaty No. 7 was signed in 1877, the Confederacy's area of control included the southern third of Alberta stretching into

Saskatchewan and Montana. The Blood, Peigan, and Siksika of Alberta and the Blackfeet of Montana recently joined together in an effort to draw the government's attention to their proposals. Included in the concerns are the honouring of Aboriginal rights, the renewal of tribal customs, and the restoration of lands they insist were wrongfully appropriated from the Confederacy (*Edmonton Journal*, 2000f).

In some instances, Aboriginal claims have received sympathetic treatment from Aboriginals. An example is the decades-long claim of the Lubicon band of northern Alberta. The band has laid claim to about 10 000 square kilometres of land where oil production is under way and the Daishowa Pulp Mill has been operating. Although a significant amount of development has been undertaken in the area in the form of new roads and drilling sites, which have had a detrimental effect on wildlife, the Lubicons have not benefited from the arrangement (Goddard, 1991).

In other instances, however, Aboriginal claims have faced strong opposition and raised fears in the non-Aboriginal community. Recent years have sometimes seen violence flare up between Aboriginals and non-Aboriginals over treaty rights. In the summer of 2000, for example, riots over lobster fishing broke out in Burnt Church, New Brunswick.

It is the settlement of comprehensive claims that has caused the most concern, however. The first comprehensive agreements were signed in the late 1970s by the Quebec government with the James Bay Cree of northern Quebec (see Chapter Eleven). The Inuvialuit agreement, dealing with lands in Canada's Far North, followed in 1984, extinguishing Aboriginal title to the western Arctic in return for ownership of 96 000 square kilometres of territory and $55 million (combined) in benefits and money for economic development (Dickason, 2002: 405). After 14 years of negotiation, a similar agreement, the Dene/Metis Western Arctic Land Claim agreement, was cancelled by the federal government, which refused to renegotiate the extinguishing of Aboriginal title (Dickason, 2002: 406; see also Geddes, 2000). This was quickly followed, however, by a series of other, smaller agreements signed with bands in Yukon and the Northwest Territories. Finally, in 1999, the territory of Nunavut was created.

Nunavut (whose name means "our land") began as a proposal submitted in 1976 by the Inuit Tapirisat of Canada organization, reinforced by the results of the NWT 1992 plebiscite and eventually accepted by the federal government. After years of exhausting negotiations, boundary disputes, and meetings with Dene and Metis representatives who had their own agendas, the residents of the NWT held their own plebiscite in 1992 (Momatiuk and Eastcott, 1995). Finally, the dream came true. Nunavut is now the permanent home of the Inuit. About 85 percent of the territory's population is of Inuit heritage. The territory's capital is the town of Iqaluit, formerly known as Frobisher Bay (Bergman, 1996).

As many of these agreements have dealt with sparsely populated northern lands inhabited heavily by Aboriginal peoples, non-Aboriginal Canadians have raised few questions. Not so, however, in the case of treaty claims and land settlements further south, especially in British Columbia.

The total area of British Columbia is 932 000 square kilometres. By October 1999, negotiations were in process for claims amounting to 703 832 sqare kilometres of the province (Frideres and Gadacz, 2001: 223). The Nisga'a people of northern British Columbia, whose claim was settled in 1999, provide a kind of case study of contemporary land claims.

The Nisga'a were never militarily defeated, nor did they ever sign a treaty with the government of Canada ceding lands. They first pressed their claims in 1887 when a group of

Nisga'a chiefs travelled to Victoria. The government ignored them and took no action until 1976. Twenty years later, in March 1996, both parties signed an agreement in principle. The agreement gave the Nisga'a a cash payment of $190 million (later increased to $500 million) and established a Nisga'a Central Government with administrative, municipal-like responsibilities for 2000 square kilometres of land in the Nass River Valley. Additionally, Nisga'a ownership of surface and subsurface resources was safeguarded as well as rights to salmon stocks and wildlife harvests. In 1999, the 5000 members of the Nisga'a First Nation ratified the treaty and, in April the same year, the British Columbia government passed the agreement into law.

Though ratified, the agreement has encountered criticism. Interestingly, not all Aboriginals are pleased with the Nisga'a agreement. They dislike the fact that federal and provincial income tax laws, the Charter of Rights and Freedoms, and the Criminal Code now apply to Nisga'a government (Frideres and Gadacz, 2001: 227). By far the strongest criticisms, however, have come from the non-Aboriginal community (Frideres and Gadacz, 2001: 184). The spring of 2001 saw the Liberal Party of British Columbia elected in part on a promise to open up the Nisga'a agreement to public input and further changes, an act some warn would renew tensions in the province between Aboriginals and non-Aboriginals.

In general, many non-Aboriginal concerns over comprehensive claims are unfounded, if not hysterical. Unscrupulous politicians and rabid talk radio hosts have sometimes fomented these fears. There is no likelihood, for example, that Aboriginals will confiscate the lands on which Vancouver sits and have non-Aboriginals evicted, as is sometimes argued. Nonetheless, there are legitimate concerns about the process and outcomes of these negotiations.

Smith (1995) has made the most cogent arguments against recent land claims. First, he argues that there is no legal basis for the claims. The Supreme Court's decision in the Calder case, used since 1973 by DIAND and subsequent federal governments to justify claims to Aboriginal title, does not provide such a basis. Second, he argues that recent land claims agreements are actually constitutional agreements that are binding upon subsequent generations and do not provide for sufficient flexibility. Third, Smith contends the agreements open the way for endless negotiations, ever-escalating demands, the creation of more bureaucracy, and mounting costs. Fourth, he suggests that the land claims agreements (and concomitant rights and benefits provided to Aboriginal peoples) are race-based and will actually hinder the chances of ordinary Aboriginals from entering fully into Canadian society. Finally, Smith raises broad jurisdictional concerns over the implications of these agreements. Specifically, he raises issues about governance and whether Aboriginals under the agreements will be subject to Canadian law, including the Constitution's Charter of Rights and Freedoms.

Despite concerns, the settlement of land claims is proceeding, albeit slowly. Of the some 450 outstanding Aboriginal land claims, only about five to ten are settled each year. In June 1996, for example, the government announced an agreement-in-principle regarding land claims with 19 First Nations in Manitoba. In March 2001, the government announced that a treaty process had also been established for the Atlantic provinces.

Residential lawsuits, the Indian Act, self-government, land claims, and treaties: these are all manageable, if complicated, issues. More intransigent of resolution is the question of preserving and even enhancing Aboriginal knowledge and culture, the bases of Aboriginal people's identity.

ABORIGINAL VERSUS NON-ABORIGINAL CULTURAL VALUES

We have previously noted (Chapter Ten) the role of the non-Aboriginal educational establishment in silencing expressions of Aboriginal culture. Over time, the process of educational imperialism had a crushing effect on Aboriginal communities. Several generations of Aboriginals lost their world views, languages, and cultures, resulting in psychological and social upheaval for Aboriginal peoples.

A growing crescendo of Aboriginal voices in recent years has emphasized the importance of renewing indigenous knowledge and spirituality (Meili, 1991; Cajete, 1994; McGaa, 1995; Johnston, 1995; Bear Heart, 1998; Weaver, 1998; Battiste, 2000; Battiste and Henderson, 2000). These writers' voices have been accompanied by those of Aboriginal elders in attempting to explain indigenous metaphysical systems. Unlike their forebears of a century or two ago, non-Aboriginals are beginning to show interest in what they have to say (Couture, 1991).

Yazzie (2000) maintains that if the First Nations are to throw off the yoke of epistemological colonialism, they must commence the process within themselves. Political self-determination begins with internal sovereignty, which means taking control of one's personal, family, clan, and community life. Essentially this means a return to tradition and a rejection of modern Euro-Canadian value systems. The latter will not be easy, however. As Findley (2000) notes:

> The task of opposing the dominant orthodoxies of modernity from a position at their ever-extending margins, or from a strategically primitivist place outside, is crucial and dangerous work....Significant numbers of Euro-Canadian scholars have become remarkably good at critiquing the pretensions and practices of modernity and defending marginalized groups, but they do so within institutions among whose faculties Aboriginal people are minimally represented.

Maintaining or even retrieving traditional Aboriginal culture is also made problematic by the fact that many Aboriginal peoples today are significantly "modernized," while others are marginalized between their traditional and European cultures. Those who remain traditional ironically find themselves joined by some elements within the dominant non-Aboriginal community who have themselves rejected modern Western values (materialism, individualism, secularism) and have sought a return to the old ways. These variations being conceded, at the macro-level of cultural analysis, there remain several areas where Aboriginal and non-Aboriginal values, beliefs, and understandings in general are at a distance.

The sacred and the profane. The early sociologist Emile Durkheim (1978) described two worlds, existing more or less side by side. One of these is the profane world. The **profane world** is *the world of the everyday, the expected, the mundane, the explainable*. The other is the **sacred world**, *a world of mystery, uncertainty, and even danger*. It existed before time, and will continue to live after; it is perpetual. Therefore, the sacred cannot and should not be approached with the idea of exploitation or domination; nor should one tamper with the elements or workings of the universe. The sacred is to be treated with awe, even reverence. This contrast between the sacred and the profane describes well a fundamental difference between Aboriginal and non-Aboriginal cultures.

The original European invaders underestimated the extent to which spirituality was valued by Aboriginal peoples in their daily lives (Friesen, 1995; Witt, 1998; Hanohano, 1999). It remains underestimated and misunderstood by non-Aboriginals today. For example, Aboriginal spirituality serves as a foundation for land claims and language revitalization programs. (Soon after government negotiators completed the signing of Treaty No. 7 with the Blood Tribe of southern Alberta, officials suggested that the tribe consider selling off some of their land to provide revenue. This idea was greeted by one chief's unequivocal announcement, "The grass is for sale, but not the earth." Implicit in this pronouncement was the belief that the resources of Mother Earth are for everyone's benefit and cannot be divided up for personal gain or ownership. For non-Aboriginals, however, land is simply a commodity.) Other differences between Aboriginal and non-Aboriginal culture follow from the former's greater acceptance of this spiritual or sacred realm.

Spiritual holism versus scientific specificity. We live in an age of specialization. It is therefore difficult for most non-Aboriginals to comprehend the implications of Aboriginal cultural beliefs in a holistic universe. Far from believing that elements are separate or can be hierarchically arrayed, Aboriginal people believe that all phenomena are connected and interconnected. Aboriginals do not adhere to a "scientific" breakdown of how people function or how the universe operates. Specialization is therefore quite foreign to the traditional First Nations' way of thinking. Aboriginals view the world as an interconnected series of only sometimes distinguishable or understandable elements.

Multiple versus singular realities. At least since the period of the Enlightenment, European thinking has emphasized the notion of a singular, empirically provable reality. By contrast, Aboriginal culture experiences no uneasiness at the thought of multiple realities simultaneously operating in the universe. Moreover, Aboriginal peoples do not differentiate or hierarchically arrange the varieties or qualities of entities; for instance, they do not sharply demarcate between material and non-material elements. For this reason, dreams, visions, and other spiritual experiences are as valid a source of knowledge as scientifically and empirically derived truths.

Cyclical versus linear notions of time. Like agrarian peoples elsewhere, many Europeans at first contact still understood time as cyclical, tied to the growing seasons. By then, however, clock towers were beginning to appear in many European cities. Subtle shifts were occurring in the European sense of time's importance and its nature, toward a linear view of it, and of history. Later, capitalism and the scientific inventions of the Industrial Revolution encouraged further conceptions of time—"wasting time," "time is money"—that were at odds with Aboriginal culture.

To give a practical example, non-Aboriginal observers unfamiliar with Aboriginal culture often joke about "Indian time" as though implying that Aboriginals who follow traditional values are always late. The fact of the matter is Aboriginals' sense of time is derived from their perceptions of the universe's rhythms, which do not adhere to any notion of exactness like hours, minutes, and seconds. Thus, while it is true that Aboriginal people *are* sometimes late—at least by non-Aboriginal standards—and sometimes do not even show up for an appointment when expected, there are times when Aboriginal people are actually *early*, depending on circumstances or purpose and the relative importance of an event. To be clear, Aboriginal peoples do not view time as irrelevant. However, they view time *per se* as neither the *only* nor necessarily the most important criterion for determining how a particular moment ought to be acted out. It is certainly not a top priority in itself. For this reason, "clock-watching" is an activity absent from Aboriginal society.

Competing notions of cause and effect. The Western world perceives the universe in terms of chains of cause and effect (Ross, 1992). Things are what they are, and do what they do, largely because antecedent phenomena did what they did and were what they were. Aboriginal people also possess a notion of cause and effect, seeing themselves as part of a great chain of existence in which all elements of creation are interrelated and interdependent. As with time, however, this chain is not linear, but rather a kind of "daisy chain." If any single element is subjected to pressures or is otherwise tampered with, there are certain to be repercussions in the grand scheme of things. The implications of these different views of cause and effect are profound.

From first contact, the European penchant for explaining and controlling every element of the universe baffled First Nations people. Europeans seemed to believe the main purpose for which humankind existed was to subdue the earth. These ideas reached new heights in the nineteenth century, the Age of Progress, and continue today largely unabated. The underlying Euro-Canadian assumption is that by designing the right tools and approaches, people can improve upon nature and perhaps tailor effects to their own advantage.

By contrast, Aboriginal culture possesses an implicit notion of what sociologists refer to as **unintended or unanticipated consequences** (Merton, 1968). Aboriginal culture includes an inherent warning not to seek to dominate or exploit nature, but to work in harmony with it. As one Siksika (Blackfoot) elder proudly explained, "There is a great deal of land on our reserve that has never seen a plow." This fact is viewed with some degree of pride, implying that the future is more secure when at least a portion of Mother Earth remains untouched, free from human bungling. Given escalating concerns over the environment, First Nations people may be correct in suspecting both the idea of progress and the further assumption that damages caused by technology can always be rectified by still another scientific discovery or adjustment.

The Aboriginal hands-off approach to the universe has two differing consequences. On the one hand, the Aboriginal would-be learner has a more open attitude toward personal growth, experiencing the universe through intuitive or spiritual, and not only scientific, means. By contrast, seldom is even the most unbiased scientist open in such ways to learn about nature's inexplicable mysteries (Suzuki, 1992).

On the other hand, acceptance that the world is "unfolding as it should" in the past has produced a deep, almost withdrawing sense of patience among Aboriginal peoples. This orientation often has worked to the advantage of governments reluctant to fulfil their legal obligations to First Nations, and to the detriment of Aboriginal communities who have dealt with problems by an attitude of "wait and see, and maybe it will disappear." This orientation of passive acceptance is changing, however, especially among better-educated, more militant, and assimilated young Aboriginals.

Family and community versus the individual. Non-Aboriginals often view Aboriginal culture as collective and conformist in contrast to modern non-Aboriginal society's extolling of individualism. (Ironically, early Europeans, accustomed to the restraints of feudal society, viewed Aboriginal societies as providing individuals with a high degree of personal latitude.) The Aboriginal relationship of individual to family and community is not as simple as sometimes imagined.

Family loyalty does have a high priority in traditional Aboriginal thinking. The individual is expected to be submissive to group and community demands. This, in turn, puts limits on one's individuality and may hinder achievements in the non-Aboriginal world. For example, a death or illness in the family may require an individual to be absent from school or work. The practice of mourning varies with each tribe, but it *is* an essential part of the life cycle, while sickness demands a similar kind of allegiance. Non-Aboriginal teachers and employers are rarely sympathetic to these cultural demands.

There is a paradox, however. Beyond these restraints, the community also guarantees the individual emotional security, support, and a particular identity. This identity is assigned, and sometimes amended, and, if need be, taken away from the individual. Generally the process also fosters a subtle kind of non-interference, though this too has limitations. The community, for example, will soon "put in line" individuals who "show off" too much. In extreme cases, individuals who step beyond community limits may find themselves shunned as punishment.

The concept of sharing displays a similar complexity regarding the individual's relationship to the whole. Aboriginal society is commonly stereotyped as a sharing society. In a certain sense, this statement is true. A dictionary definition of *sharing* means simply that those who possess things or have access to resources may use those resources to assist others in need. Implicit in the dictionary definition is the assumption that those who have resources *may* help out the needy if they so choose.

Choice, however, is seldom a relevant factor in Aboriginal culture. Aboriginal definitions of sharing lean quite heavily toward obligation, almost to the point that those who have, *had better share*. This tradition has deep historical roots, predating first contact. When a warrior returned from a successful hunt he was expected to give some of the meat to his immediate family members and relatives. Likewise, an obligation to share was enforced during times of famine through various means of disapproval ranging from humour to outright shunning (Dion, 1979). Downturns in Aboriginal fortunes, following the arrival of Europeans, reinforced the urgency of sharing (Surtees, 1969).

There is an element of a business atmosphere to consider when defining Aboriginal sharing. Many Aboriginal leaders have interpreted treaty benefits on a broader basis than the written conditions indicated. They perceive government grants and rations as a form of regular and perpetual compensation for the elimination of the buffalo and for lands taken. For this reason, some Aboriginal people do not to feel any measure of shame or chagrin for receiving welfare monies or other forms of government "handouts." These are strictly to be viewed as honourable and appropriate compensation for ceded territories and the right of unlimited occupancy (Snow, 1977).

Order, hierarchy, and legitimacy. Early Europeans were constantly frustrated with the uncertainty with which Aboriginals greeted their demands to be "taken to their leader." Aboriginal societies had complex and shifting authority rules. Europeans could not understand the generally egalitarian and democratic rules governing the Aboriginal tribes. Non-Aboriginals experience something of the same confusion today when faced with Aboriginal decision-making processes.

Few followers of *Robert's Rules of Order* could endure a traditional Aboriginal meeting. Aboriginal rules are different from those of non-Aboriginals. For example, an individual may leave a Aboriginal meeting for no apparent reason and return sporadically or not at all. Elders, chiefs, and respected spokespersons prescribe the procedures for a meeting simply by their behaviour, and no one takes issue with this. In the most traditional format, every challenge faced by a tribe must be resolved communally. Government negotiators frequently become quite impatient with such processes, especially when elders decide that a lengthy sweet grass ceremony should precede the deliberations.

EDUCATION, IDENTITY, AND CULTURAL SURVIVAL

The current resurgence of traditional Aboriginal values is the result of demands by indigenous peoples for the right to educate their youth in the ways of Aboriginal knowledge and heritage (Battiste and Henderson, 2000: 87). These demands are encased in broader understandings that Aboriginal self-esteem and survival of the community depend upon cultural renewal (Antone, 2000). At the same time, these demands are not merely to have Aboriginal components added to the content of non-Aboriginal curricula in schools. Rather, there is an understanding that Aboriginal teachings must have a broad cultural foundation (Witt, 1998: 270; also Marker, 2000). As Verna Kirkness (1998a: 12–13), a Cree professor emeritus at the University of British Columbia, argues, the survival of Aboriginal culture must move beyond mere rhetoric to the actual practice of culture in everyday life, beyond the school.

The revival of Aboriginal languages is viewed by many as key to the transmission and survival of Aboriginal knowledge and culture (Kirkness, 1998b). Likewise, many believe the Canadian government must play a great role in ensuring the vitality of Aboriginal languages. Fettes and Norton (2000), for example, argue that the federal government should establish a program for Aboriginal languages within the Department of Canadian Heritage (see also Battiste, 2000: 199).

Things are improving. Young Aboriginals are becoming aware of their past history, assisted by elders who pass on cultural lessons, often in traditional ways—through storytelling, modelling, and on-the-job training—and by Aboriginal teachers who have been trained to work in their own communities. Likewise, there have also been improvements in educational facilities, local control of schooling, counselling services, and support groups, and school curricula have been revised to include more culturally relevant content. From kindergarten to grade 12 and beyond, Aboriginal people are slowly gaining control of their own schools, their own education, and their own lives.

Mainstream Canadian society need not romanticize traditional Aboriginal culture or its values. Neither, however, can these things be ignored. The fact is, there is a large gap between the values and beliefs embedded in First Nations cultures and those of modern society. The latter has little understanding, and even less appreciation, for a lifestyle focused on living in harmony with nature, respecting the earth, believing in the interconnectedness of all living phenomena, and honouring the Creator in one's daily life (Friesen, 1995; Brascoupe, 2000). In the words of well-known architect Douglas Cardinal, Aboriginal culture amounts to a "different way of being human" (Buckley, 1993: 174). The question for non-Aboriginal Canadians at the start of the twenty-first century is whether they are open enough to accommodate, and perhaps even learn from, such a divergent world view.

CONCLUSION: A TWO-WAY LEARNING PATH?

Our world continues changing at an accelerating speed. Ironically, however, many of the biggest changes in Canada today and in the foreseeable future involve Aboriginal peoples—those who were there at the forefront of changes 400 years ago, then forgotten, now once more prominent. Nor is this situation peculiar to Canada. Throughout many parts of the world long ago colonized, Aboriginal peoples have begun reasserting their political rights and cultural identities. This has been particularly the case in former British colonies: Canada, the United States, Australia, and New Zealand (see Fleras and Elliott, 1992). But a resurgence of Aboriginal peoples is also apparent in Latin America; the Mexican Zapatista movement provides only one prominent example.

There remain many, sympathetic or otherwise, who claim Aboriginal traditions and practices have no relevance in a modern, competitive society. They claim that the way forward for Aboriginal peoples is through greater assimilation (see Flanagan, 2000: 196). It is implicit in such recommendations that Aboriginals have "much to learn" from Euro-Canadian society; that the way out of poverty and social dysfunction lies in becoming more like the dominant culture. Such assumptions are not new. They underlay early European encounters with Aboriginals in North America, even as the newcomers often borrowed Aboriginal technologies (snowshoes, canoes) and occasionally—as in the case of the American constitution, which adopted some elements of the constitution of the Iroquois Confederacy—even ideas. A more interesting, and perhaps more fruitful, avenue might be to ask, What might Canada's non-Aboriginal community gain today from knowing more about Native peoples, their values, and their heritage?

One small example comes to mind. Non-Aboriginal society regularly expresses deep concern over its inability to deal effectively with crime. Punishment alone seems often ineffective and costly. But rehabilitation seems equally ineffective. Moreover, both punishment and rehabilitation often leave victims themselves feeling unsatisfied, even re-victimized. They and others believe the perpetrators are not remorseful enough, have not repaid their debt to society or their victims, and remain on the fringes of law-abiding society, likely to commit criminal acts again.

By contrast, crime as we know it was not a problem in traditional Aboriginal societies. To the extent that wrongs were committed, such acts were considered as being against the entire community. In consequence, perpetrators, victims, and community elders would meet to discuss *both* the punishment and how community healing should proceed. Today, in an effort to deal with high Aboriginal rates of imprisonment, Canada's justice system has reintroduced sentencing circles for some offences into some Aboriginal communities. Might a similar idea work in non-Aboriginal communities?

Other areas where Aboriginal cultural beliefs might benefit non-Aboriginal society include striking a greater balance between work and leisure, community and individual rights, and humanity and nature. Above all, Aboriginal culture might provide a useful check to the hubris of modern society.

We began our search for Canadian society with a discussion of notions of country, nation, and state. We noted the problematic nature of these terms, and the uniqueness of Canada in trying to fit them into the Canadian experiment. The case of Aboriginal peoples in Canada provides perhaps the most striking example. Canada remains a country. It constitutes also – we would argue – a unique society. Part of Canada's uniqueness, however, resides in the complex manner in which the state has involved itself in its creation, and the creative manner in which more than one nation has been accommodated to that grand design. One thing is particularly clear: Canada's Aboriginal nations will play a major and important role in shaping Canadian society throughout the remaining years of the twenty-first century.

KEY TERMS

bands
comprehensive claims
profane world
sacred world
specific claims
unintended or unanticipated consequences
urban reserves

chapter fourteen

Conclusion: Canada—A Twenty-First Century Society?

Much will have to change in Canada if the country is to stay the same.
—Abraham Rotstein, 1964

We peer so suspiciously at each other that we cannot see that we Canadians are standing on the mountaintop of human wealth, freedom, and privilege.
—Prime Minister Pierre Trudeau, New Year's message, 1980

The Global Village is nothing more than Canadian culture writ large.
—author John Gray, 1994

INTRODUCTION

As Canada embarks on a new century, it is instructive to look back a hundred years to the end of the nineteenth century. Many of the same issues that bedevilled Canadians then continue to do so today (see Morton, 2000). Notable among these was the relationship of French and English peoples, fears of American domination, and related concerns over economic development. Regional alienation—though it was not so termed—was already becoming prominent, especially in western Canada. And there were, as today, worries over the problems of urbanization, the integration of new immigrants, and crime, especially among youth. At the same time, Aboriginal issues, largely ignored by mainstream society in 1900, have recently gained saliency and will likely dominate the next decades. To a degree, history does repeat itself.

In the course of the last century—through two world wars, a major economic depression, internal constitutional and political upheavals, and assorted social changes—Canadians created one of the most admired countries on earth. For seven straight years, ending in 2001, Canada in fact was ranked first in the United Nations Human Development Report. Yet, at the start of the new millennium, many Canadians also were filled with unease about their future, uncertain how long the great "social experiment" (Bernard, 1996; Saul 1997; Martin, 1999b) might continue. What are the challenges facing Canada and Canadian society today? We explore this question briefly in this final chapter.

ISSUES AND CHALLENGES IN CANADIAN SOCIETY

In Chapter One, we defined *society* in this way:

> A society is defined as the product of relatively continuous and enduring interactions, within a political territory, between people more or less identifying themselves as members of the society, these interactions being maintained by an ensemble of political, economic, cultural, and other institutions, the sum of such interactions being in excess of interactions occurring with similarly defined societies external to the given territory.

We have taken as a given throughout this text the notion that something termed "Canadian society" exists as a sociological construct amenable to study. For several hundred years, the people inhabiting the political territory of Canada have interacted, sometimes in hostility (but also in amity), more often in tolerance (but perhaps also unconsciousness). The creation of a Canadian society has meant the intensification of these interactions and knowledge (or at least imagined knowledge) of a large assortment of others, from Cape Spear to Vancouver Island to the Arctic Circle. No society remains static, however; even less so in the twenty-first century. Several issues are likely to bear particularly strongly on the nature, direction, and interconnectedness of Canadian society in future.

The issue of the state and society. A central argument of this book has been that the state and modern society are inseparable. In the case of Canada, the two expanded and thrived together. As it grew, the Canadian state created a national economy, bringing people, goods, and services together. Likewise, the state facilitated the means of transportation and communication, from the canals, railroads, highways, and skyways, to the telegraph, telephone, radio, television, and computer systems of today. And it oversaw the establishment of a host of important institutions: schools, courts, hospitals, and so on. In short, Canadian society is what it is largely because of the Canadian state, just as, reciprocally, elements within Canadian society (through both conflict and consensus) have created Canada's unique state form.

Today, however, states in general are facing pressures from all sides (see discussion in Chapter One). Local communities, regional interests, and sometimes long-suppressed subnational groups exert pressures from below. From above, pressure is exerted by the likes of free-market entrepreneurs, transnational corporations, and global political organizations such as the World Trade Organization and the United Nations (see Bell, 1993; Robbins, 1999). For Canada, specific pressures are also exerted by the United States through its enormous economic and cultural influence, not to mention obvious geographic proximity (see Clarkson, 2002a).

The state *per se* will not (*à la* Lenin) "wither away." Its functions may change, but it is here to stay (for a discussion, see Courchene, 1997). State and modern society, we say again, are inseparable. The state is merely an instrument of power. The central questions are: Who will control those instruments? What will be the state's role? Or, perhaps, as Graham Spry said in 1932 speaking before a parliamentary committee, "The question is, the State or the United States?" (quoted in Cook, 1995: 174). Will Canada remain an independent country with its own distinct state and society, will it be a backwater colony of the American empire, or will it in fact disappear entirely into the American monolith?

The issue of inclusion. Noted sociologist Daniel Bell (quoted in Swedberg, 1990: 222) has remarked that "people can only identify with society if the society feels a responsibility to them." Economic and political turmoil in the first half of the twentieth century resulted in the creation of the welfare state, at least one function of which was to equalize the life chances of Canadian citizens and (more broadly) enhance social solidarity (Chapter Eight).

Canada has made great strides in reducing social inequalities. Today, ethnicity and race no longer play as large a role as they once did in deciding life chances and social status, the situation of Canada's Aboriginal peoples providing a striking exception (see Chapters Five and Thirteen). But even in that area, there are positive signs brought about through social and labour market changes and enhanced educational opportunities. Likewise, though gender stratification remains, economic and social differences between males and females have declined over the decades.

Yet Canada cannot rest on its laurels. Beginning in the late 1980s, rising government debt (Chapter Eight) and an increased reliance upon markets saw welfare state programs steadily eroded and the real incomes and wealth of many Canadians decline. As elsewhere, the gap has increased markedly between the very rich and very poor (Kerstetter, 2002). For Canada, a key issue in the twenty-first century is how to ensure every citizen has the means to develop to his or her full potential and to participate meaningfully in society.

The issue of difference. "Birds of a feather flock together" but "opposites attract." In a simple way, these duelling aphorisms point to our ambivalence about how we view difference. On the one hand, every society exerts pressures upon its members to conform. On the other hand, most societies today allow (and often actively encourage) a degree of difference, both individually and among societal subgroups. In Canada, the Charter of Rights and Freedoms and the policy of multiculturalism underpin the rights of individuals and minority groups to hold different beliefs and practices. More broadly, diversity is widely viewed as strengthening Canadian society by making it more adaptable to change.

What is the "right" balance between diversity and conformity? On what matters is agreement (conformity) necessary? In what areas is insistence upon conformity problematic, perhaps even threatening to other important societal values, such as respect for human rights or the rule of law? What programs and policies are required to ensure sufficient positive interactions and tolerance among Canadian citizens of different backgrounds? What should be the role of educational, employment, and cultural institutions in fashioning a coherent Canadian quilt from this country's various threads?

The issue of democracy. Defined simply, **democracy** means *rule by the people*. For thousands of years, and most particularly since the great revolutions of the late eighteenth century, the pursuit of democracy has empowered societies everywhere. In recent years, however, citizens in many Western developed countries, including Canada, have signalled growing disenchantment with political institutions and practices through a decline in voting and increased extra-political actions (strikes, protests). It seems many citizens today perceive the existence of a democratic deficit.

To address political alienation within Canada, some people have suggested specific changes to the political system, such as a revamped Senate or the introduction of proportional representation (see Chapter Five). Others, however, suggest that the problem lies deeper, in economic policies that have removed (intentionally) decision-making from political institutions and placed it instead in the hands of large, unelected corporations and global markets. Clearly, this argument underlies many of the recurrent anti-globalization protests since 1997. In any case, the need seems clear to revitalize political institutions and processes in a manner that will legitimately engage Canadian citizens in seeking solutions to the country's problems. Such revitalization might begin with a few questions. What does democracy really mean? Who are "the people"? Is democracy just about voting or rule by the majority? Or is it something more? Is political democracy possible without economic democracy? What is the role of the media and schools in fostering a sense of civic-mindedness and encouraging democratic participation?

The issue of identity. For historic and cultural reasons, forging a national identity has never been easy for Canadians. In the past, critics have often viewed this as a weakness, a potential breaking point for Canada; hence, policies adopted with disastrous consequences over the years to compel French Canadians (Part One) and Aboriginal Canadians (Part Three) to abandon their distinctive identities in favour of a pan-Canadian one. Likewise, others have denounced Canadian identity, especially in English Canada, for being shallow and less than positive; for being, in particular, based on anti-Americanism (Granatstein, 1996).

More recently, however, some have suggested that Canada's lack of a strong national identity—say, in contrast to the United States—makes the country better able to meet the demands of a global, multicultural, postmodern society. Richard Gwyn (1996), for example, refers positively to the "incredible lightness of being Canadian": the relatively unfixed and adaptive quality of Canadian identity. Similarly, John Gray (1994; see quotation above) and John Ralston Saul (*Edmonton Journal*, 2000g) suggest Canadians are the first truly "global" people, able to retain a sense of being Canadian while engaging fully with the rest of the world. But does Canadian society possess enough of a cultural and psychological—even spiritual—centre to keep its disparate social elements from flying apart?

The issue of a sustainable economy. Despite—or perhaps because of—400 years of development, Canada remains largely a resource hinterland to the world economy. This has sometimes brought Canada prosperity, though it has not often been sustained, and it has sometimes been unequally dispersed by class, region, gender, and ethnicity. At the beginning of the twenty-first century, Canada possesses at least two major resources, in particular, that will continue to increase in demand: oil and water. At the same time, however, Canada and the rest of the world face a threat that has been too long ignored: environmental depletion and destruction. Canada has a major role—some would say a responsibility—to protect and nurture its resources for the good of the planet. But Canadians also want jobs and prosperity. They live in a cold and demanding climate; hence, Canadians per capita are among the heaviest energy users in the world. How will Canadians "square the circle" of maintaining a prosperous and sustainable economy while also protecting and even restoring the natural environment?

Canada is one of the world's wonders. Against many odds, Canadians through the centuries have constructed a society that for the most part is prosperous and tolerant, progressive and civil. The torch is thus passed to future generations to continue the great Canadian experiment into the twenty-first century.

KEY TERMS

democracy

Appendix 1

Canadian Federal Election Results Since Confederation

Year	Conservatives	Liberals			Other	Total
1867	101	80				181
1872	103	97				200
1874	73	133				206
1878	137	69				206
1882	139	71				210
1887	123	92				215
1891	123	92				215
1896	89	117			7	213
1900	78	128			8	214
1904	75	139				214
1908	85	133			3	221
1911	133	86			2	221
		Unionists				
1917		82	153			235
			Liberal Conservatives	Progressives		
1921		116	50	65	4	235
1925	116	101		24	4	245
			Liberal Progressives	United Farmers		
1926	91	116	9	13	11	5	245
1930	137	88	3	2	10	5	245
			CCF	Social Credit		
1935	39	171	7	17	11	245
1940	39	178	8	10	10	245
1945	67	125	28	13	12	245
1949	41	190	13	10	8	262

Appendix 1

	Conservatives	Liberals					Total
1953	51	170	23	15		6	265
1957	112	105	25	19		4	265
1958	208	48	8			1	265
			NDP				
1962	116	99	19	30		1	265
1963	95	129	17	24			265
					Créditistes		
1965	97	131	21	5	9	2	265
1968	72	155	22		14	1	264
1972	107	109	31		15	2	264
1974	97	136	17		9	5	264
1979	136	114	26		6		282
1980	103	147	32				282
1984	211	40	30			1	282
1988	169	83	43				295
				Reform	Bloc Québécois		
1993	2	177	9	52	54	1	295
1997	20	155	21	60	44	1	301
				Alliance			
2000	13	173	12	66	37		301

Sources: Lower (1983: 326-27); *Canadian Global Almanac 2000* (1999: 180), "Federal Election Results, 1867-1997" (as taken from Elections Canada), adopted and reprinted with permission from Macmillan Canada, an imprint of John Wiley & Sons Canada, Ltd.; and Elections Canada (2000).

Appendix 2

Canadian Prime Ministers, Governments, and Major Policies Since Confederation

Prime Minister	Party	Dates of Administration	Major Policies/Events
Sir John A. Macdonald	C	July 1867–Nov. 1873	Confederation; Red River Rebellion; Manitoba, British Columbia, and Prince Edward Island join Canada
Alexander Mackenzie	L	Nov. 1873–Oct. 1878	Supreme Court of Canada established; Intercontinental Railway completed; first Indian Act passed
Sir John A. Macdonald	C	Oct. 1878–June 1891	National Policy; the North-West Rebellion; Louis Riel hanged
Sir John J.C. Abbott	C	June 1891–Nov. 1892	
Sir John S. Thompson	C	Dec. 1892–Dec. 1894	
Sir Mackenzie Bowell	C	Dec. 1894–Apr. 1896	
Sir Charles Tupper	C	Apr. 1896–July 1896	
Sir Wilfrid Laurier	L	July 1896–Oct. 1911	Manitoba Schools Act; Klondike Gold Rush; Boer War; Free Trade Election (lost)
Sir. Robert L. Borden	C	Oct. 1911–Oct. 1917	First World War begins; Conscription Crisis; income tax introduced
Sir. Robert L. Borden	U	Oct. 1917–July 1920	Louise McKinney elected to Alberta legislature; war ends; Winnipeg General Strike
Arthur Meighen	U	July 1920–Dec. 1921	
W.L. Mackenzie King	L	Dec. 1921–June 1926	
Arthur Meighen	C	June 1926–Sept. 1926	
W.L. Mackenzie King	L	Sept. 1926–Aug. 1930	Great Depression begins; Cairine Wilson appointed Canada's first woman senator
Richard B. Bennett	C	Aug. 1930–Oct. 1935	Statute of Westminster; Cooperative Commonwealth Federation founded; Regina riot; Social Credit wins Alberta election

Appendix 2

Prime Minister	Party	Dates of Administration	Major Policies/Events
W.L. Mackenzie King	L	Oct. 1935–Nov. 1948	Second World War; beginning of welfare state; second Conscription Crisis
Louis St. Laurent	L	Nov. 1948–June 1957	Korean War
John G. Diefenbaker	PC	June 1957–Apr. 1963	Canadian Bill of Rights; Avro Arrow
Lester B. Pearson	L	Apr. 1963–Apr. 1968	Maple Leaf flag; medicare
Pierre E. Trudeau	L	Apr. 1968–June 1979	bilingualism, multiculturalism, the FLQ Crisis
Charles Joseph Clarke	PC	June 1979–March 1980	
Pierre E. Trudeau	L	March 1980–June 1984	Quebec Referendum; National Energy Program; the Constitution Act, 1982
John N. Turner	L	June 1984–Sept. 1984	
Martin Brian Mulroney	PC	Sept. 1984–June 1993	Free Trade Agreement; Meech Lake Accord, Charlottetown Accord and Referendum; Goods and Services Tax (GST), Oka Crisis
Kim Campbell	PC	June 1993–Oct. 1993	
Jean Chrétien	L	Oct. 1993–today	North American Free Trade Agreement; Quebec Referendum; Clarity Act

Sources: Canadian Encyclopedia (1985: 1473; 1999: 465, 1535) Used by permission from *The Canadian Encyclopedia* c 2002 Historica Foundation of Canada.

Legend: C = Conservative; L = Liberal; U = Unionist; PC = Progressive Conservative.

Bibliography

Abel, Kerry. 1993. *Drum songs: Glimpses of Dene History*. Montreal-Kingston: McGill-Queen's University Press.

Abella, Irving, and Harold Troper. 1982. *None is Too Many: Canada and the Jews in Europe, 1933–1948*. Toronto: Lester and Orpen Dennys.

Abrams, Philip. 1988. "Notes on the difficulty of studying the state." *Journal of Historical Sociology* 1 (1): 58–89.

Adams, Howard. 1989. *Prison of Grass. Canada from a Native Point of View*. 2nd Edition. Saskatoon: Fifth House Publishers.

———. 1999. *Tortured People: The Politics of Colonization*. Revised edition. Penticton, BC: Theytus Books.

Adams, Michael. 1998. *Sex in the Snow*. Toronto: Penguin.

Aitken, Hugh G.J. 1959. "The changing structure of the Canadian economy." In H.G.J. Aitken (ed.), *The American Economic Impact on Canada*. North Carolina: Duke University Press.

Albrow, Martin. 1997. *The Global Age: State and Society Beyond Modernity*. Stanford: Stanford University Press.

Alford, W.E. 1996. *Britain in the World Economy Since 1880*. London: Longman.

Alfred, Gerald R. 1995. *Heeding the Voices of Our Ancestors: Kahnawake Mohawk Politics and the Rise of Native Nationalism*. Toronto: Oxford University Press.

Allison, Derek. 1983. "Fourth world education in Canada and the faltering promise of Native teacher education." *Journal of Canadian Studies* 18(3): 102–119.

American Natural Resource Defense Council. 2002. "National security and oil: 'Dangerous Addiction' report outlines risks of import dependence, offers roadmap to save 5 million barrels per day." *Press Release*. **www.nrdc.org/media/pressReleases/020116.asp**.

Anderson, Benedict. 1983. *Imagined Communities*. London: Verso.

Angus, Murray. 1991. *And the Last Shall Be First: Native Policy in an Era of Cutbacks*. Toronto: NC Press.

Antone, Eileen M. 2000. "Empowering Aboriginal views in Aboriginal education." *Canadian Journal of Native Education* 24(2): 92–101.

Baer, D., E. Grabb, and W. Johnston. 1993. "National character, regional culture, and the values of Canadians and Americans." *Canadian Review of Sociology and Anthropology* 30(1): 13–36.

Baker, Maureen. 1996. "Social assistance and the employability of mothers: Two models from cross-national research." *The Canadian Journal of Sociology* 21(4): 483–504.

Balaam, David N., and Michael Veseth. 1996. *Introduction to International Political Economy*. New Jersey: Prentice-Hall.

Baldwin, Gordon C. 1967. *How Indians Really Lived*. New York: G.P. Putnam's Sons.

Balikci, Asen. 1970. *The Netsilik Eskimo*. Garden City, NY: The American Museum of Natural History.

Balthazar, Louis. 1993. "The faces of Quebec nationalism." In D. Taras, B.

Rasporich, and E. Mandel (eds.), *A Passion for Identity: An Introduction to Canadian Studies*. Scarborough: Nelson Canada.

———. 1997. "Quebec and the ideal of federalism." In M. Fournier, M. Rosenberg, and D. White (eds.), *Quebec Society: Critical Issues*. Scarborough: Prentice Hall Canada. Scarborough: Prentice Hall Canada.

Barber, Benjamin. 1996. *Jihad vs. McWorld*. New York: Ballantine Books.

Barman, Jean, Yvonne Hébert, and Don McCaskill. 1986. "The legacy of the past: An overview." In J. Barman, Y. Hébert, and D. McCaskill (eds.), *Indian Education in Canada, Volume I: The Legacy*. Vancouver: University of British Columbia Press.

Baron, F. Laurie, and Joseph Garcea. 1999. "The genesis of urban reserves and the role of governmental self-interest." In F. L. Barron and J. Garcea (eds.), *Urban Indian Reserves: Forging New Relationships in Saskatchewan*. Saskatoon: Purich.

Bartlett, John. 1980. *Bartlett's Familiar Quotations*. Toronto: Little, Brown and Company.

Battiste, Marie. 2000. *Reclaiming Indigenous Voice and Vision*. Vancouver: UBC Press.

Battiste, Marie and James (Sa'ke'j) Youngblood Henderson. 2000. *Protecting Indigenous Knowledge and Heritage*. Saskatoon, SK: Purich.

Bear Heart. 1998. *The Wind Is My Mother: The Life and Teachings of a Native American Shaman*. New York: Berkley Books.

Beattie, Owen, and John Geiger. 1987. *Frozen in Time. Unlocking the Secrets of the Franklin Expedition*. Saskatoon: Western Producer Prairie Books.

Bell, Daniel. 1961. *The End of Ideology*. New York: Collier.

———. 1993. "The third technological revolution: And its possible socioeconomic consequences." In K. Finsterbusch and J. Schwartz (eds.), *Sources: Notable Selections in Sociology*. Guilford, Connecticut: The Dushkin Publishing Group.

———. 1996. *The Cultural Contradictions of Capitalism*. Twentieth Anniversary Edition. New York: Basic Books.

Bellamy, Donald, and Allan Irving. 1981. "Pioneers." In J. Turner and F. Turner (eds.) *Canadian Social Welfare*. Don Mills: Collier Macmillan Canada.

Bercuson, David, and Barry Cooper. 1991. *Deconfederation: Canada Without Quebec*. Toronto: Key Porter.

Berger, Carl. 1976. *The Sense of Power: Studies in the Ideas of Canadian Imperialism 1867–1914*. Toronto: University of Toronto Press.

Bergman, Brian. 1996. "A new capital for the Arctic." *Maclean's* 109(7): 20–21.

Bernard, Paul. 1996. "Canada as a social experiment." *The Canadian Journal of Sociology* 21(2): 245–258.

Berton, Pierre. 1958. *The Klondike Fever: The Life and Death of the Last Great Gold Rush*. New York: Knopf.

———. 1980. *The Invasion of Canada, 1812–1813*. Toronto: McClelland and Stewart Ltd.

———. 1988. *The Arctic Grail*. Markham: Penguin.

———. 1991. *The Great Depression, 1929–1939*. Toronto: Penguin.

Bissoondath, Neil. 1994. *Selling Illusions: The Cult of Multiculturalism in Canada*. Toronto: Penguin.

Black, Conrad. 1977. *Duplessis*. Toronto: McClelland and Stewart.

Black, Don, and John Myles. 1986. "Dependent industrialization and the Canadian class structure: A comparative analysis of Canada, the United States, and Sweden." *Canadian Review of Sociology and Anthropology* 23(2): 157–181.

Blumer, Herbert. 1969. *Symbolic Interactionism: Perspective and Method*. Englewood Cliffs, NJ: Prentice-Hall.

Boldt, Menno. 1993. *Surviving as Indians. The Challenge of Self-Government*. Toronto: University of Toronto Press.

Bone, Robert M. 1988. "Cultural persistence and country food: The Case of the Norman Wells Project." *The Western Canadian Anthropologist* 5: 61–79.

———. 1992. *The Geography of the Canadian North: Issues and Challenges*. Toronto: Oxford University Press.

———. 2000. *The Regional Geography of Canada*. Don Mills: Oxford University Press.

Bourgault, Pierre. 1991. *Now or Never. Manifesto for an Independent Quebec*. Toronto: Key Porter.

Bowlby, G., and J. Usalcas. 2003. "The labour market: Up north, down south." *Canadian Economic Observer*, January: 3.1–3.10. Ottawa: Statistics Canada. Cat. No. 11-010-XPB.

Bowler, Arthur. 1993. "Introduction." In A.D. Gilbert, G.M. Wallace, and R.M. Bray (eds.) *Reappraisals in Canadian History. Pre-Confederation*. Scarborough: Prentice Hall Canada Inc.

Boyer, Robert, and Daniel Drache (eds). 1996. *States Against Markets*. London: Routledge.

Brascoupé, Simon. 2000. "Aboriginal peoples' vision of the future: Interweaving traditional knowledges and new technologies of the heart." In D. Long and O.P. Dickason (eds.), *Canadian Aboriginal Issues*. Toronto: Harcourt Canada.

Brimelow, Peter. 1986. *The Patriot Game*. Toronto: Key Porter.

Brodie, Janine. 1990. *The Political Economy of Canadian Regionalism*. Toronto: Harcourt Brace Jovanovich Canada.

Brody, Hugh. 1987. *Living Arctic. Hunters of the Canadian North*. Vancouver: Douglas and McIntyre.

Brookes, Sonia. 1991. "The persistence of Native educational policy in Canada." In J. W. Friesen (ed.), *The Cultural Maze: Complex Questions on Native Destiny in Western Canada*. Calgary: Detselig.

Brown, Wallace. 1993. "Victorious in defeat: The American Loyalists in Canada." In A.D. Gilbert, G.M. Wallace, and R.M. Bray (eds.) *Reappraisals in Canadian History. Pre-Confederation*. Scarborough: Prentice Hall Canada.

Brunelle, Dorval. 1999. "Free trade illusions in Quebec." *Le Monde Diplomatique*, April, 15.

Brunet, M. 1993. "The British conquest and the decline of the French-Canadian bourgeoisie." In A.D. Gilbert, G.M. Wallace, and R.M. Bray (eds.) *Reappraisals in Canadian History. Pre-Confederation*. Scarborough: Prentice Hall Canada.

Brym, Robert J. 2001. *New Society*. 3rd edition. Toronto: Harcourt.

Buckley, Helen. 1993. *From Wooden Ploughs to Welfare: Why Indian Policy Failed in the Prairie Provinces*. Montreal and Kingston: McGill-Queen's University Press.

Bueckert, Dennis. 2002. "Canadian sovereignty at risk as Arctic ice shrinks, experts say." *Edmonton Journal* 26. January: A5.

Burbach, Roger, Orlando Nunez, and Boris Kagarlitsky. 1997. *Globalization and Its Discontents*. London: Pluto Press.

Cairns, Alan C. 2000. *Citizens Plus: Aboriginal Peoples and the Canadian State*. Vancouver: UBC Press

Cajete, Gregory. 1994. *Look to the Mountain: An Ecology of Indigenous Education*. Durango, CO: Kivaki Press.

Calgary Herald. 2001a. "Abuse award insulting." 14 July, A9.

———. 2001b. "Chief fails to illustrate Native vision." 21 July, A15.

Canada West Foundation. 2001. *Building the New West*. Calgary: Canada West Foundation.

Canadian Encyclopedia. 1985. *First Edition*. Edmonton: Hurtig.

———. 1999. *Year 2000 Edition*. Toronto: McClelland and Stewart.

Canadian Global Almanac 2000. 1999. *A Book of Facts*. Toronto: Macmillan.

Cardinal, Harold. 1969. *The Unjust Society. The Tragedy of Canada's Indians*. Edmonton: Hurtig.

Careless, J.M.S. 1970. *Canada: A Story of Challenge*. Toronto: Macmillan and Company.

Carlson, Leonard. 1981. *Indians, Bureaucrats and the Land: The Dawes Act and the Decline of Indian Farming*. Westport, CN: Greenwood Press.

Carr, E.H. 1990. *What is History?* Markham: Penguin Books.

Carter, Sarah. 1993. *Lost Harvests. Prairie Indian Reserve Farmers and Government Policy*. Montreal and Kingston: McGill-Queen's University Press.

Chalmers, J.W. 1974. "Marguerite Bourgeoys, Preceptress of New France." In R.S. Patterson, J.W. Chalmers, and J.W. Friesen (eds.), *Profiles of Canadian Educators*. Toronto: D. C. Heath.

Chodos, Robert, and Eric Hamovitch. 1991. *Quebec and the American Dream*. Toronto: Between the Lines.

Chomsky, Noam. 2001. *9–11*. New York: Seven Stories Press.

Chorney, Harold. 1989. *The Deficit and Debt Management: An Alternative to Monetarism*. Ottawa: Canadian Centre for Policy Alternatives.

Citizenship and Immigration Canada. 1998. *Citizenship and Immigration Statistics 1996*. Ottawa: Minister of Public Works and Government Services.

———. 2003. *Citizenship and Immigration Statistics 2003*. Ottawa: Minister of Public Works and Government Services.

Clarkson, Stephen. *Canada and the Reagan Challenge*. Toronto: Lorimer.

———. 2002a. *Uncle Sam and Us: Globalization, Neoconservatism, and the Canadian State*. Toronto: University of Toronto Press.

———. 2002b. "What Uncle Sam wants…." *Globe and Mail* 2 December: A13.

Clarkson, Stephen, and Christina McCall. 1990. *Trudeau and Our Times. Vol. 1: The Magnificent Obsession*. Toronto: McClelland and Stewart.

Clement, Wallace. 1975. *The Canadian Corporate Elite*. Toronto: McLelland and Stewart.

Clerici, Naila. 1999. "The Cree of James Bay and the Construction of Their Identity for the Media." In Michael Behiels (ed.), *Futures and Identities*. Montreal: Association for Canadian Studies.

Cline, Michael S. 1975. *Tannik School: The Impact of Education on the Eskimos of Anaktuvuk Pass*. Anchorage, AL: Alaska Methodist University Press.

Cohen, Andrew. 1990. *A Deal Undone. The Making and Breaking of the Meech Lake Accord*. Vancouver: Douglas and McIntyre.

Cohen, J.M. and M.J. Cohen. 1985. *Dictionary of Quotations*. New York: Penguin.

Cohen, Stewart J. 1997. "What If and So What in Northwest Canada: Could Climate Change Make a Difference to the Future of the Mackenzie Basin?" *Arctic* 50(4): 293–307.

Collins, Randall. 1982. *Sociological Insight. An Introduction to Non-Obvious Sociology*. Oxford: Oxford University Press.

Colombo, John Robert. 1987. *New Canadian Quotations*. Edmonton, AB: Hurtig.

———. 1994. *Colombo's All-Time Great Canadian Quotations*. Toronto: Stoddart.

———. 2000. *Famous Lasting Words. Great Canadian Quotations*. Vancouver: Douglas and McIntyre.

Condon, Richard G. 1987. *Inuit Youth: Growth and Change in the Canadian Arctic*. Newark, NJ: Rutgers University Press.

Conrad, Margaret, Alvin Finkel and Cornelius Jaenen. 1993. *History of Canadian Peoples: Beginnings to 1867*. Toronto: Copp Clark Pitman.

Conway, John. 1994. *The West. The History of a Region in Confederation*. Toronto: James Lorimer and Company Pub.

———. 1997. *Debts to Pay*. Toronto: James Lorimer and Company.

Cook, Ramsay. 1995. *Canada, Quebec and the Uses of Nationalism*. Second Edition. Toronto: McClelland and Stewart.

Cornellier, Manon. 1995. *The Bloc*. Toronto: James Lorimer and Company.

Cornish, George H. 1881. *Encyclopedia of Methodism in Canada*. Toronto: Methodist Book and Pub. Co.

Coulombe, Pierre A. 1998. "Quebec in the federation." In M. Westmacott and H. Mellon (eds.), *Challenges to Canadian Federalism*. Scarborough: Prentice Hall Canada.

Courchene, Thomas."In quest of a new "National Policy." In J.E. Trent, R. Young, and G. Lachapelle (eds.), *Quebec-Canada. What is the Path Ahead*? Ottawa: University of Ottawa Press.

———. 1997. *The Nation State in a Global/Information Era: Policy Challenges*. Kingston: John Deutsch Institute for the Study of Economic Policy, Queen's University.

———. 1998. *From Heartland to North American Region State: The Social, Fiscal, and Federal Evolution of Ontario*. Toronto: University of Toronto Press.

Couture, Claude.1998. *Paddling with the Current. Pierre Elliott Trudeau, Etienne Parent, Liberalism, and Nationalism in Canada*. Edmonton: University of Alberta Press.

Couture, Joseph E. 1991. "The Role of Native Elders: Emergent Issues." In J.W. Friesen (ed.), *The Cultural Maze: Complex Questions on Native Destiny in Western Canada*. Calgary: Detselig Enterprises.

Creighton, Donald. 1970. *Canada's First Century, 1867–1967*. Toronto: Macmillan of Canada.

Cross, Ronald and Héléne Sévigny. 1994. *Lasagna: The Man Behind the Mask*. Vancouver, BC: Talonbooks.

Crowe, Keith J. 1974. *A History of the Original Peoples of Northern Canada*. Montreal, PQ: Queen's University Press.

Cruikshank, Julie. 1998. "Discovery of gold on the Klondike: Perspectives from oral tradition." In J.S.H. Brown and E. Vibert (eds.), *Reading Beyond Words: Contexts for Native History*. Toronto: Broadview Press.

Curtis, James, Edward Grabb, and Neil Guppy. 1999. *Social Inequality in*

Canada: Patterns, Problems, and Policies. Scarborough: Prentic Hall Allyn and Bacon Canada.

Dahrendorf, Ralf. 1958. "Toward a theory of social conflict." *Journal of Conflict Resolution* 2: 170–183.

Dawson, Michael. 1998. *The Mountie from Dime Novel to Disney*. Toronto: Between the Lines.

Deloria, Vine, Jr. 1994. *God is Red: A Native View of Religion*. Golden, CO: Fulcrum.

———. 1995. *Red Earth, White Lies: Native Americans and the Myth of Scientific Fact*. New York: Schribner.

Dene of the N.W.T. 1975. *The Dene: Land and Unity for the Native People of the Mackenzie Valley*. Brampton, ON: Charters.

Denis, Claude. 1989. "The genesis of American capitalism: an historical inquiry into state theory." *Journal of Historical Sociology* 2(4): 328–56.

———. 1993. "Quebec-as-distinct-society as conventional wisdom: The constitutional silence of Anglo-Canadian sociologists." *Canadian Journal of Sociology* 18(3): 251–70.

———. 1997. *We Are Not You. First Nations and Canadian Modernity*. Peterborough: Broadview.

Denton, Frank. 1993. "The labour force." *Historical Statistics of Canada*. Second Edition. Ottawa: Statistics Canada.

Deutsch, Karl W. (ed.). 1980. *Politics and Government: How People Decide Their Fate*. Boston Houghton Mifflin.

Dickason, Olive Patricia. 1984. *The Myth of the Savage and the Beginnings of French Colonialism in the Americas*. Edmonton: The University of Alberta Press.

———. 2002. *Canada's First Nations: A History of Founding Peoples from Earliest Times*. Toronto: McClelland and Stewart.

Dickinson, John, and Brian Young. 1993. *A Short History of Quebec*. Second edition. Toronto: Copp Clark Pitman.

Dilthey, Wilhelm. 1961. *Pattern and Meaning in History*. London: Harper and Row.

Dion, Joseph F. 1979. *My Tribe: The Crees*. Calgary: Glenbow Museum.

Doern, B., and B.W. Tomlin. 1991. *Faith and Fear: The Free Trade Story*. Toronto: Stoddart.

Drache, Daniel. 1995. "Introduction. Celebrating Innis: The man, the legacy." In D. Drache (ed.), *Staples, Markets, and Cultural Change. Selected Essays*. Montreal and Kingston: McGill-Queen's University Press.

Driedger, Leo. 1991. *The Urban Factor. Sociology of Canadian Cities*. Oxford: Oxford University Press.

Dubuc, Alain. 2001. *The Lafontaine-Baldwin Lecture: Canadian Nationalism*. **www.operation-dialogue.com/lafontaine-baldwin/e/2001_article_gm_dubuc.html**.

Dufour, Christian. 1990. *A Canadian Challenge. Le defi quebecois*. Halifax: Oolichan Books and the Institute for Research on Public Policy.

Dumond, Don E. 1977. *The Eskimos and Aleuts*. London: Thames and Hudson.

Duncan, Sarah J. 1971. *The Imperialist*. Originally published in 1904. Toronto: McClelland and Stewart.

Dunn, Christopher. 1995. *Canadian Political Debates*. Toronto: McClelland and Stewart.

Dunning, John. 1983. "Changes in the level and structure of international production: the last one hundred years." In M. Casson (ed.), *The Growth of International Business*. London: George Allen and Unwin.

Dupereau, Jean R. 1981. "L'affaire Richard: A situational analysis of the

Montreal Hockey Riot of 1955." *Canadian Journal of Sports History* 12(1): 66–83.

Durkheim, Emile. 1964. *The Division of Labor in Society.* Originally published in 1893. New York: The Free Press.

———. 1978. *Elementary Forms of Religious Life.* Originally published in 1915. London: George Allen and Unwin.

Dyck, Rand. 1998. *Canadian Politics.* Concise Edition. Toronto: Nelson.

Easterbrook, W.T., and Hugh G.J. Aitken. 1988. *Canadian Economic History.* Toronto: University of Toronto Press.

Eccles, W.J. 1993a. "The French forces in North America during the Seven Years War." In A.D. Gilbert, G.M. Wallace, and R.M. Bray (eds.) *Reappraisals in Canadian History. Pre-Confederation.* Scarborough: Prentice Hall Canada Inc.

———. 1993b. "The society of New France, 1680's–1760." In A.D. Gilbert, G.M. Wallace, and R.M. Bray (eds.) *Reappraisals in Canadian History. Pre-Confederation.* Scarborough: Prentice Hall Canada.

Economic Council of Canada. 1991. *Economic and Social Impacts of Immigration.* Ottawa: Minister of Supply and Services.

Edmonton Journal. 1999a. "Bloc's new Quebecer lives most fully in French." 12 September: A7.

———. 1999b. "Private French TV network goes national." 2 May: A3.

———. 1999c. "Ottawa wants more French online." 1 September: A11.

———. 1999d. "Quebec will strive for more francophone immigrants." 26 September: A3.

———. 1999e. "Sovereignty support lowest since '95." 19 September: A7.

———. 1999f. "Exports jumped under free trade says bank study." 2 June: A3.

———. 1999g. "Ottawa considers dismantling Indian Act." 25 September: A3.

———. 2000a. House passes Clarity Act." 16 March: A6.

———. 2000b. "Quebecers federal gov't's top fans, poll shows." 15 January: A6.

———. 2000c. "Fur trading still a part of Canada in U.S. eyes." 20 May: A6.

———. 2000d. "Canadian incomes fade in dust of U.S.—study." 29 July: A6.

———. 2000e. "Canada still best place to live—for the wealthy." 30 June: A1.

———. 2000f. "New confederacy aims to restore Blackfoot Nation." 13 August: A8.

———. 2000g. "Our culture safe from U.S. Saul claims." 19 May: A3.

———. 2001a. "Whose oil is it, anyway?" 27 September: G1.

———. 2001b. "U.S. firm snaps up Canadian Hunter for $3.3B." 10 October: G1.

———. 2001c. "The death of a diocese." 16 December: D4.

———. 2002. "Younger Quebecers shrug at sovereignty." 6 November: A6.

Elections Canada. 2000. *Report of the Chief Electoral Officer on the 37th General Election.* Ottawa: Chief Electoral Officer of Canada.

Esping-Andersen, Gosta. 1990. *The Three Worlds of Welfare Capitalism.* Princeton: Princeton University Press.

Fairchild, Henry Pratt (ed.). 1967. *Dictionary of Sociology and Related Sciences.* Totowa, NJ: Littlefield, Adams and Co.

Fanon, Frantz. 1968. *The Wretched of the Earth*. New York: Grove Press.

Fettes, Mark and Ruth Norton. 2000. "Voices of winter: Aboriginal languages and public policy in Canada." In M.B. Castellano, L. Davis and L. Lahache (eds.), *Aboriginal Education: Fulfilling the Promise*. Vancouver: UBC Press.

Finance Canada. 2003. *Federal Transfers to Provinces and Territories*. Reproduced with the permission of the Minister of Public Works and Government Services Canada, 2003. www.fin.gc.ca/FED PROV/mtpe.html#major

Findley, L.M. 2000. "Foreword." In M. Battiste (ed.), *Reclaiming Indigenous Voice and Vision*. Vancouver: UBC Press.

Finkel, Alvin. 1989. *The Social Credit Phenomenon in Alberta*. Toronto: University of Toronto Press.

—————. 1997. *Our Lives. Canada After 1945*. Toronto: Lorimer.

Finnie, Richard. 1940. *Lure of the North*. Philadelphia: David McKay Company.

—————. 1948. *Canada Moves North*. Toronto: The Macmillan Company of Canada.

Fisher, A.D. 1981. "A colonial education system; historical changes and schooling in Fort Chipewyan." *Canadian Journal of Anthropology* 2(1): 37–44.

Flanagan, Thomas. 1977. "Louis Riel: Insanity and Prophecy." In H. Palmer (ed.), *The Settlement of the West*. Calgary: Comprint.

—————. 2000. *First Nations? Second Thoughts*. Montreal and Kingston: McGill-Queen's University Press.

Fleras, Augie, and Jean Leonard Elliott. 1992. *The Nations Within. Aboriginal-State Relations in Canada, the United States, and New Zealand*. Toronto: Oxford University Press.

—————. 2002. *Unequal Relations. An Introduction to Race and Ethnic Dynamics in Canada*. 4th Edition. Don Mills: Prentice Hall.

Forbes Magazine. 2003. *Forbes World's Richest People 2003*. Forbes.com

Fossum, Jon-Erik. 1997. *Oil, the State, and Federalism. The Rise and Demise of Petro-Canada as a Statist Impulse*. Toronto: University of Toronto Press.

Fournier, Marcel, Michael Rosenberg, and Deena White (eds.). 1997. *Quebec Society: Critical Issues*. Scarborough: Prentice Hall Canada.

Fox, John, Robert Andersen, and Joseph Dubonnet. 1999. "The polls and the 1995. Quebec referendum." *The Canadian Journal of Sociology* 24(3): 411–424.

Fox, Terry and David Long. 2000. "Struggles within the circle: Violence, healing and health on a First Nations reserve." In D. Long and O.P. Dickason (eds.), *Visions of the Heart: Canadian Aboriginal Issues*. Second edition. Toronto: Harcourt Canada.

Francis, Daniel. 1997. *National Dreams. Myth, Memory, and Canadian History*. Vancouver: Arsenal Pulp Press.

Francis, R. Douglas, Richard Jones and Donald B. Smith. 1988. *Origins: Canadian History to Confederation*. Toronto: Holt, Rinehart and Winston of Canada.

Frank, Andre Gunder. 1975. *On Capitalist Underdevelopment*. Bombay: Oxford University Press.

Frank, Steven. 2001. "What next for separatism?" *Time* 22. January: 17–22.

Fraser, Blair. 1967. *The Search for Identity. Canada: Postwar to Present*. Toronto: Doubleday Canada Ltd.

Freuchen, Dagmar (ed.) 1961. *Peter Freuchen's Book of the Eskimos*. Cleveland, OH: The World Publishing Company.

Frideres, James S., and Rene R. Gadacz. 2001. *Aboriginal Peoples in Canada: Contemporary Conflicts*. Sixth edition. Scarborough, ON: Prentice-Hall Canada.

Fried, Jacob. 1969. "Boom towns... Must they bust?" In M. van Steensel (ed.), *People of the Light and Dark*. Ottawa: Department of Indian Affairs and Northern Development.

Friesen, Jean. 1986. *Magnificent Gifts: The Treaties of Canada with the Indians of the Northwest, 1869–70*. Ottawa: Transactions of the Royal Society of Canada. Series 5, Vol. 1: 41-51.

Friesen, John W. 1983. *Schools with a Purpose*. Calgary: Detselig.

———. 1991. "Introduction: Highlights of Western Canadian Native History." In J.W. Friesen (ed.), *The Cultural Maze: Complex Questions on Native Destiny in Western Canada*. Calgary: Detselig.

———. 1993. *When Cultures Clash: Case Studies in Multiculturalism*. Second edition. Calgary: Detselig.

———. 1995. *You Can't Get There From Here: The Mystique of Plains Indians' Culture & Philosophy*. Dubuque, IA: Kendall/Hunt.

———. 1996. *The Riel/Real Story: An Interpretive History of the Métis People of Canada*. Second edition. Ottawa: Borealis Press.

———. 1997. *Rediscovering the First Nations of Canada*. Calgary: Detselig.

———. 1998. *Sayings of the Elders*. Calgary: Detselig.

———. 1999. *First Nations of the Plains: Creative, Adaptable, and Enduring*. Calgary: Detselig.

Frisby, David, and Derek Sayer. 1986. *Society*. London: Ellis Horwood/Tavistock.

Fukuyama, Francis. 1992. *The End of History and the Last Man*. New York: Free Press.

Furniss, Elizabeth. 1995. *Victims of Benevolence: The Dark Legacy of the Williams Lake Residential School*. Vancouver, BC: Arsenal Pulp Press.

Gagnon, Lysiane. 2000. "The October Crisis: Singular anomaly." *The Beaver* 80(5): 6–7.

Gairdner, William. 1990. *The Trouble with Canada*. Toronto: Stoddart.

Galbraith, John Kenneth. 1969. *The New Industrial State*. Boston: Houghton Mifflin.

Gardner, Dan. 2002. "The first casualty of Hollywood... is truth." *Edmonton Journal*, 9 February: A16.

Geddes, John. 2000. "Northern son." *Maclean's* 114 (17): 16–21.

Gibbins, Roger. 1979. *Prairie Politics and Society: Regionalism in Decline*. Toronto: Butterworths.

Gibbins, Roger, and Sonia Arrison. 1995. *Western Visions. Perspectives on the West in Canada*. Peterborough: Broadview Press.

Gibson, Gordon. 1994. *Plan B. The Future of the Rest of Canada*. Vancouver: The Fraser Institute.

Giddens, Anthony. 1984. *The Constitution of Society: Outline of the Theory of Structuration*. Cambridge: Polity Press.

Giffen, Naomi Musmaker. 1930. *The Roles of Men and Women in Eskimo Culture*. Chicago: University of Chicago Press.

Gitlin, Todd. 2001. "The ordinariness of American feelings." *Open Democracy* 10 October. **www.opendemocracy. net/forum/document_ details.asp?CatID=98& DocID=723.**

Globe and Mail. 2002. "Allophones hike use of French in Quebec, census figures show." 11 December: A7.

Goddard, John. 1991. *Last Stand of the Lubicon*. Vancouver: Douglas and McIntyre.

Gonzalez, Roberto J. 2001. "Lynne Cheney-Joe Lieberman group puts out a Blacklist." *San Jose*

Mercury News, 13 December.

Gordon, Charles. 2002. "What's playing at the cinema?" *Edmonton Journal*, 10 February: A14.

Gordon, Walter. 1966. *A Choice for Canada: Independence or Colonial Status?* Toronto: McClelland and Stewart.

Government of Alberta. 2002. *A Framework for Reform*. (The Mazankowski Report.) Appendices. Edmonton: Government of Alberta.

Government of Canada. 1963. *A Preliminary Report of the Royal Commission on Bilingualism and Biculturalism*. Ottawa: Queen's Printer.

———. 1969. *The White Paper*. Statement of the Government of Canada on Indian Policy. Published under the Authority of the Honourable Jean Chrétien, Minister of Indian Affairs and Northern Development. Ottawa: Indian Affairs Branch.

———. 1979 A Future Together: Observations and Recommendations of the Task Force on Canadian Unity. Ottawa: Minister of Supply and Services.

———. 1982. *The Canadian Constitution*. Ottawa: Public Works.

———. 2003. *Federal Transfers to Provinces and Territories*. **www.fin.gc.ca/FEDPROV/mtpe.html#Major**.

Government of the United States. 2002. *The National Security Strategy of the United States of America*. Washington, D.C.: Government of the United States.

Goyder, John. 1993. "The Canadian syndrome of regional polarities: an obituary." *Canadian Review of Sociology and Anthropology* 30(1): 1–12.

Grabb, Edward, Douglas Baer, and James Curtis. "The origins of American individualism: Reconsidering the historical evidence." *The Canadian Journal of Sociology* 24(4): 511–534.

———. 2000. "Defining moments and recurring myths: Comparing Canadians and Americans after the American Revolution." *Canadian Review of Sociology and Anthropology* 37(4): 373–420.

Granatstein, Jack. 1996. *Yankee Go Home? Canadians and Anti-Americanism*. Toronto: HarperCollins Pub. Ltd.

Grant, Agnes. 1996. *No End of Grief: Indian Residential Schools in Canada*. Winnipeg: Pemmican Publications.

Grant, George. 1965. *Lament for a Nation*. Toronto: McClelland and Stewart.

Gray, John. 1994. *Lost in North America. The Imaginary Canadian in the American Dream*. Vancouver: Talonbooks.

GRES. 1997. "Immigration and ethnic relations in Quebec: Pluralism in the making." In M. Fournier, M. Rosenberg, and D. White (eds.), *Quebec Society: Critical Issues*. Scarborough: Prentice Hall Canada. Scarborough: Prentice Hall Canada.

Gresko, Jacqueline. 1986. "Creating Little Dominions Within the Dominion: Early Catholic Indian Schools in Saskatchewan and British Columbia." In J. Barman, Y. Hébert, and D. McCaskill (eds.), *Indian Education in Canada, Volume 1: The Legacy*. Vancouver: University of British Columbia Press.

Grunwald, Michael. 2002. "Security fears have U.S. and Canada rethinking life on the border." *Guardian Weekly*, 10–16. January: 29.

Gwyn, Richard. 1996. *Nationalism Without Walls. The Unbearable Lightness of Being Canadian*. Toronto: McClelland and Stewart.

Haig-Brown, Celia. 1993. *Resistance and Renewal:*

Surviving the Indian Residential School. Vancouver: Tillacum Library.

Hall, D.J. 1977. "Clifford Sifton: Immigration and settlement policy, 1896–1905." In H. Palmer (ed.), *The Settlement of the West*. Calgary: Comprint Publishing Company.

Halliday, W.M. 1935. *Potlatch and Totem and the Recollections of an Indian Agent*. London: J.M. Dent & Sons.

Hamelin, J. 1993. "What middle class?" In A. D. Gilbert, G. M. Wallace, and R. M. Bray (eds.) *Reappraisals in Canadian History. Pre-Confederation*. Scarborough: Prentice Hall Canada.

Hamilton, Robert M. and Dorothy Shields (compilers). 1979. *The Dictionary of Canadian Quotations and Phrases*. Toronto: McClelland and Stewart.

Hanks, Lucien M., Jr., and Jane Richardson Hanks. 1950. *A Study of the Blackfoot Reserve of Alberta*. Toronto: University of Toronto Press.

Hanohano, Peter. 1999. "The spiritual imperative of Native epistemology: Restoring harmony and balance to education." *Canadian Journal of Native Education* 23(2): 206–219.

Harman, Lesley D. 2001. "Gender relations." In J.J. Teevan and W. E. Hewitt (eds.), *Introduction to Sociology: A Canadian Focus*. 7th edition. Toronto: Prentice Hall.

Harrison, Brian, and Louis Marmen. 1994. *Languages in Canada*. Ottawa: Statistics Canada. Catalogue no. 96–313E.

Harrison, Trevor. 1995. *Of Passionate Intensity: Right-Wing Populism and the Reform Party of Canada*. Toronto: University of Toronto Press.

———. 1996. "Class, citizenship, and global migration: The case of the Canadian Business Immigration Program." *Canadian Public Policy* 22(1): 7–23).

———. 1999. "Globalization and the trade in human body parts." *Canadian Review of Sociology and Anthropology* 36(1): 21–36.

———. 2000. "The changing face of prairie politics: Populism in Alberta." *Prairie Forum* 25(1): 107–122.

———. 2002. *Requiem for a Lightweight: Stockwell Day and Image Politics*. Montreal: Black Rose.

Hawthorn, Harry B. 1966/67. *A Survey of the Contemporary Indians of Canada, Part II and Part I*. Ottawa: Indian Affairs.

Heilbroner, Eric. 1992. *Twenty-First Century Capitalism*. Concord, Ontario: Anansi.

Hemberger, Suzette. 1993. "Constitution." In J. Krieger (ed.), *The Oxford Companion to Politics of the World*. Oxford: Oxford University Press.

Henderson, James (Sákéj) Youngblood. 2000. "Postcolonial ledger drawing: Legal reform." In M. Battiste (ed.), *Reclaiming Indigenous Voice and Vision*. Vancouver: UBC Press.

Henderson, Robert (ed.). N.d. *A Soldier's Account of the Campaign on Quebec, 1759*. Taken from "A Journal of the Expedition up the River St. Lawrence," originally published in 1759. Manotick, Ontario: The Discriminating General. services@militaryheritage.com

Heron, Craig, and Robert Storey. 1986. "On the job in Canada." In C. Heron and R. Storey (eds.), *On the Job*. Montreal/Kingston: McGill-Queen's University Press.

Hiller, Harry. 1987. "The foundation and politics of separation: Canada in comparative perspective." *Research in Political Sociology* 3: 39–60.

Historical Statistics of Canada. 1983. Ottawa: Statistics Canada.

Hobsbawm, Eric. 1992. *Nations and Nationalism*

Since 1780. Second edition. Cambridge: Cambridge University Press.

———. 1995. *Age of Extremes. The Short Twentieth Century 1914–1991*. London: Abacus.

Hofstadter, Richard (ed.). 1958. *Great Issues in American History, Vol. I: 1765–1865*. New York: Vintage Books.

Hofstadter, Richard, William Miller, and Daniel Aaron. 1957. *The United States. The History of a Republic*. Englewood Cliffs, NJ: Prentice-Hall.

Honan, William. 1998. "Historians warming to games of 'What if?'" *New York Times*, 7 January.

Hopkins, John Castell (ed.). 1898. *Canada: An Encyclopaedia of the Country*. Toronto: Linscott.

Horowitz, Gad. 1966. "Conservatism, liberalism, and socialism in Canada: An interpretation." *Canadian Journal of Economic and Political Science* 32: 143–171.

Horsman, Reginald. 1993. "On to Canada: Manifest Destiny and United States strategy in the War of 1812." In A.D. Gilbert, G.M. Wallace, and R.M. Bray (eds.), *Reappraisals in Canadian History. Pre-Confederation*. Scarborough: Prentice Hall Canada.

House, John D. 1978. *The Last of the Free Enterprisers*. Toronto: MacMillan of Canada.

Howard, V. 1999. "Unemployment relief camps." *The Canadian Encyclopedia. Year 2000 Edition*. Toronto: McClelland and Stewart.

Hum, Derek. 1983. *Federalism and the Poor: A Review of the Canada Assistance Plan*. Toronto: Ontario Economic Council.

Huntington, Samuel P. 1996. *The Clash of Civilizations and the Remaking of World Order*. New York: Touchstone.

Hurtig, Mel. 1992. *The Betrayal of Canada*. Second edition. Toronto: Stoddart.

Hylton, John H. 1999. "Future prospects for Aboriginal self-government in Canada." In J.H. Hylton (ed.), *Aboriginal Self-Government in Canada*. Saskatoon: Purich.

Ibbitson, John. 2001. *Loyal No More: Ontario's Struggle for a Separate Destiny*. Toronto: HarperCollins.

Ignatieff, Michael. 1993. *Blood and Belonging. Journeys into the New Nationalism*. Toronto: Penguin.

———. 2003. "The burden." *The New York Times Online*, 5 January.

Indian and Northern Affairs Canada. 1996. *Highlights from the Report of the Royal Commission on Aboriginal Peoples: A Word from Commissioners*. www.ainc-inac.gc.ca/ch/rcap/rpt/wrd_e.html.

———. 2002. "Registered Indian population by region and type of residence December 31, 2001." *Registered Indian Population by Sex and Residence, 2001*. Ottawa: Department of Indian and Northern Affairs. www.ainc-inac.gc.ca/pr/sts/rip/rip_e.pdf.

Indian Chiefs of Alberta. 1970. *Citizens Plus: A Presentation by the Indian Chiefs of Alberta to the Right Honourable P.E. Trudeau, Prime Minister and the Government of Canada*. A.k.a., "The Red Paper." Edmonton: Indian Association of Alberta.

Industry Canada. 2003. *Economic Indicators— Annual Bankruptcies in Canada 1966–2001*. Ottawa: Office of the Superintendent of Bankruptcy, Industry Canada. http://osb-bsf.ic.gc.ca.

Innis, Harold. 1956. "Great Britain, the United States, and Canada." In M.Q. Innis (ed.), *Essays in Canadian Economic History*. Toronto: University of Toronto Press.

———. 1962. *The Fur Trade in Canada*. Toronto: University of Toronto Press.

———. 1995. "Recent trends in Canadian-American relations." In D. Drache (ed.), *Staples, Markets, and Cultural Change. Selected Essays*. Montreal and Kingston: McGill-Queen's University Press.

Ip, Greg. 1996. "The borderless world." *Globe and Mail,* 6 July, D1 and D5.

Irwin, R. Stephen. 1994. *The Indian Hunters*. Second printing. Blaine, WA: Hancock House.

Ives, John W. 1990. *A Theory of Northern Athapaskan Prehistory*. Boulder, CO: Westview Press.

Jackson, Andrew. 1999. "From leaps of faith to lapses of logic." *Policy Options*, June: 12–18.

Jaenen, Cornelius. 1986. "Education for francization: The case of New France in the seventeenth century." In J. Barman, Y. Hébert, and D. McCaskill (eds.), *Indian Education in Canada, Vol. I: The Legacy*. Vancouver: University of British Columbia Press.

James, Lawrence. 1997. *The Rise and Fall of the British Empire*. London: Abacus.

Jaszi, Oszkar. 1961. *The Dissolution of the Habsburg Monarchy*. Originally published in 1929. Chicago: University of Chicago Press.

Jennings, Jesse D. 1978. *Ancient Native Americans*. San Francisco: W. H. Freeman and Company.

Jensen, Derrick. 2001. "Neighborhood Bully. Ramsay Clark on American Militarism." *The Sun Magazine*, August. **www.thesun magazine.org/bully.html**.

Jensen, Philip. 2000. "A passage from India." *The Beaver* 80(3): 26–30.

Jessop, Bob. 1993. "Towards a Schumpeterian workface state? Preliminary remarks on post-Fordist political economy." *Studies in Political Economy* 40: 7–39.

Johnson, Andrew, and Andrew Stritch. 1997. *Canadian Public Opinion. Globalization and Political Parties*. Toronto: Copp Clark.

Johnson, Chalmers. 2001. "Blowback." *The Nation*, 15 October.

Johnson, William. 1999. "Ottawa must wake Quebecers from secessionist dream." *Edmonton Journal*, 17 September, A17.

Johnston, Basil. 1995. *The Manitous: The Spiritual World of the Ojibway*. Vancouver: Key Porter Books

Johnston, Charles M. (ed.). 1964. *The Valley of the Six Nations: A Collection of Documents on the Indian Lands of the Grand River*. Toronto: University of Toronto Press.

Johnston, Darlene. 1989. *The Taking of Indian Lands in Canada: Consent or Coercion?* Saskatoon: University of Saskatchewan Native Law Centre.

Josephy Alvin M., Jr. 1968. *The Indian Heritage of America*. New York: Alfred A. Knopf.

Kelly, W.E. 1997. "Canada's Black defenders." *The Beaver*, 77(2): 31–34.

Kendall, Diana, Jane L. Murray, and Rick Linden. 1997. *Sociology in Our Times*. Toronto: Nelson.

Keohane, Robert O. 2001. "The globalization of informal violence: Theories of world politics, and the 'liberalism of fear'." *Social Science Research Council*. **www.ssrc.org/sept11/ essay/keohane.html**.

Kerr, Clark, J.T. Dunlopo, F H. Harbison, and C.A. Meyers. 1964. *Industrialism and Industrial Man*. Second edition. New York: Oxford University Press.

Kerstetter, Steven. 2002. *Rags and Riches: Wealth Inequality in Canada*. Ottawa: Canadian Centre for Policy Alternatives.

Kesselman, Jonathan. 2001. "Policies to stem the brain drain—without Americanizing Canada." *Canadian Public Policy* 27(1): 77–93.

King, A. Richard. 1967. *The School at Mopass: A Problem of Identity*. New York: Holt, Rinehart and Winston.

Kirkness, Verna J. 1998a "The critical state of Aboriginal languages in Canada." *Canadian Journal of Native Education* 22(1): 93–107.

———. 1998b "Our peoples' education: Cut the shackles; cut the crap; cut the mustard." *Canadian Journal of Native Education* 22(1): 10–15.

Knuttila, Murray. 2002. *Introducing Sociology: A Critical Perspective*. Toronto: Oxford University Press.

Knuttila, Murray, and Wendee Kubik. 2000. *State Theories. Classical, Global and Feminist Perspectives*. Halifax: Fernwood.

Korten, David. 1995. *When Corporations Rule the World*. San Francisco: Berrett-Koehler.

Krahn, Harvey, and Graham Lowe. 2002. *Work, Industry, and Canadian Society*. 4th Edition. Toronto: Nelson.

Krotz, Larry. 1990. *Indian Country: Inside Another Canada*. Toronto: McClelland and Stewart.

Kurth, James. 1993. "Military-industrial complex." In J. Krieger (ed.), *The Oxford Companion to Politics of the World*. Oxford: Oxford University Press.

La Haye, Laura. 1993. "Mercantilism." In D.R. Henderson (ed.), *The Fortune Encyclopedia of Economics*. New York: Warner Books.

Lairson, T.D., and D. Skidmore. 1997. *International Political Economy: The Struggle for Power and Wealth*. Toronto: Harcourt Brace.

Lane, Jan-Erik, and Svante O. Ersson. 1994. *Politics and Society in Western Europe*. London: Sage.

Langer, W.L. 1948. *An Encyclopedia of World History*. Boston: Houghton Mifflin Company.

Laurendeau, Andre. 1985. "The conditions for the existence of a national culture." In H. D. Forbes (ed), *Canadian Political Thought*. Toronto: Oxford University Press.

Laviolette, Gontran. 1991. *The Dakota Sioux in Canada*. Winnipeg: DLM Publications.

Laxer, Gordon. 1989. *Open for Business. The Roots of Foreign Ownership in Canada*. Toronto: Oxford University Press.

———. 1991. *Perspectives on Canadian Economic Development*. G. Laxer (ed.). Toronto: Oxford University Press.

———. 1992. "Distinct status for Quebec: A benefit to English Canada." *Constitutional Forum* 3(3): 57–61.

———. 1995. "Social solidarity, democracy and global capitalism." *Canadian Review of Sociology and Anthropology* 32(3): 287–314.

———. 2000. "Surviving the Americanizing right." *Canadian Review of Sociology and Anthropology* 37(1): 55–76.

———. 2001. "Alternatives to secession." In C. Couture (ed.), *In Search of a Community: Globalization and the Canadian National Identity*.

Laxer, Gordon, and Trevor Harrrison. 1995. *The Trojan Horse: Alberta and the Future of Canada*. Montreal: Black Rose.

Lekachman, Robert. 1966. *The Age of Keynes*. New York: Random House.

Levitt, Kari. 1970. *Silent Surrender. The Multinational Corporation in Canada*. Toronto: Macmillan of Canada.

Li, Peter. 1996. *The Making of Post-War Canada*.

Toronto: Oxford University Press.

Lian, Jason Z., and David Ralph Matthews. 1998. "Does the vertical mosaic still exist? Ethnicity and income in Canada, 1991." *The Canadian Review of Sociology and Anthropology* 35(4): 461–482.

Lincoln, Kenneth. 1985. *Native American Renaissance*. Berkeley, CA: University of California Press.

Lipset, Seymour M. 1968a. *Agrarian Socialism: The Cooperative Commonwealth Federation in Saskatchewan*. Garden City, NY: Doubleday.

———. 1968b. *Revolution and Counter-revolution*. New York: Basic Books.

———. 1986. "Historical conditions and national characteristics." *Canadian Journal of Sociology* 11(2): 113–55.

———. 1990. *Continental Divide*. New York: Routledge.

———. 1996. *American Exceptionalism: A Double-Edged Sword*. New York: W.W. Norton.

Lipsey, Richard. 2000. *The Canada-US FTA: Real Results Versus Unreal Expectations*. **www.freeetradeat10.com/speeches/lipsey/html**.

Lord Durham. 1839. Report on the Affairs of British North America. London: British Colonial Office.

Lowe, Graham S. 1987. *Women in the Administrative Revolution*. Toronto: University of Toronto Press.

Lower, Arthur R.M. 1977. *Colony to Nation: A History of Canada*. Toronto: McClelland and Stewart.

Lower, J. Arthur. 1983. *Western Canada: An Outline History*. Vancouver: Douglas and McIntyre.

Lyon, John Tylor. 1998. "'A picturesque lot': The Gypsies of Peterborough." *The Beaver* 78(5): 25–30.

Macionis, John, and Linda M. Gerber. 1999. *Sociology*. 3rd Canadian edition. Scarborough: Prentice Hall Allyn and Bacon Canada.

Macionis, John, S. Mikael Jansson, and Ceciliar M. Benoit. 2002. *Society: The Basics*. 2nd Canadian edition. Toronto: Prentice Hall.

Maclean's. 1990. "Uncertain future." 2 July, 22–25.

———. 1999. "The vanishing border." 20 December, 20–49.

———. 2000. "Trudeau: His Life and Legacy." *A Special Commemorative Edition*.

———. 2002. "Why so cranky?" 30 December, 24–36.

MacLennan, Hugh. 1974. *The Rivers of Canada*. Toronto: Macmillan of Canada.

Macpherson, Don. 2000. "Sovereignty non-movement," *Edmonton Journal*, 2 November, A14.

Manchester, William. 1992. *A World Lit Only by Fire. The Medieval Mind and the Renaissance*. Boston: Little, Brown.

Manning, Preston. 1992. *The New Canada*. Toronto: Macmillan Canada.

Marchak, M. Patricia. 1988. *Ideological Perspectives on Canada*. Toronto: McGraw-Hill Ryerson.

Marchildon, Gregory. 1995. "From Pax Britannica to Pax Americana and beyond." In C. Doran and E. Babby (eds.), *Being and Becoming Canada. The Annals of the American Academy of Political and Social Science* 538: 151–169.

Marker, Michael. 2000. "Economics and local self-determination: Describing the clash zone in First Nations education." *Canadian Journal of Native Education* 24(1): 30–44.

Marquis, Greg. 2000. *In Armageddon's Shadow. The Civil War and Canada's Maritime*

Provinces. Kingston and Montreal: McGill-Queens University Press.

Martin, Ged. 1993a. "The influence of the Durham Report." In A.D. Gilbert, G.M. Wallace, and R.M. Bray (eds.), *Reappraisals in Canadian History. Pre-Confederation*. Scarborough: Prentice Hall Canada Inc.

——. 1993b. "History as science or literature: Explaining Canadian Confederation." In A.D. Gilbert, G.M. Wallace, and R.M. Bray (eds.), *Reappraisals in Canadian History. Pre-Confederation*. Scarborough: Prentice Hall Canada.

Martin, Lawrence. 1982. *The Presidents and Prime Ministers*. Markham: Paper Jacks.

——. 1993a. *Pledge of Allegiance. The Americanization of Canada During the Mulroney Years*. Toronto: McClelland and Stewart.

——. 1999a. "Canada was on brink of civil strife just four years ago." *Edmonton Journal* 10 April: A19.

——. 1999b. "Canada losing battle against assimilation." *Edmonton Journal* 2 July: A22.

Marx, Karl. 1977a. "The Communist manifesto." In D. McLellan (ed.), *Karl Marx: Selected Writings*. Oxford: Oxford University Press.

——. 1977b. "The eighteenth brumaire of Louis Napoleon." In D. McLellan (ed.), *Karl Marx: Selected Writings*. Oxford: Oxford University Press.

Massey, Don, and Patricia N. Shields. 1995. *Canada: Its Land and People*. Second edition. Edmonton, AB: Reidmore Books.

Maxim, Paul S., Jerry P. White, Dan Beavon, and Paul C. Whitehead. 2001. "Dispersion and polarization of income among Aboriginal and non-Aboriginal Canadians." *Canadian Review of Sociology and Anthropology* 38(4): 465–476.

Mayes, Hubert G. 1999. "Resurrection: Tolstoy and Canada's Doukhobors." *The Beaver* 79(5): 39–44.

McCall-Newman, Christina. 1982. *Grits. An Intimate Portrait of The Liberal Party*. Toronto: Macmillan of Canada.

McCallum, John. 1991. "Agriculture and economic development in Quebec and Ontario until 1870." In G. Laxer (ed.), *Perspectives on Canadian Economic Development*. Toronto: Oxford University Press.

McCracken, Harold, and Paul Dyck. 1972. *A Heritage of the Blackfeet*. Cody, WY: Buffalo Bill Historical Center.

McCue, William Westaway. 1999. "Crossing the line." *The Beaver*, 79(1): 16–21.

McDonald, Kevin. 1994. "Globalisation, multiculturalism and rethinking the social." *Australian-New Zealand Journal of Sociology* 30(3): 239–47.

McDonnell, R.F. and R.C. Depew. 1999. "Self-government and self-determination in Canada: A critical commentary." In J.H. Hylton (ed.), *Aboriginal Self-Government in Canada*. Saskatoon: Purich.

McDougall, John. 1903. *In the Days of the Red River Rebellion*. Toronto: William Briggs.

McGaa, Eagle Man (ed.). 1990. *Mother Earth Spirituality: Native American Paths to Healing Ourselves and Our World*. New York: Harper Collins.

McGaa, Ed Eagle Man. 1995. *Native Wisdom: Perceptions of the Natural Way*. Minneapolis: Four Directions Publishing.

McGhee, Robert. 1978. *Canadian Arctic Prehistory*. Toronto: van Nostrand Reinhold Ltd.

McKie, Craig. 1994. "A history of emigration from Canada." *Canadian Social Trends* 35: 26–29.

McMillan, Alan, D. 1995. *Native Peoples and Cultures of Canada.* Second edition. Vancouver, BC: Douglas and McIntyre.

McPherson, James. 1998. "Quebec whistles Dixie." *Saturday Night*, March: 13–14, 18, 20, 22–23, 72.

McQuaig, Linda. 1991. *The Quick and the Dead. Brian Mulroney, Big Business, and the Seduction of Canada.* Toronto: Viking.

Meekison, J. Peter. 1993. "Canada's quest for constitutional perfection." *Constitutional Forum* 4(2): 55–59.

Meili, Dianne. 1991. *Those Who Know: Profiles of Alberta's Elders.* Edmonton: NeWest Press.

Melling, John. 1967. *Right to a Future: The Native Peoples of Canada.* Toronto: T.H. Best Printing Co.

Menzies, Gavin. 2002. *1421: The Year the Chinese Discovered America.* London: Bantam Press.

Mercredi, Ovide and Mary Ellen Turpel. 1993. *In the Rapids: Navigating the Future of First Nations.* Toronto: Viking Press.

Merkur, Daniel. 1991. *Powers Which We Do Not Know: The Gods and Spirits of the Inuit.* Moscow, ID: University of Idaho Press.

Merriam-Webster, Incorporated. 2003. *Merriam-Webster's Collegiate® Dictionary, 10th Edition.* Springfield, MA: Merriam-Webster. **www.Merriam-Webster.com**.

Merritt, Christopher B. 1996. *Free Trade: Neither Free Nor About Trade.* Montreal: Black Rose.

Merton, Robert. 1968. *Social Theory and Social Structure.* New York: The Free Press.

Miliband, Ralph. 1969. *The State in Capitalist Society.* New York: Basic Books.

Miller, Alan D. 1988. *Native Peoples and Cultures of Canada.* Vancouver: Douglas and McIntyre.

Miller, Carman. 1999. "Canada's first war." *The Beaver* 79(5): 6–7.

Miller, J.R. 1987. "The irony of residential schooling." *Canadian Journal of Native Education* 14(2): 3–14.

———. 1991. *Skyscrapers Hide the Heavens: A History of Indian-White Relations in Canada.* Revised edition. Toronto: University of Toronto Press.

———. 2000. *Skyscrapers Hide the Heavens: A History of Indian-White Relations in Canada.* 3rd edition. Toronto: University of Toronto Press.

Mills, C. Wright. 1956. *The Power Elite.* Oxford: Oxford University Press.

———. 1961. *The Sociological Imagination.* New York: Grove Press.

Mittelman, J.H. 1996. "The dynamics of globalization." In J.H. Mittelman (ed.), *Globalization: Critical Reflections.* International Political Economy Yearbook, Vol. 9. London: Lynne Rienner Publishers.

Moffett, Samuel E. 1972. *The Americanization of Canada.* Originally published in 1908. Toronto: University of Toronto Press.

Momatiuk, Yva and John Eastcott. 1995. "'Nunavut' means 'Our Land'." *Native Peoples* 9(1): 42–48.

Monahan, Patrick. 1995. *Cooler Heads Shall Prevail: Assessing the Costs and Consequences of Quebec Separation.* Toronto: C.D. Howe Institute.

Moore, Christopher. 1997. *1867: How the Fathers Made a Deal.* Toronto: McClelland and Stewart.

———. 2000. "Colonization and conflict: New France and its rivals (1600–1760)." In Craig Brown (ed.), *The Illustrated History of Canada.* Toronto: Key Porter.

Morissette, Rene, and Xuelin Zhang. 2001. "Experiencing low income for several years." *Perspectives,* Summer. Cat. No. 75-001-XPE: 25–35. Ottawa: Statistics Canada.

Morrow, Ray. 1994. "History of sociological theory." In W. Meloff and D. Pierce (eds.), *An Introduction to Sociology*. Scarborough: Nelson.

Morton, Desmond. 1997. *A Short History of Canada*. Edmonton: Hurtig Publishers.

——————. 2000. "1900: A new century begins." *The Beaver* 79(6): 23–29.

Morton, William Lewis. 1970. "The Battle at Grand Coteau, July 13 and 14, 1851." In D. Swainson (ed.), *Historical Essays on the Prairie Provinces*. Toronto: McClelland and Stewart.

Mowat, Farley. 1952. *People of the Deer*. Toronto: McClelland and Stewart.

Nakhaie, M. Reza. 1997. "Vertical mosaic among the elites: The new imagery revisited." *The Canadian Review of Sociology and Anthropology* 34(1): 1–24.

National Post. 2001a. "1999 income median still below 1990." 11 August: A1 and A9.

——————. 2001b. "$20-billion pipeline to be biggest private project ever in N. America." 27 July: A1 and A8.

Naylor, R.T. 1975. *The History of Canadian Business 1867–1914*. Two volumes. Toronto: Lorimer.

Nevitte, Neil. 1996. *The Decline of Deferrence*. Peterborough: Broadview Press.

Newman, Peter C. *The Canadian Revolution, 1985–1995: from Deference to Defiance*. Toronto: Viking, 1995.

——————. 1998. *Empire of the Bay. The Company of Adventurers that Seized a Continent*. Toronto: Penguin Books.

——————. 1999. "The year of living dangerously." *Maclean's,* 20 December, 51–56.

Nickerson, Colin. 2000. "Sovereignty on thin ice." *Edmonton Journal* 26 March: E5.

Norrie, Ken, and Douglas Owram. 1996. *The History of the Canadian Economy*. Second Edition. Toronto: Harcourt Brace and Company, Canada.

OECD (Organization for Economic Development). 1997. *Economic Outlook*. June.

O'Hara, Jane. 2000. "Abuse of Trust." *Maclean's* 113(26): 16–21.

Ohmae, Ken'ichi. 1990. *The Borderless World. Power and Strategy in the Interlinked Economy*. New York: Harper Business.

——————. 1995. *The End of the Nation State: The Rise of Regional Economies*. New York: The Free Press.

Olsen, Gregg. 1999. "Locating the Canadian welfare state: Family policy and health case in Canada, Sweden, and the United States." *The Canadian Journal of Sociology* 19(1): 1–20.

——————. 2002. *The Politics of the Welfare State. Canada, Sweden, and the United States*. Oxford: Oxford University Press.

Orchard, David. 1998. *The Fight for Canada*. 2nd Edition. Westmount: Robert Davies Multimedia Publishing Inc.

Orum, Anthony M. 1989. *Introduction to Political Sociology. The Social Anatomy of the Body Politic*. Englewood Cliffs, NJ: Prentice-Hall.

Orwell, George. 1983. *1984*. In *The Penguin Complete Novels of George Orwell*. Toronto: Penguin.

Osborn, Kevin. 1990. *The Peoples of the Arctic*. New York: Chelsea House.

Ouellet, Fernand. 1993. "The 1837/38 rebellions in Lower Canada as a social phenomenon." In A.D. Gilbert, G.M. Wallace, and R.M. Bray (eds.), *Reappraisals in Canadian History. Pre-Confederation*. Scarborough: Prentice Hall Canada.

Quimet, Marc. 1999. "Crime in Canada and the United States: A comparative analysis." *Canadian Review of Sociology and Anthropology* 36(3): 389–408.

Palmer, Howard. 1982. *Patterns of Prejudice: A History of Nativism in Alberta*. Toronto: McClelland and Stewart.

Palmer, R.R., with Joel Colton. 1957. *A History of the Modern World*. New York: Alfred A. Knopf.

Panitch, Leo. 1977. The Canadian State: Political Economy and Political Power. Toronto: University of Toronto Press.

———. 1981. "Dependency and class in Canadian political economy." *Studies in Political Economy* 6: 7–33.

Panitch, Leo, and Donald Swartz. 1988. *The Assault on Trade Union Freedoms: From Consent to Coercion Revisited*. Toronto: Garamond.

Paquet, Gilles. 1997. "States, communities, and markets: The distributed governance scenario." In T.J. Courchene (ed.), *The Nation State in a Global/Information Era: Policy Challenges*. Kingston: Queen's University.

Parenti, Michael. 1995. *Against Empire*. San Francisco: City Lights Books.

Parsons, Talcott. 1951. *The Social System*. Glencoe, Ill.: The Free Press.

Parti Québécois. 1994. *Quebec in a New World. The PQ's Plan for Sovereignty*. R. Chodos (trans.). Toronto: James Lorimer and Company.

Pauls, Syd. 1984. "The case for band-controlled schools." *Canadian Journal of Native Education* 12(1): 31–37.

Pearlstein, Steven. 2000. "Canada casts a wary eye across the border." *Guardian Weekly* 14–20 September, 35.

Pentland, Clare. 1991. "The transformation of Canada"s economic structure." In G. Laxer (ed.), *Perspectives on Canadian Economic Development*. Toronto: Oxford University Press.

Perley, David G. 1993. "Aboriginal education in Canada as internal colonialism." *Canada Journal of Native Education* 20(1): 118–128.

Persson, Diane. 1986. "The changing experience of Indian residential schooling: Blue Quills, 1931–1970." In J. Barman, Y. Hébert, and D. McCaskill (eds.), *Indian Education in Canada, Vol. I: The Legacy*. Vancouver: University of British Columbia Press.

Petitot, Father Emile. 1999. *Among the Chiglit Eskimos*. E. Otto Höhn (trans.). Edmonton: Boreal Institute for Northern Studies.

Pevere, Geoff, and Greig Dymond. 1996. *Mondo Canuck: A Canadian Pop Cultural Odyssey*. Scarborough: Prentice-Hall.

Pinard, Maurice. 2003. *A Great Realignment of Political Parties in Quebec*. Montreal: Centre for Research and Information on Canada.

Plain, Fred. 1988. "A Treatise on the Rights of the Aboriginal Peoples of the Continent of North America." In M. Boldt and J.A. Long (eds.), *The Quest for Justice: Aboriginal Peoples and Aboriginal Rights*. Toronto: University of Toronto Press.

Ponting, J. Rick. 1986. "Relations Between Bands and the Department of Indian Affairs: A Case of Internal Colonialism." In J.R. Ponting (ed.), *Arduous Journey: Canadian Indians and Decolonization*. Toronto: McClelland and Stewart.

———. 1997a. "Getting a Handle on Recommendations of the Royal Commission on Aboriginal Peoples. In J.R. Ponting (ed.), *First Nations in Canada: Perspectives on Opportunity, Empowerment, and Self-Determination*. Toronto: McGraw-Hill Ryerson Limited.

———. 1997b. The Socio-Demographic Picture. In J.R. Ponting (ed.), *First Nations in Canada: Perspectives on Opportunity, Empowerment, and Self-Determination*. Toronto: McGraw-Hill Ryerson Limited.

Porter, John. 1965. *The Vertical Mosaic*. Toronto: University of Toronto Press.

Poulantzas, Nicholas. 1973. *Political Power and Social Classes*. T. O'Hagan (trans.). London: New Left Books.

Pratt, Larry. 2001. *Energy: Free Trade and the Price We Paid*. Edmonton: Parkland Institute.

Pratt, Larry, and Garth Stevenson (eds.). 1981. *Western Separatism: The Myths, Realities, and Dangers*. Edmonton: Hurtig.

Purich, Donald. 1986. *Our Land*. Toronto: James Lorimer.

———. 1992. *The Inuit and Their Land*. Toronto: Lorimer and Company.

Ralph, Diana S., André Régimbald, and Nérée St-Ama (eds.). 1997. *Open for Business, Closed to People: Mike Harris's Ontario*. Halifax: Fernwood.

Ramonet, Ignacio. 2001. "The changing face of separatism." *Le Monde diplomatique*, February, 1.

Ray, Arthur J. 1974. *Indians in the Fur Trade: Their Role as Trappers, Hunters, and Middlemen in the Lands Southwest of Hudson Bay, 1660–1870*. Toronto: University of Toronto Press.

Rea, K J. 1968. *The Political Economy of the Canadian North*. Toronto: University of Toronto Press.

Reid, Scott. 1992. *Canada Remapped*. Vancouver: Pulp Press.

Resnick, Philip. 1991. *Toward a Canada-Quebec Union*. Montreal and Kingston: McGill-Queen's University Press.

———. 2000. *The Politics of Resentment: B.C. Regionalism and Canadian Unity*. Vancouver: University of British Columbia Press.

Resnick, Philip, and Daniel Latouche. 1990. *Letters to a Quebecois Friend*. Montreal/Kingston: McGill-Queen's University Press.

Rice, James, and Michael Prince. 2000. *Changing Politics of Canadian Social Policy*. Toronto: University of Toronto Press.

Richards, John, and Larry Pratt. 1979. *Prairie Capitalism: Power and Influence in the New West*. Toronto: McClelland and Stewart.

Richburg, Keith B. 2001. "Divergent views of U.S. role in world." *Washington Post* 20 December: A34.

Rickman, H.P. 1961. "Introduction." W. Dilthey's *Pattern and Meaning in History*. London: Harper Row Publishers.

Riddell, W. Craig, and Andrew Sharpe. 1998. "The Canada-US unemployment rate gap: An introduction and overview." *Canadian Public Policy* 24: S1–S37.

Riesman, David, with Reuel Denney and Nathan Glazer. 1950. *The Lonely Crowd: A Study of the Changing American Character*. New Haven: Yale University Press.

Rioux, Marcel. 1978. *Quebec in Question*. Toronto: James Lorimer and Company.

———. 1993. "The development of ideologies in Quebec." In D. Taras, B. Rasporich, and E. Mandel (eds.), *A Passion for Identity: An Introduction to Canadian Studies*. Scarborough: Nelson Canada.

Robbins, Richard. 1999. *Global Problems and the Culture of Capitalism*. Toronto: Allyn and Bacon.

Roberts, Ian. 2003. "We are driving as to war." *Guardian Weekly* 23–29 January: 11.

Roberts, Joseph K. 1998. *In the Shadow of Empire. Canada for Americans*. New York: Monthly Review Press.

Robin, Martin. 1991. *Shades of Right: Nativist and Fascist Politics in Canada, 1920–1940*. Toronto: University of Toronto Press.

———. 1993. "British Columbia: The company province." In D. Taras, B. Rasporich, and E. Mandel (eds.), *A Passion for Identity: An Introduction to Canadian Studies*. Scarborough: Nelson Canada.

Romney, Paul. 1999. *Getting It Wrong. How Canadians Forgot Their Past and Imperilled Confederation*. Toronto: University of Toronto Press.

Ross, Rupert. 1992. *Dancing with a Ghost: Exploring Indian Reality*. Markham: Reed Books.

Rotstein, Abraham. 1978. "Is there an English-Canadian nationalism?" *Journal of Canadian Studies* 13.

Rudmin, Floyd. 1993. *Bordering on Aggression*. Hull: Voyageur Publications.

Rummel, R.J. 1994. *Death By Government*. New Brunswick: Transaction.

Russell, Bob. 1990. *Back to Work? Labour, State, and Industrial Relations in Canada*. Scarborough: Nelson Canada.

Ryan, Joan. 1995. *Doing Things the Right Way: Dene Traditional Justice in Lac La Martre, N.W.T.* Calgary: Arctic Institute of North America.

Said, Edward. 1993. *Culture and Imperialism*. New York: Vintage Books.

Sanders, D.E. 1974. "Native people in areas of internal national expansion." *Saskatchewan Law Review* 38(1): 63–87.

Sassan, Saskia. 2001. "Governance hotspots: Challenges we must confront in the post-September 11 world." *Social Science Research Council*. **www.ssrc.org/sept11/essay/sassen.html**.

Saul, John Ralston. 1997. *Reflections of a Siamese Twin. Canada at the End of the Twentieth Century*. Toronto: Penguin Books.

Saul, S.B. 1969. *The Myth of the Great Depression 1873–1896*. London: The Macmillan Press Ltd.

Savoie, Donat (ed.). 1970. *The Amerindians of the Canadian North-West in the 19th Century, as seen by Émile Petitot. The Loucheux Indian, Volume II*. Ottawa: Northern Science Group, Department of Indian Affairs and Northern Development.

Sawatsky, John. 1991. *Mulroney: The Politics of Ambition*. Toronto: Macfarland, Walter, and Ross.

Sayer, Derek. 1987. *The Violence of Abstraction: The Analytic Foundations of Historical Materialism*. Oxford: Basil Blackwell.

Schlesinger, Arthur, Jr. 1997. "Has democracy a future?" *Foreign Affairs* 76(5): 2–12.

Scott-Brown, Joan. 1991. "Native land claims." In J.W. Friesen (ed.), *The Cultural Maze: Complex Questions on Native Destiny in Western Canada*. Calgary: Detselig.

Scowen, Reed. 1999. *Time to Say Goodbye. The Case for Getting Quebec Out of Canada*. Toronto: McClelland and Stewart.

Silver, A.I. 1997. *The French-Canadian Idea of Confederation 1864–1900*. 2nd Edition.

Toronto: University of Toronto Press.

Silver, Jim. 1996. *Thin Ice: Money, Politics, and the Demise of an NHL Franchise*. Halifax: Fernwood.

Simeon, Richard (ed.). 1977. *Must Canada Fail?* Montreal and Kingston: McGill-Queen's University Press.

Skocpol, Theda. 1979. *States and Social Revolutions*. Cambridge, MA: Cambridge University Press.

Smith, Adam. 1986. *An Inquiry into the Nature and the Wealth of Nations, Books I–III*. Originally published in 1776. London: Penguin.

Smith, Dan. 1993. *The Seventh Fire: The Struggle for Aboriginal Government*. Toronto: Key Porter Books.

Smith, David, Peter MacKinnon, and John Courtney (eds.). 1991. *After Meech Lake. Lessons for the Future*. Saskatoon: Fifth House.

Smith, Donald. 1998. *Beyond Two Solitudes*. Halifax: Fernwood.

Smith, Goldwin. 1891. *Canada and the Canadian question*. Reprinted in 1971 by the University of Toronto Press.

Smith Q.C., Melvin H. 1995. *Our Home OR Native Land? What Government Aboriginal Policy is Doing to Canada*. Toronto: Stoddart.

Snow, Chief John. 1977. *These Mountains Are Our Sacred Places: The Story of the Stoney Indians*. Toronto: Samuel Stevens.

———. 1988. "Identification and Definition of Our Treaty and Aboriginal Rights." In M. Boldt and A. Long (eds.), *The Quest for Justice: Aboriginal Peoples and Aboriginal Rights*. Toronto: University of Toronto Press.

Sprague, D.N. 1988. *Canada and the Métis, 1869–1885*. Waterloo: Wilfred Laurier University Press.

Srebrnik, Henry F. 1998. "The Radical 'Second Life' of Vilhjalmur Stefansson." *Arctic* 51(1): 58–60.

Stabler, Jack. 1989. "Dualism and Development in the Northwest Territories." *Economic Development and Cultural Change* 37(4): 805–840.

Stacey, C.P., and Norman Hillmer. 1999. "World War II." *The Canadian Encyclopedia*. Toronto: McClelland and Stewart.

Stanford, Jim. 2003. "Who's outperforming whom?" *Globe and Mail* 13 January: A13.

Stanley, George F.G. 1975. *The Birth of Western Canada: A History of the Riel Rebellion*. Originally published in 1936. Toronto: University of Toronto Press.

Starnes, Richard. 2002. "Once-hostile Arctic waters will soon be fished." *Edmonton Journal* 9 March: A3.

Statistics Canada. 2001. "Aboriginal people in Canada." Canadian Centre for Justice Statistics profile series. Ottawa: Statistics Canada. Cat. No. 85F0033MIE2001001.

———. 2003a. "Earnings of Canadians: Making a living in the new economy." *2001 Census: Analysis Series*. Cat. No. 96F0030XIE2001013. www.statcan.ca/cgi_bin/downpub/freepub.cgi.

———. 2003b. "Education in Canada: Raising the standard." *2001. Census: Analysis Series*. Cat. No. 96F0030XIE2001012. www.statcan.ca/cgi_bin/downpub/freepub.cgi.

———. 2003c. "Population." CANSIM II, Table 051-0001. www.statcan.ca/english/Pgdh/demo02.htm .

———. 2003d. "Population by Aboriginal group, 1996." Census, Census metropolitan areas. www.statcan.ca/english/Pgdb/demo39_96b.htm (11.5 kb).

Stearns, P.N. 1975. *European Society in Upheaval*. Second edition. New York: Macmillan Publishing Company.

Stefansson, Vilhjalmur. 1921. *The Friendly Arctic*. New York: Macmillan.

———. 1938. *Unsolved Mysteries of the Arctic*. New York: Collier.

Strange, Susan. 1996. *The Retreat of the State*. Cambridge University Press.

Stubbs, R., and G.R.D. Underhill (eds.). 1994. *Political Economy and the Changing Global Order*. Toronto: McClelland and Stewart.

Surtees, R.J. 1969. *The Development of a Reserve Policy in Canada*. Ontario Historical Society, LXI: 87–99.

Suzuki, David. 1992. "A personal foreword: The value of Native ecologies." In P. Knudtson and D. Suzuki, *Wisdom of the Elders*. Toronto: Stoddart,

Swedberg, Richard. 1990. *Economics and Society*. Princeton: Princeton University Press.

Tajfel, Henri, and John C. Turner. 1986. "The social identity theory of intergroup behavior." In S. Worchel and W.A. Austin (eds.), *Psychology of Intergroup Relations*. Chicago: Nelson-Hall.

Taylor, Charles. 1993. *Reconciling the Solitudes*. Montreal and Kingston: McGill-Queen's University Press.

Taylor, J. Garth. 1974. *Netsilik Eskimo Material Culture: The Roald Amundsen Collection from King William Island*. Oslo, Norway: Universitetsforlaget.

Teeple, Gary. 1995. *Globalization and the Decline of Social Reform*. Toronto: Garamond Press.

Tennant, Paul. 1988. "Aboriginal rights and the Penner Report on Indian self-government." In M. Boldt and A. Long (eds.), *The Quest for Justice: Aboriginal Peoples and Aboriginal Rights*. Toronto: University of Toronto Press.

Thomas, Lewis H. 1977. "A judicial murder: The trial of Louis Riel." In H. Palmer (ed.), *The Settlement of the West*. Calgary: Comprint.

Thompson, Dale. 1995. "Language, identity, and the nationalist impulse: Quebec." In C. Doran and E. Babby (eds.), *Being and Becoming Canada. The Annals of the American Academy of Political and Social Science* 538: 69–82.

Time. 1999. *Almanac 2001*. Boston: Time Inc.

———. 2002. *Almanac 2003*. Boston: Time Inc.

Titley, E. Brian. 1992. Red Deer Industrial School: A case study in the history of Native education. In N. Kach and K. Mazurek (eds.), *Exploring Our Educational Past*. Calgary: Detselig.

Tobias, John L. 1977. "Indian Reserves in Western Canada: Indian homelands or devices for assimilation?" In D. A. Muise (ed.), *Approaches to Native History in Canada*. Ottawa: National Museum of Man Mercury Series.

———. 1983. "Protection, Civilization, Assimilation: An Outline History of Canada's Indian Policy." In Ian A. L. Getty and Antoine Lussier (eds.), *As Long as the Sun Shines and Water Flows: A Reader in Canadian Native Studies*. Vancouver: University of British Columbia Press.

Tompkins, Joanne. 1998. *Teaching in a Cold and Windy Place*. Toronto: University of Toronto Press.

Tönnies, Ferdinand. 1957. *Community and Society*. C.P. Loomis (ed. and trans.). Originally published in 1887. New York: Harper and Row.

Tracy, Frank. 1908. *The Tercentenary History of Canada; From Champlain to Laurier, MDCVIII–MCMVIII*. Three Volumes. New York: P. F. Collier and Son.

Treaty Seven Elders and Tribal Council, with Walter Hildebrandt, Sarah Carter and Dorothy First Rider. *The True Spirit and Original Intent of Treaty 7*. Montreal and Kingston: McGill-Queen's University Press.

Trent, John E. 1995. *The 1995 Quebec Referendum: A Practical Guide*. Ottawa: Dialogue Canada.

Trigger, Bruce G. 1969. *The Huron: Farmers of the North*. New York: Holt, Rinehart and Winston.

Trofimenkoff, Susan. 1993. "For whom the bell tolls." In A.D. Gilbert, G.M. Wallace, and R.M. Bray (eds.), *Reappraisals in Canadian History. Pre-Confederation*. Scarborough: Prentice Hall Canada.

Trudeau, Pierre. 1996. *Against the Current. Selected Writings 1939–1996*. G. Pelletier (ed.). Toronto: McClelland and Stewart.

Turner, Joanne. 1981. "The historical base." In J. Turner and F. Turner (eds.), *Canadian Social Welfare*. Don Mills: Collier Macmillan Canada.

Turp, Daniel. 1993. "Solutions to the future of Canada and Quebec after the October 26th referendum: Genuine sovereignties within a novel union." *Constitutional Forum* 4(2): 47–49.

Ugbor, Kez O. 1994. "Social stratification." In W. Meloff and D. Pierce (eds.), *An Introduction to Sociology*. Scarborough: Nelson.

Ungar, Sheldon. 1991. "Civil religion and the arms race." *Canadian Review of Sociology and Anthropology* 28(4): 503–525.

Valaskatis, Kimon, and Angeline Fournier. 1995. *The Delusion of Sovereignty. Would Independence Weaken Quebec?* Montreal: Robert Davies Publishing.

Vallee, Frank. 1971. "Eskimos of Canada: A minority group." In Jean Elliott Leonard (ed.), *Native Peoples*. Scarborough: Prentice-Hall of Canada.

Vallieres, Pierre. 1971. *White Niggers of America*. Toronto: McClelland and Stewart.

van den Berghe, Pierre. 1992. "The modern state: nation-builder or nation-killer?" *International Journal of Group Tensions* 22: 191–208.

van Kirk, Sylvia. 1999. *Many Tender Ties: Women in the Fur Trade Society 1670–1870*. Winnipeg: Watson and Dwyer.

Waite, P.B. 1997. "In Loyalist Ontario: A schoolboy's recollections, 1930–1933." *The Beaver*, February-March: 12–13.

Wall, Denis. 2000. "Aboriginal self-government in Canada: The cases of Nunavut and the Alberta Métis settlements." In D. Long and O.P. Dickason (eds.), *Visions of the Heart: Canadian Aboriginal Issues*. Second edition. Toronto: Harcourt Canada.

Wallerstein, Immanuel. 1997. "World-systems analysis." In A. Giddens and J. Turner (eds.), *Social Theory Today*. Stanford: Stanford University Press.

Wanner, Richard A. 1999. "Expansion and conscription: Trends in educational opportunity in Canada, 1920–1994." *Canadian Review of Sociology and Anthropology* 36(3): 409–442.

Waters, Malcolm. 1994. "Introduction. A world of difference." *Australian-New Zealand Journal of Sociology* 30(3): 229–34.

Watkins, Melville. 1963. "A staple theory of economic growth." *Canadian Journal of Economics and Political Science* 29(2): 80–100.

———. 1991. "The 'American system' and Canada's National Policy." In G. Laxer (ed.), *Perspectives on Canadian Economic Development*. Toronto: Oxford University Press.

———. 1997. "Canadian capitalism in

transition." In W. Clement (ed.), *Understanding Canada: Building on the New Canadian Political Economy*. Montreal and Kingston: McGill-Queen's University Press.

Waubageshig (ed). 1970. *The Only Good Indian*. Essays by Canadian Indians. Toronto: New Press.

Wax, Murray, Rosalie Wax, and Robert V. Dumont (eds.). 1964. "Formal Education in an American Indian Community." *Social Problems*. SSSP Monograph: 1–126.

Weaver, Jace (ed.). 1998. *Native American Religious Identity: Unforgotten Gods*. Maryknoll, NY: Orbis Books.

Webber, Jeremy. 1994. *Reimagining Canada*. Montreal/Kingston: McGill-Queen's University Press.

Weber, Max. 1958. *From Max Weber: Essays in Sociology*. H. Gerth and C. W. Mills (eds.), New York: Oxford University Press.

Westfall, William. 1993. "On the concept of region in Canadian history and literature." In D. Taras, B. Rasporich, and E. Mandel (eds.), *A Passion for Identity: An Introduction to Canadian Studies*. Scarborough: Nelson Canada.

Whitaker, Reg. 1987. "Neo-conservatism and the state." *Socialist Register*. London: The Merlin Press.

———. 1991. *Canadian Immigration Policy Since Confederation*. Ottawa: Canadian Historical Association.

White, Deena. 1997. "Quebec state and society." In M. Fournier, M. Rosenberg, and D. White (eds.), *Quebec Society: Critical Issues*. Scarborough: Prentice Hall Canada.

Whyte, Donald. 1992. "Sociology and the constitution of society: Canadian experiences." In W. Carroll, L. Christiansen-Ruffman, R. Currie, and D. Harrison (eds.), *Fragile Truths: 25 Years of Sociology and Anthropology in Canada*. Ottawa: Carleton University Press.

Widdis, Randy. 1997. "American-resident migration to Western Canada at the turn of the twentieth century." *Prairie Forum* 22(2): 237–261.

Wilensky, Harold. 1975. *The Welfare State and Equality: Structural and Ideological Roots of Public Expenditures*. Berkeley: University of California Press.

Wills, Terrance. 2000. "What if Meech had lived?" *Edmonton Journal*, 18 June: F4.

Wilson, Beth, with Emily Tsoa. 2001. *Hunger Count 2001. Food Bank Lines in Insecure Times*. Toronto: Canadian Association of Food Banks.

Wilson, C. Roderick and Carl Urion. 1995. "First Nations prehistory and Canadian history." In R.B. Wilson, and C.R. Morrison (eds.), *Native Peoples: The Canadian Experience*. Second edition. Toronto: McClelland and Stewart.

Wilson, Roger (ed.). 1976. *The Land That Never Melts: Auyuittuq National Park*. Ottawa: Minister of Supply and Services.

Winks, Robin. 1998. *The Civil War Years. Canada and the United States*. Fourth Edition. Montreal and Kingston: McGill-Queen's University Press.

Wiseman, Nelson. 1993. "The pattern of prairie politics." In D. Taras, B. Rasporich, and E. Mandel (eds.), *A Passion for Identity: An Introduction to Canadian Studies*. Scarborough: Nelson Canada.

Wissler, Clark. 1923. *Man and Culture*. New York: Thomas Crowell

Witt, Norbert. 1998. "Promoting self-esteem, defining culture." *Canadian Journal of Native Education* 22(2): 260–273.

Wittington, Michael. 1985. "Political and constitutional development in the N.W.T. and Yukon: The issues and the interests." In M. Wittington, (ed.), *The North*. Toronto: University of Toronto Press.

Wolcott, Harry F. 1967. *A Kwakiutl Village and School*. New York: Holt, Rinehart and Winston.

Wolfson, and Murphy. 2000. "Income taxes in Canada and the United States." *Perspectives on Labour and Income* 12(2). Ottawa: Statistics Canada. Catalogue no. 75-001-XPE.

Wonders, William. 1993. "Canadian regions and regionalisms: National enrichment or national disintegration?" In D. Taras, B. Rasporich, and E. Mandel (eds.), *A Passion for Identity: An Introduction to Canadian Studies*. Scarborough: Nelson Canada.

Woodsworth, J.S. 1972. *Strangers Within Our Gates*. Originally published 1909. Toronto: University of Toronto Press.

Wright, Eric Olin. 1985. *Classes*. London: Verso.

Wright, Ronald. 1993. *Stolen Continents. The New World Through Indian Eyes*. Toronto: Penguin.

Wuttunee, William I.C. 1971. *Ruffled Feathers: Indians in Canadian Society*. Calgary: Bell Books.

Wynn, Graeme. 2000. "On the margins of empire 1760–1840." In Craig Brown (ed.), *The Illustrated History of Canada*. Toronto: Key Porter Books.

Yazzie, Robert. 2000. "Indigenous peoples and post-colonial colonialism." In M. Battiste (ed.), *Reclaiming Indigenous Voice and Vision*. Vancouver: UBC Press.

York, Geoffrey. 1989. *The Dispossessed: Life and Death in Native Canada*. Toronto: Lester & Orpen Dennys.

Young, Robert A. 1995. *The Secession of Quebec and the Future of Canada*. Montreal and Kingston: McGill-Queen's University Press.

———. 1998. "Quebec succession and the 1995 referendum." In M. Westmacott and H. Mellon (eds.), *Challenges to Canadian Federalism*. Scarborough: Prentice Hall Canada.

Zinn, Howard. 1995. *A People's History of the United States 1492–Present*. New York: HarperPerennial.

Index

A
Aberhart, William, 117
Aboriginal culture
  belief systems, 176, 201
  collectivism in, 243–244
  cyclical notion of time, 242–243
  language groups, 174–175, 198
  multiple realities in, 242
  notion of cause and effect in, 243
  ocean-oriented culture, 199
  order, hierarchy, and legitimacy in, 244–245
  pre-contact lifestyles, 174–176
  present-oriented culture, 175
  sharing in, 244
  social organization, 176
  spirituality, 241–242
  survival of, 241, 245
  values of, 241–245
Aboriginal-European relations
  Aboriginal resistance, 180
  first contact, 176–177
  fur trade, 178–180, 203–204
Aboriginal land claims, 219
  comprehensive claims, 238, 239–240
  Native strategies, 239
  Oka Crisis, 224–225
  Penner Report and, 222
  public reaction to, 239
  Royal Proclamation and, 213–214
  specific claims, 238
Aboriginal peoples
  and agriculture, 181–183
  and American expansionism, 92–93
  and defeat of Meech Lake Accord, 223

disenfranchisement of, 215
economic circumstances of, 229–230
education, 188–194, 207, 230–231
and internal colonialism, 184–186
Loyalists, 90
of the North, 197–202
and North-West Rebellion, 103
population, 184, 228
Royal Commission on (RCAP), 232–233
and sexual equality, 221–222
in urban centres, 228–229
Aboriginal rights, 58
  BNA Act, 214–215
  Constitution Act, 1982, 219–221
  and legal principles of Royal Proclamation, 213–214
Aboriginal self-government, 220, 222, 236–238
Aboriginal treaties, 179, 181–182, 213–214, 215–217
Abrams, Philip, 7
Acadians, expulsions of, 26
Act of Union (1841), 34, 50
Adams, Howard, 216
Advisory Committee on Post-War Reconstruction, 124
Afghanistan war, 164
Alaska Highway, 207
Alberta
  economy, 138
  and free trade, 149
  immigration, 106
  and New Energy Program, 145
  population, 137–138
Algonquian, 174

alienation, regional, 140
American exceptionalism, 92
American Revolution, 86–89
American system, 102
  See also protectionism
Amundsen, Roald, 203
An Act for the Gradual Civilization of the Indian, 190
An Act for the Gradual Enfranchisement of Indians, 214
Anderson, Benedict, 8
Anglican Church, and residential claims, 234
Anglo-conformity, 107
annexation
  fears of, 108, 109
  movement, 96
anti-Americanism, 90–91, 108, 109, 133, 136
anti-feminist backlash, 128
anti-nationalist liberalism, 43
anti-Oriental riots, 107
Arctic region, 196–197
Argentina, and globalization, 156–157
Arnold, Benedict, 88
Articles of Confederation (American), 88
Asbestos Strike, 42
Assembly of First Nations, 223, 224, 232, 235
assimilation
  of Aboriginal peoples, 190, 207
  of immigrants, 107
asymmetrical federalism, 77–78
Athapaskan, 175, 200
Auden, W.H., 118
authority, and power, 31
Auto Pact, 133
"axis of evil," 165

283

B

Balthazar, Louis, 69
bands (Aboriginal peoples), 176, 228
Barber, Lloyd, 219
Barker, William, 110
Beauvoir, Simone de, 127
Beaver (Dene tribe), 200, 201
Bell, Daniel, 76, 229
Bennett, R.B., 116, 117
Beothuk, 177
Bercuson, David, 79
Berger Inquiry, 210
Bering Strait theory, 174
Beveridge Report, 124
bilateral kindreds, 200, 201
Bilingualism and Biculturalism, Royal Commission on, 45–46, 125
Bill 22. *See* Official Language Act (Bill 22)
Bill 101. *See* Charter of the French Language (Bill 101)
Bill C-20. *See* Clarity Act (Bill C-20)
Bill C-31, 221
Bird Commission. *See* Status of Women, Royal Commission on
Bishop, Billy, 110
blacks
 immigration, 107
 Loyalists, 90
Blakeney, William, 58
Bloc Québécois, 65, 68, 71
Boer War, 39, 108
Borden, Sir Robert, 39
Bouchard, Lucien, 64, 68, 69, 70, 71
Bourassa, Henri, 37, 39
Bourassa, Robert, 52, 209
Bourgault, Pierre, 80
Bourgeoys, Marguerite, 188
branch plants, 135
Brant, Joseph, 90
Brimelow, Peter, 79
Britain
 investment capital, 109
British Columbia
 immigration, 107
 Nisga'a land claims, 239–240
 population, 137–138
British North America
 American expansionism, 92, 103
 economy, 94–95
 immigration, 93, 94
 population, 93, 94, 104
 and reciprocity, 95–97
British North America Act (Constitution Act of 1867), 50, 51, 53, 214–215
British system, 102
 See also free trade
Brock, Isaac, 90
Brown, A. Roy, 110
Brown, George, 98
Brown Paper, 218
Brunelle, Dorval, 80
Bush, George, Jr., 164, 165
Bush, George, Sr., 150
Bush Doctrine, 165
Business Council on National Issues (BCNI), 149

C

Cabot, John, 202
Campbell, Kim, 150
Campbell, Robert, 204
Canada
 and American Civil War, 97–98
 American invasion of, 90
 American invasions, 88
 and American war on terrorism, 167–168
 bilingualism, 60
 boundaries, 92
 country, 6–7
 distribution of wealth, 161–162
 and First World War, 109–111
 health care, 162
 income inequality, 74
 incomes, 161
 and Iraq war, 168
 nation, 8
 and North-West Territories, 103
 population, 161
 postwar economy, 140–143, 161
 quality of life, 162
 religion, 60
 role of state, 123–125
 and scenario of independent Quebec, 79–80
 and Second World War, 118
 trade with United States, 108–109
 unemployment, 161
 welfare state, 126
Canada Pension Plan, 124
Canadian Charter of Rights and Freedoms, 57–58, 220
Canadian Citizenship Act, 132
Canadian imperialists (imperial nationalists), 108
Canadianization, economic policy, 143–145
Canadian Metis Society, 219
Canadian Pacific Railway (CPR), 103
Canadian Taxpayers Federation, 235
Canadiens, 27–28
Cardinal, Harold, 216, 218
Carleton, Guy, 88
Carmack, George Washington, 204
Carr, Emily, 113
Carrier, 200
Cartier, George, 99
Cartier, Jacques, 23, 177
Cents-Associés, Compagnie des, 23
Champlain, Samuel de, 23, 177
Charles II, 203
Charlottetown Accord, 64–65, 223–224
Charter of the French Language (Bill 101), 54
Chateau Clique, 31
Chauveau, Maurice, 29
Chilcotin, 200
Chinese immigration, 106
Chipewyan, 200, 201

Chrétien, Jean, 69, 72, 150, 219
Cité libre, 43
citizens plus, 217
civic nationalism, 8
Civilization and Enfranchisement Act, 190
clans, 176
Clarity Act (Bill C-20), 71
Clark, Joe, 56
class, social, 156–157
class consciousness, 157
class theory, 135
clerico-nationalism, 40–41
closed boreal forest, 197
coercive power, 31
Cold War, 121–123, 133
collective bargaining, 125
collective rights, 75–76
colonialism, 183–184
   See also internal colonialism
communism, 116
compact theory, 46
comprador elite, 135
comprehensive claims, 238
Comte, Auguste, 9
Confederation, 98–99
   Charlottetown Conference, 98
   federal system of government, 98–99
   and French minority rights, 38
   and isolation of Quebec, 37–40
   objectives of, 98
   public reception, 99
conflict theory, 12–13, 15
Conrad, Joseph, 63
conscription crises, 39, 111
conservatism, English Canadian, 136–137
conservative (maternal) feminism, 14
conservative welfare state, 125
constitution
   defined, 50
   evolution of Canadian constitution, 50–51
   language rights, 53
   role of, 50

Constitution Act, 1982, 219–221
Constitution Act of 1791, 28–29, 50
Constitution Act of 1867, 58
   See also British North America Act
Constitution Act of 1982, 53, 58
constitutional reform, 50
   Aboriginal rights and, 219–220, 221, 222, 223–224
   amending formula, 58
   complexities of, 51
   "distinct society" clause, 60, 63
   issues, 51
   Meech Lake Accord, 59–60, 63–64
   "notwithstanding clause," 58
   patriation of Canadian constitution, 57–58
Conway, John, 77
Coon Come, Matthew, 235
Cooper, Barry, 79
Co-operative Commonwealth Federation (CCF), 117, 124
corporate (monopoly) capitalism, 112, 122
corporations
   and globalization, 11
counterfactual history, 17–18
country, defined, 4
Courchene, Thomas, 78
Creighton, Donald, 46
Cross, James, 47
Crowfoot, Chief, 182
Cuban Missile Crisis, 123
cultural areas, indigenous, 174
cultural theory, 126
culture, Canadian, 113
   decline of British influence in, 132
   marketability of, 156
   music, 134
   promotion of, 133
   protection of, 155–156
   and regionalism, 156

D
debt "crisis," 163–164
decapitation thesis, 30
decentralization, 78
Declaration of Independence, 86
de-commodification, of social needs, 124, 126
democracy, 230
Denbigh people, 198
Dene, 200–202
Dene/Metis Western Arctic Land Claim agreement, 239
Denis, Claude, 4, 9, 63
Department of Indian and Northern Development (DIAND), 220
dependency theory, 134–135
Depression, 113–117
   economic crisis, 115
   political unrest, 116
   populist parties, 117
   social impact, 115
   and Western Canada, 115
Dickinson, John, 23
Diefenbaker, John, 133, 208
differences, issue of, 229–230
Dion, Stéphane, 71
direct investments, 109
disease, and Aboriginal peoples, 179
Dogrib, 200
dominant ideology, 31
Dominion-Provincial Relations, Royal Commission on, 124
Donnacona, 177
Dorset people, 198
Douglas, Tommy, 117, 124
Doukhobors, 107
Dryden Chemicals, 209
Dufour, Christian, 28, 91
Dumont, Mario, 68, 72
Duncan, Sara Jeannette, 108
Dunton-Laurendeau Commission. *See* Bilingualism and Biculturalism, Royal Commission on
Duplessis, Maurice, 42, 44

Durham Report, 33–34
Durkheim, Emile, 9, 12, 75
Dussault, René, 232
dysfunctions, 12

E
economic policy
    Canadianization, 143–145
    See also free trade; mercantilism; protectionism
Economic Union and Development Prospects for Canada, Royal Commission on, 148
Edwards, Henrietta Muir, 112
1818 Convention, 92
Eisenhower, Dwight, 167
Elgin, Lord, 96
elites, ethnicity and, 139
elite theory, 135
employment rate, 161
endogamy, 184
energy sector
    Canadianization of, 143–145
    foreign ownership in, 141, 153
English Canadian identity, 90–91
English Canadian nationalism. *See* nationalism
Erasmus, George, 232
Ericsson, Lief, 202
Erik the Red, 202
Eskimo-Aleut, 175
ethnicity, and elites, 139
ethnic nations, 8
ethnocentrism, 174
European system, 102
Evans, James, 189
extraterritoriality, 166

F
Family Allowances Act, 124
Family Compact, 31, 32
federalism
    asymmetrical federalism, 77–78
    and Canadian unity, 77
    ideology, 43

feminism, 127
feminist theory, 13–14, 15
feminization of poverty, 160
Filmon, Gary, 63
first wave feminism, 127
First World War, 109–111
fiscal crisis, 141–143
Flanagan, Thomas, 233, 236, 237
Fontaine, Phil, 233
force, power and, 31
Foreign Investment Review Agency (FIRA), 143
francophone proletariat, 42
Franklin, Sir John, 203
Fraser, Blair, 118
free trade
    1891 general election and, 104
    1911 general election and, 109
    1988 general election and, 150
    and access to American market, 152
    Adam Smith and, 95
    British trade policy, 96
    business interests and, 149
    and Canadian sovereignty, 148–149, 153–154
    and cultural identity, 155–156
    and democracy, 153–154
    and economic efficiency, 152
    exports and imports under, 151
    and foreign ownership, 153
    impact of, 150–155
    incomes under, 151
    job growth under, 151
    Mulroney and, 148–150
    and national unity, 153–154
    reciprocity with United States, 96–97
    and social programs, 153
French and Indian War (Seven Years War), 22, 24
Frobisher, Martin, 202
Front de Libértion du Québec, 45, 47–48
Frontenac, Louis, 91

fur trade
    Aboriginal women and, 178
    beaver pelts, 178
    French, 23, 178
    "gift diplomacy," 179
    guns, 178, 179
    and indigenous rivalries, 178, 179
    liquor, 179
    nature of, 178–180

G
Gaulle, Charles de, 46
General Motors stirke (1937), 117
genocide, 177
Gibson, Gordon, 78
globalization
    Argentina and, 156–157
    and cultural homogenization, 76
    debate over, 163
    heyday of, 162
    and power of states, 10–12
Gordon, Walter, 134
Gouzenko, Igor, 121
Grant, George, 134, 136, 137
Grant, George Monro, 108
Gray, John, 16, 230
"Great Compromise," 125
Greer, Gemaine, 127
Grey Nuns, 189
Groseilliers, Médard Chouart, 203
gross domestic produce (GDP), 79
Guaranteed Annual Income, 125
Gwyn, Richard, 230

H
habitants. *See Canadiens*
Hamilton, 113
Hammerstein, Alfred von, 205
Hare (Dene tribe), 200, 201
Harman, Leslie, 14
Harper, Elijah, 64, 232
Harrison, Trevor, 78
Hawthorn Report, 217
Hawthorn-Tremblay Report, 125

healing fund, 233
Heilbroner, Eric, 10
historical sociology, 16–18
Hobsbawn, Eric, 8, 118
Hudson, Henry, 202, 203
Hudson's Bay Company, 94, 123
   charter of, 50, 203
   and fur trade, 180
   and North-West Territories, 103
human rights, and constitution, 57–58
Hundred Associates, Company of the. *See Cents-Associés, Compagnie des*
Huron Confederacy, 23

I
identity
   English-Canadian, 90–91
   national identity, 230
   and Quebec sovereignty, 75–76
   and social values, 155
ideology
   defined, 42
   dominant ideology, 42
   Quiet Revolution, 43
Ignatieff, Michael, 76, 166
imagined communities, 8
immigration, 41
   from Britain, 106
   British North America, 93, 94
   competition for immigrants, 104
   Depression years, 115
   postwar policy, 129
   Prairies, 104–108
   selective policy, 106
   from United States, 93, 103, 106
   See also Loyalists
imperialism, American, 166–167
imperial nationalists (Canadian imperialists), 108
import substitution, 135
inclusion, 229
income, defined, 157

Indian Act, 217, 218, 220–221, 234–236
Indian Association of Alberta, 216, 219
indigenous elite, 135
individual egalitarianism, 199
industrial schools, 189
Innis, Harold, 134, 178
Innuit, 198–200
institutional bilingualism, 60
inter-generational social mobility, 157
internal colonialism, 184–186
International Monetary Fund, 163
interpretation, of history, 16–17
intra-generational social mobility, 157
Inuit language, 198
Inuvialuit agreement, 239
Iraq war, 165
Iroquois Confederacy, 23

J
James, Lawrence, 87
James Bay project, 209
Japanese Canadians, internment of, 118
Japanese welfare state, 125
Jaszi, Oscar, 17
Jefferson, Thomas, 89
Jesuits, 188
Johnson, Daniel, 68
Johnson, Lyndon, 125, 133

K
Kendall, Diana, 4
Kennedy, Howard Angus, 107
Kennedy, John, 133
Keynes, John Maynard, 124, 134
Keynesian welfare state. *See* welfare state
King, Mackenzie, 16, 39, 117, 122
Kirnkess, Verna, 245
Klaska (Nahani), 200
Knight, John, 202
Knuttila, Murray, 9
Komagata Maru, 108
Korean War, 121

L
labour market
   Aboriginal peoples in, 229
   and immigration policy, 129
   structure of Canadian labour market, 128
   women in, 112, 127
Lacombe, Albert, 182, 189
L'Action Démocratique du Québec, 68, 72
Laporte, Pierre, 47
latent functions, 12
Laurendeau, André, 75, 80
Laurendeau-Dunton Commission. *See* Bilingualism and Biculturalism, Royal Commission on
Laurier, Sir Wilfrid, 104, 108, 109
Laxer, Gordon, 8, 77, 78
Leacock, Stephen, 17, 108
League for Social Reconstruction, 124
Lesage, Jean, 44
Lévesque, René, 44, 47, 55, 58, 59
liberal democratic welfare state, 125
liberalism, Canadian, 137
Liberal Party (federal), 104, 143
Liberal Party (Quebec), 44, 52, 68
Lincoln, Abraham, 93
Lipset, Martin Seymour, 136
Lipsey, Richard, 152
Loucheux, 200, 201
Lougheed, Peter, 220
Louisbourg Grenadiers, 24–25
Louis XIV, 23
Louis XV, 224
Lovelace, Sandra, 221
Lower Canada
   creation of, 29
   See also Quebec (pre-Confederation)
lower tier, of service sector, 128
Loyalists, 28–29, 90–91
Lyon, Sterling, 58

M

Macdonald, Sir John A., 99, 104
Macdonald Commission. *See* Economic Union and Development Prospects for Canada, Royal Commission on
Mackenzie, William Lyon, 32
Mackenzie Valley Pipeline Inquiry. *See* Berger Inquiry
Macphail, Agnes, 111
Madison, James, 89
manifest destiny, 92
manifest functions, 12
Manitoba
  creation of, 103
  economy, 138
  immigration, 106
Manitoba Act, 53
Manitoba Schools Question, 38
Manning, Preston, 63
Marchand, Jean, 46
Marshall Plan, 121
Martineau, Harriet, 13
Marx, Karl, 8, 12, 42, 54, 75
Marxism
  and social stratification, 156–157
  and state, concept of, 7
mass consumption, 113
Massey Commission, 133
maternal (conservative) feminism, 14
McClung, Nellie, 112
McCrae, John, 110
McDonald, Robert, 204
McDougall, George, 189
McKenna, Frank, 64
McKinney, Louise, 110, 112
Mead, George Herbert, 14
Medical Care Act, 124
Meech Lake Accord, 59–60
  failure of, 223
  opposition to, 59–60, 63
  proposed constitutional amendments, 59
  ratification deadline, 59, 64
mercantilism, 22
merchants against industry thesis, 135
Mercredi, Ovide, 223, 224
Metis, 38, 103, 181, 221
Metis Nation Council, 221
Micmac, 177
Miliband, Ralph, 7
military-industrial complex, 167
Millett, Kate, 127
Mills, C. Wright, 54
miniture replica effect, 135
missionary education, 188–189
Moffett, Samuel, 83
Monroe Doctrine, 92
Montcalm, General Louis Joseph, 26
Montgomery, Richard, 88
Montreal, 113
"Montreal School" historians, 30
Morin, Claude, 59
Morrow, Ray, 14
Morton, Desmond, 24, 90
Mulroney, Brian, 59, 64, 148, 222, 232
multiculturalism, 129–132
Multilateral Agreement on Investments, 150
multilateralism, 166
multinational corporations, 11
Munk, Jens, 203
Murphy, Emily, 112
Murray, James, 27

N

nation, concept of, 7–8
National Energy Program (NEP), 144–145
National Indian Brotherhood (NIB), 219
National Indian Council, 219
nationalism
  and Canadian federalism, 35
  Canadianization economic policy, 143–145
  and economic control, 134–136
  English-Canadian nationalism, 108, 132–134, 144
  First World War and, 111
  Toryism, 136–137
  See also Quebec nationalism
National Policy
  and branch plants, 135
  economic constraints on, 103
  and immigration, 104–108
  and nation-building, 102–103
  tariffs, 102
National Progressive Party, 111
National Security Strategy. *See* Bush Doctrine
nation-state, 8
Native Brotherhood of British Columbia, 219
Native Council of Canada, 221
Nault, Robert, 225, 235
neo-conservatism, 149
neo-liberalism, 149
neo-Marxism. *See* Marxism
New Brunswick
  British immigration, 93
  economy, 94, 95
  population, 93, 94
New Deal, 117, 124
New Democratic Party, 117, 143
Newfoundland
  economy, 93, 94
  population, 93
New France
  British conquest of, 24–26
  colonization of, 23–24
  education of Native children, 188
  rivalry with British, 24
  social structure of, 29
Nisga'a land claims, 239–240
non-status Indians, 221
North, the
  economic development, 208–211
  economic transformation, 204–206
  government administration, 207–208
  peoples, 197–202
  physical environment, 196–197
  resources, 204–205
  Second World War and, 206–207

North American Air Defense Command (NORAD), 122
North Atlantic Treaty Organization (NATO), 122
North West Company, 94, 180
North West Mounted Police, 206
Northwest Passage, 202–203, 210
North-West Territories, 103
"notwithstanding clause," 58
Nova Scotia
    British immigration, 93
    economy, 94
    Loyalists, 28
    population, 93, 94
"numbered treaties," 215–217
Nunavut, creation of, 252

O

Oblates, 189
October Crisis. *See* Front de Libértion du Québec
Official Language Act (Bill 22), 54
oil and gas. *See* energy sector
Oka Crisis, 224–225
Old Age Pensions Act, 123
Old Age Security Act, 124
Ontario, and constitutional patriation, 57
OPEC crisis, 141
Oregon Treaty, 89
Orwell, George, 16
O'Sullivan, John, 92
Ottawa, 113

P

Paley Report, 122
Papineau, Louis-Joseph, 32
Parizeau, Jacques, 68, 69, 70
Parkin, George Robert, 108
Parlby, Irene, 112
Parti Québécois
    aftermath of 1995 referendum, 72
    and Bill 101, 54
    and constituitional patriation, 58–59
    1976 election victory, 52–53
    and 1980 referendum, 54–57
    and 1995 referendum, 68–70
    social reforms, 53
patriarchy, 14
Patriotes, 32
Pearson, Lester, 45, 133
Pelletier, Gérard, 43, 46
Penner Report, 216, 222
Pépin-Robarts Report, 55–56
Perry, Matthew, 166
"persons" case, 112
Pettigrew, Pierre, 71
Phips, Sir William, 91
Pike Lake project, 209
Plains of Abraham, Battle of the, 26
political values, 136
polity-centred/neo-institutional theory, 126
polygamy, 199
Pond, Peter, 205
"Pontiac's Rebellion," 180
popular culture, 113, 122, 134
populist parties, 117
Porter, John, 72, 139
portfolio investments, 109
post-secondary education, 125
Poulantzas, Nicholas, 7
poverty
    gender and, 160
    social program cuts and, 159–160
power
    exercise of, 31
power resources theory, 126
primary sector, 128
Prince Edward Island
    British immigration, 93
    economy, 95
    population, 93, 94
Privy Council, British, 51
profane world, 241
Prophet (brother of Tecumseh), 180
protectionism
    American policy, 102
    National Policy, 102

Q

Quebec Act, 27, 50, 87–88
Quebec nationalism
    anti-nationalist liberalism, 43
    Canadien identity, 27–28
    conservative nature of clerico-nationalism, 40–41, 70
    ethnicity and, 70
    globalization and, 74
    historical grievances, 34
    identity and, 75–76
    Parti Québécois, 52
    popular support for sovereignty, 74–75
    Quiet Revolution and, 43, 44–45, 70
Quebec Pension Plan, 124
Quebec (pre-Confederation)
    bloc voting, 34
    British immigration, 93
    under British rule, 26–27
    division of, 29
    economic and political impact of Conquest, 29–30
    economy, 94
    habitants, 27–28
    population, 93, 94
    Rebellions of 1837-38, 31–33
Quebec (province)
    aftermath of 1995 referendum, 72–75
    assimilation, fear of, 38, 81
    bloc voting, 38
    and conscription, 39
    and constitutional patriation, 57–58
    demographic changes, 41–42
    and devolution of federal powers, 51–52
    "distinct society," 60–63
    federal-provincial relations, 55–56, 70–72
    and free trade, 149
    French language laws, 54
    French usage, 60
    historical grievances, 34
    income distribution, 72

incomes, 72–73
industrialization, 42
isolation of, 37–40
and Meech Lake Accord, 64
and official bilingualism, 53
and pro-American feeling, 80–81
scenario of independent state, 79–80
transfer payments, 72
veto power, 58
and Victoria Charter, 52
Quebec Resolutions, 98
Quebec sovereignty referendum (1980), 54–57
Quebec sovereignty referendum (1995), 19, 22, 68–72
Quiet Revolution, 43, 44–45

R
racism, 107, 184
radio, advent of, 116
Radisson, Pierre-Esprit, 203
Ramonet, Ignacio, 80
Rand Formula, 53, 125
Reagan, Ronald, 149
Rebellions of 1837-38, 31–33
Reciprocity Treaty, 95–97
    See also free trade
Red Paper, 218
Red River Uprising, 38
Reform Party, 63, 65
Regina Riot, 116
region, defined, 140
regionalism
    defined, 140
    free trade and, 154
    nature of, 140
    New Energy Program and, 144, 145
    oil crisis and, 143
    the West, 140
reification, concept of, 3
relief camps, 116
reserves
    living conditions, 229
    reserve system, 186–188
residential claims, 233, 234
residential schools, 189, 190–194
Resnick, Philip, 77, 78

Ricardo, David, 96
Richard Riot, 37
Richelieu, Cardinal, 23
Riel, Louis, 38, 181
Riesman, David, 75
Robarts, John, 55
Robinson, Walter, 235
Roosevelt, Franklin, 117, 122
Rotstein, Abraham, 44
Royal Canadian Mounted Police, 206
Royal Proclamation of 1763, 26–27, 50, 88, 179, 213–214, 232
Rundle, Robert, 189
Rush-Bagot Convention, 92
Ryerson, Egerton, 190

S
sacred world, 241
Said, Edward, x
St. Laurent, Louis, 133
Saskatchewan
    economy, 138
    immigration, 106
    population, 137–138
Saul, John Rolston, x–230
Schlesinger, Arthur, Jr., 11
scientific management, 112–113
scientific specificity, 242
Scowen, Reed, 79
secondary sector, 128
second wave feminism, 127
Second World War, 118
Secord, Laura, 90
Sekani, 200
Senate, Canadian, 98
September 11 terrorist attacks, 164
Seven Years War, 22, 24
sexism, 14
Sifton, Sir Clifford, 104
Simpson, Sir George, 180
Skocpol, Theda, 7
Skookum Jim, 204
Slavey (Dene tribe), 5, 200, 201
Smith, Adam, 95
Smith, Goldwin, ix–79, 83, 108
Snow, John, 216

Social Credit, 117
social-democratic welfare state, 125
social mobility, 157
social norms, defined, 50
social stratification
    differential rewards and, 31
    distribution of wealth, 158–160
    ethnicity and race, 160
    gender and, 160
    language and, 34
    New France, 29
    regional disparity and, 160
    theoretical models of, 156–157
society
    conceptions of, 8–10
    defined, 10, 249
    and historical transformations, 9
    problem of definition, 3–4
    and role of state, 9, 250
socio-economic status (SES) model, of class, 156–157
sociological imagination, 54
sociology
    emergence of, 9
    historical sociology, 16–18
Soros, George, 163
sovereigntist nationalism, 43
Soviet Union, 121, 123
Special Committee on Indian Self-Government in Canada. *See* Penner Report
specific claims, 238
Spencer, Herbert, 12
spiritual holism, 242
stagflation, 143
staples theory, 134
staples trap, 134
Starblanket, Chief, 182
state
    concept of, 7
    globalization, impact on, 10–211
    and society, 9, 249
status, 31
Status of Women, Royal Commission on, 125

Statute of Westminster, 51
Steffanson, Vilhjalmur, 206
Steinhauer, Robert, 189
Stiglitz, Joseph, 163
stock market crash, 115
storytelling, 200
stratification. *See* social stratification
structural-functional theory, 12, 13, 15
Subarctic region, 197
subsidiarity, 78
sustainable economy, 230
symbolic interaction theory, 14, 15
symbolic order, 128
symbols, symbolism
  Maurice Richard, 37
syncretism, 202

T
Tagish Charley, 204
Tahlan, 200
tariffs. *See* protectionism
Task Force on Canadian Unity. *See* Pépin-Robarts Report
Taylor, Charles, 76, 77
Taylor, Frederick, 112
Tecumseh, 89, 90, 180
Teeple, Gary, 9
television, advent of, 122
territorial bilingualism, 60
terrorism
  defined, 24
  FLQ, 45
  state terrorism, 25
  war on, 164–165
tertiary (service) sector, 128
Thatcher, Margaret, 149
theories
  as conceptual tools, 12
  conflict theory, 12, 13, 15
  feminist theory, 13–14, 15
  macro theories, 13
  micro theories, 13
  structural-functional theory, 12, 13, 15
  symbolic interaction theory, 14, 15
third wave feminism, 127

Thule Inuit, 198
time, notions of, 242–243
Tolstoy, Leo, 107
Tönnies, Ferdinand, 9
Toronto, 113
Toryism, 136–137
transfer payments, 72
transnational corporations, 11
Treaty of Ghent, 89, 90
Treaty of Paris, 89
Treaty of Versailles, 111
Tremblay Report, 44
Trudeau, Pierre, 43, 46, 47, 48, 51, 55, 57, 63, 221, 222
Truman, Harry, 122
Tuchone, 200
Turner, John, 59, 148
two nations theory, 46

U
unemployment
  Canada and United States compared, 161
  Depression years, 115
  and fiscal crisis, 141
Unemployment Insurance Act, 124
unilateralism, 166
unintended (unanticipated) consequences, 243
Union Nationale, 42
Union of British Columbia Indian Chiefs, 218, 236
Union of Ontario Indians, 214
Union of Saskatchewan Indians, 219
United Church, and residential claims, 234
United Empire Loyalists. *See* Loyalists
United Farmers of Alberta, 111, 117
United Farmers of Manitoba, 111
United Farmers of Ontario, 111
United Nations, 165, 221
United States
  Civil War, 97–98
  distribution of wealth, 161–162

  economy, 161
  equality of life, 162
  health care, 162
  imperialism, 166–167
  investment capital, 108–109, 122
  justice system, 162
  military spending, 162
  population, 161
  protectionism, 102
  territorial expansion, 92–93, 103
  trade imbalance crisis, 143
  unemployment, 161
  war on terrorism, 164–165, 167–168
  See also American Revolution; War of 1812
Upper Canada
  anglophone majority, 34
  British immigration, 93
  creation of, 29
  economy, 95
  population, 93, 94
  Rebellions of 1837-38, 31, 32–33
upper tier, of service sector, 128
urbanization, 113, 138
urban reserves, 228–229
Ursulines, 188
usufructuary rights, 213

V
Vallieres, Pierre, 45
Vancouver, 113
Vander Zalm, Bill, 63
verstehen, 14
Victoria Charter, and Quebec, 52
Vietnam War, 122, 133

W
Waite, P.B., 91
Wakeham, William, 206
Wallerstein, Immanuel, 9
War Measures Act, 47–48
War of 1812, 89–90
Waters, Malcolm, 11
Watkins, Melville, 134
wealth, defined, 157

Webber, Jeremy, 77
Weber, Max, 9, 12
welfare state, 123–126
   globalization and, 163
Wells, Clyde, 64
West, the
   Depression, 115
   economic development, 139
   ethnic makeup, 129
   immigration boom, 104–108
   population growth, 137–138
   regionalism, 140, 145
   urbanization, 138
wheat, 94, 95, 103
White Paper, 217–219
wife sharing, among the Inuit, 199
Winnipeg, 113
Winnipeg General Strike, 111
Wolf, General James, 26
women
   and First World War, 110
   fur trade and, 178
   and "Indian" status, 221
   and job ghettos, 160
   labour market participation, 112, 127
   and public office, 112
   status of, 127–128
   wage gap, 160
wooded tundra, 197
Woodsworth, James S., 107, 117
Woolstonecraft, Mary, 13
World Bank, 163
World Trade Organization, 163
Wuttenee, William, 218

X
xenophobia, 107, 108

Y
Young, Brian, 23
Yukon Gold Rush, 104, 204–206